Professional Sport
in the European Union:
Regulation and Re-regulation

INTERNATIONAL SPORTS LAW CENTRE
Anglia Polytechnic University
Chelmsford, United Kingdom

Professional Sport in the European Union: Regulation and Re-regulation

edited by

Andrew Caiger
Simon Gardiner

T·M·C· Asser Press
The Hague

The INTERNATIONAL SPORTS LAW CENTRE based at the ANGLIA POLYTECHNIC UNIVERSITY in Chelmsford, England has been in existence since 1996. It is the only one of its kind in Britain. It has three main aims:

- *Research*: the Centre is involved in wide variety of research projects concerning the legal regulation of sport.
- *Consultancy*: members of the Centre have provided consultancy to a number of sports related bodies and regularly give papers at UK, European and world-wide seminars and conferences.
- *Education*: the Centre provides an unique LLM/MA in International Sports Law, which is a flexible learning programme involving tuition via the internet and attendance at two intensive study weeks at locations around the world.

For further information of the Centre's work, contact:
Simon Gardiner, Director
International Sports Law Centre
Anglia Polytechnic University
Chelmsford CM1 1LL, UK
Tel no: +44(0) 1245 493131 x3332
Fax no: +44 (0) 1245 493132
E-mail: s.j.gardiner@anglia.ac.uk
Internet: www.sportslaw.anglia.ac.uk

Published by T.M.C. ASSER PRESS,
P.O.Box 16163, 2500 BD The Hague, The Netherlands

Sold and distributed in North, Central and South America
by Kluwer Law International,
675 Massachusetts Avenue, Cambridge, MA 02139, U.S.A.

In all other countries, sold and distributed
by Kluwer Law International, Distribution Centre,
P.O.Box 322, 3300 AH Dordrecht, The Netherlands

ISBN 90-6704-126-2

Lay-out and cover: Oasis Productions, Nieuwerkerk a/d IJssel, The Netherlands
Printing and binding: Koninklijke Wöhrmann BV, Zutphen, The Netherlands

FOREWORD

This book comes at a critical time for the future development of sports law. It examines key issues of both contemporary and future importance to the administration of sporting activity in the European Union. The book is particularly pertinent coming at a time when European Community law is playing a key role in the restructuring of football's transfer system. This forms only one small, though highly significant, part of the fundamental shift that has taken place in European professional sport; away from the self-regulatory autonomy of sporting bodies towards a system more rigidly codified and governed by mainstream legal norms and rules.

The law, in particular the economic freedoms provided for under the Treaty of Rome, has become a key weapon in the armoury of those who wish to exploit sport to its full commercial potential, free of self-regulatory constraints. It is not only those desirous of exploiting the economic potential of sport, who have made use of European Community law. As sport has become increasingly commercialised and commodified, it has also attracted the attention of the institutions of the Community, which have been keen to ensure that sports regulations adhere to Community law.

However, the increasing involvement of the law has not been the sole influence on the re-regulation of European sport; the media have also had a key role to play. Indeed, many would perceive the media as being the key component in the complex processes that have redeveloped sport. New media outlets have provided significant commercial opportunities, both for sporting clubs and organisations and for the broadcasters themselves. Both parties have seized upon these opportunities, to the extent that the two have become increasingly entwined. The resultant growth in economic activity has also been the key factor in the interest that the law has taken in the sporting field. In addition the global sport-media complex has also involved the development of new forms of sporting organisation and the departure from traditional models of governance purely for the purposes of commercialism.

With this re-definition of sporting regulation the role of the state is one that is increasingly coming into question, and domestic regulators are consistently being forced to re-evaluate their role and functions in the face of the increasing internationalisation and globalisation of sport's regulatory processes.

Against this background the book engages the debate concerning the development of sports regulation in the European Union and highlights further areas ripe for investigation and development. It also seeks to draw on creative solutions to many of the regulatory problems, indeed crises, which face sport at the present time.

This book is a timely and valuable contribution to this important debate in Europe.

Leuven, November 2000   ROGER BLANPAIN

ACKNOWLEDGEMENTS

This book is the product of the insights of our colleagues to whom we are very grateful for the time they found to contribute to the debate. There are a few colleagues we would like to mention specifically for their contribution to the production of this book. Robert Siekmann for his encouragement and the support of the Asser Institute. Philip van Tongeren and Marjolijn Bastiaans at the Asser Press for their patience, fortitude and confidence in this project. We would also like to mention the assistance of Jonathan Fitchen, Dave McArdle and Simon Boyes for helping us with the revision and editing of the texts.

We thank Michael Malone-Lee, our vice-chancellor, for his continued encouragement, enthusiasm and support for the sports law project. We thank the University for providing us with the facilities to undertake this task. We thank our colleagues in the Law School and Sports Law Centre for the contributions they have made to the discussions about the book.

ANDREW CAIGER AND SIMON GARDINER

TABLE OF CONTENTS

INTRODUCTION: RE-REGULATING PROFESSIONAL SPORT IN THE EUROPEAN UNION

Andrew Caiger and Simon Gardiner

INTRODUCTION

The social phenomenon of sport not only has immense cultural significance both in terms of individual participation and spectating, it is now clearly 'big business'.[1] Sport is still seen by some as an area of activity that ought to be essentially self-regulating. The growing intervention of the law in the sports field has drawn resentment from both sport fans as well as those who administer sport. However, legal intervention in the domain of sport is a reality and is growing rather than diminishing. Yet, few questions are asked as to why this has happened or why it is necessary.

One reason clearly seems to lie in the process of the overt commercialisation of modern professional sport. There are important distinctive characteristics of the sports business world:

– it does not presuppose cut-throat competition – clubs are mutually dependant on each other's health;
– sports businesses are able to subsidise a number of losses in their quest for the periodic 'big hit';
– traditionally European clubs have primarily aimed to win competitions and not make money;
– increasing ambiguity as to who are the consumers – paying spectators or the TV viewers; and
– sport has an unusual labour market with the working life of most professional athletes being limited.

Professional sport is increasingly best understood as a commodity that has developed complex and symbiotic relationships within the global media complex and sports marketing industry. On the European regulatory level, this changing nature

---

[1] 3% of world GNP is estimated to be accounted for by sports business.

A. Caiger and S. Gardiner (Eds), Professional Sport in the EU: Regulation and Re-regulation
© *2000, T.M.C.Asser Press, The Hague, The Netherlands*

of sport has led to a number of governance issues, which will be briefly discussed.

Broadcasting Rights

The impact of the media, essentially surrounding the issue of broadcasting rights, can be used to illustrate the increasing role of legal regulation in sport and the corresponding problems that have arisen in terms of governance. This impact can be demonstrated in two ways. Throughout Europe during the 1990s the value of television rights has exponentially increased. In England, the impact of satellite TV, especially BSkyB has seen the market for television rights transformed. In 1987-1988 season, the rights for the top league were sold for £3.1 million. In 1996-1997 season, it was valued at around £185 million – an increase of around sixty times. The deal that will come into force from season 2001-2002 is worth around £1.3 billion over three years. Collective selling of TV rights by the football authorities has come under close scrutiny and it is likely that with the increasing flexibility and business opportunities that are created by digital TV technologies, there will be a move to individual arrangements.

Under the current Premiership deal, the top English club, Manchester United has only just broken through the £10 million-per-season barrier. This can be contrasted with Spanish club Barcelona, who in 1999, completed a domestic deal worth £254 million over five years – or more than £50 million a year.[2] With Manchester United having its own digital TV channel, MUTV, individual TV deals rather than shared revenues based on collective selling is extremely attractive. The current collective deal for the Premier League rights was challenged as being anti-competitive in 1998 – the investigation found that there was a cartel in operation, but concluded that it was not contrary to the 'public interest'.[3] In 1998, the argument of the Dutch club, Feyenoord, that it could sell individually the rights to home matches was upheld. In 1997, a decision of the German Federal Supreme Court ruled that clubs could not collectively sell the television rights to the home matches of clubs participating in European competition. Collective selling within Europe is clearly vulnerable to continued external regulation.

The second impact of media groups on sport is the way that sporting clubs in general and football clubs specifically have been subject to the buying of significant share interests. The bid by Rupert Murdoch's BSkyB for Manchester United is the definitive example. In autumn 1998, BSkyB made a bid of £623 million for Manchester United Football club. The referral in November 1998 of the takeover to the relevant UK regulatory body, the Monopoly and Mergers Commis-

---

[2] Henderson J, 'Cost of keeping United', *The Observer* August 15, 1999.
[3] Re F.A. Premier League Ltd. Agreement Relating to the Supply of Services Facilitating the Broadcast of Premier League Football Matches, (Restrictive Practices Court, 28 July 1999).

sion (MMC)[4] represented something far more significant than the market interests of one broadcaster and one club. Crucial questions were raised – not least the relationship between sport and competition issues. How far should the competition rules penetrate the inner sanctum of sport – especially football? In spring 1999, Stephen Byers, the Secretary of State for Trade, agreed with the MMC and ruled that the merger should not go ahead and was not in the public interest.[5] There have been other forms of resistance to media appropriation, for example attempts by governing bodies to limit the potential conflict of interest that media acquisitions of clubs can create. UEFA unsuccessfully blocked the cross-ownership of the investment company ENIC in SK Slavia Prague and AEK Athens, clubs who could have potentially competed and played each other in the same European competition.[6]

There have also been attempts in football to create rival leagues and challenge the traditional forms of governance. The threatened break-away by the top European teams in 1998, initiated by the Milan based media consultancy, Media Partners, to form a European Super League, did not materialise. UEFA reconstituted the European Champions League for the 1999-2000 season with an expansion from 24 to 36 clubs. This included four teams from Italy and Spain – hardly, strictly speaking, only restricted to champions. A European league however is not a prize that media groups will stop pursuing. It has been reported that a collaboration between Rupert Murdoch, the German Kirch group, the French company Canal Plus and the Spanish Telefonica group have been in negotiation with the top 16 European teams for the creation of a closed league, televised on a pay-per-view basis, to start in 2001-2002 season.

In other sports, there has been the acquiescence by sports governing bodies to the creation of new leagues. There are examples of this amounting to the acquisition of whole sports, as illustrated with Rupert Murdoch effectively purchasing the whole of English rugby league in the mid-1990s, with the subsequent creation of the Rugby *Superleague*. However, rival leagues usually effect the stability and integrity of the sport leading to 'turf wars' between governing bodies over competing interests. For example in European basketball, an alternative *Euroleague* backed by the Union of European Basketball Leagues and funded by the Spanish telecommunication giant, Telefonica, has broken away from the official FIBA *Suproleague*. FIBA requested the national basketball association whose clubs were involved in the *Suproleague* to sanction them. However the response of the

---

[4] Since the advent of the new Competition Act 1998, the MMC is now known as the Commission for Competition. It serves as an advisory body to the Secretary of State for Trade and Industry and the Director General of the Office of Fair Trading. It has no decision making or enforcing powers.

[5] See *BSkyB and Manchester United: A Report on the Proposed Merger* Cm. 4305, (1999) London: HMSO.

[6] AEK Athens FC and SK Slavia Prague FC v UEFA, CAS 98/200, interim order of 17 July 1998.

national associations thus far has been to permit clubs to participate in both competitions if they wish. FIBA's authority is therefore clearly compromised.[7]

The Transfer System

The *Bosman* ruling clearly showed that the UEFA and FIFA rules on the transfer of players between clubs from one Member State to another infringed the EU Treaty rules relating to freedom of mobility of workers. In addition to this the football rules regarding nationality were discriminatory and contrary to the Treaty provisions. As a result of the ruling, there has been a marked increase in the movement of professional football players between Member States. In addition, football salaries have risen substantially. The competition law implications of *Bosman* were not set out in the ruling, but have surfaced subsequently both at EU level and in the national states.[8] Over fifty competition cases relating to sport are pending with the Commission.

There are indications from the Competition Commission that the transfer system as it currently obtains is unlawful in EU law. A final decision is expected from the Commission by the end of 2000 as to FIFA's new transfer proposals. Thus competition issues relating to transfers first raised by Advocate General Lenz in *Bosman* will finally be addressed.[9]

Drugs and Doping

Where athletes or interested bodies suffer decisions, which have an adverse economic impact on professional careers or livelihoods, the law has become a primary means of redress. The use of the law to challenge disciplinary bans, enforced due to prohibited drug use, is an appropriate illustration. The regulation has been constructed as a 'war on drugs'.[10] Although there are clear health issues, drug use in sport has ceased to be a medical dilemma – it is now a legal conundrum. There are continued calls that drug use is the antithesis of sport – it is nothing other than cheating. But the cynic may well claim that the problem with drug use in sport is the financial bottom line. Its existence adversely impacts upon sponsorship and commercial opportunities. As a phenomenon assimilated within

---

[7] *Soccer Investor Weekly* September 19, 2000.

[8] See the Feyenoord case and the MMC enquiry into the BSkyB/Manchester United merger as well as the Restrictive Trade Practices Court judgement in the sale of collective broadcasting rights discussed by Spink and Morris elsewhere in this book.

[9] C-415/93 Union Royale Belge des Sociétés de Football ASBL v Bosman [1995] ECR I-4921, [1996] 1 CMLR 645. para. 237. See also Gardiner S, & Welch R, 'The Winds of Change in Professional Football: The Impact of the Bosman Ruling' and Caiger A, & O'Leary J, A New Rainbow? The promise of Change in Professional Football (1998) 3(4) *Contemporary Issues in Law*, 288-312 , 313-328.

[10] See the creation by the IOC in 1999 of the World Anti-Doping Agency, www.wada-ama.org.

sporting endeavour, its control is one of the major challenges for modern sports governance.

ENGAGING IN A DEBATE

So these are some of the issues and examples that can help us locate the debate about sports governance in the new millenium and the quest for new forms of re-regulation. What role does the law have to play within the normative framework of sport? The European Court of Justice has indicated in a number of decisions, that there are issues facing sports bodies involving 'sporting rules', that are essentially within their domain.[11] While the law may prefer that sports bodies run their own affairs it seems clear however, that this cannot be done at the expense of or against the existing framework of social and legal norms both at national and EU level.

This interaction between sport and the law has brought and is still bringing about changes in the way sport is and will be administered. The law has acted as a catalyst for changes in the sporting world. Some of these changes have been far-reaching and have forced the sports world to address certain practices that do not accord with wider societal values. At the same time there is a concern that important social aspects of sport will be sacrificed to commercialisation and other interests. Although they will not be the focus of this book, the role that sport has as a tool of education in promoting public health and fighting social exclusion is an important consideration. The European Commission recognises the importance of sport in promoting social and cultural cohesion : '[it] helps build a society that is more open and tolerant.'[12]

The purpose of this book is to engage debate regarding the mode of re-regulation of sport by examining special areas of sports law and policy. This clash between the civil laws and the *Lex Sportiva* needs to be addressed. Sports governance needs to be reformed and at the same time regain credibility and a legal space within which it can assert its once traditional role of making rules for the 'good of the game'. This book considers the current 'state of play' and offers suggestions as to how a new era will emerge with the principles of transparency and proportionality enlightening governance in a reconstituted domain.

The book does not pretend to be comprehensive in that all sports are covered – rather it offers a variety of insights into the clash between sports governance and EU law and policy. It is a timely debate in the world of sport.

---

[11] For example see Case C-176/96 Lehtonen & Castors Canada Dry Namur-Braine v FRBSB (Belgian Basketball Federation) judgment of 13 April 2000.

[12] *The European Model of Sport*, Brussels, Consultation document of DG X, chapter 3 para.11.

EUROPEAN CHARACTERISTICS OF RE-REGULATION

The re-regulation of sport is occurring within a complex milieu of national and European regularity frameworks, regional, national and international sports federations. At the European level the European Court of Justice has clearly ruled that sports organisations can no longer act in ways that are clearly contrary to the legal provisions of the Treaty. In the past, sports federations have believed themselves beyond legal control. Right up until the decision in *Bosman,* leading figures in UEFA and FIFA believed that the football authorities would win. Is it merely a question of being seen as above the law? Probably not – it is a more complex recognition of the organisational structures of sports governing bodies and the particular dynamics and cultures found within sport.

The European Model

The values and structures of European sport are vital to understand. Although there are unmistakable national and even regional specificities concerning sport, some European-wide characteristics and deep-lying traditions can be identified. The European Commission published *'The European Model of Sport'* in 1998. The focus was on the essential characteristics of European sport, the relationship between sport and television, focussing primarily on broadcasting rights and lastly sport and social policy, particularly the role of sport in promoting social inclusion.

The European Commission contends that in the future development of sport, the special features of the European model need to be carefully taken into account. These include the pyramid organisational structure. The clubs form its foundation; regional federations form the next level; national federations, one for each discipline, represent the next level and at the top of the pyramid, the European Federations are located. The system of promotion and relegation is also one of the key features. This can be contrasted with the United States, which has developed the model of closed championships/leagues and multiple sport federations.

It is clear from the *European Model for Sport* that there is a serious concern that continued legal intervention and rampant commercialisation could undermine the solidarity engendered by sport. In this regard the American model has been rejected and there is a search as to how a uniquely European vision of sport can be developed that will re-establish and demarcate an area of autonomy for sport in the future.

It has to be recognised, however, that in Europe, a new tendency can be observed: attempts to combine both the European and American systems. For example, in a recent proposal by UEFA, clubs would qualify for European competition not only by a system of promotion and relegation, but also by fulfilling economic and technical criteria.[13] In addition the proposal for a closed league outside UEFA is new and has attracted the interest of many of Europe's top clubs. Within this league there is no system of promotion and relegation. It is a new form of competition, which has no link with the existing pyramid structure. There are also moves to a franchise system for sports clubs-relocating, American-style, to take advantage of untapped markets. Wimbledon's attempt to move to Dublin is an example. Plans for rival leagues and pan-European leagues are appearing – note the aforementioned development of the basketball *Suproleague*. In football, the proposed 'Atlantic League' across several European countries has significant support. Small countries have been disadvantaged by the *Bosman* ruling. In The Netherlands, for example, the best players have left to play in bigger football markets abroad. Clubs such as Ajax find it difficult to compete on the European stage. The Atlantic League may address the economic disadvantages experienced by such clubs and expand the market within which these clubs operate and help create a level playing field in Europe.

Economic Regulation

The main underlying economic model of European professional sport can be characterised as being one of 'win-maximisation'. This can be seen as having been the traditional approach with clubs being non-profit organisations and attempting to maximise their winning percentage. There is evidence that there is a move to 'profit-maximisation' – essentially the North American economic model. For example, some professional football clubs are now listed companies. Further evidence of the influence of the North American model can be seen in the proposals for salary caps (see explanation below), revenue sharing (where income, for example from gate receipts and merchandsing, is centrally shared between the clubs in a league) and use of the draft system (where players from a pool are allocated and distributed to the clubs in an attempt to share the talent around).[14]

Are we witnessing an 'Americanisation' of the regulatory and economic framework of European sport? There is considerable evidence that this is happening. Salary caps for example have started to be used as a mechanism to counteract some of the financial pressures on clubs in professional team sports. They exist in England in both codes of rugby. Rugby League Premiership clubs are limited to an outlay of £700,000 or 50% of their projected income on players' wages. In addition clubs are further restricted to paying only 20 player salaries of £20,000 or more per year. In 1999, Rugby Union Premiership clubs voted to accept a wage cap for that season, limiting them to spending £1.8 million each per year on player salaries. Ice Hockey and Basketball leagues also operate salary-

---

[13] 'SPL welcome Uefa initiative', *BBC On-Line* September 26, 2000.
[14] See for further analysis, Jeanrenaud C & Kesenne S, *Competition Policy in Professional Sports: Europe after the Bosman case* (1999) Université de Neuchatel.

capping systems in the UK. In football, they are also under active consideration by a UEFA taskforce.

The salary cap is intended to work in two ways, firstly by maintaining the economic viability of clubs taking part in competitions and secondly by preserving competitive balance between the clubs, ensuring that the richer clubs cannot accrue all the best players and thus dominate a competition. In 1997, the ex-competition commissioner, Karel Van Miert suggested that a salary cap is one possible method of addressing the complex problems concerning both sporting and economic competition that face the modern world of professional team sports in Europe. If they were widely introduced in European sport, they would amount to revolution. They may of course be seen as a restraint of trade. There will be inevitable problems to introduce them on a European-wide basis, in European sports such as football. Presumably one argument would be that salary caps would need to be set at the same level in each national league. However there is clearly great economic distinctions between different countries and leagues in Europe. In the context of a 'European *Super League*', if there was differentiation between leagues and say it was set at the level in Italy and Spain to accommodate the likes of AC Milan and Barcelona, it would put clubs like Dynamo Kiev in the Ukraine or Galatasaray in Turkey at a clear disadvantage. This would indeed create competitive imbalance.

What is vital is that the specific traditions and forms of European sport are retained wherever possible. Although Article 3H of the Treaty requires the approximation of laws in the EU to facilitate the proper functioning of the single market, this does not mean the harmonisation of legal systems in the EU. This strategy has been abandoned as a general policy. Similarly, sports governance requires a certain degree of approximation to the principles of the EU Treaty especially for example in the areas of free mobility and competition. Approximation does not mean sameness and blandness – the 'McDonaldisation' of sport should be resisted.[15]

The re-regulation of European sport does not necessarily need to be understood as a complex process. As shown with *Bosman* and subsequent cases – this change can be achieved in a simple way with a simple mix of sport with European law and economic logic. The ability of national and European sports federations to comply with the discourse of this new re-regulation – accountability and transparency, together with compliance to external regulations – is the key determing factor. The reality for sports federations in Europe is that, *the times they are a-changin'*.[16]

---

[15] Perhaps in the context of Rupert Murdoch's appropriation of significant amounts of world sport, it could more appropriately be described as the 'Murdochisation' of sport.

[16] Taken from title of Bob Dylan song found on album of the same name *The Times They Are A-Changin'* (1964) Columbia Records.

THE CONTRIBUTIONS: ENGAGING THE DEBATE

The contributors have engaged a debate in a variety of national perspectives, reflecting different jurisdictions and traditions. For the sake of coherence the book is divided into four sections.

Section 1: Theoretical and Policy Perspectives

This first section attempts to provide an underpinning to the debate concerning re-regulation. Richard Parrish offers a detailed history of the development of the sports policy of the European Commission. He evaluates the broad-based approach that the EU has aimed for, with the attempt to balance regulation with the protection of the socio-cultural dimension of sport.

Ken Foster locates this policy within an understanding of what is the nature of regulation in sport. He argues not only that external law juridifies the internal practices of sport but that sport has to internalise legal norms in its own practices of governance and discipline in order to avoid legal intervention and/or government regulation. He sees the need for the regulatory framework to ensure that sport is 'still run partly for the love of the game and not just for the love of money'. He favours sports federations having a 'supervised autonomy' within the EU ensuring that federations have a proper 'rule of law' system of governance.

Finally in this section, Simon Boyes provides a wider international perspective of the globalising forces that are clearly visible within professional sport. Europe as a powerful focus of many world sports is *driving* many globalising tendencies. But sport is paradoxical: it fits well with theories of globalisation and the breakdown of national boundaries; it does however have an extensive regional and national cultural resonance – the localised focus of sport competes with its global ambitions.

The friction between the reality of globalisation and the reality of sports governance forms the crux of the current debate.

Section 2: The Frontiers of Regulatory Mechanisms

This second section examines the current disposition of sports governance and how this interfaces with the normative order. Klaus Vieweg develops the issues surrounding the challenges to the tradition of self-regulation of sports federations. By examining the significant case law of the ECJ and considering the practical problems found in sports associations, he identifies alternative courses of action that sports associations could adopt. He stresses there is a need for them to wake up to the regulatory problems that have emerged and adopt 'an active rather than reactive approach'.

Simon Gardiner and Roger Welch evaluate the restrictions on mobility of professional sports men and women (both EU and non-EU citizens) within the EU in the post-*Bosman* sports world. They note the increase of players from third countries and also the proposals for futher limiting mobility of players within the EU. They suggest that there are dilemmas facing the Member States with calls for the introduction of protectionist quotas in response to ever increasing legal support for mobility of workers within the EU. They argue that mobility of sports athletes once in the EU should have the same status as EU citizens. This enriches the quality of a general cultural experience and specific sporting endeavour.

Paul McCutcheon examines nationality and eligibility rules in sports participation that are increasingly nebulous and fragile within the closer European integration and the global village of sport. Conversely, national identities can become more attractive in these times of change. McCutcheon evaluates whether commercial pragmatism will not supercede birthrights as a replacement for existing eligibility criteria.

Finally David McArdle and Laura Edgar argue that sports marketing in Europe has a global impact. They challenge the ethical dimensions of the sports marketing industry. They argue that any regulation in Europe needs to take account of these considerations. They identify the Internet as posing a serious problematic for effective regulation.

Section 3: The Re-regulation of Football: A Quest for Order

This third section focuses on the major European and world sport, namely football. Paul Spink and Philip Morris evaluate the impact that television is having on football. Focusing on how the regulatory authorities have responded to a number of developments in the last few years in Britain where vast amounts of new money has come into the game from satellite television purchase of broadcasting rights, they speculate about the regulatory response to the new technologies of digital pay-per-view and internet broadcasting.

Andrew Caiger and John O'Leary examine transfers and contract stability in professional football in the light of the Anelka saga. They argue that transfers as they currently operate are illegal and contrary to EU competition rules. Further more they conclude that contract stability without a transfer system is likely to be fragile but have identified other possible legal remedies that may support such stability.

Tom Mortimer and Ian Pearl consider the rights of establishment using football as a relevant illustration. As financial viability for sports clubs becomes increasingly vital, the opportunities to re-locate in new geographical markets or compete in new geographical leagues becomes more attractive. By reviewing the EU jurisprudence in other business sectors, the tension between the exercising of the freedom of location supported under the Treaty and the restrictive control of sports governing bodies are examined.

Section 4: Localisation and Specificity: Attempts at Resistence

The fourth section engages with the specificity and variety of national sporting regulatory frameworks that need to be reconciled within the forces of 'Europeanisation' and globalisation. Andrez Szwarc details the regulatory legislation on sports clubs, sports unions and athletes in Poland. He argues that there are many remnants of state control of sport that existed in the former Eastern Europe. This is a national regulatory framework in transition, driven by the desire of the 'new' polity to prepare for future entry into the EU.

Dimitrios Panagiotopoulos and Gregory Ioannidis provide a useful contrast with the distinctions in the structure of sports clubs in Greece and its significance for sports governance. The Greeks have recognised the need for distinguishing between professional and amateur sport. Luc Silance briefly evaluates the impact that *Bosman* has had on the legal regulation of sport in Belgium and spells out the complexity of the political regime on sports governance.

Finally James Gray provides a comparison with the regulatory framework found in American sport. Although the European Commission has turned its back on the American Model of sport, its influence in reality is clearly apparent. Gray argues that the American experience may provide a useful insight to the function of different regulatory regimes. He provides details of how the major US sports have developed accommodations and in some sports, exceptions, to anti-trust legislation.

CONCLUSION

The contributions in this book illustrate the complexity facing sports governance in Europe. Different solutions are explored and the debate engaged. The complexities of globalisation are examined and its effects on the regulatory process assessed. The debate shows how modern technology and money are determining the future direction of this governance. The question arises how sports organisations, nation states and the EU should respond to these challenges. The complexity and diversity of sport indicates that the interventions of these entities are bound to be diverse, incoherent and spasmodic.

There needs to be convergence in sports governance. In the EU, this convergence needs to be towards the principles of the EU Treaty which include, the basic freedoms of mobility (people, establishment, services and capital) and free competition. In addition to these, the principles of transparency, accountability and proportionality ought to infuse any new regulatory regime in sport.

IN THE FOOTSTEPS OF *BOSMAN*: AN INTERVIEW WITH JEAN-LOUIS DUPONT – THE MAN WHO LIT THE FUSE UNDER EUROPEAN SPORT*

INTRODUCTION

The *Bosman* case and subsequent events have shown that it is likely that there will be much more legal intervention in the area traditionally regulated by independent (national and international) sporting bodies. Thus far the intrusions of the law in various states in Europe have been piecemeal and unsystematic. *Bosman* can be seen as the significant catalyst in this re-regulation of European sport. The Belgian lawyer, Jean-Louis Dupont, is synonymous with the *Bosman* ruling, a case he tackled freshly out of Law School:

'I had mastered in European law whilst my future wife lived a few doors down from Bosman's parent house ... when Bosman had the problem, he decided that rather to go to his parents lawyer – he understood that it was something about European law, a French club, and a Belgian club, and UEFA regulations- he knocked at my door and we went to the law firm and looked at the problem.'[1]

IMPACT OF BOSMAN ON BELGIUM

As a result of these discussions, Bosman took the matter to a Belgian court in Liège who sought a ruling from the European Court of Justice. But what were the consequences of the *Bosman* case? In our interview with Jean-Louis, we asked what had been the impact of *Bosman* in Belgian:

'Belgian clubs should have been prepared- a number were "most dramatically hit" by the judgement. In June 1996, six Anderlecht players were at the end of their contracts and their careers fell to be decided by the *Bosman* ruling. There was the usual reaction that *Bosman* was "the end of football", but "adjustments" were made. The quota of EC players was suppressed and more foreign players entered Belgian football. Today there are fewer Belgian nationals playing for the top teams, in fact most Belgian professional players play abroad.

---

* Telephone interview conducted on September 28, 2000.
[1] A Law Unto Himself: the Lawyer who Changed the Face of Football in Bent I, McIlroy R, Mousley K, and Walsh P (eds.) (2000) *Football Confidential*, London, BBC Worldwide.

A. Caiger and S. Gardiner (Eds), Professional Sport in the EU: Regulation and Re-regulation
© 2000, T.M.C.Asser Press, The Hague, The Netherlands

Professional football contracts since *Bosman* are longer as a whole. Good players will try to have long contracts. They want to feel more secure and clubs are ready to give longer contracts, although these are not always in their long-term interest in terms of mobility. *Bosman* was detrimental to small markets, initially the ECJ was asked in *Bosman* to allow for a five-year transitional period, so clubs and federations could adapt. As we now know the court did not agree to this idea. Longer contacts are fine. *Bosman* should not be seen as a bible. It is appropriate that individual agents should find the best solution to the players they represent. Longer contracts are not a problem because when a player wants to terminate his contract, it can be done in terms of the national law of Belgium. This is especially so when the player knows he could have a higher salary elsewhere. Naturally the player will be liable for damages for breach of contract should the player terminate his contract without agreement with the club. We should really consider what the average wage was in Member States before the *Bosman* ruling. If we compare it with the average wage since, we find it has gone up.

Bosman shifted more power to the players. Most players are better off than before. The ruling has given an 'extraordinary' opportunity to Players' Trade Unions to effectively represent footballers. In Belgium before *Bosman* there was no players union. Since the ruling a number of players joining the Union has rapidly increased. Thus far a minimum legal wage for professional footballers has doubled and collective bargaining has become a strong feature of the modern game in Belgium. Before the ruling there was also no unemployment benefit for players.

Since *Bosman*, there has been an influx of young African players who have been exploited through ridiculous contracts. The Players Union is now in the position to take care of some of these problems especially social problems encountered by these African players. The Union has been influential in protecting wages of young non-EU players. They now must be paid at least twice the minimum wage of EU players. This measure also prevents hundreds of aspirant African footballers coming to Belgium. I have acted for many African players and they are now in a better contractual position. Many people want to be agents but only a few (5 or 6 in Belgium) are professional and provide an effective service.

Since *Bosman*, there is now a much clearer borderline between real professional clubs and non-professional clubs in Belgium. The national league in Belgium has 5-6 sizeable professional clubs. Smaller ones are not out of business but find it harder to survive. In the second and third division these days, players are told not to expect special privileges and these semi-professional players are not in a strong bargaining position as far as wages.'

Post-Bosman Developments

Contrary to the view of Professor Roger Blanpain, Jean-Louis does not think the transfer system is akin to slavery and legal and moral concepts should not be mixed:

'To speak of slavery is insulting to the real victims of slavery. Before *Bosman* players had few rights, the approach was "players must shut-up". There were terrible restrictions on their freedom of movement.

The *Balog* case is due to be heard on the 21ˢᵗ November 2000 by the ECJ. Also know as the 'Bosmanovic case', it challenges the free movement of non-EU players within the EU on competition grounds. This issue was addressed by Advocate General Lenz in *Bosman* but the ECJ avoided the competition issues in its ruling. The *Balog* case directly challenges the competition issues first raised in *Bosman*.'

During the last few years, Jean-Louis has been consulted on cases involving territoriality. He sees this as the next big question in the area of European sports law: recent examples are Wimbledon's quest to establish itself in Dublin and Mouscron, the Belgium club, who wished to play a UEFA cup match in France.

'In the case of Wimbledon, UFEA resisted any move to Dublin. In the *Mouscron* case, a complaint was lodged with the European Commission. It was 'very cautious' and did not want to challenge openly the territoriality rules of UEFA. It felt that it was up to the actors to decide whether they wanted other rules. People confuse legal and moral concepts: e.g. is it right that an Italian club hires a fifteen-year old French player. It is probably morally wrong but it is a cultural question. Another question is that of the Superleague. Similar considerations apply. Can the law prevent it? The answer is no. UEFA has a monopoly over the football governance in Europe. But how can you stop someone creating a new competition? There is the evolution of the issues concerning territoriality. One must be sensible- these issues are more of a political orientation.

For example there is the issue around the promotion of an 'Atlantic League' and the proposers of this development are negotiating with UEFA over whether this is a 'formula' for future regional development. The Atlantic League represents a regional re-grouping including top clubs in Scotland, Scandinavia, Belgium, Portugal and Holland. The most important factor in the success of these developments is 'political and legal evolution' in these re-groupings. The opposition by international federations to these innovative new developments of the 'European Superleague' and Atlantic League in football, and the European Basketball League, could lead to them finding themselves politically and legally undermined leading to divisions within the sports governing structure and possibly a reconstituted regulatory order.'

GOVERNANCE

Jean-Louis opines that sports governing bodies still often believe that they are above the law and fail to accept the logic that they are subject to general legal regulation just as other business entities:

'Sports governance very much depends on the country in which it takes place. In some countries, clubs are well organised when it comes to collective bargaining. For example in the Netherlands, clubs are use to precise legal negotiations. In some cases or in some countries it is difficult for clubs to integrate economic and legal concepts. During the last one and a half years, UEFA had done a 'tremendous job' in negotiating with the EU commission. The fundamental question really is whether the traditional organisation of sport that was 'so perfect' 15 years ago is compatible with the developments in modern society and economy?

Many people have overestimated the significance of *Bosman*. It has made a big difference in football but its psychological effects are probably more profound. New technology drives football today, for example to promote a WAP driver, the companies probably need to contact the top ten-fifteen European clubs. A sport can only be big today when new technology is attracted. For example there is not much big technology interested in volleyball- football is the main player!

The organisation of sport must take account of these realities. Once upon a time, the communist system was probably an efficient way of establishing heavy industries. But as the structure of societies has evolved this structure could no longer cope with new circumstances that presented themselves. Similarly the traditional organisation of sport is no longer compatible with our modern times. It was probably a good superstructure for a time.

This evolution to the organisation of sport has taken place on a local scale in some countries. Some countries have had their 'own Bosmans', e.g. in England the *Eastham* case is always mentioned. The modern trend is for federations to lose power in favour of groupings such as the FA Premier League, the possible European Superleague and now the new European Basketball League in which the top European club have broken away to form a new superleague with the backing of Telephonica, the giant Spanish telecoms company.'

In this context, an editorial in *Soccer Investor Weekly* sent out a warning in regard to UEFA:

'UEFA is making a big mistake if it does not take on board the fact that clubs with far higher budgets than the rest need to negotiate a more satisfactory percentage of income generated by the Champions League. In the case of basketball, the Union of European Basketball Leagues (ULEB) was formed in July 2000 from FIBA after an argument with FIBA over TV income in June.'[2]

CONCLUSION

How does Jean-Louis see future developments:

'The EU will not be able to provide for the re-regulation of sport. It's more a question of national law. The EU has no competence in the area of sport, so re-regulation will have to take place at the level of national Parliaments. However it is possible for the federations and the EU Commission to make agreements in which the EU ensures or encourages these federations to make rules consistent with EU law. In The basketball case for example, FIBA, the international federation of the game, threatened to exclude all clubs who joined the new Superleague. But the national federations were happy to accept the presence of the Superleague placing FIBA in a very embarrassing position. The national clubs said they want the new Superleague to exist side by side with FIBA. This is the new reality of sports governance that needs to be grasped by international, national and regional federations.'

---

[2] *Soccer Investor Weekly* September 19, 2000, 1.

Bosman has only been the start of vast changes in the dynamics of sport. In the next few years Jean-Louis says he foresees half a dozen landmark cases, which will finally bring 'a sense of balance' to European sport.

Part One
Theoretical and Policy Perspectives

RECONCILING CONFLICTING APPROACHES TO SPORT IN THE EUROPEAN UNION

Richard Parrish

INTRODUCTION

The European Union (EU) has been characterised as a regulatory state.[1] Embedded within the EU's constitutional structure is an in-built regulatory ethos, an ideological commitment to make and enforce rules. This image has led some commentators to describe the EU as an interfering and out of control Leviathan seeking to draw into the regional integration process a whole raft of sectors never intended to be subject to supranational governance. When sport hit the European regulatory buffers following the ruling in *Bosman*,[2] many sports bodies shared this view, particularly given that sport was not mentioned in the EU's founding Treaty, the 1957 Treaty of Rome.

The emergence of a new regulatory operating environment for sport was driven by more than just internal dynamics. The actions of supply-side regulatory actors such as the European Court of Justice and the Competition Policy Directorate were indeed significant. However, equally important was the attitude of the demand-side regulatory actors, in particular those sports bodies that sought to use the supply-side actors to resolve disputes between themselves. By the end of 1998, the Competition Policy Directorate in the European Commission had received 55 complaints relating to sport.[3]

Without denying the importance and strength of the regulatory ethic in the EU, its role should be located within a wider social, cultural and essentially political governance context. EU involvement in sport is shaped by more than just the force of regulation. By locating the regulatory ethic within a wider political context it is possible to see how sports 'policy' is shaped by an equally powerful political ethic also deeply rooted within the EU's constitutional structure.

---

[1] Majone G, *Regulating Europe* (1996) London, Routledge.

[2] C-415/93 Union Royale Belge des Sociétés de Football Association ASBL v Jean-Marc Bosman [1995] ECR I-4921.

[3] Commission of the European Communities, *The European Model of Sport* (1998) Consultation Document, Directorate General X, Brussels.

A. Caiger and S. Gardiner (Eds), Professional Sport in the EU: Regulation and Re-regulation
© 2000, T.M.C.Asser Press, The Hague, The Netherlands

This chapter argues that although sport's relationship with the EU has been greatly shaped by regulatory forces (the promulgation and enforcement of rules), EU sports 'policy' is equally being shaped by a deep commitment to socio-political integration. This commitment has manifested itself in a desire to harness the socio-cultural and integrationist qualities of sport for political purposes. These include the use of sport to promote European solidarity and identity, the use of sport as a tool of urban and regional regeneration and the use of sport as a tool to combat social exclusion.[4] This approach to sport is however incompatible with the economic and essentially regulatory approach being pursued elsewhere in the EU. As such a body of opinion has emerged in the EU seeking a more broad-based approach to sport that balances regulation with the promotion and protection of the socio-cultural dimension of sport.

The reconciliation between these two forces has involved the complex interplay between key policy advocates working within a range of institutional venues in the EU. The examination of this interplay is divided into six sections. The first briefly examines the traditional patterns of nation state involvement in sport. The second reviews the historical and institutional development of the EU. The third and fourth sections examine the regulatory and socio-cultural approaches to sport in the EU. The fifth section reviews attempts to reconcile the regulation of sport with the promotion and protection of sports' socio-cultural dimension within the framework of a 'new approach' to sports policy. The conclusion examines the impact of this new approach.

Sport and the Nation State in Western Europe

A criticism often levelled at the EU is that supranational involvement in sport is eroding sporting autonomy and that sport and politics should not mix. This image of sport as an autonomous sector, capable of generating its own internal rules independent of wider political and legal developments is however questionable. Historically sport has always been caught between regulatory and political forces. All that is new is the internationalisation of this phenomenon.

Distilling the work of a number of authors,[5] four patterns of nation state involvement in sport can be identified:

---

[4] Henry I & Matthews N, Sport, Policy and European Union: The Post-Maastricht Agenda (1998) 3 *Managing Leisure* 1-17.

[5] Houlihan B, *Sport Policy and Politics: A Comparative Analysis* (1997) London, Routledge; Allison L (ed), *The Changing Politics of Sport* (1993) Manchester, Manchester University Press; Cashmore E, *Making Sense of Sports* (1996, 2ed) London, Routledge; Grayson E, *Sport and the Law.* (1994, 2ed) London, Butterworths; Gardiner S *et al*, *Sports Law, Text and Materials* (1998) London, Cavendish.

- First, sport has been used by governments as an instrument of domestic policy. In this connection sport has been employed by governments for the purposes of social control, social integration, nation building and as a tool for economic development and health promotion.
- Second, sport has been used by governments as an instrument of foreign policy. Historically sport has been an important weapon employed by states wishing to forge new international links or indeed sever them. Sport can also help increase a state's international prestige and image.
- Third, state intervention in sport may occur not as an instrument of state policy but rather as a consequence of state policy. For example, domestic economic reform programmes may affect sport unintentionally.
- Fourth, state law may seep into the internal laws of sport, either intentionally or unintentionally through a process often referred to as 'juridification'.[6] Commercial developments in sport have resulted in generic legal frameworks such as competition law, contract law and employment law increasingly being applied to sport.[7] The extent of this application has led some legal writers to identify a new body of law known as 'sports law'.[8]

Sport has become linked to state activity as both an *instrument* and a *consequence* of state policy. Although sport has been seen by the state as an activity to use instrumentally, recent commercial developments in sport have also led to increased regulatory interest from the state. This has served to internationalise a regulatory environment. The late 1980's and 1990's witnessed the rapid commercialisation of European sport. By 1998, sport accounted for 3% of world trade.[9] Running parallel to this commercialisation was the completion of the EU's Single European Market (SEM) project and the heightened desire by newly empowered EU institutions to see the economic basis of the Union respected by all commercial entities.

THE DEVELOPMENT OF THE EUROPEAN UNION

The origins of a relationship between sport and the EU can be traced to the birth of the Common Market. Although sport was not mentioned in the 1957 Treaty of Rome, the chosen 'path' of integration laid the foundations for sport to be potentially drawn into the regional integration process. Embedded within the Preamble of the Treaty of Rome is a commitment not only to remove obstacles to free trade and free movement (economic integration) but also a desire to promote social

---

[6] Foster K, Developments in Sporting Law, in Allison, supra n.5, 108.

[7] Grayson, supra n.5.

[8] Gardiner *et al*, supra n.5.

[9] Commission of the European Communities, *Developments and Prospects for Community Activity in the Field of Sport* (1998) Brussels, Directorate General X.

progress and European solidarity (socio-political integration). Common European institutions were established, some charged with the responsibility of securing economic integration whilst others pursued socio-political integration. Pinder identifies a clear relationship between these two 'engines' of European integration.[10] Not only does successful economic integration require a commitment to socio-political integration but the former is also easier to achieve than the latter because: 'free trade ideology is firmly built into the system, but the planning ethic is no more than a possibility for the future'.[11] However, since Pinder's initial thesis in 1968, the 'planning' ethos has been strengthened. To reflect this change the Maastricht Treaty established a new organisation, the 'European Union', the name change symbolising a significant movement away from a *Community* established on economic foundations to a *Union* underpinned by socio-political integration.

The institutional structure of the EU reflects this desire to balance economic integration with socio-political integration. Prior to the Single European Act of 1986 the balance favoured economic integration. Since the signing of the Treaties of Maastricht (1992) and Amsterdam (1997), the balance has shifted in favour of socio-political integration. This is because the SEM project became linked to institutional and policy reform. Those actors keen to promote socio-political integration in the EU currently have more influence over policy and legislation than at any time since their creation.

The institution with the potential to exercise the most influence over sport is the European Council, a body composed of the heads of State and Government of the Member States. Although not a legal body, the European Council is politically very significant. Meeting only two to three times a year, the European Council is centrally involved in the macro development of the EU. The Maastricht and Amsterdam Treaties were negotiated during European Council sessions. During normal European Council meetings, general declarations of principle and intent are made rather than firm policy decisions. Since the European Council inserted a Declaration on sport into the Treaty of Amsterdam, subsequent European Council and Council Presidency Conclusions have regularly made mention of EU involvement in sport. Although these conclusions do not bind the EU legally, they have proved politically very significant in guiding the actions of those involved in EU sports policy.

Acting within the Treaty framework established by the European Council, the European Commission is responsible for proposing secondary legislation and supervising the implementation of policy. The Commission consists of 24 sectoral Directorates-General (DG) and numerous specialised services with a Commissioner at the head of each DG. Due to the highly fragmented nature of EU in-

---

[10] Pinder J, Positive and Negative Integration. Some Problems of Economic Union in the EEC (1968) 24 *World Today* 88-110.

[11] Ibid. 98.

volvement in sport, most DG have some impact, direct or indirect on the operation of sport. The Competition Policy Directorate has a very significant impact on sport in Europe due to its role in investigating breaches of Article 81 and 82 of the Treaty (formerly 85 and 86).[12]

Responsibility for sport within the Commission lies with the Education and Culture Directorate. Located within this Directorate is a specialist *Sport Unit* which is designed to ensure coherence in the Commission's sports related work and foster co-operation with national and international sports interests. This is achieved through the organisation of the *European Sports Forum* and the management of *Sport Info Europe*, a Brussels based sporting telephone service. In addition to these functions, the Directorate has also traditionally managed the sports funding programmes such as *Eurathlon* and *Sports for People with Disabilities*. These programmes were however suspended following a European Court of Justice ruling in May 1998 challenging the legal base for a Community action programme to combat social exclusion.[13] The ruling required each budget item to have a legal base thus forcing the Commission to suspend its sports related funding programmes. The Commission has subsequently published a study examining ways in which sport can be integrated into Community aid programmes.

The directly elected European Parliament has been the biggest beneficiary of institutional reform in the EU. The Parliament's powers over European legislation have been significantly increased since the Single European Act. Following the Maastricht Treaty, the Parliament has been granted legislative co-decisional powers with the Council of Ministers in a range of policy areas. In addition to legislative power, the Parliament can also exert influence on sport through its budgetary and supervisory powers. As the EU does not formally pursue a common sports policy, the Parliament's influence in these areas is however restricted. Within the Parliament's committee structure, sporting issues are discussed in the *Committee on Culture, Youth, Education and Media*. The *Committee on Legal Affairs and Citizens' Rights* and the *Committee on Social Affairs* also have some input into sporting issues. These Committees have produced some influential sports related reports. The Parliament has also established a *Sports Intergroup*, a cross committee, cross party discussion forum for sports related matters. A separate consultative body, the *Committee of Regions* also discusses sporting issues through its sub-committee for *Youth and Sport*.

---

[12] Article 81 prohibits 'all agreements between undertakings, decisions by associations of undertakings and concerted practices which may affect trade between Member States and which have as their object effect the prevention, restriction or distortion of competition within the common market'. Article 82 prohibits 'any abuse by one or more undertakings of a dominant position within the common market ... insofar as it may affect trade between Member States'. Note on Treaty re-numbering- Treaty articles have been re-numbered since the Amsterdam Treaty entered into force in 1999. Post Amsterdam numbering will be used throughout unless otherwise indicated.

[13] Case C-106/96 United Kingdom v The Commission [1998] ECR I/7411.

The Council of Ministers has historically been the main legislative body in the EU although since the Maastricht and Amsterdam Treaties it increasingly shares this power with the European Parliament. The 'Council' is composed of representatives (usually Ministers) from the Member States. Each Council discusses legislative proposals in its own sectoral field. Although the Sports Ministers of the Member States have met informally, they do not pass sports related legislation because the EU does not have a Treaty base to develop a common sports policy. The general legislative activity of the Council has however had a profound effect on sport even though most of the legislation did not have sport as the intended target.

The European Court of Justice has been the most visible European institution in forging a link between the EU and sport. Court rulings have incrementally established important legal principles regulating the operation of sport within the SEM. The most significant of these rulings came in 1995 with the seismic *Bosman* ruling.

Within the above institutional structure, two broad 'advocacy coalitions' can be identified.[14] The first coalition may be termed *'regulatory'*, whilst the second, *'socio-cultural'*. Central to the belief system of the regulatory coalition is a commitment to economic integration and the protection of the four fundamental freedoms.[15] The Competition Policy Directorate and the European Court of Justice are key players within this coalition, both regarding sport as being subject to European law when practised as an economic activity. The socio-cultural coalition is composed of elements within the European Parliament and increasingly many Member States. Central to their belief system is a desire to balance the economic regulation of sport with the promotion and protection of sports socio-cultural and integrationist dimension. As such, the application of European law to the sports sector should be 'soft touch' and the EU should seek ways of harnessing the 'positive' effects of sport. The tension between these two forces is currently shaping the nature of EU sports policy. The Education and Culture Directorate has recently emerged as an important policy broker, attempting to steer a middle course between these two forces.

The Regulatory Agenda

Sport and the European Court of Justice

Embedded within the operating ethos of the European Court of Justice lies a deep commitment to establish and preserve the four fundamental Treaty freedoms.

---

[14] Sabatier P, An Advocacy Coalition Framework of Policy Change and the Role of Policy Orientated Learning Therein. (1988) *Policy Sciences* 21.

[15] The free movement of goods, persons, services and capital.

Three sports related court cases have illustrated the extent of this commitment. The first case concerned nationality restrictions in motor-paced cycling.[16] Two Dutch professional pacemakers (Mr Walrave and Mr Koch) objected to a new requirement made in 1970 by the Union Cycliste Internationale (the sports governing body) that the *pacers* and the *stayers* (the cyclists) had to be of the same nationality in order to compete in World Championships. As Walrave and Koch acted as pacers for non-Dutch stayers, they feared their careers may be jeopardised especially as they felt there was a *'paucity of good Dutch stayers'.*[17] A reference was made by the national court to the European Court of Justice under Article 234 of the EC Treaty.[18] In the case the European Court held that:

'... having regard to the objectives of the Community, the practice of sport is subject to Community law only in so far as it constitutes an economic activity within the meaning of Article 2 of the Treaty'.[19]

The second occasion on which the European Court of Justice dealt with a sports related case concerned nationality rules in Italian football.[20] Italian Football Federation rules placed a heavy restriction on non-Italian footballers wishing to play professional football in Italy. A challenge to these rules was brought by an agent who had attempted to recruit players from abroad. As in the *Walrave* case, the national court referred the case to the European Court of Justice. In particular, the court asked the European Court to establish if the nationality requirement for playing in professional football matches in Italy was compatible with Community law. In 1976, the European Court held that:

'Rules or a national practice, even adopted by a sporting organisation, which limit the right to take part in football matches as professional or semi-professional players solely to the nationals of the state in question, are incompatible with Article 7 and as the case may be, with Articles 48 to 51 or 59 to 66 of the Treaty, unless such rules or practice exclude foreign players from participation in certain matches for reasons which are not of an economic nature, which relate to the particular nature and context of such matters and are thus of sporting interest only'.

Both cases established that sport is subject to Community law in so far as it constitutes an economic activity within the meaning of Article 2 of the EC Treaty.

---

[16] Case 36/74 Walrave & Koch v Union Cycliste Internationale [1974] ECR 1405.

[17] Opinion of Advocate-General Warner, Delivered on 24 October 1974.

[18] Article 234 (formerly 177) grants the Court of Justice jurisdiction to give preliminary rulings concerning the interpretation of the Treaty.

[19] Article 2 of the EEC Treaty reads ...'It shall be the aim of the Community, by establishing a Common Market and progressively approximating the economic policies of the Member States, to promote throughout the Community a harmonious development of economic activities, a continuous and balanced expansion, an increased stability, an accelerated raising of the standard of living and closer relations between its Member States'.

[20] Case 13/76 Donà v Mantero [1976] ECR 1333.

However, exemptions from the principle of non-discrimination on the grounds of nationality are permitted but linked with the practise of sport on a non-economic basis.

The European Commission's attitude towards discriminatory practices in sport in the aftermath of *Walrave* and *Donà* was somewhat contradictory. The Commission adopted a generally consistent view that discriminatory practices in sport should be abolished but took little action to ensure sports compliance with Community law. Dialogue between the Commission and UEFA (European football's governing body) began in 1978 and culminated in the 1991 'gentleman's agreement' between the two parties. This agreement introduced the 1992 '3+2' rule permitting clubs to play three non-nationals in a team and two 'assimilated' players who had played in the country in question for five years without interruption, including three years in junior teams. The Commission's position on sport was framed at a time when sport was barely practised as a significant economic activity. The rapid commercialisation of sport in the 1990's and the ruling in *Bosman* significantly altered the Commission's position.

In the third case, Jean-Marc Bosman, a Belgian footballer, challenged UEFA's use of nationality restrictions and the international transfer system. Bosman's action was sparked by his inability to leave the Belgian first division football club SA Royal Club Liégeois (RC Liége) following his rejection of a new (and diminished) contract offer. RC Liége was permitted to demand a transfer fee for Bosman and thus retain a financial interest in the player despite his contract having ended. In August 1990, Bosman began legal proceedings in the Belgian courts in the hope of securing three main objectives. First, Bosman wanted to gain compensation from his club and the Belgian football authority. Second he wanted the transfer rules amended which allowed a club to retain a financial interest in a player even after expiry of a contract. Third, he wanted the case to be referred to the European Court of Justice for a preliminary ruling on the compatibility of international transfer rules and nationality restrictions in football with EU free movement and competition law. In June 1992 such a reference was made by the national court and although appealed, was confirmed by the Liége Court of Appeal in October 1993.

On 15 December 1995 the European Court of Justice delivered its ruling. The Court answered the questions posed by the Liége Cour d'Appel by stating...

'1. Article 48 of the EEC Treaty precludes the application of rules laid down by sporting associations, under which a professional footballer who is a national of one Member State may not, on the expiry of his contract with a club, be employed by a club of another Member State unless the latter club has paid the former club a transfer, training or development fee.'

'2. Article 48 of the EEC Treaty precludes the application of rules laid down by sporting associations under which, in matches in competitions which they organise, football clubs may field only a limited number of professional players who are nationals of other Member States.'

The impact of the ruling has been profound. The first significant effect has been felt by sports organisations. The internal organisation of professional football has been dramatically re-shaped. International and domestic transfer regimes have been dismantled and nationality restrictions relaxed in all games except in the composition of national teams. Furthermore, the ruling has confirmed sports linkage to the operation of the SEM whenever practised as an economic activity. Football is therefore not the only sport to be affected by the ruling. The second significant effect has been felt within the EU itself. In particular, the ruling sparked renewed regulatory interest in sport from elements within the European Commission. This interest served to galvanise support from within other elements of the EU who wanted sport to be afforded a higher level of protection from EU legislation. In particular, the socio-cultural coalition wanted the EU to give the socio-cultural and integrationist qualities of sport a higher priority.

Sport and Competition Policy

Although the Court chose to apply Article 39 (formerly 48) to the *Bosman* case and not Articles 81 and 82 (formerly 85 and 86), the Competition Policy Directorate within the European Commission has taken the view that the operation of sport may fall within the remit of EU competition law. In this connection the Competition Policy Directorate's scrutiny of sport has been concentrated in three key areas. First, it has examined the organisation of sport including the applicability of revised transfer rules and the continued use of nationality quotas. Second, it has investigated ticketing arrangements for major international sporting events. Third, it has examined the broadcasting of sport in Europe.

The Organization of Sport

The *Bosman* ruling required discriminatory nationality restrictions and the use of the out of contract international transfer system to be dismantled. The Competition Policy Directorate has overseen this restructuring and has closely scrutinised alternatives suggested by UEFA. In addition to this the Commission has been asked to investigate the conduct of competing sports federations. Most sport in Europe is organised on the single structure football model. One international federation controls the activities of its constituent members (usually national federations). The Commission must decide whether restrictive practises employed by federations to maintain the single structure organisation of sport are lawful and if alternative or 'breakaway' structures are established, what is the best mechanism to regulate competition between them. The likelihood of such breakaway structures being formed has increased with the growing trend for media and other investment companies to buy a stake in European football clubs. This move has greatly worried UEFA in that it may challenge their monopoly over the organisation of European football. Also concerned at the implications of this for strategic player transfers and contrived results, UEFA introduced a rule in May 1998 banning clubs with the same owner from competing in European competitions. Only one club from each 'stable' is allowed to participate. The Commission must similarly decide whether these rules are restrictive in nature and whether they can be justified on purely sporting grounds.

The tension between the commercial and socio-cultural dimensions of sport has been further highlighted by two cases involving clubs who had planned to temporarily or permanently relocate to another Member State. English Premiership side Wimbledon and Scottish league side Clydebank examined the possibility of moving to Dublin in the Irish Republic. FIFA, UEFA and national association rules prohibit this type of cross-border move. Both clubs were reported to have considered asking the European Commission to test these rules against EU competition law.[21] A similar case concerned the Belgian football club Excelsior Mouscron who wanted to stage the home leg of a UEFA Cup tie against French side F.C Metz in a larger nearby Stadium across the border in Lille, France. UEFA blocked the move arguing that the home and away structure of its competitions needed protecting. UEFA maintained that the tie must go ahead in the stadium of the home host. The two public bodies representing Lille and Mouscron complained to the European Commission that UEFA's prohibition breached the EC Treaty provisions relating to the free movement of services and competition policy. In December 1999, the Commission took an official decision to reject this complaint.[22]

The most high profile competition policy case investigated by the Commission has concerned the operation of Formula One racing. Acting on two complaints in 1997 by AETV, a German television company and the BPR organisation (known later as GTR) that the Fédération Internationale de L'Automobile (FIA) had abused a dominant market position by controlling the broadcasting of motor sport, the Commission identified four competition issues relating to the operation of Formula One:

- the Commission believes that 'the FIA uses its power to block series which compete with its own events';
- the Commission has claimed that 'the FIA has used this power to force a competing series out of the market';
- the Commission holds the opinion that 'the FIA uses its power to acquire all the television rights to international motor sports events';
- the Commission also believe that 'Formula One Administration Ltd (FOA)

---

[21] Duff A, Scottish Update: A Brief Synopsis of Newsworthy Matters Concerning Football, Rugby & Others from 1997 to Date, (1998) 6(3) *Sport and the Law Journal* 54.
[22] Infra.

and the FIA protect the Formula One Championship from competition by ty-
ing up everything that is needed to stage a rival championship'. [23]

Ultimately, the Commission can impose a fine of not more than 10% of the company's turnover in the full financial year preceding the year in which the Commission takes its decision. In addition, the abusive agreements can be required to
be terminated.

Ticketing Arrangements

Ticketing arrangements for sporting events have also been subject to scrutiny by
the Commission. It has become an established commercial practice for the
organising committees of sporting events to enter into agreements with ticket distributors guaranteeing for the distributor, often for a high price, the exclusive
right to distribute the tickets within each of the Member States. Rather than there
being one single market for ticket sales in the EU, nationally tied exclusive agreements create multiple markets. Very often, only nationals of the country in which
the exclusive ticket distributor is based can purchase tickets. In effect therefore,
each country is given a ticket quota which the exclusive distributor then sells to
the public. The alleged benefit of this system is that it guarantees a fair and equitable distribution of tickets to fans of all countries, large and small who want to
purchase tickets.

On three occasions the Commission has objected to these exclusive ticketing
contracts. In the *Italia '90* case, the Commission objected to this arrangement arguing that it contravened Article 81 of the Treaty.[24] The use of exclusive agents
effectively foreclosed the market for other travel agents. No fine was imposed on
the organisers as the offence was the first of its kind to be investigated by the
Commission and it noted that issues of safety, in particular spectator separation
had complicated matters. In the 1992 *Barcelona Olympics* case the Commission
considered Articles 81 and 82 as having been breached by the practice of territorial exclusivity. No exemption under Article 81(3) could be justified. The
organising committee subsequently amended their contractual arrangements, allowing nationals of a Member State to purchase tickets directly from the
organising Committee or from travel agents based in other Member States.[25]

In a third ticketing case the Commission objected to a proportion of tickets being sold for the 1998 World Cup held in France exclusively to the French market.

---

[23] Commission of the European Communities, *Commission Opens Formal Proceedings into
Formula One and Other International Motor Racing Series* (1999) DN: IP/99/434.

[24] Commission Decision 92/521/EEC relating to a proceeding under Article 85 and cases IV/
33.384 and IV/33.378 on distribution of package tours during the 1990 World Cup (1992) OJ L 326/
92, 12 November 1992.

[25] Coopers and Lybrand, *The Impact of European Union Activities on Sport, Study for DG X of
the European Commission* (1995).

The Commission issued a warning letter to the Comité Français d'Organisation (CFO) on February 20th 1998 requesting an adaptation of its sales policy. Following only minor amendments, on July 20th the Commission issued a formal legal decision against the CFO.[26] The Commission concluded that the CFO's discriminatory ticketing practises amounted to an abuse of a dominant position and as such contrary to Article 82 of the EC Treaty (and Article 54 of the European Economic Area Agreement). The Commission argued that discrimination against non-French residents was reinforced by the CFO advising such people that tickets could only be obtained from national football federations and tour operators. As the ticketing arrangements were similar to those adopted in previous World Cups, the Commission chose to fine the CFO a symbolic sum of just 1000 *Euros*. The Commission acknowledged that the CFO did not have case law to guide them in their decision to establish such as system. It also noted that the CFO had been co-operative and had made more tickets available to non-French customers. In the formal decision, the Commission concluded that future breaches of EU competition law in relation to ticketing arrangements would be dealt with more seriously.

The Broadcasting of Sport

The commercialisation of European sport owes much to developments in the European broadcasting sector. The proximity of sport to broadcasting has inevitably led to a closer relationship between sport and the EU. The Competition Policy Directorate has examined four aspects of sports relationship with broadcasting:

– The well-established practice of selling broadcasting rights to sports games on an exclusive basis. Although not opposed to exclusivity, the Commission has investigated the length of such contracts. The sale of exclusive broadcasting rights, sold on long term contracts, may be viewed as a barrier to market entry. It believes that exclusive deals may be exempt from competition law when they are granted for a brief time and are limited in their scope and effect.
– The joint sale of broadcasting rights on behalf of the participants. In such cases the Commission must examine whether the prevention of clubs from entering into individual agreements with broadcasters amounts to a restraint of trade and also whether the central marketing of broadcasting rights is necessary to ensure the survival of the smaller participants in the league. An exemption under Article 81(3) from cartel rules of Article 81(1) may be granted if the solidarity argument is accepted.
– The manner in which broadcasting rights are acquired. In particular, the negotiating strength of the European Broadcasting Union (EBU), a cartel of public

---

[26] Commission of the European Communities, *Commission takes action against the local organisers of the 1998 football World Cup finals competition in France* (1999) DN: IP/99/541.

service broadcasters who co-operate in order to improve their collective bidding power. In the Eurosport case the Commission found that the EBU's collaborative acquisition system gave the EBU members an unfair competitive advantage and was incompatible with Article 82 of the Treaty.[27]

– Article 14 of UEFA's statute controls he cross-border transmission of football matches. UEFA uses Article 14 in order to protect attendance at matches and indeed participation at all levels believing that these could be adversely affected by broadcasting matches from other countries at the same time as domestic games. Commission investigations into Article 14 have centred on its compatibility with Article 81 of the Treaty as cross border trade in the broadcasting of football matches between Member States is restricted. Furthermore, Article 14 prevents national football federations from freely marketing their transmission rights in the SEM. Following negotiations between UEFA and the Commission, Article 14 was amended to become less restrictive.

THE SOCIO-CULTURAL AGENDA

The Court ruling in *Bosman* and the nature of Commission investigations into sport has resulted in considerable criticism being levelled at the EU. In particular a significant body of opinion has emerged who believe the EU is insensitively applying the legal regime to sport and through its regulatory ethos has failed to appreciate the socio-cultural and its integrationist qualities. Many regard sports organisations as being best placed to decide on the future of sport. A powerful socio-cultural coalition has emerged within the EU seeking to articulate and act upon these concerns.

Although galvanised by *Bosman*, this coalition is not entirely new. Traditionally, the instrumental use of sport for socio-cultural and integrationist purposes in the EU has been linked with the concept of a 'People's Europe'. The formal launch of an institutional commitment to the concept of a People's Europe can be traced back to the 1984 Fontainebleau Summit. In response to a perceived crisis in European integration, an *ad hoc* committee (the Adonnino Committee) was established charged with the responsibility of exploring measures that could strengthen the image of the European Community in the minds of its citizens.

The Committee made eight sets of recommendations, one of which concerned the symbolic use of sport.[28] The spirit of Adonnino has lived on, particularly within the European Parliament's *Committee on Culture, Youth, Education and Media* and with many Member States. *Bosman* opened a window of opportunity

---

[27] Collins, R, *Broadcasting and Audio-Visual Policy in the European Single Market* (1994) London, John Libby, 149.

[28] Ibid.

for these actors to push for their particular approach to sport to be more widely adopted.

The European Parliament

Although the Parliament has consistently argued for the EU to recognise the socio-cultural and integrationist qualities of sport, its approach has become more active since *Bosman*. This is consistent with the Parliament's aim of establishing an ever-closer union among EU citizens. Parliament's operating ethos reflects a desire to promote socio-political integration in the EU as a complimentary counterbalance to economic integration and has been active in a range of sports related issues.

Two reports illustrate the Parliament's approach to sport. Both the 1994 '*Larive Report*' on the European Community and Sport and the 1997 '*Pack Report*' on the Role of the European Union in the Field of Sport. These demonstrate a desire to balance the economic regulation of sport with the promotion of sports' socio-cultural and integrationist qualities.[29] Parliament has also exploited the co-decision legislative procedure to insist on the adoption of a socio-culturally minded sporting amendment to the second Television Without Frontiers directive (TWF) in 1997.[30] The initial 1989 TWF project sought to liberalise the European broadcasting sector. In a subsequent amendment to this directive, Article 3a of the new directive permits Member States to draw up lists of protected sporting events that will have to be made available to the public on free-to-air television.

Re-directing EU Sports Policy: The Involvement of the Member States

Following *Bosman*, calls intensified within the European sports sector for sport to be granted a legal base within the European Treaty. The proponents of this move, including National Olympic Committees, European sports federations, the European Parliament and some Member States, hoped to achieve three broad objectives:

– they wanted to ensure that sports organisational autonomy remains intact;
– that EU institutions consult with the sports sector when sporting issues are discussed;
– that sport is taken into account in the framing of other EU policies.

---

[29] European Parliament, *Report on the European Community and Sport (The Larive Report)* (1994) Document A3-0326/94/PartA (27/4/94) Part B (29/4/94); European Parliament, *Report on the Role of the European Union in the Field of Sport (the Pack Report)* (1997), Document A4-0197/97 (28/5/97).

[30] Council of the European Communities, Recitals to the Directive 97/36/EC of the European Parliament and of the Council of 19/6/97, amending Council Directive 89/552/EEC on the Co-ordination of Certain Provisions Laid Down by Law, Regulation or Administrative Action in Member States Concerning the Pursuit of Television Broadcasting Activities, 89/552/EEC.

In short, it was hoped that a legally based article for sport would limit what was perceived as the insensitive application of EU law to sport and protect sports' traditional and autonomous structures.

Proposals were submitted to the 1996 intergovernmental conference, a conference charged with the task of preparing a new Treaty designed to reform the Maastricht Treaty. Despite the strength of support, the issue of sports' incorporation into the Treaty became secondary to weightier political concerns. Crucially, the European Commission did not support the legal incorporation of sport into the Treaty for fear of setting a precedent for allowing certain professions exemptions from the Treaty. As a result, the heads of State and Government meeting in Amsterdam in June 1997 attached a non-binding Declaration on sport to the Amsterdam Treaty. The Declaration read:

> 'The conference emphasises the social significance of sport, in particular its role in forging identity and bringing people together. The conference therefore calls on the bodies of the European Union to listen to sports associations when important questions affecting sport are at issue. In this connection, special consideration should be given to the particular characteristics of amateur sport.'

The Declaration disappointed those who wished to see legal competence for sport to be established within the Treaty. Inspite of appearing 'fairly banal',[31] it has had a significant impact on the course of EU sports policy. Through the Declaration, the Member States have given some political guidance to the EU institutions on how they wish to see sports policy develop. In particular, the Member States have signalled that the socio-cultural and integrationist qualities of sport should be given a higher priority.

Since the Declaration, each Council Presidency has discussed sport in some form.[32] During the Luxembourg Presidency in the second half of 1997 sport was discussed as a vehicle in tackling unemployment through the provision of sporting activities and facilities. The British Presidency in the first half of 1998 promoted the role of sport in combating social exclusion, regenerating communities and reconnecting the EU with its citizens. The Austrian Presidency continued discussing these social dimensions of sport during the second half of 1998. At the Vienna Council meeting in December 1998, the Commission was requested to "submit a report to the Helsinki European Council with a view to safeguarding current sports structures and maintaining the social function of sport within the Community framework'.[33] In addition to the fight against doping in sport, the

---

[31] Henry & Matthews, supra n.4, 2.

[32] The Presidency of the Council of Ministers rotates every six months. The Presidency combines an administrative role with a political function. This political function allows the Presidency to prioritise pre-existing items on the EU's agenda. At the end of each Presidency (June / December) a European Council meeting is convened.

[33] Austrian Presidency Conclusions (11-12/12/98), *The Vienna European Council Presidency Conclusions*.

Vienna summit stands as a significant milestone as it formally requests the Commission to examine approaches to safeguard sports structures. This demonstrated for the first time that the Amsterdam Declaration had teeth.

This significant policy development was continued by Germany during their Presidency in the first half of 1999. At an informal meeting of the Sports Ministers of the EU in Paderborn in early June, a range of issues concerning doping in sport, employment and sport and improving the portrayal of sport for the disabled in the media was discussed. The Sports Ministers concluded that the particular concerns of sport should be supported especially the application of competition law and internal market rules and EU measures relating to sport and television. This advanced the Amsterdam Declaration significantly. The Ministers requested the Commission to examine ways of how the concerns of sport could be taken into account in the EU Treaty.[34]

The Paderborn Conclusions once again reflect a growing socio-cultural attitude towards sport in the EU and a move away from a purely regulatory approach. The willingness of the Member States to specify those areas of EU law to be applied to the sports sector with a 'soft touch' is a significant development and one designed to place political pressure on the Commission to take note.

The Finnish Presidency (in the second half of 1999) declared that it wished to:

'carry on the discussion on the status of sports in Community law, emphasising the social significance of sports and the need to take the special characteristics of sports into account in the application of legislation'.[35]

In a thinly veiled criticism of the EU's regulatory approach to sport, Sports Directors meeting as part of the Presidency programme concluded:

'sport is an important resource that promotes people's well-being and health, the cultural dimension and social cohesion. Therefore, sport in its social significance should be seen as a broad-based sector.[36]

The 'Helsinki Report on Sport'[37] indicates that the Amsterdam Declaration on sport and subsequent Presidency meetings have had a significant effect on the Commission's approach to sport. The Report attempts to provide a more struc-

---

[34] German Presidency Conclusions (31/5-2/6 1999), *Conclusions of the German European Council Presidency on the Occasion of the Informal Meeting of the Sport Ministers of the European Union, 'the Paderborn Conclusions'.*

[35] Finnish Ministry of Education, *Priorities: Ministry of Education* (1999) Finnish EU Presidency Website.

[36] Finnish Presidency Conclusions (18-20/10/99), *Sports Directors Meeting. Conclusions of the Presidency.*

[37] Commission of the European Communities, *Report from the Commission to the European Council with a View to safeguarding Sports Structures and Maintaining the Social Significance of Sport Within the Community Framework (the Helsinki Report on Sport)*, Com (1999) 644.

tured relationship between sport and the EU and represents something of a 'new approach' to EU sports policy.

At the end of the Portuguese Presidency (in the first half of 2000) the Ministers held on 10 May. At this meeting the Ministers recommended five developments in the field of EU sports policy:

- the establishment of an informal working group with the aim of proposing to the Member States forms of participation with the World Anti-Doping Agency;
- that, '... the specific aspects of sport, namely its social dimension, should be taken into consideration in the implementation of Community policies'; [38]
- Third: 'the creation of a joint working group with representatives of the EU and the Commission, charged with studying the harmonisation of the specific aspects of sport within the Treaty of the Union';[39]
- Fourth, the creation of training and exchange programmes for young sportspersons;
- Finally, the creation of a sports information network between Member States that would act as a mechanism for the dissemination of information.

The Presidency Conclusions relating to sport read:

> 'the European Council requests the Commission and the Council to take account of the specific characteristics of sport in Europe and its social function in managing common policies'.[40]

RECONCILING CONFLICTING APPROACHES: THE 'NEW APPROACH'

Through the institutions of the European Council, Council of Ministers and Council Presidency, the Member States have signalled a clear desire to adopt a more broad-based approach to sport. In this connection, the Education and Culture Directorate has emerged as a key institution attempting to construct a more balanced approach to sport. In 1998, as part of its response to the Amsterdam Declaration on Sport, DG X published a Commission working paper entitled, *'The Development and Prospects for Community Action in the Field of Sport.'*[41] It identified sport as performing an educational, public health, social, cultural and recreational function. Sport is the key vehicle through which policy objectives in these fields could be pursued. It recognised that sport plays a significant economic role in Europe and the Commission as guardian of the Treaties had a re-

---

[38] Portuguese Presidency Conclusions (17/3/00), *Troika Meeting. Presidency Conclusions.*

[39] Ibid. In a footnote below this passage it was noted that the United Kingdom had refused to approve the establishment of a working group for the inclusion of a new paragraph in the Treaty.

[40] Ibid.

[41] Commission of the European Communities, *Developments and Prospects for Community Activity in the Field of Sport* (1998) Directorate General X, Brussels.

sponsibility to ensure the even implementation of Community law. The paper advocated a dual approach to sport: on the one hand the integration of sport into different Community policies whilst on the other ensuring the implementation of Community law.

Shortly after the working paper, DG X published a consultation document entitled, *'The European Model of Sport'*.[42] This was an attempt by the Commission to conduct a more structured dialogue with the world of sport, to canvass opinion and to communicate to the sports world its approach to sport and also to assist sports organisations to re-frame sporting rules in line with Community law. The document comprised three chapters:

– the European 'model' of sport which argued that commercial pressures in the world of sport are putting pressure on this model;
– the relationship between sport and television
– the socio-cultural dimension of sport.

Attached to the consultation document were a series of questionnaires designed to canvass opinion on the future structure of European sport, the future relationship between sport and television and to identify the social dimension of sport. Issues relating to doping in sport received a particularly high priority. The findings of this exercise were used by the Commission to prepare the first EU Conference on Sport held in Greece in May 1999. The conclusions of the Conference were then used by the Commission to prepare the Helsinki Report on Sport, outlining an approach to safeguarding current sports structures and maintaining the social function of sport within the Community framework.

The Report was submitted to the December 1999 Helsinki European Council. It signals the establishment of a new approach to sport in the EU. At the heart of this is a framework for applying EU law to sport: 'this new approach involves preserving the traditional values of sport, while at the same time assimilating a changing economic and legal environment.'[43]

CONCLUSIONS: EVIDENCE OF A 'NEW APPROACH'?

Although only a very recent development, evidence suggests that this 'new approach' to sport, which balances regulatory with socio-cultural forces, is beginning to have an affect on the development of EU sports policy. Three examples illustrate this point.

---

[42] Commission of the European Communities, *The European Model of Sport. Consultation Document* (1998) Directorate General X, Brussels.

[43] *The Helsinki Report on Sport*, supra n.37.

The Application of EU Competition Law

First, the new approach has affected the workings of the Competition Policy. In February 1999 the Competition Policy Directorate published a paper on the application of competition rules to sport.[44] In the paper, the Commission made a distinction between purely sporting situations and wholly commercial situations to which Treaty provisions will apply. However, even in the application of these provisions to such commercial situations, the Commission recognised that the particular characteristics of sport must be taken into account. Without granting sport a general exemption from EU law, the general principles are identified to guide the application of EU competition law to the sports sector. These include:

- safeguarding the general interest in relation to the protection of private interests;
- restricting Commission action to cases which are of Community interest;
- applying the so called *de minimis* rule, according to which agreements of minor importance do not significantly affect trade between Member States;
- applying the four authorisation criteria laid down in Article 81(3) of the EC Treaty, but also refusing an exemption to any agreements which infringe other provisions of the EC Treaty and in particular freedom of movement for sportsmen;
- defining relevant markets pursuant to the applicable general rules;
- adapted to the features specific to each sport.[45]

In the Helsinki Report, the Commission employed these principles to provide examples of instances where competition law would or would not apply and instances where exemptions are likely to be granted. Significantly, the Report concluded that agreements between professional clubs, or decisions by their associations that are designed to achieve a balance between clubs and to encourage the recruitment and training of young players, may be exempt from the application of EU law. Indeed, the same would be true of a revised transfer system based on 'objectively calculated payments that are related to the costs of training, or of an exclusive right, limited in duration and scope, to broadcast sporting events'.[46]

Although not 'reversing'[47] some of the effects of *Bosman*, the paper does provide greater legal certainty than previously existed. In addition it indicates a greater willingness on the part of the Competition Policy Directorate to exempt certain sporting practices from the application of EU law. The Commission's Re-

---

[44] Commission of the European Communities, *Commission Debates Application of its Competition Rules to Sport* (1999) IP/99/133.

[45] Ibid.

[46] *The Helsinki Report on Sport*, supra n.37.

[47] Europe to Protect Clubs from Bosman (1999) The Guardian October 20. Vivek Chaudhary wrote: *The European Commission has given its strongest hint yet that it may reverse some of the effects of the Bosman ruling because of their damaging impact on smaller football clubs'.*

port clearly indicates the adoption of a more 'soft touch' application of competition law to sport.

The Report must be placed in context:

- First, the Competition Policy Directorate is keen to reduce its existing sports related competition policy caseload. This has expanded greatly in recent years and is placing pressure on an over-stretched bureaucracy.
- Second, although the Competition Policy Directorate's approach to sport can be described as 'regulatory', it has been far from ultra-regulatory, as many have claimed. The policy shift is not huge, and even though the recent approach to sport has been labelled 'new', the principles employed by the Commission have followed a well-trodden path.
- Third, the framework approach for applying EU law to sport is still problematic. The Commission will need to distinguish between purely sporting situations and wholly commercial situations. Can a framework accommodate such diversity? If a more flexible approach is adopted by the Commission in applying competition law to situations that are considered to be 'unique characteristics' of sport, who is to define these characteristics? Restrictions purporting to protect these characteristics must also respect the principle of proportionality whilst subsidiarity cannot be employed by sports bodies to mask anti-competitive practices. If a flexible approach is to be adopted, perhaps supported by the greater use of exemptions, a framework approach can only develop incrementally as principles emerge on a case-by-case basis. A policy shift in this field is therefore likely to take time.
- Finally, the Commission is still committed to the development and consolidation of the internal market and officials are keen not to set a precedent for allowing certain professions exemptions from the Treaty.

In December 1999 the Competition Policy Directorate adopted two decisions demonstrating its willingness to employ the above framework.[48] In the first case the Commission rejected the complaint made against UEFA in the *Mouscron* case. The Commission argued that, 'the UEFA Cup rule to the effect that each club must play its home match at its own ground is a sports rule that does not fall within the scope of the Treaty's competition rules'.[49] As such the case contains no Community interest. In the second case, the Commission has taken the preliminary decision that UEFA rules limiting multiple club ownership could also fall outside the Treaty's competition rules. The Commission may in time confirm this view by adopting an exemption decision.

It would, however be incorrect to view these moves as an ideological shift on the part of the Commission. The Commission has, after all failed to take action in

---

[48] Commission of the European Communities, *Limits to application of Treaty competition rules to sport: Commission gives clear signal* (1999) DN: IP/99/965.

[49] Ibid. 1.

sports related matters before.[50] In other cases, particularly relating to ticketing arrangements in sport, the Commission has adopted a very soft touch approach. The significance of the 'new approach' in terms of applying competition law is based on a pragmatic response to administrative and political pressures for a structured approach.

Jurisprudence of the European Court of Justice

It is also likely that the 'new approach' has affected the European Court of Justice's view in recent sports related cases. This is a controversial claim and one rejected by those who adopt an overly legalist interpretation of the role of the Court. Contextualist studies of the Court's treatment of sports issues have found evidence of a more sensitive approach to the prevailing political environment.

The Court has recently been requested to consider two further sports related disputes, one concerning judo, the other basketball: the *Deliège* and *Lehtonen* cases.[51] In both cases the Court confirmed the practice of sport as an economic activity but having done so stepped back from further extending the principle of free movement in the sports world. The Court's rulings took place within the context of an on-going discussion in the EU on how best to reconcile the economic and socio-cultural dimensions of sport within the EU structure. By acknowledging the existence of the concept of sporting interest in the composition of sports rules, the Court has been sensitive to this debate. For instance, the Court held that without transfer deadlines, late transfers could substantially change the sporting strength of a team thus calling into question the comparability of results between the teams taking part. This could therefore affect the whole functioning of the championship at a critical time in the season.[52] In short therefore, the Court argued that in both cases there existed a public interest in maintaining rules that *prima facie* may be considered restrictive.

The Intergovernmental Conference (IGC) Process

Finally, the new approach to sport may find more formal and institutionalised expression in the revised Treaty currently being negotiated. The Amsterdam Treaty was designed to prepare the EU for the necessary deepening that was to take place prior to the successful widening of the Union. In the event, the summit postponed many of the difficult decisions. Throughout much of 1999 and the first half of 2000, the EU has embarked upon a further revision to the Treaty. This process has provided the socio-cultural actors with another opportunity to push

---

[50] As in the Belgium Indoor Football dispute.

[51] These cases are fully considered by Foster K, elsewhere in this volume.

[52] Case C-176/96 Jyri Lehtonen and Castors Canada Dry Namur-Braine v Fédération Royale des Sociétés de Basketball and Ligue Belge-Belgische Liga, 13 April 2000, para. 54.

for more formal measures concerning the Treaty's status of sport. The current debate on the status of sport in the Treaty has been heavily influenced by the debate within European football on the impact foreign players are having on domestic and international football. Towards the end of 1999 and during the first half of 2000, it was widely reported that governing bodies, FIFA and UEFA were examining ways of re-imposing nationality restrictions within the framework of the EU.[53] This issue was discussed under the Portuguese Presidency at Lisbon, which as a result of this a Committee was established to consider the special status of sport and to examine the merits of a protocol in the revised Treaty.[54]

The protocol idea is not entirely new. On occasion, the EU has adopted such protocols to:

– First, address specific Member State concerns (as with the *social* protocol)
– Second, to provide exemptions to Treaty principles (as with the *Danish Second Homes* protocol) or
– Third, to limit the effects of a Court ruling (as with the *Barber* protocol).

Clearly, all three instances pose problems. In the first instance a precedent for a more flexible 'a la carte' Europe is set. In the second instance, a precedent is set for allowing a range of industries to claim 'special status'. In the third, a potentially undemocratic precedent is set whereby Member States interfere in Court rulings.

The French Presidency (June-December 2000) has continued these discussions. In particular, the French Presidency has expressed the desire that the conclusions of the working group should form the basis of discussions at the 9th European Sports Forum held in Lille on 26th and 27th October 2000 and that the conclusions of this meeting will lead to the adoption of 'significant' steps by the European Council of Nice on 7 and 8 December, 2000. The appearance (or not) of sport in the new Treaty will tell us much about the strength of the new approach. The willingness of the EU to discuss the Treaty status of sport at a high level indicates the seriousness and determination of some Member States to adopt a more broad based approach to sports policy. However, Treaty incorporation will require unanimous agreement and this may prove difficult to achieve.

---

[53] See Gardiner & Welch in this volume.

[54] UEFA Chief Executive, Gerhard Aigner explained ... *'We are not seeking to change EU law by having the Bosman ruling repealed but what we do want is a sporting protocol to the European Treaty which would allow the EU to apply certain exemptions in sport'* (UEFA News Release 13/4/00).

CAN SPORT BE REGULATED BY EUROPE?: AN ANALYSIS OF ALTERNATIVE MODELS

Ken Foster

INTRODUCTION

What role is there for the regulation of sport at the European level? Sport has traditionally been an arena of self-regulation in which the courts and the legislature have respected the autonomy of the governing bodies of sport. This autonomy has been eroded over the past decade.[1] Sport has become more commercialized, especially as the deregulation of the broadcasting industry has allowed new entrants to use sport as a way of gaining a foothold in the marketplace. This has brought the law into play as a method of challenging decisions made by governing bodies. National courts have made some important decisions, especially concerning the legitimacy of the collective selling of broadcasting rights by football leagues.[2] Yet there are limits to the scope of national legal regulation. National courts are restricted in what they can do to control the activities of transnational governing bodies, such as UEFA and FIFA in football. Greater international competition in most sports has made issues such as the player's right to move freely across national borders more significant. International legal regulation of sport however is in its infancy and so far has been limited to minor issues. So the regulation of international sporting federations has to date mainly been the province of the European regulatory authorities. Football is the most international and popular sport in Europe and thus the activities of UEFA have been the principal focus of the European Commission since the landmark decision in *Bosman*.[3]

The traditional model of governance in European sport had a single federation that created institutions, regulated the sport, promoted competitions usually by

---

[1] On the erosion of sporting autonomy see Foster K, Developments in Sporting Law, in Allison L (ed.), *The Changing Politics of Sport* (1993), Manchester University Press.

[2] See the German decision in 1997, overturned by legislation from 1st January 1999 and the decision by the Restrictive Practices Court in 1999, Re the supply of services facilitating the broadcasting on television of Premier League football matches.

[3] C-415/93 Union Royale Belge des Sociétés de Football ASBL v Bosman [1995] ECR I-4921, [1996] 1 CMLR 645.

A. Caiger and S. Gardiner (Eds), Professional Sport in the EU: Regulation and Re-regulation
© 2000, T.M.C.Asser Press, The Hague, The Netherlands

sanctioning events, and organized the commercial exploitation of broadcasting and other rights. The commercial activities of governing bodies have expanded and it is these activities in particular that have come under regulatory scrutiny. Competition policy is the main area of conflict. The Commission has tried to formulate a vision of what constitutes the wider public interest in sport, taking as its touchstone that Europe has a distinctive model of sport. This differs from the more commercialized American model and helps to preserve the social role of sport. European governing bodies of sport are changing from their traditional role of self-governance to a more hybrid role that tries to expand and organize their revenues for the collective good of the sport.

European regulation of sport has had four periods, each of which illustrates a different regulatory tactic. There was a long period of relative non-intervention that lasted until the judgment in *Bosman*. Early judicial decisions recognized that the Treaty of Rome governs sport in principle in so far as it involves economic activity. These decisions nevertheless suggested that amateur sport was not necessarily covered and that selection for national teams could be an exception to the Treaty.[4] The Commission as a regulator intervened very little in sport. It limited itself to peripheral issues such as the sale of package tours linked to the purchase of tickets for the 1990 World Cup in Italy.[5] It had also begun to be interested in the sale of broadcasting rights by sporting bodies. There was some inter-governmental action in the Council of Europe on football hooligans[6] and doping in sport.[7] The Council adopted a European Sports Charter in 1992 but this contains only vague aspirations about co-operative measures. Overall the pattern was one of minimum regulation with little desire to intervene. A report in 1995 for the European Commission was a catalogue of piecemeal measures that hardly suggested widespread intervention in sport.[8]

The *Bosman* decision marked the start of a second phase.[9] The implications of the judgment for professional football were far-reaching. The legality of the transfer system was questioned. A labour market in which players out of contract could move without restriction was allowed, and the legality of transfer fees for players under contract questioned.[10] *Bosman* also declared national quotas that

---

[4] Case 36/74 Walrave and Koch v Association Union Cycliste Internationale, [1974] ECR 1405; case 13/76 Donà v Mantero, [1976] ECR 1333.

[5] Italia 90, OJ 1992 L326/31.

[6] European Convention on Spectator Violence and Misbehavior at Sports Events and in particular at Football Matches. (Adopted at Strasbourg 19th August 1985).

[7] Anti-doping Convention (Adopted at Strasbourg 16th November 1989).

[8] Coopers and Lybrand, *The Impact of European Activities on Sport* (1995).

[9] On *Bosman* see Foster K, Games Without Frontiers: Free Movement in Sport, in Wilson G and Rogowski R (eds.), *Challenges to European Legal Scholarship* (1996), Blackstone, London.

[10] In December 1998 the Commission informed FIFA that all transfer fees were illegal under Article 81. The Commissioner for Competition Policy, Mario Monti, said in April 2000 that 'in the absence of any structured and clear proposals from FIFA for new regulations bringing the transfer rules into line with Article 81, a negative decision will be prepared.' (DN: Speech/00/152).

limited the number of foreign players illegal. This made the preservation of local and national identity in sport more difficult. The principle of the single market that allowed no discrimination based on national origins overrode the sporting values of teams made up of mainly domestic players. The significant feature of *Bosman* was that it was a private right action brought by an individual player. By relying on Article 39 of the Treaty,[11] *Bosman* was able to bypass the cosy regulatory regime that existed previously. The direct enforcement of the basic freedoms in the Treaty was a means of regulation that sidestepped the slow-moving Commission. They had been considering *Bosman*-type issues for many years and had only moved UEFA part of the way towards a free non-discriminatory labour market for footballers.

Bosman also highlighted the implications of competition law. Whilst not using Articles 81 and 82 of the Treaty[12] as the basis of their decision, the European Court of Justice made it clear that when acting as a business, football was subject fully to competition law and policy. This began a third phase, that of Commission activity. It is much easier and cheaper to file a complaint with the Commission against sporting federations for acting in an anti-competitive manner that it is to bring a private right action. Suddenly the Commission became reactive as a flood of complaints reached it and proactive as they debated the automatic application of the competition rules to sport. To treat sport purely as a business implied that the ideology of the free market was the appropriate one for sport. The logic of a free and single market underpins Europe's competition policy. As Hoehn and Szymanski have argued,[13] football does not have a single European market. It lacks a European league and is still segmented into national leagues. They propose that a 'transnational league' is the 'most plausible market solution'.[14] But the question remains – can sport be regulated like any other business?

The Amsterdam Treaty of 1997 began a fourth period with a different strategy. The Treaty had a protocol emphasizing the social aspects of sport and its unique features. This was a political initiative with two aims. One was a warning shot across the bows of the Commission, encouraging it to develop policies that limited the automatic application of the competition rules to sport. The other purpose was to develop a separate policy strand of regulation that argued for sport's distinctive cultural and social importance. This purpose could be achieved by exempting sport from the Treaty entirely or by having a special competence for sport akin to the existing one for cultural affairs. The Helsinki Report on Sport in 1999 furthered this 'social role of sport' approach.[15]

---

[11] Formerly Article 48.

[12] Formerly Articles 85 and 86.

[13] Hoehn T, and Szymanski S, The Americanization of European Football, (1999) *Economic Review*, April, 205-40.

[14] Ibid. 206.

[15] Com (1999) 644. For a summary of the report, see Weatherill S, in (2000) 25 *European Law Review* 270.

A final regulatory model that has been little discussed is the harmonization of national legal regimes. Many Member States have introduced measures that support or reform sporting federations, especially with the aim of better governance. The protection of consumers from exploitation by clubs and the protection of players from arbitrary disciplinary measures by governing bodies are two areas that may be better controlled at national level. Harmonization of these measures can have benefits. This approach, can however, flounder because different national traditions have developed as to the desirable degree of state intervention in sport. The development of a single Community sports policy may be some distance away but there are signs of it emerging. Each of these regulatory strategies is now examined.

PRIVATE RIGHTS REGULATION

One potential source of regulation for European sport is the European Court of Justice. The fallout from *Bosman* has illustrated its potential power. Its chief legal impact has been to assert the primacy of the fundamental freedoms. It upheld freedom of movement for workers under Article 39 as necessarily applicable to sport and said that this can only rarely be ignored. Despite the considerable impact that *Bosman* has had, the private right strategy of regulation has several limitations. It depends on the willingness of individuals to pursue claims. Players with a short professional career may not be prepared to risk the disapproval of those governing bodies of sport on whom they ultimately depend for their livelihood. For the individual, litigation is expensive and lengthy. It can only have a wider impact on sport if the sporting authorities respond to the judgments of the Court. It is a crude form of regulation that can only allow a yes/no answer by the Court. The negotiated settlement under the threat of enforcement that the Commission can use is not directly available to the Court. Finally because it is direct enforcement by an individual, it is restricted to the basic freedoms of the Treaty. Yet it was the Court of Justice that first recognized that when sport is an economic activity it is governed by European law.

Early decisions of the Court confirmed that the Treaty governs sport. In 1974 in *Walrave*[16] the Court held that Article 39 was directly enforceable against a sporting federation. This was because they had 'rules ... aimed at regulating in a collective manner gainful employment and the provisions of services'. In 1976 in *Donà*[17] the Court held that semi-professional footballers were workers for the purposes of Article 39. The combined effect of these two decisions was that most players who received some payment had a directly effective right against their

---

[16] Supra n. 4.
[17] Ibid.

governing bodies. However *Donà* also introduced into the Court's jurisprudence the distinction between economic and social activities. In selecting national or regional teams, governing bodies could insist on geographical qualifications because these were reasons 'not of an economic nature, which relate to the particular nature and context of such matches and are thus of sporting interest only'. This dichotomy between economic and sporting activities persists in *Bosman*. In a key passage the Court recognized the social importance of sport within the community. It spoke of 'the considerable social importance of sporting activities and in particular football in the Community'[18] as the basis for a possible exception to Article 39. In retrospect this paragraph can be seen as the genesis of the Court's attempt to formulate a policy of non-intervention in sport.

Two recent decisions of the European Court of Justice advance this policy of trying to create an area of non-intervention, especially by using the Treaty's concept of public interest. In *Lehtonen*,[19] a Finnish basketball player was signed by a Belgian club for the play-offs of the Belgian championship. The Belgian Basketball Federation had rules that imposed deadlines on the transfers of players. Players signed after these deadlines were ineligible to play in the current season. The purpose of these rules was to prevent clubs buying in new players late in the season specifically to play in the play-offs. This was said to distort the outcome of the season-long competition. However the Basketball Federation had staggered deadlines. The transfer of players between Belgian clubs was not permitted after the start of the season. International transfers from non-Belgian clubs had later deadlines. Players who had played in other European countries could be transferred before February 28 and still be eligible to play for the rest of the season. Players who had played in non-European countries, such as the USA, had a later deadline of March 31. Lehtonen, who had played in the Finnish championship, signed for his Belgian club on March 30 and was therefore ineligible under the rules. The Belgian Basketball Federation penalized the club when they did play him by awarding the game to the other team. Lehtonen's club thereafter decided not to play him in the remaining play-off games.

The original ground of complaint was that the transfer deadlines were unlawful because they hindered free movement within Europe. The Advocate-General in his opinion did not accept an argument claiming the 'organizational autonomy of sporting federations'. This would have prevented any effective investigation of the justification for any sporting rule. The European Court of Justice confirmed this non-immunity in its judgment. It said that the Treaty applied 'to sporting activities and to rules laid down by sports associations'.[20] The private nature of sporting federations was irrelevant. The Court said that 'the abolition as between

---

[18] Para. 106 of the judgment.
[19] Case C-176/96 Lehtonen and Castors Canada Dry Namur-Braine v FRBSB (Belgian Basketball Federation) judgment of 13 April 2000.
[20] Para. 36.

Member States of obstacles to freedom of movement for persons and freedom to provide services would be compromised if the abolition of State barriers could be neutralized by obstacles resulting from the exercise of their legal autonomy by associations or organizations not governed by public law'.[21] This is interesting in view of the English courts' reluctance to allow judicial review, a public law remedy, of decisions made by governing bodies.[22]

The Advocate-General was ready to accept, on the other hand, that the Basketball Federation could have legitimate sporting reasons for imposing transfer deadlines. The Court itself described these reasons thus: 'late transfers might be liable to change substantially the sporting strength of one or other team in the course of the championship, thus calling into question the comparability of the results between the teams taking part in that championship'.[23] The legal basis for this 'sporting justification', at least in the Advocate-General's opinion, is the 'public interest' exception contained in Article 39 itself. This interpretation could be unsound. Council Directive 64/221 provides that 'public policy' exceptions must relate exclusively to the personal conduct of the individual concerned. It is hard to see how a general argument that late transfers can distort the outcome of a championship is related to the personal conduct of the player.

The European Court of Justice was not however convinced that there was a need for staggered deadlines for transfers. There was no obvious sporting justification for the different deadlines. These discriminated against players moving from other European leagues as they had the earlier deadline. The principle of proportionality, whereby any restriction on the free movement of workers has to be effective to achieve its objective and to go no further than is necessary, was offended. Article 39 therefore prohibited such differential treatment of transfers for there was no good 'objective sporting reasons'.

The conclusions for sporting federations from the *Lehtonen* decision are fourfold. First, that sport cannot claim to be immune from regulation or be free to make its own rules. Second, that even fundamental rights such as the right of free movement can be interfered with by the rules of sport such as those on transfer deadlines. Third, that such interference must be justified as being necessary for sporting reasons and proportional. Fourth, that the rules permitting such deviations from the fundamental rights must not themselves discriminate between players on the grounds of national origin.

There are qualifications to the *Lehtonen* decision. Neither the European Court of Justice nor the Advocate-General fully explore the sporting justifications permitting transfer deadlines as an exception to Article 39. As long as the rules are the same for each club, why are deadlines in themselves objectionable? Is it be-

---

[21] Para. 35.

[22] As confirmed by the Court of Appeal in R v Disciplinary Committee of the Jockey Club, ex parte Aga Khan [1993] 2 All ER 853.

[23] Para. 54.

cause otherwise the richest clubs can buy success at a crucial stage of the season? This maybe the reality, but the Court does not offer this as an explanation. The sole reason advanced by the Court is 'the comparability of results'. This means that some clubs will play a stronger team from one club later in the season than other clubs who have already played that same club. Again this may occur, but where is the 'objective' evidence that such transfers do alter a team's prospects for the better? If this were the main reason the logic would be to prevent any transfers during the season so that each club plays every other club during the season with the same squad of players. The Court did note that there was greater risk of skewing the outcome of a championship where there was a play-off format as in this case. A single imported star player could tip the balance in knock-out games, even in a single game. The Advocate-General in his Opinion did recognize that the particular nature of knockout competitions could justify special eligibility rules. The likelihood of affecting the result with one star player is greater in a six-man game like basketball than say a fifteen-man game like rugby union. Whether 'sporting justifications' as an exception apply as strongly to league all-play-all formats is questionable. Some sports do distinguish between knockout competitions, where a player cannot play for two clubs in the same season, and league competitions, where this is allowed. The general legality of transfer deadlines *per se* cannot safely be assumed from this judgment.

Another limitation to *Lehtonen* is the question of discrimination. The Court decided that different deadlines as between transfers from European clubs and non-European clubs were illegal. There was no discussion of the other aspect of discrimination, namely that players already with Belgian clubs at the beginning of the season could not move at all during the season. If most basketball players play with their domestic clubs, this implies that Belgian players cannot move clubs during the season whilst players from other European countries can move from their country to a Belgian club during the season but before the transfer deadline. This appears therefore to be a difference based on nationality. The Court was careful to avoid this conclusion, pointing out that the rules referred only to transfers between clubs in different countries, irrespective of the players' nationality.

The European Court of Justice's attempt to draw a distinction between economic and sporting issues is also evident in the *Deliège* case.[24] This concerned the freedom of sporting federations to select teams for international competitions. Deliège was a judoka, who felt that she was being denied top-class competition, and so her chances of Olympic participation were prejudiced. The international federation imposed quotas on participation in top international events. National federations in turn decided who of their judokas was to be selected to fill their quota. Deliège was not selected by her national federation when she felt that her

---

[24] Cases C-51/96 and C-191/97 Deliège v Liège Ligue Francophone de Judo, judgment 11 April 2000.

performances merited it. The case raised two important legal questions. One was the status of 'amateurs' as workers under the Treaty and the other was whether, and on what grounds, organizers of sports events could restrict entry.

The Court was not prepared to automatically accept the distinction between amateurs and professional players. It declared that Deliège was able to claim her fundamental rights under the Treaty, even though she was technically an amateur, because she was engaged in economic activity. She was effectively a full-time athlete who trained continually and had no other job. She received grants from sports organizations that were based on her past results and were more than necessary to improve her performance. In other words she was being subsidized as an elite performer. In that sense she was 'earning' from her sport. She was also sponsored because of her celebrity status. The Court rejected the argument that her classification as an amateur by her sports federation was relevant.[25] This conclusion seriously undermines the autonomy of sports federations. The European Court of Justice can scrutinize their activities whenever they have an impact upon the economic prospects of the athletes under their jurisdiction. The Court even thought that any indirect commercial advantage to the promoter of an event was sufficient to subject the sporting organization to account. Even if the athletes are unpaid, they still add value so that the organizers of the event can have commercial opportunities through gate receipts, sponsorship or broadcasting rights.[26]

The Court was more circumspect on the central question, which was how far is a national sports federation free to set criteria of qualification for international competitions. It accepted that some criterion of selection was inevitable in top-class sport and that unrestricted open entry was unworkable. But the criteria had to be justified and not arbitrary. The preliminary order of the Belgian court below had been that the sporting federation should not restrict the freedom to enter and to compete unless there were objective standards. These standards were to be based on 'physical ability' or on 'a comparative assessment of her merits' against other judokas. The European Court of Justice endorsed this position. This means that sports bodies must have justifiable principles of selection and the Court can consider these principles. The Court will however not intervene if these criteria have been properly applied. This allows a limited autonomy to sporting organizations.

Two important questions remain. One is what are objective standards and how can they be supervised by a court? In most individual sports there are relatively objective measures of sporting performance and these are frequently used to control entry. World tennis is a good example where a player's ranking not only allows entry to the top tournaments but is also used automatically to determine their seedings.[27] Even golf's 'Open' championship requires a minimum handicap

---

[25] Para. 46.

[26] Para. 57.

[27] Except at Wimbledon. In 2000 two Spanish players withdrew in protest at not being seeded according to their world ranking.

qualification. Many Olympic sports, such as swimming, have minimum times that must be bettered before a swimmer can qualify for selection in that event. What if a national federation consistently failed to select their fastest swimmer for international competitions? Could the national federation then rely on a subjective 'comparative assessment'? For individual combat sports, such as judo, it would be easy to arrange elimination contests so that a national federation could determine their best representative. In team sports, on the other hand, objective criteria may be more difficult to measure and apply. Moreover the blending of a successful side may mean that picking the 'best' players is not necessarily the way to pick the best team. The second question is, who decides these issues of selection? The European Court of Justice cautioned against the automatic assumption that the national federation is the only body which can decide.[28] They will however be the appropriate organizations where there is a single national federation that normally has 'the necessary knowledge and expertise'.

The final judgment in *Deliège* avoided directly the issue of selection for national teams. Behind Deliège's complaint was her fear that she was being ignored for Olympic selection. In Olympic and world championships, even in individual sports such as judo, entry is restricted to a maximum number of athletes from each country. These national quotas can discriminate against elite athletes who are excluded from strong national teams in favour of poorer performers from weak countries. The fourth best Austrian ski jumper would normally beat the best British one but is prevented from competing in the Winter Olympics because only three athletes are permitted from each country. These Olympic quotas can restrict the economic opportunities of some athletes because in many minor sports a good performance in the Olympics is the main opportunity for better sponsorship. But in *Deliège* it was conceded that the basis of selection for other international tournaments was not nationality but affiliation to the appropriate national federation. This avoids the issue. Athletes cannot normally affiliate to two federations. They will normally affiliate to their home federation. Affiliation is essentially the same as nationality. The Advocate General's Opinion was based on wider criteria than those used by the Court. He argued that national sporting federations function to organize and promote their national teams and athletes, especially for international and Olympic events. This allows them a 'limited power of self management and self-regulation'. This is justified in the public interest. This he interpreted as the interests of the national team and the 'need to ensure the representative nature of the competitions'.

This conclusion is not necessarily consistent with *Lehtonen*. In that case the 'public interest' was in fair play-offs. That was equated to 'the sporting interest', which in turn was assumed to be the consumer's interest. Clubs buying in top players for crucial games should not manipulate the integrity of the competition, and therefore the fans' interest, in the destination of the championship. In

---

[28] Para. 67.

Deliège, the Advocate General's view treats nationality as a key element in sport. National quotas in the Olympic are justifiable because they are 'representative', which presumably means that every nation has a chance to compete. This is not self-evidently in the public interest. Why nationality and not merit should be paramount in world championships designed to find the best performer is not immediately obvious. The European Champions League in football has recently moved away from the idea of a single national representative, qualifying by winning their national league, to allowing the stronger national leagues to have multiple (up to four) representatives. This has arguably made the event more attractive and more commercially valuable through the sale of broadcasting rights.

'Private rights' regulation has been advanced by these recent two decisions. The European Court of Justice has refused to give governing bodies immunity when they interfere with the fundamental rights under the Treaty. These judgments show that sport can be an economic activity even if the competitors are unpaid amateurs. This leaves very little in the realm of non-economic activities that cannot be scrutinized by the Court. The real test of sporting autonomy will however be the manner in which exceptions are allowed on the grounds of 'objective justification'. The issues in these two cases – the imposition of transfer deadlines and selection for national teams – are central to the autonomy of a national federation. Yet in both cases reasons for interfering with an athlete's right to move clubs freely or to compete wherever they wish had to be defended as in the public interest.

The danger in future cases is that courts will too readily accept the sporting federation's own assessment of what is in the best interests of the sport and allow that 'sporting interest' to be equated with the 'public interest'. The purpose of Article 39 after all is to protect the interests of workers. To continue to deny these interests by using the vague notion of 'sporting interest' or the dubious nationalism of representative sport would be regrettable. While the purpose of Article 39 is to protect workers, the interests of consumers are protected by the enforcement of competition law under Articles 81 and 82. It is noticeable that in both the *Lehtonen* and *Deliège* cases that the European Court of Justice refused to consider the competition aspects raised by the monopoly control of sporting matters that most national federations have. In identical terms[29] they state that there is insufficient information about the definition of the relevant market, the number of undertakings operating in the market, or the degree of cross-border movement of players.

---

[29] Para. 28 of the judgment in Lehtonen and para. 38 of the judgment in Deliège.

REGULATION BY THE COMMISSION

The work of the Commission in regulating sport is almost entirely based on their role in enforcing European competition law. Their attitude to sport before the *Bosman* decision could at best be described as one of 'education, advice and persuasion.'[30] Their position on quotas for overseas players in football is a good example. This had been the subject of Commission interest since 1968 when the Community rules on free movement of workers became fully operative. Over twenty years later there was a report prepared for the European Parliament. In 1991 the '3 + 2' foreigners rule was introduced by UEFA and made mandatory in all European national leagues. This was the result of a compromise between the Commission and UEFA. The slow pace of reform achieved by this regulatory strategy was one of the factors that led to a challenge to the rule in *Bosman*. Professional footballers and their unions became frustrated and encouraged a private right challenge to the system. The European Court of Justice declared the quota system illegal, thereby achieving more quickly the desired result.

Bosman initiated a new phase of Commission activity. This was sparked by the suggestion in the European Court of Justice's judgment that Articles 81 and 82 applied to sport. Previously, the Commission's interest had been limited to cases where sports federations were acting purely as businesses.[31] One example was the Danish Tennis Federation (DTF) case.[32] The DTF had allowed three manufacturers the right to label their balls as 'official'. Only official balls could be used in tournaments organized by the DTF. This label had no preconditions that the balls were to be tested to show superior quality. The arrangement was purely a revenue-raising scheme by the DTF. The Commission has forced the DTF to revise its agreements to allow other manufacturers greater opportunities to participate.

What *Bosman* highlighted was that sports federations are monopoly regulators of sport and so potentially have a dominant position over the sport. *Bosman* had exposed the business of sport to the logic of the free market. If players could be free to move in an unrestricted labour market, what other consequences followed? In particular the governing bodies of sport, and the sports leagues that they organized, could be seen as cartels of clubs and their centralized marketing of broadcasting rights as an anti-competitive practice. Lewis and Taylor say, 'in the resulting struggle for control over the revenue streams of a particular sport ... competition law has emerged as the weapon of choice.'[33] The application of Eu-

---

[30] The phrase comes from Baldwin R and Cave M, *Understanding Regulation* (1999), Oxford University Press.

[31] The Cooper and Lybrand Report, supra n. 8, gives a good overview of the Commission's level of activity in 1995 just before *Bosman*.

[32] See Commission press release IP/98/355.

[33] Lewis A and Taylor J, The Impact of European Competition Law on Sport (May 2000), at www.townleys.co.uk

ropean competition law assumes a free market model,[34] that the dominant values in sport are those of the market place and that sport is organized like any other business. One conclusion that could therefore be drawn from competition law was that sports clubs could not be prevented by a national federation from exercising their right of establishment by moving abroad, and that breakaway leagues and federations could not legally be prevented as this would be anti-competitive.[35]

The problem with this approach to regulation is that sport is not a free market. As producers of sport, sports federations and sports leagues are 'natural monopolies'. Fans prefer a single professional league in each country as this shows who is the best team. World championships are better when open to all and not just the athletes under the jurisdiction of one of several rival federations. Rival leagues are unusual in European sport and have been short-lived. An existing federation can implement an effective international boycott against anyone who participates in a breakaway league. Traditional structures of governance in sport have survived the challenge of rival organizations, even if considerably modified, in several sports. Professional cricket was seriously spilt in the 1970s when Kerry Packer introduced a rival 'World Series'. The resulting litigation in *Grieg v Insole*[36] led to a compromise and cricket continued to be governed by a single governing body. Professional darts split in the 1990s with two rival organizations. Each had a 'world championship' which were sold to different broadcasters. A limited compromise so that players could compete in the other federation's championship without fear of reprisal was agreed after a brief visit to the courts. Sport does not have a market structure in which many producers organize competing events, which are then offered to the consumer.

Sports fans are also not consumers in the normal free market sense. They do not behave as rational economic actors. They are consumers of adhesion, bound to a single club. It has been argued that support for football clubs is a culturally determined irrational choice but represents 'fan equity.'[37] The fan is emotionally committed to one club and a transfer of their support to a rival club is unthinkable. The consumer has no viable choice other than to withdraw from the market. This makes sport a peculiar market. This is reflected in the answer to the question: what is the relevant product market, a central question for the purposes of

---

[34] For a discussion of the different models that are used in different styles of regulating sport see Foster K, How Can Sport be Regulated? in Greenfield S and Osborn G (eds.), *Law and Sport in Contemporary Society* (2000) Frank Cass, London.

[35] On these issues see Foster K, European Law and Football: Who's in Charge, in Garland J, Malcolm D, and Rowe M, (eds.), *The Future of Football: Challenges for the Twenty-First Century* (2000) Frank Cass, London.

[36] [1978] 1 WLR 302; an excellent description of the litigation and its context is given in Greenfield S and Osborn G, *Contract and Control in the Entertainment Industry*, (1998) Ashgate, Aldershot.

[37] Hamil S, A Whole New Ball Game? in Hamil S, Michie J, and Oughton C, *The Business of Football – A Game of Two Halves* (1999) Mainstream, Edinburgh.

Articles 81 and 82, in sport? In the 'ticketing cases',[38] such as the 1998 World Cup, the Commission had assumed that there is a single market for the tickets. However for media companies, as buyers of broadcasting rights, the relevant market may be different. Here viewers can treat sports as interchangeable and substitutable. The relevant market may be not just sport, it could even be the wider entertainment market. There is some evidence however that the popularity of football makes it a single market for broadcasters. This was a key finding in the report of the Monopolies and Mergers Commission into the proposed take-over of Manchester United by BSkyB.[39]

There are alternatives to not applying competition law fully to sport. One is to reassert that self-regulation by the governing bodies of sport is acceptable. Another is to try and modify the application of European competition law in such a way that the special features of sport and the importance of social values in sport are recognized. The application of the anti-trust laws in the USA to sport is instructive.[40] American sport has historically been more commercialized and has operated with closed leagues that govern themselves as an alliance of clubs. Sport has been exempted in many ways from the anti-trust laws. The Supreme Court in 1922 confirmed that baseball was exempt from the operation of the anti-trust laws.[41] Recent judicial decisions have tried to limit this immunity but it remains largely intact. The US courts refused to extend baseball's immunity to other professional sports but Congress has also intervened. In 1966 they approved the amalgamation of two rival American Football leagues by granting a statutory exemption from the anti-trust laws for an alliance that otherwise could have been construed as creating a monopoly.[42] There was widespread political support for the idea of a single league as the most effective and profitable form of organization for the sport. Similarly in 1961 Congress had allowed sports leagues to sell their collective broadcasting rights on an exclusive basis by legislating that such sales did not infringe the anti-trust laws.[43]

The combined effect of this judicial and legislative effort was to exempt the core activities of the sports leagues from regulatory interference. This preference for self-regulation and governance was reinforced by a series of judicial decisions in the 1980s. These developed the theory that sports leagues were 'single enti-

---

[38] Football World Cup, decision 2000/12; OJ. L5/55-74. On this decision see the helpful article by Weatherill S, Fining the Organisers of the 1998 Football World Cup (2000) *European Law Review*, 275. There were previous inquires into the ticketing arrangements at the 1990 World Cup (Italia 1990; Commission Decision 92/521 and OJ 1992 L326/92), the 1992 Olympic Games (Press Release IP/92/593) and for the 1996 Olympic Games (*Competition Report* 1996, 144).

[39] Cm 4395.

[40] A good summary of the current position of sporting bodies under US anti-trust law is available at 18 A.L.R. Fed. 489.

[41] Federal Baseball Club v National League of Professional Baseball Clubs (1922) 259 US 200.

[42] Football Merger Act of 1966 (USC s.1293).

[43] Sports Broadcasting Act of 1961 (USC s.1291).

ties'. Under this doctrine a sports league is treated as a joint venture for the purpose of anti-trust law. Clubs in the league cannot legally be deemed to be a cartel and cannot be guilty of a conspiracy because they are not separate legal entities. The American experience suggests that there are routes by which the collective interest of sports leagues can be protected from the full vigorous application of competition laws. But two features, both recognized by the courts, of American sports that are very different from European sport have been crucial in allowing this broad immunity. One is that American sports have much more extensive collective revenue sharing and the other is that they are typically governed by a single Commissioner to whom the teams cede a great deal of their executive power.

Anti-trust law has nevertheless been used to protect the interests of the players. In a series of cases the American courts have asserted a *Bosman*-type principle of free agency for players. Whilst not achieving full freedom of movement for players, these decisions have modified some of worst excesses of labour practices within American sport. The draft system in American football where new professional players are effectively assigned to one club has been regularly challenged. It has been slowly modified under this judicial onslaught. A related development has been the use of the 'labor exemption' in the US anti-trust laws. This allows enterprises to avoid some of the anti-trust laws if they establish that they have proper collective bargaining arrangements with their labor unions. This form of protection for professional players has created structured salary scales, better safety and better pensions. The European Commission's regulatory policy to date has shown little interest in protecting the interests of workers and players. The explicit beneficiary of competition policy is the consumer. Unlike the USA the Commission has not yet made favourable regulatory treatment or modification depend up on some link with the players' unions.

After a brief flirtation with the undiluted free market model the Commission has begun to search for an intermediate position. They have recognized that sport is not solely about economic values. Its major goals are social and cultural. Despite commercialization, modern European sport is still not driven by the purely economic purpose of making a profit. Sports clubs continue to function even when insolvent,[44] amateurs still compete unpaid. The Commission is in part responding to an increasing recognition of the social role of sport. The Amsterdam Treaty of 1997 contained a the non-binding declaration on sport.[45] This acknowledged 'the social significance of sport, in particular its role in forging identity and bringing people together'. It further called on 'the bodies of the European Union to listen to sport associations when important questions affecting sport are at is-

---

[44] The current European football champions, Real Madrid, are reported to be £100 million in debt even though they paid £37 million to Barcelona for Luis Figo in the summer 2000.

[45] Amsterdam Treaty.

sue. In this connection special consideration should be given to the particular characteristics of sport.'[46]

This was a clear signal to the Commission that a free market model was unacceptable and that a modified application of competition law was called for. It also signaled the belief that European sport had two specific characteristics that justified a different treatment from other businesses. One, that sport in Europe is usually based on national leagues and that international sport, especially in team sports like football, is culturally important. This is the clear import of the phrase about 'forging identity and bringing people together'. Two, that governing bodies of sport have a general social role in promoting the overall interests of the sport. To achieve this objective, it is necessary for them to exploit the commercial value of sport and to redistribute some of this revenue downward towards the grassroots of the game.[47]

These two characteristics of European sport are very different from the commercial model of American sport, which has minimal international competition and no organic link with the grassroots of the game. It usually has a separate professional league with no promotion from lower leagues. These differences have been highlighted by the Commission's attempts to formulate a coherent ideology as to the distinction between the economic and social functions of sport. A report on the European model of sport,[48] and the differences between this model and the American model of sport, has been influential and widely discussed.[49] Briefly the American model is of a closed league to minimize the risk of financial loss arising from sporting failure. The European model is a pyramid of open leagues with promotion and relegation between divisions on sporting merit. American leagues are self-governing and have very little relation with international governing bodies. The European model is more global with a hierarchy of governance and regulation up to an international sports federation based on national governing bodies. There is far more international competition as a result. The American model is that international expansion of the sport is an economic venture based on franchising the original homegrown model abroad. Ultimately the American sports league is a capitalist venture. If it does not make a profit, it ceases business. The European model is a powerful antidote to the free market model represented by the American model.

This European model of sport has now begun to influence the Commission's thinking on creating what I will call 'supervised autonomy'. In an important

---

[46] Ibid. Article 29.

[47] This is a process that has been described as 'vertical solidarity' as opposed to 'horizontal solidarity' which is a process where elite clubs redistribute income among themselves to achieve greater sporting balance. The two processes are not mutually exclusive.

[48] *The European Model of Sport*; Consultation Document (DG X, Brussels, 1998).

[49] See Hoehn and Szymanski, supra n. 11; Gratton C, The Peculiar Economics of English Football in Garland J, Malcolm D, and Rowe M, (eds.) *The Future of Football: Challenges for the Twenty-First Century* (2000), London, Frank Cass.

document in 1999 the Commission stated its views.[50] It began by drawing a distinction between 'sporting activity in the strict sense' and 'economic activities generated by sporting activity'. The former performs a 'social, integrating and cultural function' that needs to be preserved and is to be protected from the Treaty's competition rules. These sporting activities are later defined as those aspects of sport that are merely to do with 'the internal organization and regulation of sport'. This in principle is unexceptionable but the scope of this non-intervention is vague. To take but one example, suppose the governing bodies of golf banned a new type of golf club because it makes the ball go further. They claim that this alters the essential character of the game and makes existing golf courses play in a different manner. Is this a mere sporting matter that is purely a regulatory decision or is it a commercial decision that can have enormous financial implications for a company which has developed and marketed the new club?

At the other extreme, the Commission states that the economic activities of sport are subject to the competition rules in the same way as any other industry. To judge from the examples that the Commission itself uses, this principally means business-to-business transactions. The sale of broadcasting rights by sports federations to media companies has attracted the Commission's regulatory gaze. The two main concerns here have been exclusivity and collective selling. The Commission dislikes exclusive contracts where sports rights are sold to only one broadcaster. While accepting exclusivity in principle, they have opposed long contracts and required open tendering.[51]

Collective selling of broadcasting rights by sports federations rather than allowing the individual clubs to market and exploit their own rights has also attracted the Commission's attention. These are an example of the Commission's intermediate position, where the policy of 'supervised autonomy' is most evident. The competition rules in principle apply to this category of cases but it may be possible for the sporting federations to apply for exemption under Article 81(3). UEFA has applied for clearance for the central marketing of the commercial rights to broadcast and to sponsor the European Champions League. They argue that the Champions League is a larger entity, with its own distinct identity, that has been created and promoted by UEFA alone. It is therefore 'entirely distinct from the identities of the competing clubs'.[52] The Commission has itself given examples of practices that are anti-competitive but may be exempted under Ar-

---

[50] Preliminary Guidelines on the Application of the Competition Rules to Sport, draft Commission paper, February 1999. The conclusions are summarized in a press release, IP/99/133 and discussed in Pons, Sport and European Competition Policy.

[51] One year deals are acceptable as it is the season long package that is the valuable commodity. Compare the reasoning in the RPC case where it was said that the total package of a championship was greater than the sum of its parts. The Commission has disapproved of a seven year deal (KNVB/Sport7, OJ 1996 C-228/4) but allowed a three year deal but partly because the company was launching a new premium sports channel (Audiovisual Sport, OJ 1997 C-361/5 and C-161/7).

[52] OJ C363.

ticle 81(3).[53] These include measures to maintain competitive balance between clubs in a league, transfer fees if they are a genuine assessment of training costs incurred, exclusive broadcasting contracts if limited, and sports quality certification schemes. All such exemptions must be effective to achieve their purpose and go no further than is necessary to achieve that purpose. It is important to note that the Commission alone can exercise this 'supervised autonomy' via Article 81(3) not national courts and so it is a distinct level of European regulation.

The Commission is also aware that governing bodies of sport are monopoly regulators. This in principle gives them market dominance. The abuse of a dominant position is illegal under Article 82. Nevertheless the Commission accepts that 'rules that are inherent to sport ... or are necessary to sport' may not be caught under Article 82. One sporting case where the Commission has proceeded under this Article is Formula One motor racing.[54] Here the Commission considers the commercial exploitation of international motor sport to be unlawful and the international sports federation (FIA) to be abusing its dominant position. The FIA is the sole regulator of motor sport in Europe. It licenses events, their organizers and the drivers. Participation in unauthorized events can lead to drivers being stripped of their license to compete. Therefore rival events to the FIA's own cannot succeed without FIA cooperation. The FIA has used this monopoly power to force rival promoters out of the sport. In addition to being the regulatory body, FIA also promotes Formula One. It further claims the broadcasting rights to all motor sports events. Teams in Formula One must assign their broadcasting rights to FIA as a condition of competing.

One of the features of motor racing is that the FIA is both the monopoly regulator of the sport and the sole promoter of Formula One, its most attractive and valuable product. A similar confusion of roles is beginning to emerge in European football. Here UEFA has departed from its traditional role as regulator and passive organizer of competitions. It is increasingly the active promoter and commercial exploiter of its flagship tournaments such as the European Champions League. The Commission's stance on several key issues is vital to the future structure of European football and the form of its governance. The battle over revenues between the elite clubs and UEFA, which claims to be the trustee of the whole game, will be crucially affected by the Commission's interventions. Key questions include:

– Can UEFA use its dominant position to prevent a breakaway superleague of the top clubs in a manner similar to that used by FIA to kill off its rivals?
– How far can UEFA market collectively the broadcasting rights to its competitions by insisting on the assignment of those rights to it from the clubs?
– Is the European model of sport influential enough to allow national leagues,

---

[53] see IP 199/133 supra, n. 50.
[54] See Commission press release, IP/99/434. 30th June 1999.

existing European competitions and national team championships to survive the market logic of a single Community-wide market for football?

The danger is that the Commission will exercise its regulatory powers weakly and give precedence to national leagues and some vague notion of 'sport's social role'. This would be to waste the opportunity that 'supervised autonomy' offers. UEFA's limited attempt to redistribute revenues to support football in the weaker footballing nations of Europe has so far been limited.[55] The Commission should use its powers to insist on much greater redistribution as a condition of granting exemptions under Article 81(3).

POLITICAL APPROACHES: THE 'EXCEPTION SPORTIVE'

Whether sport can be exempted from the Treaty is a political as well as a regulatory question since *Bosman*. The Commission's approach emphasizes sporting justifications as exceptions to the competition rules. This approach tries to keep non-economic factors ring-fenced within a regulatory framework of free market economics. The political approach has stressed the social and cultural functions of sport; especially in so far as it contributes to a sense of identity, both national and European. This approach was given political impetus by the declaration on sport to the Amsterdam Treaty. The ultimate goal of these political pressures is either the creation of a special competence for sport or a total exemption of sport from the Treaty, an 'exception sportive'. Not unnaturally this is the favoured option of sports bodies such as UEFA for it would restore their traditional position of self-regulation. After Amsterdam the Commission responded with its consultative paper on the European model of sport. This was contrasted with the over-commercialized American model in which fans' interests are so subservient to the profit motive that teams can leave town and move hundreds of miles because the economic grass is greener. The European Council meeting in Vienna in December 1998 requested the Commission to prepare a report on sport within Europe. The conservative nature of this request is evident from the language, which spoke of 'safeguarding current sports structures' and 'maintaining the social functions of sport'.

The Report was presented to the Helsinki Council in December 1999.[56] The Report began by criticising the commercialization of sport. It claimed that there were too many events in the sporting calendar. It also suggested that there was a danger that the elite clubs in sport would break free from the existing governing bodies. The Report then stressed the values upheld by existing governing federa-

---

[55] IP/99/965; OJ C-99/23.

[56] Commission of the European Communities, Report from the Commission to the European Council with a View to Safeguarding Sports Structures and Maintaining the Social Significance of Sport Within the Community Framework (the Helsinki Report on Sport), Com (1999) 644.

tions. They regulate open leagues, implement vertical solidarity, and uphold ethics and sporting values. The Report concludes by calling for a new partnership between the sporting federations, the Member States and the European Community. This requires that the Commission as the principal regulatory organ will 'take account of the specific characteristics of sport'. Member States need to create a clearer legal framework 'to safeguard the current structures ... of sport.'[57]

There is a consensus of aims between the governing bodies and the European Commission on this analysis. Instead of direct regulation by what Baldwin and Cave[58] call 'command and conquer', this model is much closer to what Hancher and Moran[59] call 'sharing a regulatory space'. This can best be described as a move from supervised autonomy to benign guidance. Instead of regulating the sports federations, this approach starts from the position of protecting the monopoly of governance that sports federations have from the corroding forces of commercialization. The difficulty that the Commission has is that its regulatory powers are limited to enforcing competition law. Whilst in this area it can follow the lead of the European Court of Justice in *Bosman* and recognize the special features of sport that make it different from other industries, it has no special competence to act in a proactive role. It wants to pursue a wider agenda that protects sport from the full application of European competition law.

This strategy depends upon permitting sports federations to keep much of their traditional autonomy and self-regulation. The Commission may find it difficult to regulate issues of unfair economic discrimination against top clubs who find that too much of their revenue is redistributed. The Helsinki Report is based upon an analysis of sport that uses football as the paradigm case. Many minor sports would love to have the problems of commercialization. The nominal beneficiary of regulation, the sporting consumer, figures only slightly. The football fan does not necessarily approve of the present set-up of world and European football which is run by unaccountable and undemocratic federations that give no formal representation to fans.[60] Protecting such institutions is not obviously in the best interests of consumers. Likewise the football fan's sporting and contractual link is with the club. The governing bodies have rarely used their regulatory powers to protect the fans from exploitation by the clubs over matters like ticket prices, ground safety and expensive merchandise.

---

[57] Ibid., conclusions.

[58] Supra n. 30.

[59] Hancher L and Moran M, (eds.), *Capitalism, Culture and Regulation* (1989) Oxford University Press.

[60] See Sugden J and Tomlinson A, *FIFA and the Contest for World Football* (1998) Polity Press, Cambridge.

Towards a Community Sports Policy

The Commission has widened its agenda beyond trying to regulate the economic aspects of sport and to distinguish the non-economic sporting aspects that can be left to self-regulation. The Helsinki Report marks a move to safeguarding the wider social function of sport. There are also emerging signs of another strand of policy which has as its goals the harmonization and co-ordination of sports policy among the Member States. There are areas where the Community thinks that harmonization of national policies is desirable. These include the legality of collective selling of broadcasting rights, anti-doping policies, the legal control of football hooligans and the taxation treatment of sporting clubs and players. The link between these issues is the fear that different policies in the Member States will produce a patchwork of legal regimes they can be exploited by enterprises for their own commercial advantage. Broadcasting companies may be able to buy up the rights to football games in countries that legally permit the individual clubs to retain their rights. Using the Television without Frontiers Directive,[61] they could beam games elsewhere within the Union. Those countries that insist on collective selling of rights could therefore be ignored or bypassed. Likewise if some countries have more favourable tax regimes, then players will be more attracted to playing in those countries. If the legality of doping procedures differ across the Union, then the effect of international efforts against doping will be undermined. All these examples show the need for greater harmonization at Community level.

One difficulty with harmonization is that different countries have different approaches towards legal intervention in sport and the degree of autonomy that is legally allowed to sporting federations. A recent study by the Council of Europe has divided countries into interventionist and non-interventionist.[62] 'Interventionist' is defined as a country that has 'specific legislation on the structure and mandate of a significant part of the sports movement.' The state has a central role in such countries. It endows sports federations with their right to exercise regulatory and disciplinary functions. These are thus public powers which are only delegated to federations so long as they comply with criteria of independence, legality, and democracy. The powers can be withdrawn if these criteria are not met or the powers are abused. It is argued that interventionist sports policies produce uniform regulation, better governance, greater public accountability and prevent alternative governing bodies proliferating. Where state intervention is reinforced with state funding, the threat of derecognition is a powerful regulatory tool for the state.

By comparison, non-interventionist states regulate sports federations under the general private law of associations. This allows them greater freedom from state interference but makes them less accountable. Many English governing bodies

---

[61] 89/552 EEC as amended by 97/36/EC.
[62] *Study on National Sports Legislation in Europe*, (1999), Council of Europe, Strasbourg.

were originally clubs, such as the Jockey Club and the Marylebone Cricket Club. The chief advantage of non-interventionism is said to be greater flexibility. Each sport can adapt its institutions and structures to its own particular needs. Non-interventionist models are more organic, protecting the grassroots of the game and adapting to circumstances rather than being controlled from above. They are said therefore to be more resistant to the state's demands to allocate resources in particular ways such as towards elite sport. These different patterns across Europe will make harmonization difficult to achieve. The latest policy documents outline limits to this approach. The principle of subsidarity, means that measures should be taken at the lowest feasible level rather than at Community level.

CONCLUSIONS

European regulation of sport has taken several different routes. It has focused to date mainly on football, the most popular and transnational sport in Europe and therefore on the activities of its European regulatory authority, UEFA. The rights of players have been enforced by the 'private rights' route of litigation before the European Court of Justice. *Bosman* confirmed that the fundamental freedom of movement of players must be protected. But the decision also confirmed that the Court would apply a conceptual distinction between sporting and economic issues. This distinction may prove difficult to apply. It is artificial and assumes that sport had an original amateur purity that has been sullied by the invasion of money into sport. What may be more useful to the players' interests in the long run is the development of a more human rights based approach to their legal protection, so that players have freedom of expression and the right to a fair trial in disciplinary proceedings.

The second route of Commission regulation by use of Articles 81 and 82 has emerged rapidly after the *Bosman* judgment. This route has been dominated by discussions over the automatic application of competition law to sport. This has also conceptualized a distinction between economic and sporting matters, but by using the Amsterdam Treaty's concept of 'social and cultural values.' This is an important concept because it forms the legal base for the Commission's regulatory approach to sport. This relies upon the exception procedure under Article 81(3) as a way of allowing sporting federations 'supervised autonomy'. The weakness of this approach lies in the possible interpretation of 'social and cultural values'. It is agreed that there are technical decisions in sport that must be immune from regulatory interference, but what are social and cultural values? In European football, this seems to mean more vertical solidarity by UEFA redistributing money towards amateur sport and more horizontal solidarity by supporting the poorer footballing nations. UEFA's record to date is poor. By encouraging a league format in their flagship competition, the Champions League, they have reduced unpredictability – the enemy of rich clubs.

The sporting pattern that is emerging is that the more profitable later stages are being dominated by teams from the rich leagues of Italy, Spain, Germany, and England, and the poorer teams are eliminated at an earlier stage. This does little to prevent the concentration of wealth. The attitude of the European Commission to sport has been heavily influenced by the fear of a breakaway European Superleague outside the regulatory framework of UEFA. This is the 'rational' market solution. Competition policy is supposed to be for the benefit of the consumer. They may prefer transnational football leagues rather than the artificial preservation of national leagues. Fans of Glasgow Rangers may wish to see better and more competitive football against teams from Portugal and the Netherlands than their team achieve easy one-sided victories against poor Scottish clubs. Fans of middle-of-the-table clubs in England, such as Coventry, may prefer a Premier League that they have some chance of winning in the absence of, say Manchester United and Arsenal. The 'consumer interest' is ambiguous and the Commission needs to be careful in assuming it is understood. The third route of regulation is the 'sporting exception'. It is clear why this is the preferred option of the sports federations. It would give sport a blanket immunity. Despite some political expressions of support of this route, it is unlikely to happen; if only because it would need unanimous support from the Member States for an amendment to the Treaty. It is also the policy option that offers least protection to the players and the fans.

The best route seems to be supervised autonomy by the Commission as this offers a legally based independent protection of the widest constituencies. The counter-balance to commercialism in sport should be the regulatory authorities of sport. They have shown that they cannot be trusted to have sole autonomy and self-governance over their sport. But the Commission needs to use its powers widely. Self-regulation should only be permitted subject to a proper 'rule of law' system of governance. This would have three minimum conditions:

– One, that there is a compulsory independent appeal for those whose sporting and economic interests are prejudiced by the activities of sports federations. They cannot continue to act as judge and jury. This appeal does not necessarily have to be to the courts, although this may be necessary if basic human rights are denied, but could be to an arbitrator.
– Two, that the internal constitutions of sports federations are reformed and democratized to give greater representation to the players.
– Three, that the interests of fans as consumers of sport are better protected.

The governing bodies of sport have not prevented fans' commercial exploitation by their clubs, to whom they are emotionally tied. An independent regulator or Ombudsman should be appointed to protect them. Without these minimum conditions for limited autonomy, sports federations should expect further legal regulation to ensure that sport as a business is still run partly for the love of the game and not just for the love of money.

GLOBALISATION, EUROPE AND THE RE-REGULATION OF SPORT

Simon Boyes

INTRODUCTION: SPORT AS A GLOBAL ENTERPRISE

The Olympic Games is perhaps the ultimate embodiment of the conduct of sport at a truly global level. At the Sydney Summer Olympic Games competitors from 199 nations, participating in 28 sports were brought together in one location in order to compete in sporting events. This not only emphasises that sporting inter-action is taking place between competitors from an increasing number of the World's nations, but that it is also deepening and taking place in a seemingly ever increasing number of sports. Whilst the Olympic Games may present the most obvious example of the system of global sport in operation, such a system clearly exists at a number of different levels. It is indisputable that sport is something that is rapidly coming to concern individuals, organisations, companies and na-tions spread increasingly across the globe. Maguire illustrates the numerous ways in which sport has become a global enterprise:

> 'Consider the example of basketball. Citizens of countries spread across the globe regularly tune in by satellite broadcasts to National Basketball Association (NBA) games. In these games perform the best male players drawn from North America and Europe. The players use equipment . . . that is designed in a range of European and North American locations, financed in the USA and assembled in the Pacific Rim . . . then sold on to a mass market across the globe.'[1]

Sport's provision of three percent of world trade is one, which further emphasises its growing importance in the world order as a whole. Not only is sport being in-creasingly played between actors from geographically disparate locations, but also it is coming to be regarded as one of the world's most significant commodi-ties. At the highest level sport is big business and the economic benefits which it brings are eagerly sought. This is most obviously evidenced by the seemingly limitless ends to which cities will go in order to win the right to host events such

---

[1] Maguire J, *Global Sport: Identities, Societies, Civilizations* (1999) Cambridge, Polity Press, 14.

A. Caiger and S. Gardiner (Eds), Professional Sport in the EU: Regulation and Re-regulation
© 2000, T.M.C.Asser Press, The Hague, The Netherlands

as Olympic Games and FIFA World Cups.[2] Nowhere is this commodification of sport more apparent than in its relationship with the media. There is a growing demand for what have been termed 'global media-sports' products.[3] This refers to the transmission by the broadcast media of sporting events across the globe.

The global spread of sport has not only had effects on culture, sociology and economics, but inevitably as popularity spreads the involvement of lawyers and politicians is increasing exponentially. Events such as the recent *World Conference on Doping in Sport*, organised by the International Olympic Committee (IOC), and convened in order to address the problem of the regulation of doping practices, signify the growing influence of global factors in the regulation, or perhaps more significantly, re-regulation of sport.

With this general context in mind, this chapter seeks to consider the extent to which the theory and practice of globalisation can help us in understanding the way in which sport has been regulated and is subsequently being re-regulated. There are three particular perspectives that will be examined in this context. Firstly, European influences on the initial regulation of sport at a global level. How did Europe contribute to the development of global structures for the development of sport? Secondly, to what extent has the growth of the global sport-media complex and the resultant commodification and commercialisation of sport contributed to its re-regulation? Thirdly, how has European Union action in the field of sporting activity impacted upon sporting systems of global governance?

GLOBALISATION

In order to make an assessment of this kind it is necessary to first understand what is meant by the term 'globalisation'. It is a concept that has proven itself to be particularly problematic for academics from a broad range of disciplines. The result of the difficulty that commentators have experienced when dealing with the idea of globalisation is reflected in the vast array of approaches that have been taken to it. However, there appears to exist some common, core characteristics, identified by a significant number of those authors. These are perhaps best reflected in two passages seeking to arrive at a definition of the term 'globalisation':

'A social process in which the constraints of geography on social and cultural arrangements recede and in which people become increasingly aware that they are receding.'[4]

---

[2] Boyes S, International Olympic Committee Corruption and Bribery Scandal [1999] 2(2) *Sports Law Bulletin* 14.

[3] Maguire, supra n.1, 144-5.

[4] Waters M, *Globalization* (1995) London, Routledge, 2.

'Globalisation refers to the multiplicity of linkages and interconnections between the states and societies which make up the modern world system. It describes the process by which events, decisions and activities in one part of the world system can come to have significant consequences for individuals and communities in quite distant parts of the globe.'[5]

The key themes seem clear: restrictions imposed by geographical boundaries disappear; activities take place at a global level; the importance of domestic systems diminish as external activities have an increasing impact; and there is a growing degree of interaction between actors based in geographically disparate locations. Further practical impacts of this are emphasised by Delbrück:

'[I]t seems that globalization, as distinct from internationalization, denotes a process of *denationalization* of clusters of political, economic and social activities. Internationalization, on the other hand refers to cooperative activities of *national* actors, public or private, on a level beyond the nation state, but at the last resort under its control.'[6]

GLOBALISATION AND THE DEVELOPMENT OF ORGANIZED SPORT

European nations, in particular Britain, were key actors in the initial development of the system of global sport and its regulation.

The sporting world is one that naturally lends itself to, and in fact depends upon, becoming 'globalised'. The nature of sport is such that there is an absolute requirement of physical proximity in order that sporting activity can be engaged in. This is true whether competition is taking place between individuals living in different villages or at a football world cup where teams represent different nations. There are a number of parallels that can be drawn between the definitions of globalisation highlighted above and the processes that fostered the initial development and spread of organised sport.

The development of sport beyond a largely localised and un-codified practice is often described as coinciding with the industrial revolution period in Britain. Though it could never be claimed that Britain was responsible for the invention of many sports,[7] it was during this period that the British took them and moulded them into a codified form which was then either mimicked or exported. This led to the adoption of the British form as a norm for international competition across

---

[5] McGrew A, Conceptualising Global Politics in McGrew A and Lewis P *et al*, *Global Politics* (1992) Cambridge, Polity Press, 23.

[6] Delbrück J, Globalization of Law, Politics and Markets – Implications for Domestic Law: A European Perspective, 11 *Indiana Global Legal Studies Journal*, available on-line at, http://www.law.indiana.edu/glsj/vol1/delbruck.html.

[7] Birley D, *Sport and the Making of Britain* (1993) Manchester University Press, 10.

a range of different sports.[8] Elias characterised this period as one of 'sportisation'.[9] The 'sportisation' theory links the codification of sport with a broader societal shift towards the introduction of rules and norms to govern behaviour.

Common rules were initially developed as a result of increasing interaction and interdependence between participants in sporting activity and in society more generally.[10] The industrial revolution and the subsequent shift away from individual subsistence to reliance upon the activities of others engendered a 'network' of social interdependence. Individuals did not simply rely on their own efforts in order to survive, but those of a great many members of society. In order for any system of collective interdependence to survive, there is the requirement for certainty, stability, organisation and direction. This spawned the rise of organisations with the express purpose of governing the conduct of these relationships in an efficient manner.[11] This is particularly helpful in explaining the adoption of universal rules for the conduct of sporting activity.

Sport as a spectacle or a participatory event, becomes unintelligible and largely unplayable where the participants are not playing to at least substantially similar sets of rules. In order for a sport to be understood by competitors from different localities, it becomes important that the rules of the game become universal, in order to facilitate this interaction. A further catalyst for the tenor of the development of sporting codes stemmed from broader, overriding societal aims. The sportisation period encompassed a period of significant growth in state regulation of personal conduct, primarily concerned with the maintenance of reducing tolerance thresholds of violence and disorder. While this does not account for the need to adopt universal rules, it does help to explain their substance.

Uniform rules and regulations demand a parallel development of institutional foundations, organising bodies with responsibility for the implementation, maintenance and application of rules. These were in the form of rationalised sporting structures, the creation of codified and documented technical and moral regulations and of organisational bureaucracies. This rationalisation of course took place in the context of the increasing 'civilisation' taking place in British society as a whole during the final quarter of the nineteenth century.

This 'sportisation' paradigm has been subject to criticism on the basis that it gives too much weight to the emergence of the football codes.[12] Racing, rowing, cricket and pugilism – 'gentrified' sports – were codified and organised much earlier.[13] However, as with the 'sportisation' process, this codification was prima-

---

[8] Hutchinson R, *Empire Games: The British Invention of Twentieth Century Sport* (1996) Edinburgh, Mainstream, 60.

[9] Elias N, The Civilizing Process (1978) Oxford, Blackwell; Elias N, and Dunning E, Quest for Excitement: Sport and Leisure in the Civilizing Process (1986) Oxford, Blackwell.

[10] Birley, supra n.7, 211.

[11] Cashmore E, *Making Sense of Sports* (1996, 2ed) London, Routledge, 79.

[12] Holt R, *Sport and the British: A Modern History* (1992) Oxford, Clarendon Press, 28.

[13] Hargreaves J, *Sport, Power and Culture*, (1986) Cambridge, Polity Press, 17.

rily in an effort to allow an element of certainty, in this case for those wishing to wager on the outcome of sporting competition. However, this serves only to demonstrate the need for codification and the universal application of rules in sport. The fact of the need or impetus for codification itself is of sufficient interest here, the particular circumstances of its advent in the context of particular sports is of secondary importance. Both accounts are synonymous with the models of globalisation highlighted above, albeit within a reduced geographical area.

The British pre-disposition to, and passion for, the codification and regulation of sport appears to have extended beyond its shores and followed the expansion of the British Empire across the globe:

'[The British] refined and they invented, and this very process – which came to be conducted with an almost manic energy – honed itself into an imperial mission. The most unusual of legislations occurred. The British modernization of sport was a complex process. Just as several of their own early games . . . were transported by the British overseas, so in many instances the old native sports of other lands encountered on the imperial trail were adopted by the British abroad, brushed down, and offered back to the world (including their own countries of origin) in a presentable state.'[14]

From this it is possible to determine that the playing of organised sport across the globe owes much to initial efforts to codify and regulate sport, primarily by the British, though as is noted below, as the process developed the British approach was adopted, developed and exported by other European nations. Although within Europe there were competing models of both the sports themselves and the methods of their regulation, it was the British version of both that was adopted. Indeed Frenchman Pierre de Coubertin's concept of the Olympic ideal, characterised as being Eurocentric in nature and subsequently exported across the globe, had its foundation very much in the ideals developed during the 'sportisation' period.[15]

This appears to be very much a case of internationalisation as outlined by Delbrück. Internationalisation is an inevitable milepost on the way to true globalisation. Indeed, Maguire makes the connection between the processes of sportisation and globalisation. He notes that the growth in global communications and interaction that took place more generally during the period from 1870 to 1920 were reflected in a similar growth in international interaction in sporting terms.

Here the same requirements of commonality of understanding and stability of regulation and organisation apply whether the relevant geographical area is a nation, continent or the globe as a whole. Increased interaction between participants

---

[14] Ibid. 87.

[15] See Tomlinson A, De Coubertin and the Modern Olympics, in Tomlinson A and Whannel G, *Five Ring Circus: Money, Power and Politics at the Olympic Games*, (1984) London, Pluto Press, 84-97.

in sporting events is again the key element fostering the development of a uniform code of regulation for sport. It also appears that similar factors have acted as a catalyst in the processes. On a global scale improved transport and communications technologies facilitate interaction between those involved in sport and related activities. Indeed, the requirement that participants in sport have proximity means that improvement in transportation technology must in fact be key in this process. Rapid and reliable communications give organisers a greater capacity to manage and administer the sport. An early example is given by Birley, who highlights the crucial role of the railways in facilitating sporting interaction between geographically distant competitors.[16] So a clear link between the processes of sportisation and globalisation is established. Communications technologies must in fact be seen as *the* essential facet in both.

Unsurprisingly, as the sports that had been codified by the British and Europeans spread across the globe, as a result of processes of cultural imperialism[17] and ludic diffusion,[18] the administrative and organisational structures that surrounded them were also adopted by the recipient cultures. The growing interaction that had led to the development of the domestic regulator and the adoption of common codes was replicated at international level. As interaction between sporting participants from different nations on the sports field became increasingly common, so too did the need for those relationships to be regulated, thus where regulators had sprung up at domestic level, they emerged at a global level as a means by which to manage this international interaction. Up to this point the degree of independence with which domestic actors were able to act meant that this activity could not yet be considered as being truly globalised.

Having spawned and taken a principle role in the diffusion of association football, the British were unusually reticent in their involvement at international level. Despite the first ever international game being played between England and Scotland in 1872, the British initially declined to be involved in the establishment of an international governing body, the *Fédération Internationale de Football Association* (FIFA) formed in 1904 by a number of continental European football associations.

Despite this, during its early years FIFA retained the old colonial approach – three of the Association's presidents have been English. Whilst the British Associations were no longer dominant, they shared power with their European partners, and for the most part the influences on the regulation of football remained firmly Eurocentric. This is not to suggest that some kind of homogenisation of world sporting culture took place. The reception, which the codified sports have received in disparate cultures, has been widely varied:

---

[16] Birley, supra n.7, 260.

[17] Heinemann K, Sport in Developing Countries, in *The Sports Process: A Comparative and Developmental Approach* (1993) Champaign, IL, Human Kinetics, 144.

[18] Ibid. Ludic diffussion can be understood as the interactive processes that facilitate the spread of sport and the way in which they are received and developed by particular cultures.

'Despite its British origins, soccer has been adopted around the world. The rules of the game are international, but the associated rituals are often the product of native culture. The folklore of Brazilian soccer is unlike that of the German game; watching Santos of São Paolo is not the same as a visit to the terraces of Schalke 04. Among the Zulus of South Africa, pre-game ceremonies include incantations, dances and ritual incisions performed on the players by witch doctors. The room allowed for national and ethnic variation has undoubtedly done a great deal to allay resentments aroused by cultural imperialism.'[19]

It was with the emergence of a power bloc amongst the South American members of FIFA that the Europeans began to perceive that their grip on the game was weakening. This led to the creation of the European Union of Football Associations (UEFA), with the prime aim of unifying the approach of the European Associations in order to defend their interests.[20] Indeed it seems that the successful diffusion of soccer throughout the world ultimately undermined the position of power enjoyed within FIFA by the European Associations, who had largely indulged in what amounted to "neo-imperialism" in their relations with FIFA's non-European members.[21]

The increasing Third World membership of FIFA, with each association being given a vote of equal proportion to its more established brethren, the ability of the non-European nations to dominate grew. The eventual result was a complete shift in power within FIFA – the non-European nations gained control of several important committees and for the first time in 1974 the members of FIFA elected a non-European president: João Havelange. Havelange's election was based primarily on the support of non-European nations and the promises of support and development that he offered them. This appears to be, when viewed from a European perspective, representative of a de-nationalisation of power. Inversely, those countries empowered by the appointment of Havelange, might well perceive it as being empowering. Either way, it does illustrate the huge significance of the global power dynamic in the global sports system.

By way of contrast with the FIFA experience, the International Olympic Committee has largely maintained its Eurocentric power base, though this does not detract from the importance that can be attributed to the concept of the global power dynamic.

---

[19] Giulianotti R, *Football: A Sociology of the Global Game*, (1999) Cambridge, Polity Press, 131.

[20] Sugden J, Tomlinson A, and Darby P, FIFA versus UEFA in the Struggle for the Control of World Football, in Brown A (ed.) *Fanatics! Power, identity and fandom in football* (1998) London, Routledge,13.

[21] Ibid.

The Media – Commodification and Re-regulation of sport

Thus far, this chapter has highlighted the importance of improvements in transport technologies as being a key part of the initial globalising processes that led to the international regulation of sport. However, communications technologies in their aspect as a means of relaying images of sporting activity across the globe have, over the previous decade, become significant and should not be underestimated.

The commercialisation and commodification of sport has developed hand in hand with increased media coverage. A key example is the development of UEFA's European Champions' League. This has been closely associated with an increased capacity to broadcast and demand to view football games featuring Europe's best club sides. The financial power of the broadcasters has affected the very structure of the competition. The perceived threat that Europe's premier club sides would abandon UEFA's competition in favour of a (media funded) *European Super League*, led to the restructuring of the Champions' League in order to ensure an increase in games, a reformulation of the entry criteria such that firstly, more clubs were involved, and secondly, that those clubs would be Europe's largest.

The significant growth in income experienced as a result of increased media involvement has contributed markedly to the increased commodification of sporting activity. In the UK football and both rugby codes have enjoyed lucrative associations with Rupert Murdoch's BSkyB organisation. Rugby union, in particular, has been catapulted from amateur to fully professional status within the space of a few years on the basis an underpinning of media finance. In some instances media companies can be seen as effectively 'hijacking' particular sports. This can be most obviously seen with Murdoch's News Corporation's effective 'buyout' of professional rugby league across the globe, with the development of *Superleague* in both Europe and New Zealand/Australia. This effectively gives News International 'ownership' over the whole of the world game. Similarly, BSkyB's attempted purchase of Manchester United Football Club highlights this move away from sport as an activity for its own sake, to sport as a product to be exploited and marketed.

It may not be immediately obvious how the concept of re-regulation is related to this. However, it is clear that the opening of new markets for their product has allowed sports to effectively re-finance themselves. Not only does this present new commercial opportunities across the globe, it also provides the economic capacity to attract the best players from around the world. The economic strength provided by media finance effectively fuels the globalisation process.

The significance of sport's emergence as a valuable commodity has also acted as a catalyst for re-regulation. The increasing requirement that the viewer pays in order to gain access to sporting events has led to concern that viewers, unable or unwilling to pay the associated costs will be deprived of access to sporting events perceived as being of cultural or historical significance. In the United Kingdom this has prompted statutory protection of some events, guaranteeing their availability on 'free to air' broadcasters.[22] Domestic action has received support at European level both from the Council of Europe[23] and the European Union.[24]

Perhaps more significantly, the economic activity prompted by the commodification of sport has provided EU law with an entrée into sporting regulation in relation to the competency to ensure effective competition. This has involved the EU in regulating not only economic activity relating to the broadcasting of sports,[25] but also ticketing,[26] marketing[27] and sponsorship.[28]

The involvement of the European Union in sporting activity is founded on Article 2 of the Treaty of Rome, which provides for the regulation of economic activity. As noted earlier, contemporary sport constitutes a not insignificant proportion of world trade, and though there is no specific competency under the Treaty of Rome for the EU to involve itself in sport, associated economic activity has proved sufficient justification.[29] This was first acknowledged in the case of *Walrave and Koch v Union Cycliste Internationale*[30] concerning nationality restrictions placed upon participants in professional paced cycle racing. The combination of sport and economic activity as a means for providing the European Court of Justice with an entrée into the sporting world was affirmed by the Court in the case of *Donà v Mantero*.[31] Nationality restrictions imposed on Italian

---

[22] S. 97 Broadcasting Act 1996.

[23] Council of Europe Convention on Transfrontier Television (1989), Article 9 notes the obligation of signatory states to:

'avoid the right of the public to information being undermined due to the exercise by a broadcaster of exclusive rights for the transmission of an event of high public interest and which has the effect of depriving a large part of the public in one or more other parties of the opportunity to follow that event on television.'

[24] The 'Television Without Frontiers' Directive, Dir 89/552/EEC, as amended by Dir 97/36/EC.

[25] European Broadcasting Union/Eurovision System [1993] OJ L179/23; [1995] 4 CMLR 56. See also, Parrish R, Sport and Policy or Sports Policy? The Broadcasting Of Sporting Events in the European Union, (1998) 6(3) *Sport and the Law Journal*; Wachtmeister A-M, Broadcasting of Sports Events and Competition Law, (1998) *Competition Policy Newsletter*, number 2, June.

[26] Pauwels Travel Bvba v FIFA Local Organising Committee Italia 1990 [1994] 5 CMLR 253; see Weatherill S, Fining the Organisers of the 1998 Football World Cup [2000] *European Competition Law Review* 275.

[27] Danish Tennis Federation case, 1996 OJ C138/7; Dunlop Slazenger International Ltd v EC Commission T-43/92; [1994] ECR II-441 (CFI).

[28] See Griffiths-Jones D, *Law and the Business of Sport* (1997) London, Butterworths, 91.

[29] Though N.B. the non-legally binding declaration appended to the Treaty of Amsterdam that notes: "The conference emphasises the social significance of sport, in particular its role in forging identity and bringing people together. The conference therefore calls on the bodies of the European Union to listen sports associations when important questions affecting sports are at issue. In this connection, special consideration should be given to the particular characteristics of amateur sport."

[30] Case 36/74 [1974] ECR 1405; [1975] 1 CMLR 320.

[31] Case 13/76 [1976] ECR 1333; [1976] 2 CMLR 578.

league football teams were outlawed as being in breach of Community provisions relating to discrimination on the grounds of nationality.

Perhaps the most significant decision taken by the European Court of Justice is that in the *Bosman* case.[32] The *Bosman* decision[33] is the real starting point for any consideration in relation to the concept of globalisation. Even though the EU represents a small percentage of the global populace its role in re-regulating global sport should not be underestimated. It has become clear that European Union action is having an increasing impact upon the organisation and administration of sporting activity.[34]

THE FACILITATION OF GLOBALISATION AND EUROPEAN LAW IN SPORT

EU intervention on the basis of economic activity appears more significant when it is considered that the role of economics has been one of the most significant elements in the facilitation of globalised activity.[35] With the advent of professional sport, the economic attractiveness of a particular jurisdiction is a key factor in encouraging labour migration. Interaction and interconnectedness increase thus increasing the need for an organisation of the sport at level that can encompass each of the affected national regulators. Association football is perhaps most illustrative of this process in action:

'Professional players criss-cross the continent of Europe. In this case, the elite of soccer talent is purchased mainly by the national leagues of Italy and Spain. This labour is drawn from donor countries spread across Europe ... Soccer labour movement flows across the continent with those more economically powerful leagues attracting a standard of player commensurate with their ability to pay transfer fees and the salary of the players concerned.'[36]

It is notable that the above comments were made *prior* to the decision in the *Bosman* case and it appears that the increased interaction and interconnectedness characteristic of the globalisation process has grown as a result of that decision. Giulianotti has highlighted the 'internationalisation' that has been experienced in the European transfer market in the post-*Bosman* era, noting that the new free-

---

[32] Case C-415/93 Union Royale Belge des Societes de Football Association ASBL v Jean Marc Bosman [1995] ECR I – 4921; [1996] All ER (EC) 97.

[33] See Ken Foster's contribution to this collection for a more detailed analysis.

[34] Parrish R, The Path to a 'Sports Policy' in the European Union (1998) 1(1) *Sports Law Bulletin*, 10.

[35] Bretherton C, Introduction: Global Politics in the 1990s, in Bretherton C and Ponton G (eds.) Global Politics: An Introduction (1996) Oxford, Blackwell, 9.

[36] Maguire J and Bale J, Introduction: Sports Labour Migration in the Global Arena, in Bale J and Maguire J (eds), *The Global Sports Arena: Athletic Talent Migration in an Interdependent World*, (1994) London, Frank Cass, 2.

doms granted to players have allowed them to move between European clubs with the utmost ease.[37] This is further emphasised by the recent comment of Colin Hutchison, Chief Executive of Chelsea Football Club, that Chelsea are a "continental team playing in England". Giulanotti stresses that the *Bosman* ruling has had a globalising impact beyond the increased mobility of footballers with EU nationality to move within it:

> 'In Spain, the problem is complicated by the large number of *canarinhos* (Brazilians) and other South Americans recruited by clubs like Deportivo La Coruña. These 'foreigners' acquire dual nationality after two years in Spain, and no longer count in calculations aimed at limiting the number of non-EU players in each team.'[38]

This 'internationalisation' of EU citizen status is further emphasised by two recent examples of abortive transfers of South American footballers to English Premier League Clubs. The case of the Argentinian, Esteban Fuertes – whose transfer to Derby County was called off after he was discovered to be in possession of a forged Portuguese passport – illustrates, albeit in a negative fashion, the increased mobility that EU citizenship can confer on a sportsman. Similarly, the transfer of the Brazilian, Edu, to Arsenal collapsed on the basis of his failure to provide adequate evidence of his status as having dual Portuguese-Brazilian nationality. These examples illustrate that significant barriers to movement still exist for professional sportsmen, but also reinforce that the *Bosman* ruling has broadened the horizons not only of EU nationals, but also those sportsmen from further afield. The importance of the acquisition of EU national status is due to the restrictions that are still put in place in terms of work permits and international clearance issues on non-EU or EEA[39] nationals.[40]

THE RE-REGULATING EFFECT OF EU ACTION ON THE GLOBAL SYSTEM

Even though, as has been highlighted above, sport may be subject to particular receptions and interpretations dependent upon the nature of the recipient culture, the need for a uniform system of regulation is maintained. It is in the very nature of sport that a 'level playing field' exists, that competitors take part on equal terms and that one party does not have a significant advantage over the other. It appears that sports regulations can withstand a certain amount of latitude in terms of their interpretation and application, relative to the local cultural, economic, social and legal context of their conduct, this is what is recognised in globalisation terms as 'resistance'. However, where that 'resistance' imposes a difference so

---

[37] Giulianotti, supra n.18, 122.
[38] Ibid. 123.
[39] *Balog* OJ C-99/23.
[40] Maguire, supra n.1, 118.

great that the theoretical 'level playing field' becomes unworkable, two possible outcomes arise. In the first instance, where the resistant locale is relatively weak, it appears that the global regulator will, in effect be able to ignore that resistance, and the locale will either have to accept the imposition of the global standard or, alternatively, isolation within the world system. This is the process of denationalisation outlined above. The second scenario is one where the local or in the case of the EU, regional resistance has sufficient sway to influence the operation of the global system. Which scenario applies depends upon the power dynamic in operation within that system. In relation to the system of global sport, Maguire is certain where this power vests:

> 'At the core of most team and individual based sports lie the countries of Western Europe, North America – excluding Mexico – and former 'White' Commonwealth countries . . . Whereas the West may be challenged on the field of play by non-core countries, the control over the content, ideology and economic resources associated with sport still tends to lie within the West.'[41]

It may be the case that the power of the European Union in the world system as it relates to sport may represent a reassertion of sovereignty of its member nations rather than the depletion of it, so often feared at a domestic level.[42] This was reinforced by the European Court of Justice in the recent *Lehtonen*[43] case when it rejected the argument that International Sporting Federations ought to be granted organisational autonomy.

It appears that the European Union, intentionally or otherwise, may be about to demonstrate European sport's predominance in the global system in relation to the renewed challenge being posed by the European Commission to football's transfer system, even after the *Bosman* imposed reforms. Initial reports suggested that transfer fees would be outlawed completely within the European Union. This would be the case even if the player were still under contract where, even post-*Bosman*, transfer fees are currently payable.[44] The European Commission have engaged with *FIFA* and *UEFA* in discussions, in order to find a compromise position. In addition, the European Court of Justice is due to consider a case concerning the Italian *Serie A* club, Perugia, who have refused to compensate a Belgian club for a player signed whilst still under contract to his original club.[45] It now appears unlikely that the transfer system will be abolished altogether, but that it is likely to undergo what has been described by an EU spokesperson as

---

[41] Ibid. 91.

[42] Wiener J, *Globalization and the Harmonization of Law* (1999) London and New York, Pinter, 37.

[43] C176/96 Jyri Lehtonen v Fédération Royale Belge de Sociétés de Basketball ASBL (FRBSB).

[44] Scrapping of transfer fees could lead to anarchy *The Daily Telegraph*, July 16, 2000.

[45] Alarm bells for FIFA and transfer system *The Guardian*, August 7, 2000.

'development'.[46] Whatever opinions exist as to the practical impact of this action on the regulation of football within the EU, there exists clear potential for an imbalance to be created between those affected by EU action and external parts of the global system of sports regulation. Giulianotti highlights the vast disparity that exists across different domestic regulatory regimes:

'Elsewhere, in contractual matters, the clubs effectively own the players. Brazil's tortured history of slave trading and feudal servitude is replicated within professional football. Young players wishing to carve a career in professional football must give up their *passe* (labour market pass) to the club, effectively removing all their wage bargaining and transfer rights until they reach thirty years of age and again become free agents. Players who challenge the *passe* system are shunned by other clubs and ignored when selecting the national team. The *passe* provides players with few financial securities during difficult times. Those failing to play to the expected standard or suffering debilitating injuries have their *passe* returned by the club, and are thus discarded as exhausted labour power.'[47]

It appears that, in terms of football at least, Europe has become the most powerful bloc, possessing the most economically powerful clubs, leagues and nations[48] and that this gives events in Europe a greater significance for the world system, at least in relation to the regulation of that sport. EU regulations in relation to the transfer system are likely to be externalised, that is absorbed by the global system, because of the gulf which will be created between the regulatory regimes in the EU and those such as the Brazilian example highlighted above. Clearly any pretence of a 'level playing field' would be seriously undermined as competitors from different jurisdictions would be subject to varied rules. The absorption will take place because of the economic and political power that vests in European football prevents the global system from simply riding roughshod over it. This much has been acknowledged both by *FIFA* and *UEFA*, with *FIFA* President Sepp Blatter commenting recently:

'FIFA remains committed to the adaptation of the *international* transfer system by way of a dialogue taking into account the interests of all parties – including clubs and players and national associations – concerned, not *just* at continental level but *globally* as well.'[49] (emphasis added)

Though many of the governing bodies' protestations have been founded on a concern over the impact of the regulation on the 'good of the game', the cynical

---

[46] EU will not abolish football transfers *BBC On-line*, September 22, 2000. Available from http://news.bbc.co.uk/sport/hi/english/football/newsid_936000/936883.stm

[47] Giulianotti, supra n.18, 113.

[48] Maguire, supra n.1, 91.

[49] International transfer System: FIFA pleased with positive reaction from European Commission, FIFA press release, available from http://www.fifa.com

may well observe a certain resentment of the diminution of the powers of these global and regional regulators. [50] Governing bodies have previously expressed their horror at being subjected to this type of regulation at all:

> 'Football has always been remarkably successful at looking after its own affairs. It is difficult to understand why regulatory authorities feel they now have to become involved.'[51]

However, it has also become clear that the extent to which the EU is able to wield its influence in this way is heavily dependent upon the nature of the sport it is trying to regulate. While football is now 'globalised', tradition and business efficacy demands that clubs are located in particular geographic areas. Formula One, by way of contrast, is not subject to these geographical constraints. It is highly mobile and the governing body of the sport, the FIA, (Fédération International de l'Automobile) has not been slow to realise this:

> "The Commission is being naïve . . . The bottom line is that the FIA is not a European organisation and if the EU tries in this unsubtle way to impose its regulations it will accentuate the trend to have more races elsewhere in the world."[52]

CONCLUSIONS

Traditionally, the approach of law has been one of cautious intervention in relation to the regulation of sport,[53] courts have been reluctant to interfere overly in an area that is perceived as being essentially self-regulating. Lord Denning famously noted in relation to the regulation of sport that:

> 'justice can often be done better by a good layman than by a bad lawyer. This is especially so in activities like football and other sports where no points of law are likely to arise and it is all part of the proper regulation of the game.'[54]

With the occasional exception,[55] those bodies charged with the regulation of sport have been granted the capacity to conduct their regulatory activities with a large degree of autonomy. In English law at least, it appears that re-regulation by the courts has taken place only where key rights involving natural justice or the

---

[50] EU move would be 'doomsday', *The Daily Telegraph*, August 16, 2000; European law and disorder leaves clubs feeling the worst, *The Daily Telegraph*, August 20, 2000.

[51] *Financial Times*, January 23, 1998.

[52] *The Guardian*, December 23, 1997.

[53] Nafziger J, Globalizing Sports Law (1999) 9 *Marquette Sports Law Journal* 225, 230-1.

[54] Enderby Town FC v Football Association [1971] 1 Ch 591, 605.

[55] See for example, Eastham v Newcastle United FC [1963] 3 All ER 139; [1964] Ch 413, involving a fundamental re-regulation of the system of 'retain and transfer' in English football.

ability to earn a living are in question.[56] This has been particularly true in relation to sport's relationship with European Community law as the Communities' founding treaties grant them no explicit competencies regarding the regulation of sport. In addition, international governing bodies can effectively choose to ignore domestic law except where they are based within a particular jurisdiction or wish to operate therein.

However, the globalisation process has brought about a sea-change in this situation. Rapid improvements in communications technologies have brought about increased interaction on the sports field and brought about the need for global regulation. More than this, they have increased the monetary value of sporting activity, which has led to the re-financing of sport at the highest level. Sport has become a valuable commodity, which the media use in order to sell their product. This has itself resulted in increased regulation, as domestic governments become concerned that broadcast sporting events should not be restricted to the few who can afford the appropriate dish or box.

These two factors have contributed greatly to the re-regulation of sport at the hands of the European Union. The economic growth associated with media re-financing of sport has provided European Law with a gateway into the sporting world and resulted in a significant re-regulation within Europe. Furthermore, the pivotal position which Europe holds in the power dynamic of the world sports system has resulted in European Law exerting an influence beyond its own jurisdictional boundaries.

---

[56] See Morris P and Little G, Challenging Sports Bodies' Determinations, (1998) 17 *Civil Justice Quarterly* 128.

Part Two:
The Frontiers of Regulatory Mechanisms

THE LEGAL AUTONOMY OF SPORT ORGANISATIONS AND THE RESTRICTIONS OF EUROPEAN LAW[*]

Klaus Vieweg

INTRODUCTION

The self regulation of sport associations, which has sometimes led to problems for both clubs and individual athletes (for instance regarding doping), has in the last few years gone through a number of changes. The reasons for these changes can be summarised as professionalisation and commercialisation. The former fear of contact with the economy is no longer a factor. Sponsoring, in its varied forms has had a particular effect on all levels of sport. Television is probably the most important factor contributing to the increase in the economic aspects of sports events. While many associations have to pay for television coverage of their events the television rights for the Olympic Games were sold for more than $1.3 billion.[1] Sport associations and clubs now compete not only for members and spectators, but also for funding. They have increasingly become participants in the economic market, whether this was desired or not. A similar change of scene has occurred through the professionalisation of coaches, athletes and officials. Through the changeover from amateur to professional status and from honorary officials to managers, the way into the labour market has been opened. Due to this development sport not only becomes subject to rules of the economic market, but also to a stronger integration into the legal system. The legal autonomy of clubs and associations is visibly becoming subject to closer scrutiny by the judiciary.

Club life as a 'law free area' came to an end in the Federal Republic of Germany with the so-called Bundesliga scandal in the 1970/71 season.[2] The then main prosecutor for the German Football Association Mr Kindermann stressed, quite seriously, at the time that sport law has priority over state law. Nowadays this appears to be an anachronism. On a European level, the *Bosman* ruling of the

---

[*] The author wishes to thank Frank Oschuetz and Andrea Murray for their valuable assistance.

[1] *International Herald Tribune* March 3, 2000.

[2] See Rauball R, *Bundesliga-Skandal*, (1972) Berlin/New York, as well as *Frankfurter Allgemeine Zeitung* June 5, 1996, 40.

A. Caiger and S. Gardiner (Eds), Professional Sport in the EU: Regulation and Re-regulation
© 2000, T.M.C.Asser Press, The Hague, The Netherlands

European Court of Justice[3] follows a similar pattern to the Bundesliga scandal of that time. The irritations expressed by the sport associations following this decision were surprising for legal experts. The sport organisations obviously did not focus sufficient attention outside their national boundaries.

Some might still recall the bitter discussion which was created by a judgment of the Bundesgerichtshof of 11th December 1997[4] concerning the inadmissibility of the centralised marketing of German teams' home games in the UEFA Cup on competition law grounds. It became clear that sport, in the economic sense, can not evade commercial law and in particular competition law rules. The intended exception of sport in the amendment relating to monopolies is due to political reasons and its effect in relation to the European sports market is limited. The comments of the former Competition Commissioner van Miert[5] made it clear that the European Commission is not in general prepared to place sport outside the scope of Articles 81 and 82 of the EU Treaty. The current Competition Commissioner, Mario Monti, who has stated that competition policy is of application to sport because sport related business is now 'big business', has followed his views.[6]

It is therefore important to clarify the effects of European Law on the autonomy of sport organisations. The following paragraphs will first of all discuss three decisions of the European Court of Justice (ECJ) relating to sport. There then will be a description of the basis of the autonomy of the clubs and associations in relation to national and European law and an attempt to make a prognosis. In addition the recognisable conflicts between the autonomy of the clubs and associations on the one hand and European law on the other will be systematised. In doing this reliance will be placed on the European law provisions regarding the basic freedoms and the ban on subsidies. The most important competition law regulations and their limitations will then be examined. Finally some possible solutions for the conflict will be presented.

---

[3] Case 415/93 (Bosman) [1995] ECR I-4921. Cf. Arens W, *SpuRt* 1996, 39 et seq.; Hilf M, Pache E, *Neue Juristische Wochenschrift* 1996, 1169 et seq.; Westermann HP, Die Entwicklung im bezahlten Fußballsport nach dem Bosman-Urteil, in Württembergischer Fußballverband e.V (Ed.), *Sport, Kommerz und Wettbewerb*, Stuttgart 1998, 27.

[4] BGHZ (Decisions of the Federal Court of Justice in civil cases)137, 297 et seq.; *SpuRt* 1998, 28 et seq.; *Neue Juristische Wochenschrift* (1998), 756.

[5] See *Frankfurter Allgemeine Zeitung* July 14, 1998, 35.

[6] Monti M, *Sport and Competition*, Excerpts from a speech given at a sports conference organised by the Commission, Brussels April 17, 2000, SPEECH/00/152: http://europa.eu.int/rapid/start/cgi/guesten.

RECENT DECISIONS OF THE EUROPEAN COURT OF JUSTICE: *BOSMAN, DELIÈGE, LEHTONEN*[7]

Facts

In 1990 the Belgian professional footballer Jean Marc Bosman entered into a contract of employment with the French Second Division club US Dunkerque. His contract with the Belgian First Division club RC Liège had expired. The transfer broke down because RC Liège prevented the release due to doubts as to whether US Dunkerque could pay the agreed transfer price. RC Liège refrained from asking the Belgian Football Association to send the release certificate to the French Football Association.

In Bosman's complaint against RC Liège and URBSFA, and later UEFA, which was raised in the Belgian Court, he asked for the transfer rules and the foreigners clause to be declared inapplicable to him and demanded damages caused by the enforcement of these regulations upon him.

The Belgian judo competitor Christelle Deliège sued the national sport organisation Ligue Francophone de Judo and the Ligue Belge de Judo because they did not nominate her for an international qualification tournament for the 1996 Olympic Games. Her amateur status had been challenged because she was a candidate for professional or rather semi-professional status due to her receiving reimbursement for her activities. The Belgian Court of First Instance in Namur referred the following questions under Article 234 to the ECJ: whether or not it is contrary to the Treaty of Rome, in particular Articles 49, 81 and 82 of the Treaty, to require professional or semi-professional athletes to be authorised by their federation in order to be able to compete in an international competition? In particular, is it in accordance with the Treaty on the European Union, that only a limited number of athletes of the same nationality can take part in international competition?[8]

The third case concerned Jyri Lehtonen, a basketball player of Finnish nationality. He also had been transferred to a Belgian club. The transfer did not take place within the transfer periods, which were established by FIBA and were applied by the national basketball association. The national association therefore imposed a fine on the player's new club because of a violation of the rules. In the trial Mr. Lehtonen contested the validity of the FIBA rules under European Law.

---

[7] Supra n. 3.; Cases C-51/96 and C-191/97 Deliège [2000] ECR I; Case C-176/96 Lehtonen [2000] ECR I .

[8] Ibid. Deliège (TN 22 and 16).

Grounds for the Judgments

In the *Bosman* case the European Court of Justice (ECJ) came to a decision about compensation for the transfer of a professional footballer from a Member State which was designated in the club rules. These rules would wrongly interfere with his right of free movement, guaranteed by Article 39, if he desired to move to another club in another Member State after the expiry of his contract. A professional footballer is classified as a worker under Article 39. However the decision states that there was no breach of the discrimination rules under Article 39 because the same transfer rules were applicable for national players. Article 39 however contains a complete ban on restrictions. Regulations which are prohibited are those which make it more difficult or ultimately prevent the exertion of the right of free movement.[9] The transfer rules in this respect would hinder a player from moving to a club in a Member State if this club did not pay a compensatory fee.[10] A violation of the limitation ban is only permissible if the transfer rules have a purpose which is agreeable with Community law and which is justified by specific reasons in the general interest and which adhere to the principle of proportionality. The ECJ in the *Bosman* ruling refused to accept that a violation of the limitation ban is permissible, because of both the aspect of maintaining a sporting and financial balance between the clubs as well as compensation for the training and demand of players. In addition the ECJ declared the limitation on the employment of foreign players from Member States as incompatible with Article 39. This means a club can employ as many players from other Member States as it wishes. However in practice this right is waived in as much as the club – due to the foreigners clause – could not field these players. In this lies discrimination towards other players elsewhere in the EU in comparison with national professional footballers.[11] In regard to the foreigners clause the ECJ also did not accept any justifying factors. The foreigners' clause concerns the core area of the work of a professional footballer and can therefore not be seen as a particular exception just because it is specific to sport. Foreigners clauses cannot be justified on the grounds of protecting the character of the national professional

---

[9] Supra n. 3, (5069) (TN 96).

[10] With regard to compensation for transfers, the quote from the judgement was as follows: 'Article 48 (now Art 39) is an obstacle to the application of rules and regulations made by the sports associations, by which a professional footballer who is a citizen of a Member State, after the expiry of his contract which ties him to a club can only then be employed by a club of another Member State if this club pays the previous club a transfer fee, training fee and a release fee.'

[11] Supra n. 3. (TN 120). With regard to the foreigners clause the quote from the judgement was as follows: 'Article 48 (now Art 39) is an obstacle to the application to the rules and regulations made by the sport associations in so far as the football clubs, in the competitions arranged by these associations, are only allowed to field a specific number of professional footballers from another Member State.'

leagues in the individual Member States, or as a basis for protection of the national team.[12]

In the more recent *Deliège* case the ECJ, in reviewing its earlier decisions, stressed again that sport is subject to Community law only in so far as it constitutes an economic activity within the meaning of Article 2 of the Treaty.[13] The Court pointed out that the mere fact that a sport association or federation unilaterally classifies its members as amateur athletes does not in itself mean that those members do not engage in economic activities within the meaning of Article 2 of the Treaty.[14] Community provisions on the free movement of persons and services do not only apply to the action of public authorities but extend also to any other rules regulating gainful employment and the provision of services generally. The abolition as between Member States of obstacles to freedom of movement for persons and to freedom to provide services would be compromised if the abolition of State barriers could be neutralised by obstacles. For example, the exercise of powers, by autonomous associations or organisations not governed by public law.[15]

expansion of Bosman ③ + ⑤

The ECJ, however, reiterated that the Treaty provisions concerning freedom of movement for persons do not prevent the adoption of rules or practices excluding foreign players from certain matches for reasons which are not of an economic nature. These rules and practices relate to such matches, which are only of a sporting interest, such as, matches between national teams from different countries.[16] The Court decided that the rules in question did not relate to events between teams or selected competitors from different countries and thus did not fall in the scope of the exemption. The Court went on to examine whether Ms. Deliège's sporting activities constituted an economic activity under Article 2 and, more particularly, the provision of services under Article 49 of the Treaty. The Court indicated that sporting activities and, in particular, a high-ranking athlete's participation in an international competition are capable of involving the provision of a number of separate, but closely related, services. Such services may fall within the scope of Article 49, even if some of those services are not paid for by those for whose benefit they are performed.[17] However, this question was left to the National Court.

In providing the National Court with guidance on interpretation, the Court went on to assess whether the contested rules could constitute a restriction on the freedom to provide services. The Court recognised the special character of sport in organising its own competitions by observing that although selection rules like

---

[12] Supra n. 3 (TN 131 et seq.); see Case C-13/76 Donà v Mantero [1976] ECR 1333 (1340 et seq.).

[13] Cases C-51/96 and C-191/97 Deliège [2000] ECR I (TN 41).

[14] Ibid. (TN 46).

[15] Ibid. (TN 47).

[16] Ibid. (TN 43).

[17] Ibid. (TN 56).

those at issue inevitably have the effect of limiting the number of participants in a tournament. Such a limitation is inherent in the conduct of an international high-level sports event, which necessarily involves certain selection rules or criteria being adopted.[18] Furthermore, and in the words of the Court:

> 'it *naturally* falls to the bodies concerned, such as organisers of tournaments, sports federations or professional athletes' associations, to lay down appropriate rules and to make their selections in accordance with them.'[19]

The Court concluded that rules do not in themselves constitute a restriction on the freedom to provide services, as long as they derive from a need inherent in the organisation of such a competition.[20]

The 6th chamber of the ECJ in delivering the judgement in *Lehtonen*, also referred to the aforementioned cornerstones for an application of European Law and its limitations. The Court stressed that a professional basketball player can be regarded as a worker in terms of Article 39 and that transfer rules may constitute an obstacle to freedom of movement for workers, prohibited by that Article.[21] In exploring the limitations of Article 39, the ECJ stressed again that rules can be justified on non-economic grounds concerning only sport itself.[22] The Court went on to point out that measures taken by sports federations with a view to ensuring the proper functioning of competitions may not go beyond what is necessary for achieving the aim pursued.[23] Here the ECJ expressed its doubts over the rules being able to pass the test of proportionality as they impose different transfer periods for players coming from outside and within Europe. This important final point was once more left to the National Court to determine.

It is noteworthy that, in the two previous decisions, the ECJ took the social significance of sport into consideration, as was expressed in Declaration No. 29 on Sport, which was annexed to the final act of the Conference which adopted the text of the Treaty of Amsterdam. As a practical consequence the ECJ did not decide the cases entirely on their merits. The examination of important questions has been left to the National Courts. The ECJ stressed that in the context of judicial co-operation between National Courts and the ECJ in connection with references for a preliminary ruling, it was for the National Court to establish and evaluate the facts of the case and for the Court of Justice to provide the National Court with such interpretative information as may be necessary to enable it to decide the dispute.[24]

---

[18] Ibid. (TN 64).
[19] Ibid.(TN69) emphasis added.
[20] Ibid. (TN 69).
[21] Ibid. (TN 47).
[22] Ibid. (TN 52).
[23] Ibid. (TN 56).
[24] Ibid. (TN 50) and ECJ Case C-176/96 Lehtonen 2000 ECR I (TN 40).

In all three cases the ECJ left open the question of whether the foreigners clauses and the transfer rules violate the provisions on the restraint of competition regulated by Article 81. In *Bosman* the ECJ stressed that an examination was not necessary since the contested rules already violated the basic freedoms.[25] In the cases *Deliège* and *Lehtonen* the Court held that the question referred to it under Article 234 was inadmissible in respect of EC competition law since the claimants did not provide sufficient information to examine this challenge.[26] The views of the Advocate General[27] in *Bosman* and the majority of legal writers[28] indicate that the rules do violate the Article 81 prohibition.

For legal experts the three decisions described above were of no surprise. Earlier decisions of the ECJ, i.e. *Donà*[29] and *Walrave*[30] gave indications that the Court would take this view. As a result of the *Bosman* ruling, there has been a reduced number of newly recruited German sportsmen in the top divisions.[31] This was a foreseeable market reaction.

BASIS OF THE AUTONOMY OF CLUBS AND ASSOCIATIONS IN NATIONAL AND EUROPEAN LAW

National Law

The autonomy of clubs and associations is a matter of national law. Autonomy is widely understood as the authority to set rules concerning their own affairs, to make use of these rules and, if need be, to enforce these rules, for example to ban doping and to enforce bans. The legal basis of this autonomy differs depending on the type of club or association. The different concepts make it necessary to examine this problem more closely. The examples of German and French law will now be considered below.

Sports associations and clubs, which are characterised as German, due to them being based in Germany or due to the majority of members being German, are protected by Article 9(1) of the German Constitution (Grundgesetz).[32] All Germans have the right to form associations and societies. The continued existence

---

[25] Supra n. 3 (TN 138).

[26] Deliège (TN 36) and Lehtonen (TN 28).

[27] See Advocate General C.O. Lenz, Opinion to C-415/93 (Bosman), *Europaeische Grundrechte-Zeitschrift (Journal of European Basic Rights)* (1995), 459.

[28] Streinz R, *Zeitschrift für Sport und Recht* (Journal of Sport and Law) 1998, 89.

[29] Case C-13/76 Donà v Mantero [1976] ECR 1333.

[30] Case C-36/74 Walrave and Koch v Union Cycliste Internationale [1974] ECR 1405.

[31] A particularly drastic example is given by the Saar Judo club. The women's Bundesliga team consists exclusively of English sportswomen. Cf. *Frankfurter Allgemeine Zeitung* September 16, 1997, 39.

[32] For the autonomy of associations in German as well as foreign law see Vieweg K, *Normsetzung und -anwendung deutscher und internationaler Verbaende*, (1990) Berlin, 154.

of the organisation and its operation of legitimate activities are also protected.[33]
On a basic legal level, paragraph 25 of the German civil code (Burgerliches
Gesetzbuch – BGB) forms the central basis of the autonomy of clubs and associations. Paragraph 25 states: 'The constitution of a club with a legal personality will
be determined by the club rules, as long as it is not based on the following regulations.' Moreover cases of actual compulsory membership, for instance like that
which exists in monopolised associations, the autonomy of clubs and associations
needs to be reinforced by the Courts. In the past few years the Courts have had a
tendency to expand the parameters of the judicial checks on club and association
decisions. The yardstick is the principle of good faith (para. 242 BGB).[34]

Very different to the German concept is the law relating to sports associations
in France. Here the autonomy of clubs and associations does not stem from constitutional principles, but is delegated by non-constitutional law. The whole area
of sport ranging from the organisation of clubs to television rights and the education and licensing of trainers is regulated by 'Law No. 84-610 of the 16th July
1984 relating to the organisation and promotion of physical and sporting activities.'[35] According to Article 16 of this law the federations that are recognised by
the Minister for Sport have a duty to fulfil a public service whilst still retaining a
certain degree of independence. To obtain recognition their statutes have to be in
accordance with a model statute issued by the Conseil d'Etat. Only one federation
may be recognised for each type of sport. This federation is then entrusted with
disciplinary powers and the right to set technical rules for its discipline.

These two examples show how crucial the discussion about autonomy for
sport is. While a German might have a very strong idea of independence and autonomy for sport rules and regulations and therefore wishes no interference from
the state law or the Courts,[36] this idea might be less developed for a Frenchman.

European Law

European law does not recognise its own 'Sport Article'. In the conference discussing reform ('Maastricht II'), one was discussed[37] but it did not come into being. Despite the lack of a direct transfer into Community law, the social significance of sport, in particular the role in finding its identity and contact with
people, was emphasised in Declaration No 29 of the Treaty of Amsterdam. The

---

[33] Ibid.

[34] See Roehricht V, Chancen und Grenzen von Sportgerichtsverfahren nach deutschem Recht,
in: Roehricht V (Ed.), *Sportgerichtsbarkeit*, Stuttgart et alia. (1997), 9 with further references from
case law.

[35] Loi n 84-610 du 16 juillet 1984 relative à l'organsiation et à la promotion des activités physiques et sportives.

[36] See the recent article from Steiner U, Doping aus verfassungsrechtlicher Sicht, in Roehricht/
Vieweg (Ed.), *Doping-Forum*, Stuttgart et alia (2000), 127.

[37] See Hilf M, & Pache E, *Neue Juristische Wochenschrift* (1996), 1169.

autonomy of sport organisations is also recognised by the European Commission.[38] There have also been requests to the decision-makers within the European Union to give sports associations advice where questions that are of importance to sport are concerned. The characteristics of amateur sport should be given special consideration.[39]

The European legislature has up until now not established any specific regulation of the autonomy of clubs and associations. It is questionable whether the European Community has legislative powers to regulate sport, in particular the problems connected with doping.[40] However, a draft of a Regulation was requested from the Council concerning a European Club Statute.[41] The difficulties caused by the working together of clubs across borders should be eliminated by legal instruments being put at the disposal of the clubs. Article 1(2) of the proposal for a Council Regulation (EEC) on the statute for a European association states, that subject to the application at national level of the legal and administrative rules governing the carrying on of an activity or the exercise of a profession, the European association shall be free to determine the activities necessary for the pursuit of these objects. These need to be compatible with the objectives of the Community as well as with the public interest of the Community and the Member States. These association or clubs shall pursue these activities in accordance with the principles derived from the characteristics (legal or otherwise) which are derived from its character as a sport – and these do not include business interests.

The ECJ recognised the freedom to form associations as a basic right in two of its decisions.[42] It used Article 11 of the ECHR as its legal basis, which protects mergers and activities of associations within the framework of the freedom to form associations.[43] Furthermore the ECJ bases the freedom of association on the constitutional traditions common to the Member States, which according to Article 6(2) of the Treaty, due to a lack of a list of basic rights, are general principles of Community law.[44] The internal authority of the clubs to set their own

---

[38] Andreu J, Plan für den Beitrag der Gemeinschaft zur Dopingbekämpfung in: Roehricht and Vieweg (Ed.), *Doping-Forum*, Stuttgart et alia (2000), 101.

[39] OJ 1997 No. C 340/136. For the protection of sport in community law also see Streinz R, *Zeitschrift für Sport und Recht* (Journal of Sport and Law) (1998) 96.

[40] With special regard to doping see Roethel, A Kompetenzen der Europaeischen Union zur Dopingbekaempfung in Roehricht/Vieweg (Ed.), *Doping-Forum*, Stuttgart et alia (2000), 109.

[41] Amended proposal for a Council Regulation (EEC) on the statute for a European association COM (93) 252 final – SYN 386, OJ 1993 No. C 236/3.

[42] Case C-175/73 (Gewerkschaftsbund) [1974] ECR 917 (925); Case C-414/93 (Bosman) [1995] ECR I-4921 (5065) (TN 79).

[43] See Frowein J and Peukert W, *Europaeische Menschenrechtskonvention, Kommentar*, (1996, 2nd Ed), Kehl/Straßburg, Article 11, Rdnr. 6.

[44] Case C-415/93 Bosman [1995] ECR I-4921 (5065) (TN 79). See. Article 9 of the German Constitution, Article 27 of the Belgian Constitution, Article 78 of the Danish Constitution, Article 12 of the Greek Constitution, Article 40 VI c of the Irish Constitution, Article 18 of the Italian Con-

provisions belongs to the freedom of association in the Community law sense.[45] The continued existence of the clubs and its operation of legitimate activities are protected. The collective freedom of association embraces the rationale of the club, and how the club's rationale will be realised through its establishment and development.[46]

Systematisation of Recent Conflicts Between the Autonomy of the Clubs and Associations and European Law, in Particular in Relation to the Basic Freedoms

In relation to sport, the legal dimension of the difficulties becomes evident, if one systemises several recently decided cases of conflict between (club/or associations) autonomy and European law. In this respect it has proven to be a great advantage that conflicts in the area of sport have frequently been made public by the media.

Freedom of Movement (of Persons) (Article 39)

Article 39(1) states that the freedom of movement for workers is one of the basic freedoms. Every worker can enter any Member State of the European Union and stay there permanently for the purposes of gainful employment. According to Article 39(2) the worker enjoys the same rights as the workers of the host country. All discrimination based on nationality, which relates to employment, pay and other working conditions is prohibited within the European Union. With this requirement of equality for all citizens, which is also effective on a private law level (horizontal effect),[47] the general ban on discrimination under Article 12 is put in concrete terms. A further specification comes from Article 4 of Council Regulation 1612/68 concerning the free movement of workers within the European Community.[48] The Article states that national provisions, which restrict by number or percentage the employment of foreign nationals, shall not apply to nationals of other Member States.[49]

---

stitution, Article 26 of the Constitution of Luxembourg, Article 8 of the Dutch Constitution, Article 46 of the Constitution of Portugal, Article 1 Number 5 of the Swedish Constitution and Article 22 of the Spanish Constitution (see Tettinger P, Die Dopingproblematik im Lichte der europäischen Grundrechtediskussion, in Vieweg K, (ed.), *Doping – Realität und Recht,* Berlin 1998, 93.).

[45] Case 415/93 (Bosman) [1995] ECR I-4921 (5065) (TN 81); Krogmann M, *Grundrechte im Sport,* (1998) Berlin, 196.

[46] Gramlich L, *Die Öffentliche Verwaltung* (Journal of Public Administration) (1996), 801.

[47] See Jarass H and Pieroth B, *Grundgesetz, Kommentar* (1995) 3rd Ed. München, Art. 1, Rdnr. 24 with further references.

[48] OJ 1968 L 257/2.

[49] See Hilf M and Pache E, *Neue Juristische Wochenschrift* (1996), 1169.

The strict application of the freedom of movement could lead to unwanted outcomes.[50] For this reason Article 39(3) and (4) lists as exceptions limitations justified on grounds of public policy, public security or public health. In addition, restrictions can be justified as being in the 'necessary general interest'. These limitations have three requirements: equally applicable measures, legitimate general interest and recognition of the principle of proportionality.[51]

In addition to the foreigners' clauses and transfer rules relevant in the *Bosman* ruling, the following cases make the difficulties apparent:

The Use of Sportsmen in Another Member State, Who are Banned in Their Own Country for Doping Reasons

The Handball club SG-Hameln, which plays in the Bundesliga (German national league) was stripped of four points by the German Handball Federation because Finur Johannsson, who was banned in his own country, Iceland,[52] because of doping until 9th September 1998, was played in January of that year. The reason for the ban was that he was said to have allegedly taken cocaine in 1996 when he was a track and field athlete. Nevertheless in December 1997 the European Handball Association gave him permission to play, which it then withdrew on 22nd January 1998.[53] This poses interesting questions as to whether the varied applications of the association rules and regulations relating to doping can be seen as a limitation on the freedom of movement. Also, whether the doping rules and regulations in general can be regarded as a justification for the limitation on the freedom of movement.

The Ban on Negotiations Whilst a Contract is Valid

Ajax Amsterdam accused Barcelona FC of violating the FIFA regulations which states that players who are still under contract with a club can not be approached by other clubs. Barcelona wanted to 'buy' the twin brothers Frank and Ronald de Boer, who were still under contract with Ajax until 2004, for the equivalent of DM35 million (approximately £12 million).[54]

---

[50] It is therefore questionable whether it is desired that a team that consists only of foreign nationals can become the German champions, supra n. 31.

[51] Case 415/93 (Bosman) [1995] ECR I-4921 (5071) (TN 104); to Article 28 (former Article 30), see Geiger R, *EG-Vertrag, Kommentar*, 2nd Ed, München 1995, Art 30, Rdnr 19.

[52] Although Iceland is not a Member State of the European Community, the case provides a good example because the same problem could arise with associations of Member States.

[53] *Frankfurter Allgemeine Zeitung* January 20, 1998, 34; *Frankfurter Allgemeine Zeitung* January 24, 1998, 33, *Frankfurter Allgemeine Zeitung* March 7, 1998, 33.

[54] *Frankfurter Allgemeine Zeitung* August 15, 1998, 30 & *Frankfurter Allgemeine Zeitung* September 9, 1998, 31. Recently the European Commission has indicated on a few occasions that FIFA's international transfer system for professional football players is not in line with the principle of free movement. FIFA have until the end of the year 2000 to change the system. If it does not then the Commission will bring appropriate sanctions against it.

Freedom of Establishment (Article 43)

Freedom of establishment guarantees the reception and exercise of self-employment in another Member State, wherein a permanent business will be set up.[55] In this respect it is also a question of the principle of equal treatment of citizens. Whether a violation of Article 43 occurs is judged on the exceptions laid down in Articles 45 and 46 or by the ECJ[56]:

– Execution of a public service (Article 45);
– Public policy, public security or public health grounds (Article 46);
– The application of the restrictive national measures in a non-discriminative way, justification on necessary grounds of general interest as well as the suitability and necessity of the measures in order to fulfil their purpose.[57]

The application of the freedom of establishment is also considered in the following, still hypothetical theoretical circumstances:

– The founding of a marketing company for the purposes of better merchandising or a television company[58] by a club which has its seat in another Member State;
– The founding or take-over of a Football Club Ltd. in Great Britain from a German Bundesliga club, for example in order to stimulate and retain talent in the German Bundesliga club.

Freedom to Provide Services (Article 49 et seq.)

The freedom to provide services guarantees that a service provider can supply his service for a fee – cross border – in another Member State, as in the one in which he is resident, without him setting up permanent residence there.[59] This is also a question of the principle of equal treatment of citizens. Whether there is a violation of Article 49 is decided by the references in Article 55 to Articles 45 and 46 regarding the limits of the freedom of establishment. Further limitations such as the general interest can also be relevant.[60] The practice is, in this respect, not yet certain.[61]

---

[55] See Nikolaysen G, *Europarecht II*, Baden-Baden (1996), 185; Lenz CO, *EG-Vertrag, Kommentar*, Köln (1994), Art 52, Rdnr. 2.

[56] For a discussion of whether Article 43 (formerly Article 52) entails a hidden discrimination or a general ban on limitation, see Troberg P, in Groeben, Thiesing, Ehlermann (eds.), *Kommentar zum EU-/EG-Vertrag*, Bd. I, 5th Edition, Baden-Baden (1997), Art 52, Rdnr. 46 Nikolaysen G (see footnote 55),185.

[57] See Case C-19/92 Kraus [1993] ECR I-1689 (1697) (TN 32); Case C-55/94 Gebhard [1995] ECR 4165, (4197) (TN 37).

[58] According to the press report in *Frankfurter Allgemeine Zeitung* August 11, 1998, 27, Manchester United was the first football club in the world to set up its own television station.

[59] Bleckmann A, *Europarecht*, 6th Ed, Berlin 1997, Rdnr. 1672.

[60] See Case C-288/89 Stichting Gouda [1991] ECR 4035 (4040 f.) (TN 13 et seq.).

[61] For the comments of the former Competition Law Commissioner K. van Miert, see 84 supra.

A number of recent cases illustrate the practical significance of the 'mobile service provider' in the area of sport.[62]

– The idea of a Superleague for the top European football clubs:

UEFA criticised the plans of the top European football clubs to play in their own Superleague from the year 2000, and threatened to exclude the clubs from UEFA competitions.[63] Behind these plans were considerations to replace the Champions League, which is run by UEFA, with a new competition that would secure increased earnings through sponsorship and the sale of television rights.[64]

– The holding of home games in a stadium, which is located in another Member State:

The English Premier League club Wimbledon FC has not had its own stadium for six years. During this time the home games were played at its neighbouring stadium Selhurst Park which belongs to Crystal Palace FC. During the time in question, the chairman of Wimbledon FC was Sam Hammam, originally from the Lebanon. In 1997 Hammam sold the majority of the shares to two Norwegian businessmen for the equivalent of DM75 million (approximately £25m). Wimbledon, with the support of the lawyer that represented Bosman, Jean-Louis Dupont, are now trying to get their home games held in Dublin. Wimbledon wants to invest almost DM300 million in a new stadium in Dublin.[65] It is expected that the stadium will always be at full capacity because Dublin has no major resident football club. With its wish to move to Dublin, Wimbledon FC has met with huge resistance from FIFA, UEFA and the Irish Football Association (FAI).[66]

– The allocation of Football World Cup 1998 tickets through the organisation committee:

The former EU Competition Commissioner, Karel van Miert, noticed that in the sale of tickets to the football associations of the 32 participant countries and to the French spectators there was a predominant discrimination against ordinary spectators outside France. Infringement of Article 82 (abuse of a dominant position), as mentioned by van Miert,[67] foreign spectators were disadvantaged in being able to buy tickets for the matches.

---

[62] In relation to the horizontal effect of Article 49, see Streinz R, *SpuRt* 1998, 45 with further references from the case law of the ECJ.

[63] *Frankfurter Allgemeine Zeitung*, July 28, 1998, 31.

[64] In the meantime the clubs have agreed to a new structure of the Champions League with UEFA, which should lead to higher incomes for the clubs. See *Frankfurter Allgemeine Zeitung* December 3, 1998, 39 and *Frankfurter Allgemeine Zeitung* December 15, 1998, 32.

[65] *Frankfurter Allgemeine Zeitung* February 13, 1998, 31.

[66] *Frankfurter Allgemeine Zeitung* February 11, 1998, 25.

[67] *Frankfurter Allgemeine Zeitung* March 25, 1998, 19; *Frankfurter Allgemeine Zeitung* July 14, 1998, 35.

– The participation of foreign teams in the leagues of other Member States:

It has been agreed that Austrian ice-hockey teams will play in the German ice-hockey league (DEL) from the 1999/2000 season.[68]

– The use of a professional foreign referee in the leagues of another Member State:

There has been an agreement amongst the DEL clubs that professional foreign referees can officiate in the ice-hockey games.[69]

– The requirement of authorisation for the organisation of an international competition:

The rules of relevant national as well as international sports associations provide that international sport events – in other words the providing of services – can only take place, if the application from the organisers has been previously approved by them.[70]

– The exclusion of national sports associations and its clubs from competitions of the international association:

The Polish Football Association and its clubs were excluded from international competition because of the influence of the Polish State, which is forbidden in the UEFA regulations.[71]

– The licensing of trainers:[72]

Problems can arise for trainers, sport teachers, and coaches etc. if their national qualifications are not recognised in another Member State.[73]

---

[68] Information given by the then Commissioner of the DEL clubs and the chairman of the league company, the lawyer Bernd Schaefer III.

[69] Ibid.

[70] Authorisation of club events: Article 50(3) FIFA regulation (International competitions between clubs are in principle to be authorised by the executive committee); Article 9(5) FIFA regulation as well as Article 28(4) IHF-constitution (International club games require the authorisation of the respective national associations).See also Article 10(1) of the FIFA regulation (The approval of FIFA in tournaments that include more than two national teams).

[71] *Frankfurter Allgemeine Zeitung* August 10, 1998, 28 and *Frankfurter Allgemeine Zeitung* December 1, 1998, 46.

[72] See DG X of the European Commission (Ed.), *Studie über den Einfluß der Tätigkeit der Europäischen Union auf den Sport* (1995), produced by Coopers & Lybrand, 36.

[73] According to a press report in the *Frankfurter Allgemeine Zeitung* November 14, 1996 the sports ministers and sports presidents from Luxembourg, Lothringen, the German speaking community of Belgium, Saarland and Rheinland-Pfalz signed a European sport pool charter. In this charter the common education of trainers and coaches as well as the mutual acceptance of qualifications are laid down and the opinion expressed that to promote competitive sport they would exchange trainers or training centres would work together. The financing of this co-operation will be from the European programme 'EURATLON' as well as from funds from the regional sports federations. (see Fritzweiler J, Pfister B and Summerer T, *Praxis-Handbuch Sportrecht*, München (1998), 488). For

Free Movement of Goods (Article 28)

The Treaty of Rome provides for the total abolition of all national measures, which restrict intra-Community trade. The free movement of goods is guaranteed in particular through the ban on quantitative restrictions and measures having equivalent effect (Articles 28–31).

Derogation from the Article 28 prohibition is governed by Article 30. Accordingly, limitations can be acceptable if they are justified, for example, on grounds of public morality, public policy or public security or the protection of national treasures or industrial or commercial property. In addition the ECJ[74] has ruled that 'necessary requirements', for example the protection of the environment and the protection of the consumer, can justify the limitation on the free movement of goods.

The following situations could, for example, lead to conflict:

– The authorisation of sport equipment according to the technical regulations and specifications and both international and national sports associations.

This would mean that only footballs with the FIFA trademark, which costs 1sfr., would be allowed to be used in official competitions.[75]

The Fédération Internationale de Basketball Amateur (FIBA) stipulated in its rules and regulations the exclusive use of certain equipment (in particular baskets, scoreboards and balls) which is approved by FIBA.[76] If a club wishes to use products made by a manufacturer authorised by FIBA, it does not need to carry out any further approval. However if a club wishes to use products belonging to another manufacturer, it must register this separately in addition to the payment of an approval fee.

Regulations of sports associations, which specify that only sports goods produced by a certain company, may be used for official tournaments, due to a necessary high standard of quality and which requires the payment of a fee to the association by the company (such as in the case of the Swiss Tennis Association) may lead to difficulties.[77]

---

more information on the EURATLON programme DG X of the European Commission (ed.) (see note 72), 109. Kreiß F, gives an overview of the situation in Mitarbeitsstrukturen im Sport in Deutschland und Europa, in Europäische Akademie des Sports (ed.), *Lokale und kommunale Sportstrukturen in Europa*, Velen (1998), 68.

[74] Case C-120/78 Cassis de Dijon [1979] ECR 649 (662) (TN 8); Case C-302/86 Commission v Denmark [1988] ECR 4607 (4630) (TN 6).

[75] *Frankfurter Allgemeine Zeitung* March 6, 1996, 39. Due to pressure from the European Commission a restriction of the FIFA regulation ensued, in that for international games, footballs with the imprint 'International Matchball Standard' (which costs nothing) were permitted, see *Sportartikel-Zeitung* (Journal of sport articles) March 11, 1996.

[76] See 128.2, 130.2, 131.3 and 132 of the FIBA Regulations 1995.

[77] See Jenny, *Zeitschrift für Sport und Recht* (Journal of Sport and Law) (1998), 173; in the case itself, however, Article 28 did not apply, because Switzerland did not join the European Economic Area and therefore the basic freedoms of the EC Treaty were not valid; see Oppermann T, *Europarecht*, 2nd ed, München 1999 (TN 137).

The changing of the rules and regulations of an association regarding the specifications of sport apparatus, which prevents the producers from selling the warehouse stock should also be noted.[78]

There is also the issue of the inadmissibility of new sport apparatus for sport competitions, e.g. the International Skiing Federation (FIS) recently banned the use of newly developed skis in ski jumping competitions.[79]

Further problems arise here regarding the competition rules in Article 82.[80]

– The requirement of authorisation in respect of the sale of goods at international sport events.

The sale of goods (videos, books) relating to the Football World Cup needed the authorisation of FIFA.[81] It is possible that through this the free movement of goods was restricted in order to take into account the economic interest of the French organisers.

Free Movement of Capital (Article 56 et seq.)

Article 56 in particular guarantees the free movement of capital as one of the basic freedoms of the Common Market.[82] Limitations on the free movement of capital are prohibited, i.e. all rules which are capable of hindering directly or indirectly, actually or potentially the flow of capital between Member States.[83] Limitations have to be justified on either necessary grounds or grounds of general interest.[84]

The following conflicts have recently arisen:

– Ruling regarding participation in foreign joint-stock sport companies.

Despite the successful qualification of the Greek club AEK Athens, the club was not allowed to take part in the UEFA Cup in the 1998/1999 season. UEFA brought in a rule in May 1998, which stated that only one club per owner was

---

[78] See e.g. women's javelin, see *Frankfurter Allgemeine Zeitung* May 20, 1999, 46.

[79] See *Frankfurter Allgemeine Zeitung* March 20, 2000, 45.

[80] See DG X of the European Commission (Ed.) (supra n. 72), Rdnr. 4063. (regarding tennis balls which were recognised as 'official' by the Danish Tennis Association); in addition the freedom to provide services is in this respect affected when the ban on competing products is relevant at the time of the allocation of the event.

[81] *Frankfurter Allgemeine Zeitung* July 14, 1998, 35.

[82] The phrase 'free movement of capital' is not defined in the Treaty. In the legislation of the Council it is widely interpreted and includes all financial transactions which are not directly qualified by the free movement of goods and services. See Geiger (supra n. 51), Article 73 b, Anm. 3.

[83] Ress G, & Ukrow J, in Grabitz E, & Hilf M, *Kommentar zur Europaeischen Union*, München, May (1998), Article 73 b, para. 11.

[84] Lenz CO, EG-Vertrag, *Kommentar*, (Köln 1994), Article 73 b, para. 10; see Case C-120/78 Cassis de Dijon [1979] ECR 649 (662) (TN 8); Case C-302/86 Commission v Denmark [1988] ECR 4607 (4630) (TN 6 et seq.).

allowed to take part in European Club competition.[85] AEK Athens are controlled by a British investment group, the English National Investment Company (ENIC), who also have control of, inter alia, Slavia Prague. The company allocated the place in the UEFA Cup to the runners up in the Championship of the Czech Republic.[86]

According to Article 15-1 of the French 'Law No. 84-610 of 16th July 1984 relating to the organisation and promotion of physical and sporting activities,'[87] it is forbidden for a natural person to hold shares, directly or indirectly, or voting rights in more than one sport company that is active in the same discipline.[88]

– A ban on advertisement for foreign sponsors of clubs.

The German Football Association (Deutscher Fußball-Bund DFB) came to an agreement with the majority of the Bundesliga and the Bundesliga clubs, which meant that sponsors specific to one club are not allowed to advertise during the home games which go out live on television.[89] In relation to foreign sponsors, the free movement of capital was affected.

Ban on Subsidies (Article 87 (1))

Article 87(1) prohibits state aid, which distorts competition in trade between Member States, by the favouring of certain undertakings or manufacturers, as long as it is not justified by special social or other factors.[90] The press reported a problematic situation:

For the use of a piece of land, which is said to have a market price of over DM100 million, the city of Munich asked Bayern Munich FC for a mere rent of DM6,079.50 per annum.[91]

---

[85] Letter from UEFA to the member associations on May 26, 1998 concerning the integrity of European club competition.

[86] As to CAS 98/200 – AEK Athens and Slavia Prague vs. UEFA, see below VI.; see *Frankfurter Allgemeine Zeitung* June 29, 1998, 40; see also *Spiegel* 43/1997, 165 and Schwarz D, (2000) *Zeitschrift für Sport und Recht* (Journal of Sport and Law) 83.

[87] Loi n 84-610 du 16 juillet 1984 relative à l'organisation et à la promotion des activités physiques et sportives.

[88] A similar approach can be found in Polish law. According to the 1996 Polish law governing physical education, a capital provider can only contribute 1% to a second joint stock sport company. Article 32, No. 5 of the law concerning physical education passed on the January 18, 1996 is published in Szwarc A, in Scherrer U (ed.), (1998) *Sportkapitalgesellschaften*, Stuttgart, 94.

[89] For the legal dispute between the sponsor Gerry Weber and Arminia Bielefeld, see *Frankfurter Allgemeine Zeitung* August 14, 1998, page 34.

[90] Supra. n.51, para. 10.

[91] See *Frankfurter Allgemeine Zeitung* January 29, 1997, 13. To the legal position in particular, see Vieweg K, Auswirkungen des Europarechts auf den Sport – Europaweite Ausschreibung und Vergabe von Bau- und Architektenleistungen sowie Zulässigkeitsgrenzen kommunaler Subventionierung, in: Europäischer Akademie des Sports (ed.), (1998) *Lokale und kommunale Sportstrukturen in Europa*, Velen, 110.

COMPETITION LAW

The competition law of the European Community – regulated by Article 81 et
seq. – has as its purpose the realisation of the internal market, which means that
competition within the Community has to be protected from distortion, restriction
and elimination.[92] Article 81 prohibits agreements between undertakings, decisions by associations of undertakings and concerted practices, which prevent, restrict or distort competition. Article 82 prohibits the abuse of a dominant position. These provisions are of exceptional practical significance to commercialised, and – because of the so-called one-place principle – to a large extent,
monopolised sport. The one-place principle means that for each state and each
sport only one association is accepted by the respective international association.[93]

The competition law prohibitions in Articles 81 and 82 are, however, not
without exceptions. In this respect there has until now been no unified practice.
Following the rule of reason doctrine in American Antitrust law, European competition law has approved restrictions relating to the facts.[94] The Commission and
the ECJ have dealt with the concept from time to time, and in balancing advantages and disadvantages of a certain restraint of competition, they have not applied the ban on cartels.[95] In addition to this, individual and block exemptions,
given by the Commission in accordance with Article 81(3), have to be taken into
consideration.[96] However, an exemption always requires that the restriction does
not go beyond what is necessary to achieve the objects of the agreement.

It has often been argued that sport as a whole should be exempt from competition rules because of its particular character. On the one hand it is recognised that
the basic aim of sports associations is to organise competition. Sports events can
only be carried out if the competitors follow certain rules that may restrain them
from 'free' competition. One must bear in mind that these rules make sport what
it is and therefore form the basis for the existence of sportsmen and women them-

---

[92] Case C-6/72 Europemballage & Continental Can v Commission [1973] ECR 215.

[93] See Vieweg K, *Normsetzung und -anwendung deutscher und internationaler Verbaende*,
(1990) Berlin, 61.

[94] See Fleischer H, *Wirtschaft und Wettbewerb* (1996), 473.

[95] Case C-234/89 [1991] II-977, 983; Case C-395/87 [1989] 2565; Hannamann I and Vieweg K,
Soziale und wirtschaftliche Machtpositionen im Sport – Rechtstatsächliche Situationen und (kartell)-
rechtliche Grenzen, in: Württembergischer Fußballverband e.V. (ed.), *Sport, Kommerz und Wettbewerb*, (1998) Stuttgart, 49.

[96] In his presentation 'Sport and Community law' held on the May 5, 1997, the former European
Competition Law Commissioner K. van Miert said that the system of balancing the rights of the
clubs according to Article 81(3) can be freely determined. There he is thinking of exemption de-
pending on the conditions, especially the use of income and the support of young sportsmen. See
Frankfurter Allgemeine Zeitung July 14, 1998, 35. According to a notice in the *Frankfurter
Allgemeine Zeitung* August 5, 1998, 32, the European Commission have sent a reminder to the Ger-
man Football Association to finally announce the marketing model for the television rights of the
Bundesliga games.

selves. They enhance competition between competitors rather than restrict it. The idea to create a restriction on the scope of the competition law provisions is evident. The associations often stress that all their rules and regulations are inevitably necessary to organise sports events and that primarily they have no economical implications. Articles 81 et seq. apply only if the challenged conduct falls within the scope of Article 2 – it must constitute an economic activity. This limitation may exclude rules concerning the size of the playing field or the length of a race track. However, provisions for the size and the quality of a ball do not only concern the players but also its manufacturers. Anti-doping rules might have the effect of preventing a professional sports athlete – who is a worker or a provider of services – from performing his or her professional activity. Professionalisation and commercialisation increasingly reflect the important economic implications of sport rules and regulations.

This ambivalent nature of sport rules and regulations has also been recognised by the European Commission:

> 'The Commission notes that sport comprises two levels of activity: on the one hand the *sport activity strictly speaking*, which fulfils a social, integrating and cultural role that must be preserved and to which in theory the competition rules of the EC Treaty do not apply. On the other hand a series of *economic activities generated by the sport activity*, to which the competition rules of the EC Treaty apply, albeit taking into account the specific requirements of this sector. The interdependence and indeed the overlap between these two levels render the application of competition rules more complex ... Sport also has features, in particular the interdependence of competitors and the need to guarantee the uncertainty of results of competitions, which could justify that sport organisations implement a specific framework, in particular on the markets for the production and the sale of sport events ... However, these specific features do not warrant an automatic exemption from the EU competition rules of any economic activities generated by sport, due in particular to the increasing economic weight of such activities.'[97]

This need for a balance[98] between necessary co-ordination of conduct and the requirements of free market competition has already been addressed by former Competition Commissioner K. van Miert. In answering questions put by the European Parliament on behalf of the Commission he suggested as follows:

> '(...) it is necessary to determine whether these ... rules are limited to what is strictly necessary to attain the objective of ensuring the uncertainty as to results or whether there exists less restrictive means to achieve it. Provided that such rules remain in proportion to the sport objective pursued, they would not be covered by the competition rules laid down in the EC treaty'[99]

---

[97] EC Commission Press Release of February 24, 1999, IP/99/133, emphasis added.
[98] Hannamann I, *Kartellverbot und Verhaltenskoordinationen im Sport*, (2001) Berlin (to be published).
[99] OJ EC, 1999, C 50, 143.

In a recent speech Competition Commissioner Mario Monti expressed that the Commission is prepared to apply three general principles when looking at competition law issues in the field of sport:[100]

- Firstly, sports federations and clubs operate as undertakings only to the extent that they are carrying out economic activities.
- Secondly, regulations drawn up by sports federations which lay down rules without which a sport could not exist should not, in principle, be subject to the application of EC competition rules. This includes rules, which are inherent to a sport or which are necessary for its organisation or for the organisation of competitions: the so-called 'sport rules and regulations'. Sport rules and regulations applied in an objective, transparent and non-discriminatory manner do not constitute restrictions of competition.
- Thirdly, the Commission is willing to take into account the social and cultural functions of sport as expressed by the Declaration on Sport annexed to the Amsterdam Treaty. Therefore, the exemption of arrangements, which provide for a redistribution of financial resources, e.g. to amateur sport from competition rules may be justified if necessary to retain those benefits.

The ECJ has so far refused to address the issue of EC competition law and sport. The International Court of Arbitration for Sport (CAS) in a recent decision[101] upholding the multiple ownership clause in the UEFA Rules, carefully examined the question of EC competition law. The CAS observed that the ECJ had held in several judgements that restraints on competitors' conduct do not amount to restrictions of competition within the meaning of Art. 81(1) provided that such restraints do not exceed what is necessary for the attainment of legitimate aims.[102] As was stressed in the *Bosman* ruling, the aim 'of maintaining a balance between clubs by preserving a certain degree of equality and uncertainty as to the results ... must be accepted as legitimate.'[103] The CAS, by drawing an analogy to franchising systems, acknowledged that the need to preserve the reputation and quality of the football product may bring about restraints on individual club owners' freedom. The CAS satisfied itself that the rule was necessary to provide the consumer with a credible sport contest. Applying the test of proportionality the arbitrators concluded that the contested rule was proportionate to the legitimate aim pursued.[104]

Thus the problem whether a certain type of conduct is a violation in the sense of Articles 81 or 82, or whether it is justified on the facts, is to be judged on a comprehensive weighing up of the interests with consideration given to the ob-

---

[100] Supra n. 6.
[101] Supra n. 86- not yet published.
[102] Ibid. (TN 156).
[103] Supra n. 3 (TN 106).
[104] Supra n. 86 (TN 161).

jects of the agreement within the freedom of competition.[105] Specific issues relating to the organisation of sport and its contests, as well as the special social and cultural role and bringing people together should not be underestimated for the determination of a violation of EC competition law.

To give further examples, consider the following problem areas:

- Transfer rules and foreigner clauses;[106]
- Limitations on marketing laid down in the association rules.

As a current example the centralised marketing of the television rights to the UEFA Cup home games by the German Football Association[107] and Motorsport events by the FIA should be mentioned.[108]

- The utilisation of foreign advertising rights and an integrated general sponsorship concept.

After the so-called Treviso decision of 27th May 1995, the International Bobsleigh Association (FIBT) reserved for themselves advertising spaces on the bobsleigh and clothing of the competitors without the approval of the owners and athletes.[109]

The Competition Directorate of the European Commission has instructed the representatives of the German Eighths (Rowers), the French and the German Rowing Association to submit a complaint against the International Rowing Association (FISA). According to the views of the rowers, FISA is abusing its dominant position. At their congress in 1997, the decision was reached to claim the first meter of the boats as well as the arms of the athletes' jerseys – by far the most important areas in terms of advertising – for the logos of their own sponsors at FISA organised events.[110]

- The compulsory purchase of equipment from certain manufacturers or dealers.[111]

---

[105] Supra n. 95, 49 (75) with reference to the area of sport.

[106] See Advocate General C. O. Lenz, Opinion to ECJ C-415/93 (Bosman), *Europäische Grundrechte-Zeitschrift* (Journal of European Basic Rights) 1995, 459. See the position taken by the former Competition Law Commissioner K. van Miert on November 27, 1997- http://www.europa.eu.int/comm/dg04/speech/seven/fr/sp97069.htm

[107] In relation to German competition law ruled on by Decisions of the Federal Court of Justice in civil cases 137, 297. *Zeitschrift für Sport und Recht* (Journal of Sport and Law) (1998), 28; *Neue Juristische Wochenschrift* (1998), 756. (Centralised marketing of the UEFA Cup home games).

[108] *Frankfurter Allgemeine Zeitung* March 19, 1998, 34; *Frankfurter Allgemeine Zeitung* March 20, 1998, 40; *Frankfurter Allgemeine Zeitung* July 29, 1998, 26; LG Frankfurt, Zeitschrift für *Sport und Recht* (Journal of Sport and Law) (1997), 129; *Wettbewerb in Recht und Praxis* (Competition in Law and Practice) (1997), 1108, with comments by Hohmann H, 1011.

[109] See Vieweg K, Sponsoring und internationale Sportverbände, in Vieweg K, (ed.) *Sponsoring in Sport*, (1996) Stuttgart, 53.

[110] *Frankfurter Allgemeine Zeitung* July 17, 1998, 33.

[111] Supra n. 94, 482.

– Exclusive sales of tickets (for example in the Football World Cup 1998).[112]

POSSIBLE SOLUTIONS – THE GLOBAL APPLICATION OF THE PROPORTIONALITY
TEST

The systematic recording of the existing, or rather the recognisable conflicts, illustrates the tense relationship between the autonomy of the associations and
clubs on the one hand, and European law – the basic freedoms and the competition provisions in particular – on the other. As it is not clear from the outset
which deserves priority, this conflict is not easy to resolve. Due to this considerable uncertainty arises. It poses the question as to how far the special features of
sport give cause for a derivation from the practice concerning general commercial
law.

The concept of a general exception for the area of sport may seem desirable
but doubts, especially in relation to the practical feasibility have already been expressed.[113] As one identifies more and more sport rules and regulations that are
able to effect economic activities, the idea of a general restriction on the scope of
EU provisions will remain theoretical.[114] Although the ECJ always states from its
earlier decision in *Donà*,[115] that there might be a place for a restriction on the
scope for reasons of a non-economic nature and which relate to the particular nature and context of such matches and are thus only related to sport, it became apparent in the *Deliège* decision that the Court is only willing to apply this exception to purely national team competitions.[116] Thus sport has to be regarded as a
wide economic activity that nevertheless deserves a distinctive treatment due to
its organisation and social implications. However the way of dealing with this
special treatment is best done by way of a justification.

It therefore appears that the provisions of the EU Treaty do not exist without
limitations. There is a concept of justification for a constraint of the basic freedoms due to certain non-economic reasons or issues of public interest. The competition law provisions permit practices that do not exceed what is necessary for
the attainment of legitimate aims. The aim of maintaining a certain degree of
equality between competitors and the uncertainty as to the results of contests has
already been identified as a legitimate, non-economic reason. Thus the organi-

---

[112] Summerer T, in Fritzweiler J, Pfister B and Summerer T, (eds.), *Praxis-Handbuch Sportrecht*, (1998) München, 510.; *Frankfurter Allgemeine Zeitung* July 14, 1998, 35.

[113] Supra n. 86, (TN 116).

[114] In relation to the unsuccessful attempt in section 31 of the Law Against Restrictions on Competition (Gesetz gegen Wettbewerbsbeschränkungen) to exempt the central marketing of television
rights from the requirements of German competition law, see supra. n.98.

[115] Case 13/76 (Donà v Mantero) [1976] ECR 1333 (TN 14 and 15).

[116] Supra n. 7 (TN 44).

sation and the social function of sport are capable of setting limits on the provisions of the EU Treaty.

Certain sport rules and regulations – even those with economic effects – may not violate the Treaty if they can be justified by the organisation of the sport itself. However, it is not enough just to pursue legitimate aims. Furthermore, every rule will have to meet the high standards of the proportionality test formulated by the ECJ.[117] The Courts will scrutinise the rules of sports organisations to see whether these exceed what is necessary to pursue the legitimate aims of the sport. These aims are balanced against the rights of sportsmen and women under European Law. If the rule meets these high standards and thus passes the test of proportionality, it will remain in force even if it contains a restriction on the basic freedoms or free competition.

The current most practical solution is to allow rules which are purely technical. They have to be identified and weighed against the aims of sport and the aim of a common market with free competition.[118]

CONCLUSIONS AND FINAL WORD

Basically, three practical ways of solving the conflict can be brought into consideration. A first, and from a legal point of view, the only approach to recommend, would be that the rules and regulations of the national and international sports associations undergo a revision, taking into consideration the basic freedoms and the competition law provisions. In this respect there is a considerable need for conformity. A second option exists through negotiations with the European Commission regarding individual and block exemptions. This tackles the competition law issues but the difficulties regarding the basic freedoms could remain unsolved. The third, more traditional, solution consists of waiting to see what happens. In particular, waiting to see which cases come before the ECJ, and – even if a negative outcome is foreseeable – pretend to be surprised at the given time. The ambivalent situation in which lawyers often find themselves in is visible. If they analyse the legal situation and forecast problems, they are regarded as *doubting Thomas'*. If they do not make their views of the problems clear, they possibly come up against the accusation that despite knowledge of the difficulties they did not warn everyone else in time. However, an active rather than a reactive approach should always prevail. Sport organisations should be prepared to explain in great detail the importance of a contested rule by showing the consequences for the sport in the case of its abolition. Reasons specific to sport must be identi-

---

[117] See for example Case 120/78 Rewe-Zentral AG v Bundesmonopolverwaltung für Branntwein [1979] ECR 649.

[118] See EU Commission, Press Release of Febrary 24, 1999, IP/99/133.

fied with greater care.[119] One always has to bear in mind that there might be only a few judges or Commission officials that have previously encountered sport and its problems. It is thus necessary to stress the importance of sport rules and regulations for the organisation of the sport itself or the social implication abolition might cause.

The hope that the significance of sport will receive adequate consideration when the tense relationship between the autonomy of the clubs and associations and European law provisions is resolved, is justified in the comments of the former Competition Commissioner van Miert:

> 'Other aspects belong to sport, which have nothing to do with economic activity – I am thinking of its social, integral and cultural significance. The rules and regulations of the sport organisations also do not pursue economic, but rather sport aims. Because of the special features in this area, limitations exist when it comes to the holding and organisation of sport events, which are not acceptable in other industry or service providing areas. These special features do not, however, justify the restriction of the basic freedoms laid down in the Treaty on the European Union, as long as the same legitimate aims can be achieved through less restrictive measures. This principle of proportionality is one of the corner stones of the application of Community law.' [120]

The identification of whether a specific rule pursues merely sport aims or has too many economic implications will take some years. During this period the uncertainty might prevail. The sooner sport accepts its existence within a certain legal framework, the sooner it will recognise the limits imposed on it.

---

[119] Supra n. 98.
[120] Supra n. 106 Van Miert K.

'SHOW ME THE MONEY': REGULATION OF THE MIGRATION OF PROFESSIONAL SPORTSMEN IN POST-*BOSMAN* EUROPE

Simon Gardiner and Roger Welch

INTRODUCTION

Europe prides itself as being at the hub of much of world sport.[1] It is true that in many professional sports, Europe is the main economic powerhouse. In terms of football, Europe (and UEFA) is still football's 'core economy'.[2] Therefore, football will be the main focus of this chapter. It most obviously exemplifies the tensions that can be located in elite professional sport around issues of power, regulation and accountability. The right of the individual sports athlete to have mobility and to be freely able to sell his or her labour has become an issue of major significance.

This chapter will chart the impact of the *Bosman* ruling on the migration patterns and mobility of professional sportsmen and women intra the European Union and inter the European Union and countries outside of its borders. Subsequent case law that has extended this part of the ruling will be evaluated, as will current arguments for the reintroduction of protectionist measures that attempt to remove or at least dilute what are seen as undesirable effects for the post-*Bosman* sports world. In the case of team sports such as football, this is invariably in the guise of quotas on non-national and foreign players and current demands for their re-introduction will be critically evaluated. Essentially these are calls for a partial reversal of the *Bosman* ruling. The legality of this move back in time under EU law is highly questionable and would certainly need political consensus.

As with other related issues concerning freedom of movement into and within the EU, notably the perceived increase in asylum seekers, a catalyst for this move is a fear of the 'sporting other' most obviously in the context of issues of national identities and the success of the national team. Close analogies can be made be-

---

[1] See *The European Model of Sport* Consultative Documents of DGX, November 1998, especially para.1.3.

[2] Maguire J, and Stae D, Border Crossings: Soccer Labour Migration and the European Union, *International Review for the Sociology of Sport*, 33 (1998), 59-73.

A. Caiger and S. Gardiner (Eds), Professional Sport in the EU: Regulation and Re-regulation
© 2000, T.M.C.Asser Press, The Hague, The Netherlands

tween the skills and entrepreneurial energy that immigrants can bring to the workplace economy and the qualities that foreign players can bring to particular sports. Conversely this can be displaced by a xenophobia which too easily lays blame at the door of the outsider. The response is invariably protectionist measures that intervene to restrict mobility. The major paradox is whether these protectionist demands make any sense in the context of the Europeanisation of sport – particularly football.

This chapter will argue that, in addition, on-going legal developments within Europe, largely caused by the greater role that the European Commission has assumed in regulating sport, are having a major impact on sports labour migration. This is with respect both to EU and non-EU nationals moving from club to club within the European Union, and to migration into the European Union by players from the rest of the world.

Sports Migration

Migration of elite professional sports athletes has become an increasingly active process in the 'sporting global village'. Many different patterns have developed in specific sports and between geographical areas. The dynamics of these migration patterns are multi-faceted and not only financially motivated. Elite sports athletes are not solely economic migrants. As Maguire and Pearton suggest, determining factors include 'political, historical geographical, social and cultural'[3] ones too. Sporting motives often play an important role with the desire to improve as a player and assume a greater playing status. The particular sports business characteristic of the short duration of the professional player's career has however clearly increased the roaming inclinations of the football mercenary. Lazio's Fabrizzio Ravenelli and Chelsea's Jimmy Floyd Hasselbaink are prime examples.

Patterns of mobility are multi-faceted. Membership of the European Union and the freedom of movement provisions under Article 39 have principally aided intra-European movement. Allied to this are geographical proximity, increasingly effective methods of communication and transportation and a greater acceptance of cultural diversity within Europe. Historically, in football there have been some noticeable migratory patterns. Perhaps one of the oldest routes of sports immigration is that between Scotland and England. Stretching back to the end of the nineteenth century, thousands of Scots have played in English professional football. Lay's study of the origins of English players from 1946 to 1981 found 1,653

    [3] Maguire J, and Pearton R, Global Sport and the Migration Patters of France '98 World Cup Final Players: Some Preliminary Observations, in Garland J, Malcolm D, and Rowe M, *The Future of Football: Challenges for the Twenty First Century*, (2000) London, Frank Cass & Co.

Scots had played in England during that period.[4] Echoing the Chelsea team of nearly half a century later with its 11 non-English players, in the 1955-1956 season, English third-division side Accrington Stanley often fielded a team of 11 Scots.[5] There has been a marked decline in the southward migration of Scots in recent years. Since the Second World War, there has also been a steady supply of players from both Northern Ireland and the Republic of Ireland. However until the 1990s, there were few non-British or Irish footballing immigrants.

In mainland Europe, the patterns of football migration have not surprisingly been historically much more complex. As Maguire and Bale state: 'professional players criss-cross the continent of Europe.'[6] In the first 50 years after the creation of the French professional league in 1932, over 1000 foreign players came to France to play professional football, around 20% of the total players. They came from such countries as Britain, Austria, Hungary, Czechoslovakia, Spain and Argentina. Especially in the latter half of the twentieth century, inter-European mobility on the world stage increased. This was invariably a consequence of pre-existing colonial links. Thus players from ex-French colonies such as Senegal have played in France.[7] Similarly, Spain and Italy have historically had strong links with South America.

BOSMAN AND PLAYER MOBILITY

Migration patterns within the EU have entered a new phase as a result of *Bosman*.[8] This has significantly enhanced the ability of players to move between clubs in different European countries. The background of the *Bosman* ruling has

---

[4] Lay, D (1984) cited in Moorehouse H, Blie Bonnets over the Border: Scotland and the Migration of Footballers in Bale J, & Maguire J, *The Global Sports Arena: Athletic Migration in an Interdependant World* (1994), London, Frank Cass.

[5] Ibid. Moorehouse H, (1994).

[6] Maguire J and Bale J, Introduction: Sports Labour Migration in the Global Arena, in Bale J and Maguire J (eds), *The Global Sports Arena: Athletic Talent Migration in an Interdependent World*, (1994) London, Frank Cass, 2.

[7] Lanfranchi P, The Migration of Footballers: The Case of France 1932-1982 in Bale J, and Maguire J, *The Global Sports Arena: Athletic Migration in an Interdependant World* (1994), London, Frank Cass.

[8] ASBL Union Royale Belge des Societes de Football Association and others v Jean-Marc Bosman [1996] 1 CMLR 645 (Case c-415/93). For further discussion see: Blainpain R, and Inston R, *The Bosman Case: The End of the Transfer System* (1996) London, Sweet and Maxwell; and Gardiner S, Felix A, James M, Welch R, and O' Leary J, *Sports Law* (1998) London, Cavendish, 98-99, 364-379, 438-442. For analysis of the ongoing impact of *Bosman* see: Gardiner S, and Welch R, 'The Winds of Change in Professional Football: The Impact of the Bosman Ruling' and Caiger A, and O'Leary J, A New Rainbow? The promise of Change in Professional Football (1998) 3(4) *Contemporary Issues in Law*, 288-312, 313-328 respectively.

been discussed in detail at other points in this book.[9] Bosman's main argument was that the transfer system violated his rights of freedom of movement as provided by Article 39 of the EC Treaty as it prevented him from taking up employment with clubs in other Member States.

Bosman's second complaint was that UEFA's '3+2' rule violated Article 39. This rule restricted the number of foreign players whose names could be included on a team-sheet in a UEFA competition to three. Additionally, two players could be included if they had played in a country for five years uninterruptedly, including three years in junior teams. The practical problem associated with the application of the rule can be exemplified by the problems that Manchester United had in fielding its strongest side in European/UEFA Cup competitions in the early 1990s. Players such as Schmeichel and Irwin could not be played in certain matches.

In support of his legal argument, Bosman argued that this restricted the freedom of movement of players who are EC nationals as clubs with their 'full quota of foreign players' are likely to restrict new contracts to indigenous players. The ECJ agreed and ruled that the '3+2' rule offends the legal requirement that all EC nationals must be treated on an equal basis.

In giving the above rulings the ECJ relied on the Opinion of Advocate General Lenz. This Opinion remains of significant interest because a number of arguments that have arisen in the wake of the *Bosman* ruling, primarily in favour of restricting its impact, were considered and rejected by Lenz. Acts of discrimination which are contrary to Article 39 are unlawful unless they can be justified. Justification requires the identification of legitimate objectives which are secured by the practices forming the subject-matter of the complaint and which satisfy the principle of proportionality, in that they do not go beyond what is necessary for attaining those objectives.[10] The following attempts at justification were rejected by the Advocate General. One argument was that it was necessary to maintain a sporting and financial balance between professional clubs, and smaller clubs are only able to secure the financial resources to flourish or even survive by selling their best young players to the wealthier and more successful clubs. A second argument was that clubs have a legitimate interest in securing compensation for the expense of having trained and developed a player prior to his move to another club.

With respect to the '3+2', rule it was argued that teams must have a number of national players to guarantee that the club's supporters are identifying with the team. As a matter of legal principle Lenz stated:

'Even if the 'national aspect' had the significance which many people attribute to it, however, it could not justify the rules on foreign players. The right to freedom of

---

[9] See Richard Parrish's and Ken Foster's contributions to this book.

[10] This approach to justification can be found in a number of rulings of the European Court, e.g. *Sagar* [1991] ECR I-4221 (Case 76/90).

movement and the prohibition of discrimination against nationals of other Member States are among the fundamental principles of the Community order. The rules on foreign players breach those principles in such a blatant and serious manner that any reference to national interests which cannot be based on Article 48(3) must be regarded as inadmissible as against those principles.'[11]

Moreover as a matter of sporting reality he wryly observed:

'As the Commission and Mr Bosman have rightly stated, the great majority of a club's supporters are much more interested in the success of their club than in the composition of the team. Nor does the participation of foreign players prevent a team's supporters from identifying with the team. Quite on the contrary, it is not uncommon for those players to attract the admiration and affection of football fans to a special degree. One of the most popular players ever to play for TSV 1860 Munchen was undoubtedly Petar Radenkovic from what was then Yugoslavia. The English international Kevin Keegan was for many years a favourite of the fans at Hamburger SV. The popularity of Eric Cantona at Manchester United and of Jurgen Klinsmann at his former club Tottenham Hotspur is well known.'[12]

An argument that continues to be heard, particularly in the UK, is that an influx of foreign players has adverse implications for a Member State's national team, as it restricts the ability of the nationals of a Member State to become professional footballers at the highest level of the game. Lenz was not convinced by this position. He replied:

'Nothing has demonstrated that the development of young players in a Member State would be adversely affected if the rule on foreign players were dropped. Only a few top teams set store on promoting their own young players as, for instance, Ajax Amsterdam do. Most talented players, by contrast, make their way upwards via small clubs to which those rules do not apply. Moreover, there is much to support the opinion that the participation of top foreign players promotes the development of football. Early contact with foreign stars "can only be of advantage to a young player".

It is admittedly correct that the number of jobs available to native players decreases, the more foreign players are engaged by and play for the clubs. That is, however, a consequence which the right to freedom of movement necessarily entails. Moreover, there is little to suggest that abolition of the rules on foreign players might lead to players possessing the nationality of the relevant State becoming a small minority in a league. The removal of the rules on foreign players would not oblige clubs to engage (more) foreigners, but would give them the possibility of doing so if they thought that promised success ...

Moreover, the national teams of the Member States of the Community nowadays very often include players who carry on their profession abroad, without that causing par-

---

[11] Para. 142.
[12] Para. 143.

ticular disadvantages. It suffices that the players have to be released for the national team's matches, as is also provided for in the current rules of the associations. The best example is perhaps the Danish national team which won the European Championship in 1992. In the German national team which became world champions in 1990 there were several players who played in foreign leagues. It is therefore not evident that the rules on foreigners are necessary in order to ensure the strength of the national team.'[13]

At the root of the Advocate General's rejection of these purported justifications was the view that neither the transfer system nor the '3+2' rule constituted the best method of enabling smaller clubs to compete with the larger richer clubs. Lenz argued that redistributing the income, acquired by clubs through ticket sales and the money received from television companies, would be much more effective in preventing the top clubs from monopolising the top players.

One immediate consequence of *Bosman* was that players who were EU or EEA[14] nationals, and who were at the end of their current contracts, were free to negotiate a new contract with a club in a different Member State. The second immediate consequence was that clubs from EU Member States have been able to field as many foreign players as they wish to in European competitions, providing such players are EU (or EEA) nationals. The '3+2' rule continues to apply to non-EU nationals, although as will be considered below this has in itself generated further litigation.

Taken together the two limbs of the ruling have impacted on sporting migration patterns by increasing the number of players who are able to negotiate a move to another club by virtue of their being out of contract, and increasing their attractiveness to clubs by virtue of the fact that they can be played in all competitions. Essentially a club can field a team composed of 8 EU nationals and 3 foreign players. It is not necessary that any of those players should be nationals of the Member State in which the club is based. The practical significance of *Bosman* was further enhanced by a voluntary decision by FIFA, in April 1997, that the ruling would be extended to the nationals of any country who were out of contract and wished to move from a club in one Member State to a club in a different Member State. However, as will be discussed below, such players are still subject to the immigration rules of the Member State concerned.

One issue that remains unclarified is whether *Bosman* applies to the situation where an out of contract player seeks to move to a different club in the same Member State. There is nothing in the ruling itself that explicitly indicates this is the case, and transfers between Member States have remained the focal area of concern. However, another significant development, which was clearly in response to the ruling, was the decision by the footballing authorities in the UK, with effect from the 1998/99 season, to give complete freedom of contract to

---

[13] Para. 145 and 146.

[14] EU law also applies to nationals of Member States of the European Economic Area – that is Iceland, Liechtenstein and Norway.

players who have attained the age of 24 and are out of contract. At the time of writing, much attention has been directed to the failure of FIFA to engage in a substantial reform of its transfer rules. As shall be seen, this voluntary reform of the UK transfer system has influenced the way in which the international transfer system may be reformed.

EC competition law has provided some of the impetus for such reform. Indeed one section of the Opinion of Advocate General Lenz was devoted to an examination of whether the transfer system constituted a violation of Articles 81 and 82 of the EC Treaty.[15] Lenz was of the view that both the rules on foreign players and the transfer system constituted a breach of Article 81, but not Article 82. The essence of his reasoning was that the aim of Article 81 was to prevent undertakings (including professional clubs) from engaging in anti-competitive practices which impeded the development of the single market. The transfer system and the '3+2' rule prevented clubs from competing for the services of out of contract players and thus were unlawful.

It must be emphasised that the European Court's ruling was based solely on Article 39; indeed the Court made no comment whatsoever on that part of the Advocate General's Opinion which was concerned with competition law. However, more recently the European Commission has indicated that EU law on freedom of movement and competition policy is intertwined. Moreover, and this takes the law in a new direction, the transfer system enables clubs to retain control of players through contractual devices and thus the whole system may be in violation of EU law – not just in the specific context of a player whose contract has already expired. This position connects with a number of problem situations, which have emerged since *Bosman*, such as the applicability of the ruling to non EU nationals and, as exemplified by the *l'affaire Anelka*, the right of players to move to another club in breach of both the transfer rules and their own contracts of employment. These issues and current proposals for reform will be discussed below.

PLAYER MOBILITY IN THE POST-*BOSMAN* EUROPE

Bosman has played a definitive role in redrawing the map of sports labour migration patterns in Europe. It clearly has increased the mobility of EU players around the community. Some of these patterns of migration have been accelerated by the ruling rather than initiated by it. An example of the former would be increasing movement of players from Nordic countries to English and Scottish football and the importing of Dutch talent into Italian football. However, new patterns have emerged, with significant numbers of French and Italian footballers moving to the English game. In addition, non-EU players have increasingly been seen as

---

[15] Formerly Articles 85 and 86.

cost effective. The signing of two Moroccan players by Coventry City in 1998 can be cited as an example. Increasingly, European clubs are looking to develop links more widely around the world in an attempt to exploit local talent.

This phenomenon needs to be understood as not just the product of *Bosman* alone. Certainly, the ruling has generated clear financial attractions for both clubs and players. For the former, there is the knowledge that transfer fees cannot be required for out of contract players; and for the latter, new contracts negotiated with new clubs are likely to involve significant signing-on fees alongside very attractive wage levels. However, other contributing factors include the presence of foreign coaches and managers who have attracted players from their own countries and beyond – Arsene Wenger at Arsenal and Ruud Gullit and Giofranco Vialli at Chelsea are notable examples. In addition, top players have been one of the main beneficiaries of the vast amounts of new money that have entered football during the 1990s – particularly from satellite TV companies, the emergence of pay-per-view technology and the marketing opportunities available to the top clubs with the exploitation of their brand. Certain clubs, such as Manchester United have been clear winners during this period.

International Alliances

In a similar fashion to how the United States has been able to attract outstanding players by the offering of attractive salaries in, for example, Major League Basketball from the Caribbean and in the professional ice hockey leagues from Canada and Scandinavia, European soccer clubs have reaped a rich harvest from South American and African nations. An analogy may be made with the natural resources that were shipped out to the metropolitan countries during colonial times. Similarly, modern third world athletic talent can be seen as a commodity to be exploited by businesses in the richer nations of the world.

 A number of intra-European alliances have also developed. In September 1999, Internazionale of Milan signed a player exchange agreement with Charlton Athletic of the English first division.[16] The logic of the relationship is that, should someone like Ronaldo ever need it, after injury for example, he could be eased back into the game through a stint in one of the lower English leagues. In return, Charlton, will be able to take advantage of the commercial and playing power of such players. This is not the first exchange agreement that has been signed. Crewe Alexandra and Liverpool have agreed to exchange players and information about commercial developments in football.[17] Meanwhile, Arsenal and Saint Etienne, Coventry City and Juventus, and Manchester United and Royal Antwerp have all agreed similar deals. Some of these alliances, for example the latter agreement between 'United' and Antwerp, have been criticised for allowing

---

[16] Pierson M, Charlton link up with Italian Giant Inter, *The Independent* September 17, 1999.

English clubs to exploit the opportunity provided by the more permissive nationality and work permits rules that exist in other Member States such as Belgium. This enables English clubs to gain access to talented players who, although they are not originally EU nationals, gain EU status in another European country.

In addition, strategic alliances have developed by European sides on a wider international stage reflecting the globalisation of player migration and the search for talent. Ajax of Amsterdam has recently entered into a franchise agreement in South Africa.[18] On the instructions of the Dutch club, two South African clubs, Cape Town Spurs and Seven Stars, merged to form Ajax Cape Town. In response, Ajax took a 51% share in the newly formed club and will be able to claim first call on their promising new players. Ajax Cape Town are now financially stable and are identified by an internationally recognised brand name. Interestingly, the Dutch bank, ABN AMRO, the sponsors of Ajax of Amsterdam, assisted them in setting up the franchise. This franchise agreement was founded upon links that already existed, in part because of the transfer of Benedict McCarthy. There is thus a historic dimension to collaboration, although this was initially motivated by trust based on cost. The Dutch club is unable to compete with the larger European clubs and has to access cheaper playing resources from elsewhere. In many ways, this continues to be the case; the Dutch club has to trust the South African club if it wants to access these players.[19]

Such patterns of migration do not develop without social costs. The tremendous increase in young African players migrating to Europe has been described by Issa Hayatou, president of the Confederation of African Football (CAF), as 'a hideous slave trade that plunders the continent'.[20] It started slowly in the late Eighties when African teams started to excel at the under-17 and under-20 World Cups. It is not uncommon for 15 and 16 year-olds to move to French, Dutch and Belgian clubs. In both France and Belgium there have been inquiries and government action to regulate this movement. FIFA have stated that new regulations will be introduced whereby no player under the age of 18 will be allowed to transfer to Europe.[21]

The activities of un-licensed player agents are viewed as a contributory problem. However the financial requirements needed to be licensed by FIFA are seen as discriminatory against those operating in the African market. In addition the opportunity to move and play in Europe is a rational economic decision. African national leagues on the whole are in deep economic problems. Players are often not paid. Being an economic migrant for a 15-year-old makes sense for the player

---

[17] Morris C, Crewe sees gold in red alliance, *Financial Times*, April 18, 1997.

[18] Milner M, Cape Town soccer club goes Dutch, The *Guardian* January 12, 1999.

[19] Chadwick S, A Research Agenda For Strategic Collaboration In European Club Football, 7 *European Journal for Sport Management* (2000), 6.

[20] Oliver B, Slaves on a Fortune *The Observer* 13 February 2000, 8.

[21] Ibid.

and his family. But for every player who succeeds, there are many that do not.[22]

The human rights organisation, *Sport and Freedom*, have investigated up to 1,000 similar cases, involving young players from Africa, South America and Eastern Europe.[23] As with other forms of trade in human labour within Europe, such as prostitution, and in traditionally low-paid industries, such as agriculture and clothing, this form of football migration can indeed be perceived as a modern form of slave trade. The problem for migrant workers is clearly exacerbated by the existence of immigration controls, and these impact upon professional sports participants as much as any other type of worker. Immigration laws constitute a fundamental constraint on all forms of economic migrancy.

Foreign Players and Work Permits

Bosman clearly overrides the immigration laws of Member States as far as the migration of EU nationals is concerned. However, it remains within the jurisdiction of national government as to whether nationals from outside of the EU and EEA will be permitted to play for a club within that country. Legal developments discussed below may well result in a further weakening of national law in this respect. However, it is useful to consider briefly the role of immigration law in professional sport before analysing these more recent developments. This will be done in the context of the work permit system for professional footballers which operates in the UK. It should be noted that these rules were changed in 1999.

Anyone seeking a work permit in the UK must meet criteria issued by the Department for Education and Employment. The scheme is administered by the Department for Education and Employment's (DEE) Overseas Labour Service under the Immigration Acts 1971, 1988. Thus work permit rules apply to all areas of employment including professional sports. There are, for example, rules relating to cricket, ice hockey and rugby that are analogous to the rules governing football.

Prior to July 1999, a foreign footballer would not generally have been eligible for a work permit unless he was an international player who had played for his

---

[22] See *BBC News On-line*, Belgium's Football 'Slave Trade', March 10,1999 www.bbc.co.uk

The example is given of Serge Nijki Bodo, 17, arrived in Belgium from his native Cameroon to pursue the dream of many young African football players – to make it big in Europe. An adolescent who showed great promise, Serge was discovered by a talent scout while training in Yaounde, the Cameroonian capital. He was promised a contract with the French side, Montpellier, and professional training. With his parents' blessing, Serge arrived in Europe to seek his fortune. It all went wrong just one month into training with Montpellier, when he was again talent-spotted, this time by a Belgian first division side who offered him a professional contract. Serge accepted, and arrived in Belgium on a three-month visa. But after three months of training, his new side dropped him without ever having been paid. It was then, with his visa about to run out he found himself penniless and almost home less.

[23] See Soccer Slaves: the Young Men Dumped on the Street by Ruthless Agents, in Bent I, McIlroy R, Mousley K, and Walsh P, *Football Confidential* (1999) London, BBC Worldwide, 143.

country's 'A' team for approximately 75% of competitive matches in the previous two seasons. He was also required to be one of the six highest earners for the British club concerned. The work permit only applied to a single season unless an extension was granted on the basis that the player had proven himself to be a regular player for the club, and was thus making a significant contribution to the British game.

Under the new current regulations the wage requirement has gone and work permits apply to the whole of the player's contract. The requirement to be an international player is retained, and the FIFA ranking of the player's national side will now be taken into account. In *R v Secretary of State for Education and Employment ex parte Portsmouth Football Club* it was held that the 75% test must not be applied too rigidly, as, for example, a player having missed international matches through injury should be taken into account. The new rules permit the requisite flexibility through provision of an appeals committee to consider an application where the player does not meet the criteria, but a club has provided evidence that he is of the highest calibre.[24]

At the level of government these changes were hailed by the (then) Minister of Sport, Tony Banks as establishing criteria which 'strike a sensible balance between allowing clubs to recruit the best available international talent and the need to provide opportunities for home grown young players.' The Employment and Equal Opportunities Minister, Margaret Hodge, described the new system as 'straightforward, open and transparent' which would 'ensure a faster and fairer application process.'[25] On the other hand, these changes were immediately criticised for constituting a relaxation of the rules. Thus Gordon Taylor, on behalf of the PFA, stated that the changes 'will open the way for cheap, foreign imports' and Frank Clark, on behalf of the League Managers' Association also expressed concern about 'the number of foreign players currently in the British game.'[26]

It is clear that there are, today, a much larger number of foreign players in the English game than has ever before been the case. Since *Bosman* there has been a 1,800 per cent increase in foreign players in the Premiership.[27] As predicted by Gordon Taylor,[28] the 1998 World Cup finals have also contributed to this devel-

---

[24] [1988] COD 142. Ironically perhaps in light of the 1988 decision, Portsmouth FC were prevented in September 2000 from signing the Zimbawean defender Norman Mapeza as Zimbabwe were outside of the top 70 FIFA rankings. Developments in EU law will make no difference whatsoever to such a situation. It does however perhaps reveal the restrictive nature of work permit requirements. The performance of Portsmouth FC hardly impacts on the fortunes of the English national side, and despite being a mid-ranking first division side Portsmouth have found it very difficult to persuade English players to come to the South coast. All the work permit rules have achieved in this situation is prevent Portsmouth from resolving its player shortage problem by recruiting an overseas player.

[25] See DEE press release 307/99.

[26] See *The Guardian*, July 3, 1999.

[27] See *The Guardian*, July 18, 1999.

[28] 'The World Cup, foreign players and work permits' 1998 5(4) *Sports law Administration and Practice*.

opment. However, whether the new rules really represent a relaxation, which will generate an even greater number of 'foreign imports', remains debatable. Certainly, the consequences of taking into account the FIFA ranking of a player's national side still need to be fully evaluated.[29] The fact that a permit can now last for the period of a player's contract will make the prospect of playing in the UK more attractive to the overseas player. But then it seems fair and just that if a player is offered and accepts a contract his job security should not be jeopardised by the possibility that his work permit will not be renewed at the end of a given season. Ironically, one FIFA proposal for reforming the transfer system, which is to put players onto annual contracts, would weaken this newly acquired job security (see below).

Discussion that restricts itself to establishing whether work permit requirements should be tightened or relaxed assumes the presence of foreign players constitutes a problem. In our view this is erroneous. This is similarly the case with proposals based on the introduction of a system of quotas. Much attention has been focused on whether the increase in foreigners in the Premiership is deleterious to the international prospects of the English team. The essence of the argument is that fewer Englishmen are able to play club football at the highest level and are forced to ply their trade in the lower divisions. Thus they do not develop the skills required at international level.

However, casual observation appears to indicate that a significant number of foreign players currently in the Premiership, probably the majority, come from EU/EEA countries (not to mention other countries in the UK). Assuming the European Commission will not agree to a modification of *Bosman*, such players will continue to be able to enter the UK without work permits. Moreover, and contrary to the observations of Advocate General Lenz, there is an assumption that the paying public collectively prioritise the success of the English team over the success of the club they support week in and week out, and pay good money to watch in all weathers. It is suggested that the Advocate General's perception that the majority of football supporters put club before country is more accurate.

Whether or not this position is accepted, it is the reality that, if anything, the number of foreign players who will able to play for clubs without a work permit is likely to increase significantly. This will be the case if the European Court ever rules, for example in cases such as *Balog* and *Malaja* as discussed below, that Article 39 applies to any country within EU trading areas. Alternatively, the introduction of new EC legislation could, of course, achieve the same result.

Subsequent Case Law – Extending the Boundaries of Bosman

European professional team sports are facing contradictory developments. Two cases that are to be heard by the ECJ in the future, *Balog* and *Malaja*, are likely

---

[29] Supra n. 24 above.

to have a significant impact upon European professional sport almost of *Bosman* proportions. Conversely, there is also pressure to re-impose the type of quotas for EU national players that were successfully challenged in the *Bosman* case.

The *Balog*[30] case involves Hungarian footballer Tibor Balog who was a footballer at Belgium first division side, Charleroi. At the end of his contract he refused an extension and sought a move to another club, claiming that he was a free agent. However, Charleroi refused to grant him a free transfer and demanded a fee which made Balog significantly less attractive to potential employers. The club relied on the fact that Balog was not an EU national as Hungary is not part of the European Community. Balog commenced an action in Charleroi arguing that although Hungary was not a part of the EU, it was part of an EU economic trading area and therefore he had the same rights as if he were an EU national, including a free transfer pursuant to *Bosman*.

Charleroi subsequently granted Balog a free transfer, but the court referred the case to the European Court of Justice for a preliminary ruling under Article 234. The case has become popularly known as, *Bosman 2* or *Bosmanovic*; it is due to be heard by the ECJ in November 2000. It is extremely likely that the ECJ will grant the same rights to nationals from countries part of the EU economic trading area, as EU nationals possess.

Similarly in the *Malaja* case, heard at the Nancy Cour d'Appel, Polish basketballer Lilia Malaja has won an appeal, which effectively recognises the right of associate members of the European Union to be regarded in the same light as EU nationals. Lilia Malaja was denied a transfer to Strasbourg by the French Basketball Federation because of restrictions on foreigners. She claimed that because Poland was part of an EU economic trading area guaranteeing free movement of labour, the foreigner limit was illegal and did not apply to her. The French court agreed that according to Community law once such nationals are legally employed in a Member State they must be viewed in the same light as EU nationals. Thus they must be allowed to work in and move about freely in the countries of the EU without discrimination.

Potentially, *Balog* and *Malaja* extend the protection of Article 39 to workers from countries that have been granted associate status by the EU. There are 22 countries that are in the same position as Hungary and Poland. They include: Armenia, Azerbaijan, Belarus, Bulgaria, Czech Republic, Estonia, Georgia, Kazakhstan, Kirgistan, Latvia, Lithuania, Moldova, Romania, Russia, Slovenia, Slovakia, Ukraine and Uzbekistan. This geographical scope is not limited to Europe because the North African countries of Algeria, Tunisia and Morocco also have associate status. Thus, the number of nationalities within the scope of Article 39 will be extended from 18 to around 40.

---

[30] Balog OJ C-99/23. See Bailey D, 'Bosman 2' (1999) *Sports Law Administration and Practice* March/April, 11 and copy of transcript of case in (1998) *Sport Zaken*, 50.

Workers from these countries, whilst working within the EU, will enjoy the same rights as EU-nationals. The decision will not allow athletes (or indeed other workers) to come to EU countries to begin employment, and initially they will continue to be subject to national rules requiring work permits. However, once athletes from the above countries have secured employment in a Member State they will enjoy exactly the same post-*Bosman* freedom, as enjoyed by EU nationals, to cross borders once their existing contracts come to an end. In terms of football, and other sports, these greater rights of mobility within the EU, is likely to make the financially lucrative sports markets of Western Europe more attractive and lead to increased migration of eastern European athletes.

Indeed, there has been a fear by many in professional team sports, particularly football, that decisions such as these will lead to a breaking down of national boundaries in Europe, and thus release a new 'flood' of foreign players into national leagues. With respect to the UK, work permit restrictions on nationals from countries with associate status may well need to be rethought. In the past, such nationals, once in the country, have still been subject to restrictive criteria, and they have been obliged to leave if the criteria have not been met. For example, in 1993 Hungarian Istvan Kozma was obliged to leave Liverpool because he did not play enough games. If *Balog* and *Malaja* are correct in their interpretation of EU law a player such as Kozma would today be able to challenge his enforced deportation in the UK courts.

LEARNING TO LIVE WITH *BOSMAN*

Protectionist Quotas

Over the last two years or so, there have been calls within a number of Member States for restrictions on non-nationals (EU and non-EU) players playing in club sides. In March 2000, twenty national associations met at a joint FIFA / UEFA conference in Amsterdam to discuss this.[31] Following this meeting, a troika of representatives of FIFA, UEFA and EU Sports Ministers met in Lisbon. It was reported that FIFA / UEFA wanted sport to be granted a 'special status' within the Treaty thus allowing foreigner limits to be re-imposed. This meeting yielded two conclusions. Firstly, a working committee was established by the Portuguese Presidency to discuss this proposal. Secondly, following the meeting, Senôr Gomez, the Portuguese Minister for Sport, remarked that there was a 'need to safeguard sport, notably soccer, from the perverseness that has emerged from the (*Bosman*) ruling.'[32]

---

[31] UEFA news release, March 1, 2000.
[32] *BBC on-line* March 17, 2000 (www.bbc.co.uk/news).

The football authorities suggested proposals that would restrict the ability of clubs to play more than five foreigners in a competitive match, as a team should always be compelled to have six players eligible for the national team on the field of play. This would clearly impact upon teams such as Chelsea who regularly field teams with a majority of non-English players. In 1998-99 season against Southampton, they became the first club to field a team with no English players in a Premiership match.

Such proposals are seen as necessary to challenge the *Bosman* ruling given that its rationale is based on economic rather than sporting situations. The argument is essentially that there is a clear conflict of interest between the needs of sport and more general EU treaties guaranteeing the free movement of goods and people. The main problem is to reconcile the EU's insistence on freedom of movement with concerns that big-money transfers are widening the gulf between large and small clubs, creating an environment of 'survival of the richest'. However the major problem will be for FIFA and UEFA to secure special treatment for soccer under European Union law.

Are such calls for the imposition of playing quotas another example of national xenophobia? In England, sports such as rugby, ice hockey, cricket and football have all benefited from the recruitment of foreign nationals. The presence of foreign players can improve the skill and strategy of their national counterparts. They can also generate increased fan and media interest, game attendance and television ratings. However when there are too many foreign players on a team, the danger is national players become mere spectators on the sidelines.

The English FA have in recent times supported the introduction of such quotas. Renewed calls were made in the wake of England's early departure from the Euro 2000 championships.[33] EU foreigners have clearly had a significant impact upon English football. During the 1995-1996 season, 102 non-British players appeared in the Premiership and Nationwide Leagues; by 1999-2000 season that figure had reached 185. Increasing concern in footballing and political circles has not been restricted to Britain alone. Other EU countries have also expressed concern over the influx of foreign players. For example, in 1999, Spanish MPs passed a motion calling on players, clubs and league associations to agree limits on foreign players to attempt to encourage home-grown talent.[34]

The Contractual Tie – Anelka

In a dialectical counter-position to calls for the re-imposition of a quota system, it may be the case that player mobility could be extended under Article 39 to players still under contract to a particular club. This possibility was identified as a result of the announcement by Nicolas Anelka in the summer of 1999 that he no

---

[33] Wilson J, Wintour P, and Chaudhary V, *The Guardian,* June 22, 2000.
[34] See *The Guardian,* March 20, 2000.

longer wanted to honour his contract to play for Arsenal. Anelka wished to leave the UK and play for the Italian club, Lazio. At the time of this announcement Anelka had another 4 years of his contract to run. The problem for Anelka was that Arsenal was not prepared to release him from his contractual obligations, and Lazio was not prepared to pay the sizeable transfer fee that Arsenal required.

This situation generated legal debate[35] (initiated by Jean-Louis Dupont, the Belgian lawyer who advised Bosman) that to prevent a player from terminating his employment contract, as the transfer system does, is as much a restraint on a player's freedom of movement as the situation in Bosman, where a player is prevented from moving to another club on the expiry of his contract. The argument on behalf of Anelka was that he should have the right to break his contract providing he was prepared to pay compensation to Arsenal by reference to the normal contractual principles for calculating damages. The function of damages is to put the injured party in the position that it would have enjoyed had the contract been carried out. Thus Arsenal would have been able to recover the cost of a replacement striker, minus Anelka's wages, for the remainder of the period of his contract. Interestingly, estimations of the actual amount of compensation to which Arsenal would have been entitled varied from around £5 million to a figure nearer the £22 million transfer fee that Arsenal required.

The position with respect to Anelka was ultimately resolved when Arsenal accepted a transfer bid submitted by Real Madrid. However, the incident has cast doubt on the original assumption, in the aftermath of *Bosman*, that Article 39 only applied to out of contract players. The authors have argued that, irrespective of the Anelka situation, English law might view an excessively long contract imposed on a player as constituting a restraint of trade. This would be particularly the case where the length of the contract was designed to circumvent Article 39.[36]

All the above legal points remain open. Other legal considerations to take into account include the presence in a player's contract of a negative stipulation whereby a player agrees to play for a particular club for a period of time and not for any other club during that period. Such clauses can be enforced by courts at their discretion, providing the effect of the granting of an injunction is to encourage, but not compel, performance of the employment contract.[37] An injunction could not be granted, of course, if an English court was persuaded that holding a player to his contract would constitute a breach of EU law.

---

[35] For a general discussion of the issues see: Caiger A and O'Leary J, contribution elsewhere in this book; Tsatsas N, 'Anelka's costly walk-out case has a hole in it' *The Guardian* July 23, 1999.

[36] English courts will release an employee from a contract if a combination of its length and other terms constitute an unconscionable bargain – see *Schroeder Music Publishing Co Ltd v Macaulay* [1974] 3 ALL ER 616. For further analysis see Gardiner and Welch (1998), supra n. 8

[37] For discussion of the effectiveness of such clauses see McCutcheon P, 'Negative Enforcement of Employment Contracts in the Sports Industries' (1997) *Legal Studies* 65.

More problematic, even if the argument over freedom of contract is accepted, would be the situation where a player was induced by another club and/or agent to break his contract of employment. This would constitute the tort of direct inducement to act in breach of contract as established in *Lumley v Gye*.[38] The elements of the tort require the plaintiff to establish the following five conditions:

- that the defendant persuaded or procured or induced the breach of contract;
- that the defendant when so acting knew of the existence of that contract;
- that the defendant intended to persuade, procure or induce a breach of that contract;
- that the plaintiff had suffered more than nominal damage; and
- that the plaintiff could rebut any defence of justification put forward by the defendant.[39]

Unless, and this would be extremely novel, justification could be pleaded successfully by reference to upholding a player's freedom of movement this tort would be committed where a player's desire to move came not from within (as was almost certainly the case with Anelka) but was the product of external inducement. It seems doubtful that, arguments over freedom of movement notwithstanding, a court would accept that this long established tort has been overridden by EU law.

In general, references to *Bosman* by EU institutions have not suggested that Article 39 applies during the currency of a player's contract, or indeed to the situation where a player wishes to move to another club in the same Member State.[40] However, a complaint to the Commission by the Italian club Perugia will almost certainly result in significant changes to the transfer system as it stands. The basis of the club's complaint was that it wished to recruit an Italian player, Massimo Lombardo, from the Swiss club, Zurich Grasshoppers. Although Lombardo was at the end of his contract with Grasshoppers, *Bosman* did not directly apply to his situation, as Switzerland is not covered by EU law. In December 1998 the Commission indicated that the transfer system in its entirety, not just on expiry of a player's contract, violated EU competition law. Since that date FIFA has been under considerable pressure to formulate proposals for reform, although the Commission has also emphasised it is not seeking the complete abolition of the transfer system as it recognises the 'specificity of sport'.[41]

---

[38] (1853) 2 E&B 216

[39] These elements of the tort were most recently confirmed in Timeplan Education Group Ltd v NUT [1997] IRLR 457.

[40] See *The Helsinki Report on Sport*, European Commission (COM(1999)644 – C5-0088/2000) and the Opinion to the European Parliament of the Committee on Legal Affairs and the Internal Market (A5-0208/2000).

[41] For an account of the 'Lombardo case' see 'Sports Focus: The End of Transfer Fees', *The Observer*, 3 September 2000. For reference to the Commission's views on the compatibility of the transfer system with EC law see the speech of Commission Member Viviane Reding to the European Parliament on 7 September 2000 (Speech/00/290).

At the time of writing proposals include capping transfer fees by reference to a player's current salary and the length of time his contract has to run; and, most recently, abolishing the requirement for transfer fees altogether for players aged 24 or over. With respect to the latter, FIFA has suggested that players' contracts should be for no longer than one year, and players should be able to terminate them during that period through the provision of notice. Both UEFA and national governments have criticised FIFA on the basis that its most recent proposals would have a negative impact on professional football.[42]

Ironically some of the argument in favour of such a change has focused on the notion that professional sports participants should be in exactly the same position as employees in general. In fact, the doctrine of restraint of trade apart, UK employment law places no restrictions on the length of fixed term contracts. Nor is there any requirement that such contracts contain terms permitting their termination through the provision of notice. Indeed EU employment law remains silent on the issue of termination of employment contracts and it thus continues to be an issue that is completely within the domain of domestic law.[43]

Footballers would thus enjoy a significant advantage over other employees if they were to be granted rights to terminate fixed term contracts prior to their date of expiry. The advantage they would enjoy would be even greater if it is taken into account that it can be lawful to restrain an employee from working for a competitor for a period of time after the contract has terminated. Whilst such post–employment restraints must be reasonable in terms of their geographical scope and duration, they are by no means rare and can apply to the relatively lowly milkman and hairdresser as much as the senior executive and computer whizzkid.[44]

Some Conclusions and Tentative Proposals

All the statements that have emanated from the European Commission and the European Parliament since the *Bosman* ruling indicate that there should be no retreat from its principles.[45] It is thus extremely unlikely (and it is argued undesirable) that there should be any re-introduction of a quota system for players protected by Article 39. Indeed the dynamic is to the contrary. Mobility of labour

---

[42] See the joint statement of Gerhard Schroder and Tony Blair of 10 September 2000 (http://europa.eu.int/comm/dg10/sport). The most hostile reaction to FIFA's proposals came from the Arsenal Manager, Arsene Wenger, who was reported as having called for a strike if the transfer system is abolished – see *The Guardian* September 2, 2000.

[43] Article 137(3) of the EC Treaty empowers the Commission to draft legislation regulating the termination of employment contracts. However, such legislation requires the unanimous agreement of Member States, and, to date, no such legislation has been proposed.

[44] See, for example, Home Counties Dairies v Skilton [1970] 1 ALL ER 1227.

[45] See n. 40 above.

will be increased if and when it is clarified by a ruling of the ECJ and/or EC leg-islation that Article 39 of the EC Treaty can be applied to the nationals of a num-ber of countries which are outside of the EU. However, even this significant move would not remove work permit restrictions, as these would continue to ap-ply to most African players and players from the other continents of the world. In the view of the authors this is unfortunate as arguably one of the few beneficial aspects of globalisation for ordinary people would be the internationalisation of the movement of labour.

Player mobility will also clearly be increased through whatever form any re-form of the transfer system ultimately takes. Ideally perhaps, the transfer system should be abolished providing the survival of the smaller clubs and their strong links to and significance for local communities could be ensured. As propounded by Advocate General Lenz this would be the case if football itself established a voluntary system for the effective redistribution of income.

Until and if this occurs it seems that some form of transfer system remains a necessary evil. One possibility would be to retain the transfer system for players below the age of 24 and then permit the continued use of fixed term contracts of up to, for example, three years and to allow transfer fees – possibly subject to a capped limit – whilst the contract subsisted. However, players could be permitted to submit notice of resignation during the currency of the contract. It could be specified that the notice would apply for the remainder of the season in which it was given.[46] A club or clubs wanting that player's services could then choose be-tween waiting for the season to expire before seeking to recruit that player, or seeking to negotiate a transfer fee to permit that club to secure the player's ser-vices immediately. It must be emphasised that such a system benefits players too by continuing to provide for a degree of job security during the currency of the contract. It is also consistent with the norms of employment law in other sectors of the economy.

An alternative would be to generalise the use of clauses in players' contracts that specify the amount of money to be paid to a club if the player leaves during the currency of the contract. The player's mobility is then dependent on whether there is a club prepared to pay the stipulated amount. It should be noted that un-der the English law of contract, if such a clause provides for the payment of an excessive sum of money a court will regard it as an unenforceable penalty, and strike it down accordingly.

It is argued that it is undesirable to allow players to move – à l'Anelka – as and when they think fit. This is detrimental to the employer but this is not the central problem. The key specificity with respect to professional football is the relationship between club and supporter and the wider local community

---

[46] The provision of a long notice period would not offend current UK employment law provid-ing a club did not seek to coerce a player into withdrawing it by, for example, refusing to select him for competitive matches – see supra. n. 8, Gardiner and Welch (1998).

(Manchester United supporters apart). For many football supporters their sense of self-identity is fused with the identity of their club. Loyal fans of football clubs – big and small – should be allowed some sense of security through the knowledge that players under contract cannot just leave the club at the drop of a hat.

NATIONAL ELIGIBILITY RULES AFTER *BOSMAN*

J. Paul McCutcheon

Introduction

International competition represents the apex of athletic endeavour in the principal sports practised in Europe. Elite athletes aspire to compete at that level and to pitch their talents against those of their rivals from other nations. Moreover, the opportunity to represent one's country is considered to be amongst the highest of honours that an athlete might achieve during the currency of his or her career. At the same time international competition holds a special attraction for spectators and television viewers (the consumers within the sports industry) with World Cups, European championships and the like holding a unique place in their hearts. The fundamental attraction of sport at this level is that nations are presented with the opportunity to field their finest athletes against those of rival countries. This may be seen to contribute to a sense of national identity and to promote national pride and well-being. Few will forget the memorable remarks of the Norwegian television commentator when his country defeated England in a football match some years ago. The success of the French football team in the World Cup was taken to be significant in that its composition reflected the multi-ethnic nature of that nation. Likewise, the South African rugby and cricket teams are seen to contribute to the building of a 'rainbow' nation in the post-apartheid era.

Eligibility Criteria

Eligibility to participate in international competition is governed principally by rules and practices adopted by the relevant international federation. While the rules vary from one sport to another two general features may be noted. The first is that they seek to identify a link between the athlete and the country that he or she wishes to represent. Different criteria are employed including nationality, place of birth and residence in the territory for a prescribed period of time.[1] It is

---

[1] E.g. the International Rugby Board Regulation 8.1 provides that 'a Player may only play for the senior National Representative Team or the next senior National Representative Team of the Union of the country in which (a) he was born; or (b) one parent or grandparent was born; or (c) he

A. Caiger and S. Gardiner (Eds), Professional Sport in the EU: Regulation and Re-regulation
© *2000, T.M.C.Asser Press, The Hague, The Netherlands*

conceivable that an athlete's sports nationality and legal citizenship[2] might differ but the general underlying theme is to ensure some basic national affiliation on his or her part. Nevertheless, it is obvious that a number of athletes will qualify to represent more than one country; for example, an athlete might be born in country A, be a national of country B, be married to a national of country C (and thus be entitled to citizenship of that country) and have resided in country D for the relevant qualifying period. This multiplicity of sports nationalities is not uncommon and the second general feature of eligibility rules seeks to regulate the number of countries that an athlete might represent. Again different criteria are used: some rules confine eligibility to one country only; others allow an athlete to select once he or she has reached a certain age or has reached senior status; and yet others allow an athlete to qualify for a second country on the fulfilment of certain criteria, such as residence in the relevant country.[3] The existence of rules that regulate eligibility in this fashion is central to modern international sport and it is considered obvious that the right to represent a nation should be confined to those who in one way or another are connected to the country in question. Likewise, it

---

has completed thirty six consecutive months of Residence immediately preceding the time of playing.' The International Cricket Council Regulation 4 stipulates that '[a] cricketer is qualified to play in Tests, one-day internationals and any other representative match for the country of his birth provided that he has not played in Tests, one-day internationals or, after October 1, 1994, in any other representative cricket match for any other Member country during the two immediately preceding years.' The regulation goes on to provide that '[a] cricketer is qualified to play in Tests, one-day internationals and any other representative match for any Full or Associated Member country in which he has resided for at least 183 days in each of the four immediately preceding years provided that he has not played in Tests, one-day internationals or, after October 1, 1994, in any other representative cricket match for any other Member country during that period of four years.' The regulation also provides for qualification in 'exceptional circumstances'; see *Wisden Cricketers' Almanac* 137th ed. (2000) Guildford, John Wisden & Co., 1473. The Olympic Charter (Rule 46) requires an athlete to be 'a national of the country' of the National Olympic Committee that enters him or her.

[2] For present purposes we can leave aside the special position that obtains in the United Kingdom which is represented by four national teams at international level in many sports.

[3] E.g. the International Rugby Board Regulation 8.3 provides that '[a] Player who has played for the senior National Representative Team or the next senior National Representative Team of a Union is not eligible to play for the senior National Representative Team or the next senior National Representative Team of another Union.' However, by virtue of Regulation 8.2 a player is deemed to have played for a national side, and thus to be debarred from playing for another country, where he has been selected for that side in a full international, is present at the match as a player, replacement or substitute *and* has reached the age of majority. A cricketer may re-qualify for another Test side if he satisfies the residency requirement of the eligibility regulation noted in n. 1. Many international federations have modelled their criteria on the Bye-Law 2 to Rule 46 of the Olympic Charter which provides that '[a] competitor who has represented one country in the Olympic Games, in continental or regional games or in world or regional championships recognised by the relevant [International Federation], and who has changed his nationality or acquired a new nationality, shall not participate in the Olympic Games to represent his new country until three years after such change or acquisition. This period may be reduced or even cancelled with the agreement of the [National Olympic Committees] and [International Federation] concerned and the approval of the [International Olympic Committee] Executive Board.'

is felt that the opportunity to compete for more than one country should be restricted; the prospect of athletes changing their national affiliations as fortunes change is viewed by many to be at odds with all that international sport is taken to represent.

These considerations are evident in several arbitral decisions of the Court of Arbitration for Sport (CAS). That body has recognised that legal nationality and sports nationality are distinct: the former involves an individual's personal status that derives from his or her citizenship of one or more states while the latter defines the eligibility of an athlete to compete in international competition. These concepts involve 'two different legal orders – one of public law, the other of private law – which do not intersect and do not come into conflict.'[4] Where an athlete is dually qualified he or she is typically required to choose his or her sporting nationality in accordance with conditions contained in the applicable international federation rules.[5] The CAS has also enforced change of nationality rules. It has observed that:

> '... regulations on the uniqueness of the sporting nationality ... are not arbitrary. They answer the legitimate concern to prevent changes of [sporting] nationality from being dependent on the wishes or interests of the players and reserve the option of choosing another sports nationality.'[6]

In the same decision it also concluded that the three-year interval prescribed as the qualifying period for the acquisition of a second sporting nationality constituted only a 'partial limitation' on an athlete's activities and that that restriction did 'not seem manifestly disproportionate.'[7] These opinions very much reflect the general principles underlying national eligibility rules but the possibility that the CAS would refuse to apply a rule that it considers to be 'manifestly dispro-

---

[4] Arbitration CAS 92/80, B./International Basketball Federation (F.I.B.A.), award of March 25, 1993 in Reeb (ed.), *Digest of CAS Awards 1986-1998* (1998) Berne: Stæmpfli Editions SA, 304. These remarks must be qualified somewhat. Public laws determining a person's citizenship might have an effect on that individual's sporting nationality especially where the latter is defined in terms of citizenship. This is particularly pertinent where a state does not recognise dual nationality with the result that nationality of that state is lost when a second nationality is acquired. An example occurred during the 1998 Winter Olympics: a member of the Swedish ice hockey team (who played in the NHL) lost his Swedish nationality, by operation of Swedish law, on his becoming a naturalised US citizen; the International Ice Hockey Federation bye-law governing eligibility provided that 'each player must prove [his eligibility] by an individual passport confirming [that] he is a citizen of the country he represents'; the point is that his ineligibility stemmed from the operation of Swedish public law; see Arbitration CAS ad hoc Division (O.G. Nagano) 004-005, Czech Olympic Committee, Swedish Olympic Committee and S./ International Ice Hockey Federation (IIHF), award of February 18, 1998 in Reeb (ed.) 435.

[5] See Arbitration CAS 94/132, Puerto Rico Amateur Baseball Federation (PRABF)/USA Baseball (USAB), award of March 15, 1996 in Reeb (ed.) supra. n.4, 53.

[6] Arbitration CAS 92/80, B./International Basketball Federation (F.I.B.A.), award of March 25, 1993 in Reeb (ed.) supra. n.4, 305.

[7] Ibid.

portionate' is left open. The compatibility of eligibility rules with European law or with the domestic law of a particular state is a separate question that does not appear to have arisen in any of the CAS adjudications and, in any event, is likely to be determined in a different forum.

The Legal Perspective

In general, international federations and national governing are free in law to adopt the eligibility criteria they consider appropriate subject, of course, to any relevant anti-discrimination and equal opportunity statutes. But those broad parameters aside the autonomy of sports bodies is legally protected.[8] Nevertheless, as far as professional athletes are concerned eligibility rules restrict the exercise of their livelihoods or, in the European idiom, their rights to free movement as workers and their freedom to provide services. It follows that those rules must be reconsidered in the light of the decision in *Union Royale Belge des Sociétés de Football Associations ASBL v Bosman*.[9] Despite the reaction of the sports community, and in particular of many football authorities, the decision in *Bosman* should have been expected. It was clear from the jurisprudence of the Court of Justice that European Community law applied to sport in as much as the latter constituted an economic activity and the autonomy of sports bodies was accordingly circumscribed.[10] Moreover, the impugned rules (the requirement for a transfer fee and the '3 + 2' rule) imposed an undoubted limitation on workers' freedom of movement within the European Community. Thus, the principal issue that remained was whether these restrictions could be justified under European law, a question that was resolved in favour of the plaintiff. *Bosman* has resulted in an appreciable body of literature and I do not propose to add to it.[11] Instead I wish in briefly to consider the status of national eligibility rules in the wake of that decision.

---

[8] In Cowley v Heathley, *The Times* July 24, 1986 the plaintiff swimmer sought a declaration that she was eligible to compete for Great Britain on the rounds of 'domicile' which was the applicable eligibility criterion. In finding against her contention the court was called on to interpret the rule, not to consider its validity or the capacity of the governing body to enact the rule.

[9] Case C-415/93 [1995] E.C.R. I-4921.

[10] See Walrave and Koch v Association Union Cycliste Internationale Case 36/74 [1974] E.C.R. 1405; Donà v Mantero Case 13/76 [1976] E.C.R. 1333; Union Nationale des Entraineurs et Cadres Techniques Professionels du Football v Heylens Case 222/86 [1987] E.C.R. 4097.

[11] See generally Morris P, Morrow S and Spink P, 'EU Law and Professional Football: *Bosman* and its Implications' (1996) 59 M.L.R. 893; Fernández Martín, (1996) 12 E.L.Rev. 313; Weatherill S, (1996) 33 C.M.L.Rev. 991; Uilhoorn, 'The Bosman Case: Freedom of Movement for Sports Players and Its Implications' 1998 *European Current Law Year Book* lvi; Blanpain and Instone, *The Bosman Case: the End of the Transfer System* (1996) Leuven, Peeters/Sweet and Maxwell; Campbell and Sloane, *The Implications of the Bosman Case for Professional Football* (1997) Aberdeen, University of Aberdeen Dept. of Economics.

National eligibility rules limit the freedom to compete in international competition and as far as professional (and semi-professional) sport is concerned they impede an athlete's opportunity to pursue his or her livelihood. In the European context this has the consequence of depriving a professional athlete of the opportunity to offer his or her services to other national teams within the European Union. At the same time the rules restrict the ability of teams to select and therefore to employ or engage the services of nationals of other European Union states who are not eligible with reference to the relevant criterion. Thus, the French rugby team may not field a talented Spanish scrum-half nor may the English football team employ a gifted Greek play-maker. From the sporting perspective elite athletes from less successful nations are deprived of the chance to compete at the highest level. At the same time, spectators are denied the possibility of witnessing and enjoying the efforts of those athletes. Neither George Best nor John Giles was afforded the opportunity to participate in a World Cup or European Nations finals series; in the modern era it is probable that Ryan Giggs will be similarly excluded. This difficulty is not confined to the case of talented players from 'minor' nations. Many athletes who are eligible but not selected for a 'major' nation are denied the opportunity to represent another nation. It is not difficult to imagine that a player who is not selected for Italy or Spain might wish to compete with another team participating in a World or European championship.

From a legal perspective restrictions imposed on the right to pursue one's profession are troubling. At common law eligibility rules amount to a restraint of trade, but in all likelihood, they would be upheld as being reasonable.[12] Such rules are more difficult to reconcile with Articles 39 and 40[13] of the Treaty of Rome which guarantee the free movement of workers and the freedom to provide services, respectively. These fundamental freedoms are designed to ensure that workers and providers of services are free to move across national frontiers within the European Union. The freedoms are not concerned solely with the elimination of discrimination based on nationality; of equal if not greater importance, they are also designed to facilitate the integration of the European market through the removal of barriers that are not capable of being justified by the invocation of what are termed 'compelling reasons of the general interest.' This proposition lies at the heart of *Bosman* and although the nationality rules in that case concerned eligibility to play for a club side rather than a national team the general philosophy at least raises the issue of national eligibility. *Prima facie*, national eligibility rules represent a barrier to free movement that if not justified would fall foul of Articles 39 and 49, as the case may be.

---

[12] I am unaware of any case in which national eligibility rules were challenged on restraint of trade grounds. However, in Macken v O'Reilly [1979] I.L.R.M. 79 the Irish Supreme Court upheld a national federation rule that required Irish show-jumpers in international competition to compete on Irish-bred horses.

[13] Formerly Article 48 and 49 respectively.

COMPATIBILITY WITH EC LAW

Despite the foregoing considerations the balance of juridical opinion is that national eligibility rules do not violate European Community law. In *Walrave and Koch* it was stated that European law did 'not affect the composition of sports teams, *in particular national teams*, the formation of which is a question of purely sporting interest and as such has nothing to do with economic activity.'[14] In *Donà* v *Mantero* the Court of Justice expressed the view that:

> 'those provisions [i.e. freedom of movement] do not prevent the adoption of rules or of a practice of excluding foreign players from participation in certain matches for reasons which are not of an economic nature, which relate to the particular nature and context of such matches and are thus of sporting interest only, such as, for example, matches between national teams from different countries.'[15]

These sentiments were echoed in *Bosman*. The Court of Justice reiterated the observation made in *Donà* and accepted the rider in that case that 'the restriction on the scope of [EC law] must remain limited to its proper objective.'[16] The Court did not spell out what the 'proper objective' entails but some paragraphs later it noted, without objection or qualification, that national teams must be composed of players having the nationality of the country in question.[17] At the very least this lends support to the view that the Court considered that such rules do not violate European law.

Advocate General Lenz came to a similar conclusion in his opinion in *Bosman*. He discerned a difference between the decisions in *Walrave and Koch* and *Donà*. The earlier decision exempted the composition of teams, especially national teams, from the prohibition of discrimination contained in the Treaty of Rome. In the later case the exclusion of foreign players from certain matches would be permissible if it was motivated by reasons that were not of an economic nature. He concluded that the proposition in *Donà* was narrower than that in *Walrave and Koch*; the earlier case considered that the composition of a team was exclusively a sporting issue while the later decision acknowledged, correctly in his opinion, that the composition of a team might be driven by non-sporting considerations. The Advocate General accepted that neither the basis of exception created by the two cases nor its extent could be deduced with any certainty but he concluded that whatever doubts might be entertained '[i]t is plain, however, that in those judgments the court expressed the view that rules which prescribe that only players who possess the nationality of a state can play in that country's national team are consistent with Community law'. He added that this proposition is

---

[14] [1974] E.C.R. 1405 at 1417-1418, para. 8 (emphasis added).
[15] [1976] E.C.R. 1333 at 1340, para. 14.
[16] [1995] E.C.R. I-4921 at I-5076, para. 127.
[17] Ibid. at I-5077, para. 133.

'obvious and convincing' but acknowledged the intellectual difficulty posed by conceding that it 'is not easy to state the reasons for it'.[18]

Strictly speaking the question of national eligibility did not fall for decision in *Bosman* and did not require exhaustive analysis. On the other hand the clear preponderance of opinion is that national eligibility rules are compatible with Community law and it is difficult to imagine the Court of Justice entertaining a challenge to their validity in the foreseeable future. As Advocate General Lenz observed, the view that a rule that restricts eligibility for a national team to citizens of that state is 'obvious and convincing'. It certainly matches current practice and sporting expectations and the point might be made that the special character of international sport would be significantly diluted were the link between an athlete and the country he or she represents undermined. However, in as much as national eligibility rules curtail freedom of movement they are compatible with Community law only if they are capable of being justified by compelling reasons of general interest. A number of possible grounds of justification might be identified but none is wholly convincing.

On one view the composition of a national team is purely a sporting matter and does not invoke economic considerations or as Weatherill put it 'national identity, not money, predominates.'[19] However, as far as professional sport is concerned a distinction between the sporting and the economic is difficult to draw.[20] In some circumstances money is the predominant consideration underlying national representation especially where international fees represent the bulk of an athlete's income. This is most clearly evident in the issuing of central contracts by national governing bodies, as is the case in English cricket and Irish rugby. The same might be said of sub-national representative sides: Irish provinces and Scottish super-districts compete in the European Rugby Cup alongside club teams from England, Wales France and Italy. In any event, free movement considerations are not excluded where the income earned from international competition accounts for a lesser part of an athlete's earnings.[21] In *Bosman* the contention that the economic aspects of football were 'negligible' was rejected: what was important was that the impugned rules affected the free movement of workers within the European Union, not the amounts of money that might be involved.

A related consideration is the so-called sporting exception from European Community law.[22] The jurisprudence clearly establishes that Community law ap-

---

[18] Ibid., at I-4978, para. 139.

[19] Weatherill, supra n. 11.

[20] See also Griffith-Jones D, *Law and the Business of Sport* (1997) London, Butterworths, 125.

[21] Compare the common law doctrine of restraint of trade which is capable of applying to semi-professionals and in some cases amateurs; see Buckley v Tutty (1971) 125 C.L.R. 353; Johnston v Cliftonville [1984] N.I. 9 (semi-professionals); Gasser v Stinson Queen's Bench Division, unreported, 15 June 1988 (amateurs).

[22] See Beloff M, 'The Sporting Exception in EC Competition Law' (1999) 10 *European Current Law*, xi.

plies to sport only to the extent that it is an economic activity. Accordingly the non-economic aspects of sport lie beyond the domain of Community law. The expressions employed differ slightly: in *Walrave and Koch* the Court of Justice spoke of 'question[s] of purely sporting interest'; in *Donà* v *Mantero* the Court referred to reasons 'not of an economic nature ... and are thus of sporting interest only'; in *Bosman* the exception reached 'non-economic grounds which relate to the particular nature and context of certain matches.'

The policy underlying these remarks is obvious: European law should recognise that issues which primarily concern the organisation and playing of sports lie outside its sphere. However, while the principle can be expressed with ease its application is a different matter. As I observed earlier, it can be difficult to draw a distinction between the economic, which is subject to Community law, and the sporting, which remains immune from its rigors. The examples of purely sporting matters provided by Advocate General Lenz in *Bosman*, namely the duration of a match and the number of points to be awarded for a win, are uncontroversial but provide little insight into the extent of the exception.[23] In particular, we await an explanation for including national eligibility rules within the exception. It can be accepted that sports rules and practices that have no economic impact lie at the core of the exception. These present no real problem and the difficulty is faced where rules that lie in the exception's penumbra are involved. When viewed from one angle some rules might seem to be purely sporting in nature yet when evaluated from a different perspective they assume an economic dimension. National eligibility rules provide an example *par excellence*. In one sense the concern of those rules is solely to determine who may represent a nation in certain competitions but in another they determine the conditions under which athletes are permitted to pursue their livelihoods. This leads to a point that awaits conclusive resolution, namely whether rules should be considered according to their purpose or their effect.[24] The dilemma is that while eligibility rules might be motivated by a sporting purpose their effects are potentially economic.

English authority tentatively supports the proposition that a rule or practice may be classified as an exclusively sporting matter if its purpose is sporting even though it might have consequences of an economic nature. In *Wilander* v *Tobin* the Court of Appeal noted, but did not decide, the point that the International Tennis Federation's doping rules are matters of an exclusively sporting nature that do not attract the application of the provisions of the Treaty of Rome.[25] The later decision in *Edwards* v *British Athletic Federation* is more decisive in that Lightman J felt that he was compelled to decide the issue as a matter of law. He concluded that the International Amateur Athletics Federation doping rules were

---

[23] [1995] E.C.R. I-4921 at I-5013, para. 215.

[24] See Beloff M, Kerr T, and Demetriou M, *Sports Law* (1999) Oxford, Hart Publishing, 86 *et seq*.

[25] [1997] 1 Lloyd's Rep. 293 at 300.

matters of an exclusively sporting nature and thus fell outside the scope of Community law:

> 'As it appears to me, [the rules] merely regulate the sporting conduct of participants in athletics ... Necessarily the imposition of the sanction may have serious economic consequences for those who breach the rules, and the IAAF and all concerned must obviously at all times have appreciated this. But this is a mere incidental and inevitable bye product [*sic*.] of having the rule against cheating. A rule designed to regulate the sporting conduct of participants does not cease to be such a rule because it does not allow those who break it to earn remuneration by participating the sport for what is (by common consent) an appropriate period.'[26]

This classification of doping rules as being exclusively sporting in nature facilitated the conclusion that no issue of European law arose. Whether those rules should be so classified is questionable especially since they restrict athletes' access to the employment market. Of course, the decisions in *Wilander* v *Tobin* and *Edwards* must be read in the context of their subject matter, namely a challenge to the validity of strict liability doping rules[27] and little is to be discerned from them in relation to the validity of national eligibility rules. But for present purposes the significance of those cases lies in the view expressed in the judgments that a rule might have serious economic consequences for those affected by its operation yet retain its status as being exclusively sporting in nature thus rendering it less susceptible to judicial scrutiny. On this basis it would be contended that an eligibility rule has economic consequences but since its motivation is to determine the composition of teams in international competition it is exclusively sporting. However, this would arguably be an unduly narrow reading of the decision in *Bosman* where it would seem that the Court of Justice was as much concerned with the effects of the impugned rules as their purpose. It follows that the English decision cannot be taken to be conclusive on this issue.

Nevertheless, even if eligibility rules are considered to be economic in character because of their effect on the free movement of athletes within the European Union it is possible that they might be held compatible with Community law. It is improbable that a national governing body or international federation could invoke the exceptions stipulated in Article 39(3), namely public policy, public security and public health, but other grounds might be available. It is accepted that the fundamental freedoms guaranteed by the Treaty may be limited for compelling reasons of general interest. Moreover, as Advocate General Lenz observed, the freedoms 'form a unity' and the same criteria should apply to the interpretation of each.[28] There is judicial support for the proposition that the protection of

---

[26] 141 SJLB 154, *The Times* June 30,1997.

[27] See further McCutcheon JP, 'Sports Discipline, Natural Justice and Strict Liability' (1999) 28 Anglo-Am. L. Rev. 37.

[28] [1995] E.C.R. I-4921 at I-5066, para. 200.

cultural interests is a legitimate limitation to the free movement of goods[29] and given the unity underpinning the freedoms it might also apply where the free movement of workers is concerned. In *Groener* v *Minister for Education*[30] the Court of Justice held that a rule requiring teachers in certain publicly funded schools in Ireland to pass an Irish language proficiency test was compatible with Community law. A significant point is that Irish was not the medium of instruction in the school in question and the validity of the rule is evidence of sensitivity on the part of the Court to the protection of cultural diversity and national identity. Nevertheless, it is clear from the terms of the judgment in that case that the measure adopted must be proportionate to the objective that is being pursued. It might be contended that sport, especially where it involves national representation, should be taken to fall within this broad notion of protection of cultural interests or as an analogue thereto that merits equal legal recognition. However, in *Bosman* the Court of Justice rejected an argument advanced by the German government that sport 'has points of similarity with culture'[31] and that by virtue of Article 151(1)[32] the Community is obliged to respect national and regional cultural diversity. While this argument was directed towards a general sporting immunity from Community law, rather than the question of the compatibility of a particular rule with the free movement of workers, it could prove to be an insurmountable obstacle. Nevertheless, the argument that might prevail is that international sport is an objective worthy of protection; the question would then be whether a particular eligibility rule that might be impugned is proportionate to that objective.

It must be admitted that none of the arguments canvassed in this paper convincingly explains the presumed compatibility of national eligibility rules with Community law. The best explanation might just be that they are an anomaly tolerated by the law. This is not entirely satisfactory but sometimes it is better to recognise that a legal principle is anomalous rather that to invoke a strained rationale. By way of comparison one might point to Lord Mustill's suggestion in *R* v *Brown* that the lawfulness of boxing is a special case that 'stands outside the ordinary law of violence because society chooses to tolerate it',[33] an explanation that is to be preferred to the exhaustive but not entirely compelling analysis in *Pallante* v *Stadiums Pty Ltd (No. 1).*[34]

---

[29] Cinétheque v Féderation Nationale de Cinemas Françaises Case 60 and 61/84 [1985] E.C.R. 2605.

[30] Case C-379/87 [1989] E.C.R. 3967.

[31] [1995] E.C.R. I-4921 at I-5063, para. 72.

[32] Formerly Article 128(1).

[33] [1994] 1 A.C. 212 at 265.

[34] [1976] V.R. 331.

THE INTERNATIONAL DIMENSION

It is obvious that national eligibility rules involve an international dimension that extends beyond the European Union. This feature might be invoked to prevent the application of Community legal standards. In short, the argument presented would be to the effect that E.U. law ought not to intervene on a matter that is regulated at a global level by international federations. From this perspective, it might be argued that inordinate difficulties would be posed were a dual, or indeed multi-layered, set of eligibility criteria to emerge shaped by different national and regional laws. It would follow, according to this view, that the prudent course would be to adopt a deferential approach by holding eligibility rules not to be affected by European law. Similar arguments were heard at the time of *Bosman*. It was suggested that football authorities were not subject to control by E.U. law on the grounds, *inter alia*, that they were headquartered in Switzerland and that their membership included non-E.U. countries; the supposed effect that a ruling would have on the organisation of football in parts of Europe outside the European Union, it was thought, should inhibit the application of Community law.

This of course was to seek immunity from European law or, to put it more starkly, it evinced an attitude that sports authorities were above E.U. law. Were a non-European multi-national corporation trading within the Union to advance the same argument it would be met with well-deserved scorn. The important point is that once an entity, be it corporate or sporting, operates within the European Union it is subject to Community law regardless of its non-E.U. activities. It will not avail a governing body to invoke the international aspect of sport to avoid the demands of European law. In as much as eligibility rules inhibit the free movement of workers and the freedom to provide services they fall to be evaluated according to the standards of European law despite the extra-European aspects of those rules. The potential conflict between accepted international sporting norms (as reflected in eligibility criteria and endorsed by the decisions of the Court of Arbitration for Sport) and the freedoms guaranteed by the Treaty of Rome might yet demand resolution. To date the CAS has managed to circumvent that thorny issue. In one case it referred to Community law (in particular, to old Article 48 and the decision in *Walrave*) but it concluded that freedom of movement considerations did not arise and rested its decision on the interpretation of the relevant eligibility rule.[35] In another case, involving dual qualifications, it concluded that a dually qualified American-born basketball player who played for a German

---

[35] See Arbitration CAS 92/80, B./International Basketball Federation (F.I.B.A.), award of March 25, 1993 in Reeb (ed.), supra n.4, 297.

club had adopted German sports nationality.[36] A consequence was that the relevant provisions of E.C. law did pertain to this player.

It can only be a matter of time before either the CAS or a court of law is faced with a case that requires definitive clarification of the status of national eligibility. In the current Olympic year it is not surprising that questions of eligibility have assumed a greater prominence.[37] It is reported that Cuba has prevented Niurka Montalvo, a Cuban-born athlete who has acquired Spanish citizenship through her marriage to a Spanish national, from competing in Sydney for Spain. Cuba has invoked the three-year qualification rule to ensure her exclusion arguing that she was the 'fruit of Cuba's sports movement' and equating the acquisition of a new sporting nationality with 'the theft of athletes' by rich countries that operates to the detriment of third world sport.[38] Morocco has adopted a similar stance in relation to three naturalised French athletes who wish to compete for France.[39] At the same time questions were raised about the eligibility of Sarah Reilly, an international sprinter who sought to switch her allegiance to Ireland on her marriage to an Irish national.[40] As it transpired, following political 'assistance', Ms Reilly's application for an Irish passport was processed with a speed that is rarely witnessed and as a result she became eligible to compete for Ireland in Sydney.[41] These cases exemplify the dilemma posed by eligibility rules. The desire to ensure a genuine link between athlete and country, to prevent the poaching of athletic talent and the adoption of 'flags of convenience' is balanced against the view that elite athletes should be afforded opportunities to exploit their talents and maximise their commercial potential, the latter raising questions of athletes' rights as employees or service providers. These matching concerns represent competing values that might well prove impossible to reconcile.

CONCLUDING OBSERVATIONS

The difficulty in rationalising the supposed validity of national eligibility rules prompts a further consideration, namely whether they should be retained in the modern era. On one hand, the uncertainties implicit in increasing globalisation and closer European integration can boost the attractions of national identity. A national sports team symbolises that identity and in the popular imagination is often considered as much an indicium of sovereignty as formal legal instruments.[42]

---

[36] See Arbitration CAS 94/123, International Basketball Federation (FIBA), W. & Brandt Hagen e.V., award of September 12, 1994 in Reeb (ed.) supra. n.4, 317.

[37] See *Le Monde*, August 22, 2000, p. 21.

[38] See *Sunday Telegraph* August 20, 2000, Sports Section p. 16.

[39] See *Le Monde*, August 22, 2000, p. 21.

[40] See *Irish Times* August 19, 2000, Sports Section p. 8.

[41] See *Irish Times* August 22, 2000, Sports Section p. 2.

[42] See Beloff et al. supra n.24, 2.

Indeed it is significant that in recent years the tendency has been to tighten up eligibility criteria and to insist on a closer link between athlete and country. On the other hand, the essence of globalisation is to move beyond national identity and to emphasise the universality of humanity – our shared attributes are more important than our differences. Moreover, in practice the link between athletes and nations is more ambiguous as the following examples suggest. Jamaican-born John Barnes played for the English football team. The current English cricket team fields players born in Australian and New Zealand, as do the Scottish, Welsh and Irish rugby teams. The Jordan Formula One team is based in England but competes under an Irish licence, reflecting the nationality of team principal Eddie Jordan. English coaches have guided the Irish and Swiss football teams to World Cup finals. Many English and Scottish born players have qualified for the Irish team through their ancestry; this might be taken to represent the Irish Diaspora, the nation overseas, but at times the national link has been tenuous. At the same time some athletes have represented more than one nation. Keppler Wessels played cricket for both Australia and South Africa while the Nawab of Patudi Senior represented both England and India. Brian Smith played rugby for Australia before qualifying for Ireland. Jim Hogan represented Ireland in the 1964 Olympic Games and Great Britain in the 1966 European Championships and the 1968 Olympic Games. Ferenc Puskas played international football for both Hungary and Spain while Alfredo Di Stefano travelled even more widely representing Argentina, Columbia and Spain. In all these cases, however, few would question the commitment of those athletes to the cause of the nation they represented nor was there any reason to differentiate them from their native-born team-mates. What the list illustrates is that national affiliation can be fluid and it is arguable that more subtle eligibility criteria are warranted. In the modern era it is difficult to justify a rule that insists on a formal link such as nationality or birth to the exclusion of other factors such as affiliation or even straightforward commercial opportunity. Whether change will be achieved through the action of governing bodies or judicial decisions remains to be seen.

SELLING YOUR SOLE: *e*-EUROPE, EU LAW AND SPORTS MARKETING

Laura Edgar and David McArdle

INTRODUCTION

A number of recent initiatives from the European Union,[1] along with domestic law and certain international protocols, have had important impact upon sports organisations' use of the World Wide Web as a marketing and retail tool. It pays particular attention to recent legal developments that cover the activities of those organisations who wish to take advantage of the benefits of electronic commerce and market or sell their products via the Internet to customers within the United Kingdom and elsewhere in the European Union. This chapter considers recent initiatives from the European Commission that will (it is hoped) facilitate electronic commerce; it also discusses some theoretical perspectives that are pertinent to successful sports goods retailing on the Internet. The strategies deployed in successful sports marketing are briefly discussed in order to provide both a practical and a theoretical background to the discussion of some of the legal issues that face sports marketing organisations that decide to incorporate the Internet into their sales and marketing strategies.

Before those issues are discussed it should be pointed out that many of the most successful sports goods marketing companies have received adverse publicity as a consequence of questionable employment practices and human rights violations in the states where their manufacturers are based and these organisations' complicity therein. Nike, Adidas and Reebok's activities in Indonesia, Pakistan and elsewhere are – to say the least – problematic. However, despite the adverse publicity that their employment practices have attracted, the impact on the sports goods sector of lawsuits,[2] increased competition within the sector and changing

---

[1] In this paper we have not discussed some of the slightly less recent, but no less important, developments. These include, inter alia, the UNCITRAL model law, the provisions relating to charge-back clauses and certain provisions relating to Internet commercial contracts. For discussion of these matters, see Brownsword R and Howells G, 'When Surfers Start to Shop: Internet Commerce and Contract Law' 19(3) (1999) *Legal Studies* 287 – 315.

[2] In the United States punitive damages awards in tort cases have devastated certain sectors of the sports goods industry. For example, between 1980 and 1988 one single manufacturer of grid iron

A. Caiger and S. Gardiner (Eds), Professional Sport in the EU: Regulation and Re-regulation
© *2000, T.M.C.Asser Press, The Hague, The Netherlands*

trends among consumers, they remain the biggest players in the sports goods market. Accordingly, an additional purpose of this paper is to explain why these particular organisations' marketing campaigns have ensured their continued commercial success despite their well-publicised collusion in unacceptable employment practices.

SPORTS MARKETING: AN INTRODUCTION

At the risk of stating the obvious, the commercial success of these companies has very little to do with the quality of their products or whether they offer 'value for money' according to any objective criteria. Rather the key to their success lay in their ability to use highly sophisticated marketing strategies, which enable these companies to portray themselves as members of a 'sporting family'. The family consists of the particular company itself, the customers and the high-profile athletes whom it endorses, and it stands in opposition to over-hyped, over-commercialised sport that Nike and their ilk purport to eschew.[3] This ability to generate a sense of 'family' through innovative advertising allows the market leaders to appeal to sports participants' need to be part of a sporting community. As Pierre Bourdieu would have it, Nike, Reebok and the others have successfully taken account of the peculiar characteristics – the lifestyle, habitus and self-perceptions – that consumers in the sports market possess, and have successfully integrated them into their marketing strategies.

It can strongly be suggested, notwithstanding some recent high-profile failures within the Internet sector, companies working within the sports firmament (and particularly sports apparel retailers) should still be able to carve a niche for themselves on the Web if they learn from some of the strategies that Nike *et al* have used to create their 'sporting communities.' Those companies should also give due consideration to the demographics of Internet users. The need to determine whether or not an Internet presence would actually enhance the quality of service they can give to their customers before they take the plunge, invest heavily in creating an Internet presence and solicit the necessary legal advice. A company

---

football helmets – Rawlings Sporting Goods Co. – paid out over $39 million in punitive damages awards, including one case where damages of $14 million were awarded after a thirteen-year old boy was rendered paraplegic by a collision. Such cases resulted in spiralling insurance premiums, while huge out of court settlements and damages awarded by juries threatened the entire industry. Indeed, the number of manufacturers of football helmets dropped from eighteen in the 1960s to only two by the 1980s. Other sectors in the US sports industry which have been particularly hard-hit hit by litigation and its consequences have included skiing, trampoline, diving and golf: Fried G, 'Punitive Damages and Corporate Liability Analysis in Sports Litigation' 9(1) (1998) *Marquette Sports Law Journal*, 47.

[3] Nike wants to enter a £300m sponsorship deal with Manchester United, according to news reports on 28th September 2000: http:/www.ananova.com/sport/soccer/PREM/ManUtd/ManUtd _970113189_2.htm

which feels it could use the Internet effectively as part of its marketing strategy should also appraise itself of the European Commission's *e*-Europe initiative, which will influence how the law in this area will develop over the next few years. It should be stressed that although some of these issues are now dealt with at European Union level, others remain the responsibility of national legislatures.

Given that the Nike Corporation remains ahead of the pack in the sports marketing game, it is worth paying particular attention to the marketing strategies that it deploys. The Nike Corporation's core activity is 'the design, development and world-wide marketing of high quality footwear, apparel and accessory products.'[4] It sells its products to over 18,000 retail outlets in the United States and it has a network of independent distributors, licensees and subsidiaries in more than 100 other countries.[5] However, Nike does not *make* sports shoes or other sports apparel. Its products are manufactured by independent contractors in developing nations, with the bulk of production taking place in Indonesia, Vietnam, the People's Republic of China and other Asian nations where human rights are not particularly high on the government's political agenda.[6] In 1996, children in Pakistan were discovered to be making footballs for Nike at 10p per hour[7] and there have been plenty of well-founded allegations[8] that Nike is indirectly involved in slavery and child labour.[9]

None of this has impacted upon Nike's commercial success. This is founded upon its relationship with an advertising agency, Wieden and Kennedy (hereafter WK), which is recognised as one of the most innovative agencies in the US. In the late 1980s, WK and a few other leading edge advertising agencies recognised that media-literate consumers in the United States rejected the use of traditional advertising strategies – the kinds used to sell toothpaste or second-hand cars – when choosing sporting commodities such as trainers and t-shirts. WK devised a distinctive advertising strategy that enabled Nike to distance itself from this advertising mainstream. Accordingly, Nike's advertising campaigns have set the company apart because of the way it addressed its target audience. For example, through its well-documented appropriation of cultural forms to create adverts designed to appeal to viewers who understand the references they contain,[10] Nike's consumers are positioned as intelligent, sophisticated, media literate individuals

---

[4] According to its 1996 US Securities and Exchange Form 10-K filing: Goldman R and Papson S, *Nike Culture* (1999) Sage Publications, 6.

[5] Goldman and Papson, ibid.

[6] Many of those factories and subcontractors also manufacture goods for Reebok, Adidas and others.

[7] Johnson S, '"Excuse me, but is that football 'child-free'"? Pakistan and Child Labour' (2000) 7(1) *Tulsa Journal of Comparative and International Law* 163.

[8] www.cleanclothes.org/companies/nike.htm.

[9] Nike goes to considerable lengths to deny these allegations and (when necessary) justify their manufacturers' employment practices: http://www.nikebiz.com/labour/index/html.

[10] Spike Lee's films, Iggy Pop's music, film and television personalities such as Dennis Hopper and Jan Hooks, Disney cartoons and nursery rhymes have all been used to peddle the Nike message.

familiar with the forms and faces of popular culture. The inference is that these are urbane people, quite capable of recognising the commercial intent behind advertising, and that Nike understands and respects them too much to use the tired old advertising formats to try and sell merchandise to them.

WK's most successful campaigns for Nike have been those where high-profile athletes have been used to peddle the Nike image to its actual and potential customers. WK adopt the premise that individuals who ignore traditional advertising strategies are also likely to be sympathetic to Nike's purported lamenting of the perceived debasement of sport for commercial purposes. Nike thus places the athletes it endorses[11] in opposition to 'the corrupting influence of television on sport, (its) crass commercialisation'[12] and the tired old techniques utilised by other advertisers. By thus addressing viewers as sports insiders with access to and an appreciation of sport's cultural capital, a boundary is drawn around the 'Nike community', the members of which are playing the same game, are on the same side and all understand the rules. Put another way, Nike *metacommunicates* with its audience. It uses 'shared, but usually unstated, taken-for-granted assumptions about the nature of communication itself. It (uses) communication about communication.'[13]

Other sports apparel marketers, notably Reebok, Adidas, Fila, have learned much from Nike over the past decade. In addition to using the same manufacturers with the same exploitative employment practices and thereby drawing upon cheap labour in countries with little regard for human rights, they have set themselves up as members of a 'sporting family' alongside their customers and their endorsed athletes. But successfully developing such a strategy required these companies to fundamentally reconsider how they marketed their merchandise.[14] If Pierre Bourdieu is right to aver that 'it is possible to consider the whole range of sporting activities and entertainment offered ... as a supply intended to meet a

---

[11] For example Michael Jordan, Tiger Woods and Andre Agassi.

[12] Goldman and Papson, supra n.4, 31.

[13] Goldman and Papson, supra n. 4, 33.

[14] Attempting to understand the subtleties of sports participation requires one to take account of individuals' perceptions of both the costs and the benefits of the sporting pursuits in which they engage. In the process of 'choosing' a sport, in determining how one plays it and with whom one plays, self-perception and the social *cachet* associated with particular sports practices are more significant than one's actual playing ability. A person whom is willing to spend time and money learning to play, and then actually participate in, highbrow sports such as fencing, golf or tennis is making a very specific statement about their lifestyle, their aspirations and their self-perceptions. Taking these into account is an important aspect of successful sports marketing. Although rapid changes in technology and consumer preference have stimulated competition in the sports apparel market in particular, product value has less to do with the material properties of those products than with the symbolic properties they carry. Nike has excelled at acquiring symbolic value for its merchandise, and the real value of the Nike product is the *swoosh* that appears on all its products. The *swoosh* has become a form of social and cultural currency. The successful marketing of Nike merchandise has involved a sophisticated understanding of what drives individuals to identify with that particular symbol rather than with the myriad alternatives.

social demand',[15] then Nike and WK were the first to understand the process by which that social demand is produced and successfully apply it to sports marketing. Participants adhere to 'what sports players call a 'feel for the game' – a mastery acquired by experience... and one that works outside conscious control and discourse.'[16] Acquiring this 'feel for the game' promotes one's acceptance within the sporting and social circle and gives a sense of 'belonging'. Nike tapped into that 'family feeling':

> 'Nike ads create a community of athletes who share the Nike philosophy: they play intensely because they love the game. (The ads) construct a Nike community based on sports talk. This includes media hype, advertising discourse, shop talk – strategies, evaluation of players, statistics and predictions. These stars have become part of the sports fan's family and he/she part of theirs – at least within the spectacle. But there is also an informal discourse that defines the community – trash-talking, jiving and teasing. ... Viewers are positioned as part of this camaraderie. We are included in the playful exchanges. We are invited into the conversation, and into the community.'[17]

The complex relationship that exists between manufacturers/marketers and consumers in the sports sector is exacerbated in respect of companies that wish to develop an Internet presence. The Internet has 'rules of the game' of its own and players have to acquire a 'feel' for it.

SPORTS MARKETING ON THE INTERNET

The failure of Internet enterprises such as Boo.com have been well documented, but hitherto such failures have been the exception. Worldwide *e*-commerce sales are expected to grow forty times over between 1998 and 2003, by which time (it is estimated) they will account for over 15% of all sales.[18] In 1999, £6.2 billion in venture funding was raised by Internet start-ups in the UK alone, a 63% increase on the previous year. However, a sudden plunge in share prices on the United States' Nasdaq stock market in April 2000 has made investors far more wary of *e*-commerce. The Internet sector will probably see many more failures and plenty of mergers as the market readjusts, and many observers are still to decide whether the Internet is a golden goose or a poisoned chalice.

These recent failures should not occasion surprise, for 40% of all new businesses fail within their first five years of operation. But in its recent initiatives the European Commission has noted that in the United States this particular sector of

---

[15] Bourdieu P (1990) *In Other Words: Essays Towards a Reflexive Sociology* London, Polity Press, 63.

[16] Ibid.

[17] Goldman and Papson, supra 66.

[18] European Commission (2000) '*e*-Europe Progress Report' ('The Report') COM (2000) 130 Final at 22.

the economy continues to punch above its weight. It is worth noting, for example, that 2.5 million Americans are employed in the dot.com economy (significantly more than are employed in the European Internet sector) and in the seven months to August 2000 there were fewer than 7000 lay-offs within United States Internet companies. In contrast, the Bank of America alone plans to make 10,000 employees redundant in 2000/2001.[19] Many of the failures have been due to the kind of profligacy within the companies' management that Boo.com epitomised, while others have failed as a consequence of the considerable start-up costs that beset Internet enterprises. The ongoing costs thereafter are far from negligible too. For example, when it ceased trading in September 2000[20] health products retailer Clickmango was achieving weekly sales of £2000, but it had to spend £25000 per week just to stay on-line.[21]

The relationship between sport and the Internet would appear to provide grounds for cautious optimism for 'e-tailers' notwithstanding those failures. The web has revolutionised the provision and analysis of the statistics, averages and other data upon which sports participants (in the broadest sense) thrive. It facilitates access to scores and other information with an immediacy that can rarely be obtained through other media, while e-mail and discussion groups facilitate the sharing of ideas, opinions, strategies and information among the cognoscenti. Back in 1996, in the earliest days of electronic commerce, the Wall Street Journal reported that:

> 'professional leagues, major media, on-line services and fantasy game operators are voraciously assembling material and courting advertisers and partners in the unshaken belief that sport is one of the few sure things in cyberspace.'[22]

On September 27th 2000, it was reported that the official Olympics website had recorded 7.2 billion visitors – a record number of visitors to any Internet site, and there was still the best part of a week of the competition remaining.[23]

The demographics of Internet users provide the grounds for this optimism. At the end of 1998, there were over 100 million Internet users worldwide. But more than 50% of these are in the United States: in the US in the mid-1990s, the number of adult users of the Internet had been estimated to be in the region of 45 mil-

---

[19] 'You Call This a Bust?' *The Economist* August 5, 2000, 71.

[20] Clickmango to Close After Last-ditch Bid for Funds Collapses' *The Independent* September 6, 2000, 23.

[21] Europe's Internet Drought' *The Economist* August 5, 2000, 71.

[22] 'Getting in the Game'. *The Wall Street Journal* April 19, 1996, 1.

[23] Olympic Roundup *The Guardian* Sports section, 27th September 2000 p. 21. The article also reported that 'many people have gone to www.olympics.com only to find themselves checking out the latest line in wood seals and paints. Despite the paint company generously providing a link to the Olympics, IOC control freaks say the site is precisely the kind of cashing in on the games they want closing down'.

lion.[24] Around the same time Gladden discovered that in the United States 'males represent 66% of Internet users and 77% of Internet usage. Twenty five per cent of all Internet users have income of more than $80,000 and 64% have at least a college degree.'[25] Among European users, 54% are in, or have completed, a course of higher education and their mean average annual income is in the region of $55,000.[26] Other surveys have predicted that this will increase to 175 million users by the end of 2002 and that Internet commerce will grow from $2.6 billion in 1996 to a staggering $220 billion by that time.[27]

This particular community of media-savvy and technologically literate individuals is vast and burgeoning; and it has money to spend. While it is impossible to say precisely what percentage of on-line business will result from sport-related transactions it is undoubtedly the case that since the demographics of the on-line community are a sports marketer's dream the value of these transactions will certainly account for a considerable proportion of that figure. Commercial Internet companies are invariably keen to establish the characteristics of their sites' users, and many sports sites try to achieve this by establishing free draws for sports merchandise or tickets but which require participants to furnish their names, addresses, income and other information. However, the more sophisticated sites explain precisely what use this information will be put to.[28] These organisations can recoup some or all of the costs incurred by selling this information to other organisations that use it for direct marketing purposes.[29]

On sports sites, comparatively well educated, young adult male users with disposable income predominate. When the United States television company ESPN discovered in 1996 that 96% of visitors to its ESPNET SportZone were male and 80% were between the ages of 18 and 34, it had no difficulty in recruiting banner advertisers at a charge of nearly $500,000 per year.[30] Banner adverts direct potential customers to the advertiser's own website, where more detailed information about goods and services can be given, and placing such advertisements on sites that have particularly high traffic represent many companies' greatest outlay in terms of advertising their Internet presence. On the majority of sites the outlay is no more than a few hundred dollars per month, but the demographics of

---

[24] Ibid.

[25] Gladden J, 'SportsMarket Bytes: The Ever Expanding Impact of Technology on Sport Marketing, Part I' (1996) 5(3) *Sports Marketing Quarterly* 13-14.

[26] http://www.nua.ie/surveys/index.

[27] Duncan M and Campbell, R 'Internet Users: How to Reach Them and How to Integrate the Internet into the Marketing Strategy of Sport Businesses' (1999) 8(2) *Sport Marketing Quarterly* 35 – 41.

[28] See for example the Nike website at http://www.nike.com and Golf Web at http://www.golfweb.com/privacy.

[29] So long as the parties accord with the terms of the relevant EU Directives, as incorporated into UK law by the Data Protection Act, 1998.

[30] Gladden, supra. The cost of a banner advert depends upon the number of hits the site receives each month.

ESPNET's users meant that many potential advertisers were convinced that this particular price was one worth paying. The ultimate test of a banner advertisement's success lay in the 'click-through rate' (i.e. how many visitors to the host site click on the banner and access the advertiser's) and, ultimately, of course, the number of sales generated.

But in order to take advantage of the benefits the Internet potentially has to offer business-to-customer sports sector retailers, those organisations will need to understand the disposition of their potential customers in the way that Nike have; they will also need to appreciate the demographics of Internet users. The major benefits of the Internet include the cheap and rapid dissemination of extensive or technical data, a more efficient means of comparing different products and the speedier completion of transactions. This means that the customers' search and transaction costs are reduced, at least in terms of time and quite often in terms of money because online sales are cheaper for the business to transact. If these savings are passed on to the purchaser there is an immediate incentive to shop online. Internet transactions also enable customers to exercise a greater degree of control over the whole purchasing process than is normally the case – a guaranteed way of improving both customer service and satisfaction.

More importantly, the Internet provides those contemplating the purchase of sports equipment the opportunity to compare brands, styles and prices at their own pace, perhaps supplemented by the chance to read on-line reviews or to solicit the opinions of other aficionados through discussion groups. The mountain biking magazine *MTB Review*, for example, carries reviews of over $30,000 worth of mountain biking equipment on its website,[31] and it enjoys enormous prestige among manufacturers who appreciate the difference that a favourable review can make to the success of a particular product. For smaller manufacturers seeking to create awareness of and outlets for their products, favourable reviews and comment on discussion groups frequented by the on-line cognoscenti can be invaluable. However, the company then needs to capitalise on the favourable impression that has been created by devoting sufficient resources to the development of a website which those interested in its products can access. The site needs to be easy to navigate, with a comprehensible layout and clear graphics (no overly-sophisticated but complex wizardry just for the sake of it) and with an on-line purchasing facility that consumers find easy to use and have confidence in. Of course, many organisations have restricted their attempts to market their merchandise online to the creation of sites that provide information photographs, technical data, prices, lists of stockists (with hypertext links if appropriate) and favourable reviews of their products.[32]

---

[31] Kahle L and Meeske C, 'Sports Marketing and the Internet: it's a Whole New Ball Game' (1999) 8(2) *Sports Marketing Quarterly* 9 – 12.

[32] http://www.planetreebok.com.

To the concern of the European Commission, the majority of online retailers have not provided a facility through which customers can actually purchase goods online because Internet commerce is initially expensive (the high start-up costs being compounded by the expense of premises and the recruitment of employees) and because of the Internet's perceived lack of security. However, the Commission's new *e*-Europe initiative suggests it is willing to take significant steps to help companies overcome these problems, while many of the regulatory issues are dealt with under recent EU laws which seek to ensure that online transactions are conducted accurately, securely and reliably.

THE EUROPEAN UNION AND THE *e*-ECONOMY

The European Union's recent pronouncements and current policies on sport make little reference to the issues that are under consideration here. This should occasion no surprise, for the big players within the European Commission's sports portfolios (most notably Competition Commissioner Mario Monti and Education and Culture Commissioner Viviene Reding) are properly concerned with the issues that are dealt with elsewhere in this book. That said, 'The European Union and Sport'[33] contains an acknowledgment that sport is 'a sector with job creation potential' and that sport 'cuts across several Community policies including ... competition, audiovisual media, culture, research and education.'[34] However, the potential economic and other benefits that may accrue specifically from sport's relationship with the Internet have yet to be appreciated. While Commissioner Monti has commented upon the fact that 'the sports industry understands the challenges and opportunities of the new economy, and in particular of the Internet,'[35] sports organisations have been particularly slow to grasp the Internet nettle.[36] The issues to which Commissioner Monti alludes have far more to do with the need to understand the broadcasting potential of the Internet than with an awareness of the issues under consideration here. One must look elsewhere for pertinent pronouncements on the matter, and specifically at the recent initiatives hailing from those within the Commission who are concerned with enhancing the EU's involvement in the electronic commercial sector as a whole. However, even here the relationship between sport and the Internet receives no particular attention.

There is undoubtedly a pressing need to facilitate Internet trade throughout all economic sectors within the European Union, and the Commission appears to be keenly aware that this is so. If one turns again to the United States for compari-

---

[33] http://europa.eu.int/scadplus/leg/en/lvb/l35001.htm.

[34] Ibid. 2.

[35] Monti M, *Sport and Competition* paper presented at the Brussels Conference on Sports, 17th April, 2000: http://europa.eu.int/rapid/start/cgi/guesten.ksh.

[36] Beech J, Chadwick S, & Tapp A, 'Towards a Schema for Football Clubs Seeking an Effective Presence on the Internet' 7 (2000) *European Journal for Sport Management (Special Issue)* 30 – 50.

sons, the economy there has enjoyed eight years of continuous growth. Inflation is less than 2% at present[37] and the unemployment rate is 4%.[38] It has been argued that the United States' current economic success is due in large part to the growth of electronic commerce. The European Commission has noted that:

'increased productivity growth in the US began in 1995, a date which coincides with the beginning of the World Wide Web, which effectively marked the beginning of the Internet as a mass market medium. It has been suggested, although it is difficult to prove, that the Internet allowed the decades of technological accumulation to finally generate higher productivity. This assertion is supported by strong *a priori* arguments that the Internet plays a key role in lowering business costs, making markets more efficient and thereby increasing productivity in the economy.'[39]

So far as the Commission is concerned, the EU is playing catch-up with the United States in the whole area of electronic commerce, and although an Internet-driven 'new economy' is emerging the citizens and Member States of the European Union had been slow to respond to the opportunities it offered. Furthermore, time is of the essence because 'the windows of opportunity are short lived. Market entry soon becomes extremely costly because of the strong branding of certain *e*-commerce services.'[40]

With this in mind, the European Commission in 1999 took new steps to promote the development and use of electronic commerce throughout the European Union. In December 1999 it launched its '*e*-Europe' initiative, which 'aims at accelerating the uptake of digital technologies across Europe and ensuring that all Europeans have the necessary skills to use them'.[41] As a first step, the Commission adopted a Communication entitled '*e*-Europe – an Information Society for All'[42] (hereafter '*e*-Europe'). Subsequently, acting at the behest of the Helsinki European Council,[43] it prepared an Action Plan and a Progress Report[44] which were presented at the Lisbon European Council.[45] Over two hundred interest groups from industry, academia, governmental and non-governmental organisations responded to *e*-Europe.

The Progress Report stated that in the few months since publication of '*e*-Europe', 'the level of interest in the impact of the Internet and awareness of the 'new economy' had increased significantly.'[46] It suggested that the Internet could

---

[37] At the time of writing, i.e., September 2000.
[38] Economic Indicators *The Economist* September 9, 2000, 178.
[39] The Report, supra at 21.
[40] The Report, supra at 3.
[41] Ibid.
[42] http://europa.eu.int/comm/information_society/eeurope/index_en.htm.
[43] 10 and 11December 1999.
[44] http://www.europa.eu.int/eur-lex/en/com/pdf/2000/com2000_0130en01.pdf.
[45] 23 and 24 March 2000.
[46] The Report, supra at 20.

provide opportunities for economic growth 'through the exploitation of new activities and by the increased productivity of existing activities.'[47]

Proponents of Internet commerce argue that the development of digital technologies 'represent a shift of equal significance to the other major technological developments in the history of industrial societies: steam power, electricity and the internal combustion engine.'[48] They argue that the Internet could be the driving force behind a successful economic policy for the whole of the EU. However, the March 2000 Progress Report states that at present Europe is not realising the full potential of the Internet because there is inadequate support for new start-ups and the workforce lacks the necessary skills and flexibility. Furthermore, 40% of the populations of Finland and Sweden use the Internet at home while in Greece and Spain the figure is little more than 10%; within the EU as a whole only 12% of all homes have Internet access. These marked differences in uptake of the Internet between European states 'raises problems for social cohesion as well as economic growth potential.'[49] In an attempt to make up lost ground, *e*-Europe recommends, inter alia, that by the end of 2001 all schools should have access to the Internet and multimedia resources. By the end of 2000, various steps should be taken that will make access cheaper (for example by a significant reduction in leased line tariffs). Additionally, the Report stressed the need to have all the remaining *e*-commerce Directives in place by the end of 2000,[50] and that measures to improve and encourage on-line dispute settlement had to be taken.[51]

SPORT, THE INTERNET AND *e*-COMMERCE LAW

As mentioned earlier, the last five years have seen the Internet transformed from being predominantly a source of information to a sophisticated sales and marketing tool. The new technology, although bringing with it many positive business developments, also creates a host of legal uncertainties. The increase in international commercial transactions, which will become as commercially important to global-brand sports organisations like Manchester United as they are to the likes of Nike and Reebok, will give rise to a greater number of potential cross-border disputes. This will inevitably lead to the need to consider which laws are applicable to disputes in this emergent market. While in some areas it is simply a case of interpreting existing laws, in others it is clear that new rules must be developed to deal with this sales forum and the marketing possibilities that it creates.

---

[47] Ibid.

[48] The Report, supra at 20.

[49] The Report, supra at 5.

[50] Specifically, the Directives relating to Copyright and related rights; legal aspects of e-commerce; e-money; and the distance selling of financial services. And the Regulations pertaining to jurisdiction and the enforcement of judgments; and the dual use export control regime.

[51] The Report, supra, passim.

Advertising online provides a retailer with access to a far wider customer base than could ever be achieved through traditional shop retailing or even mail order. Rather than selecting and targeting a particular customer base by geographical location or common interest (e.g. through a magazine) the Internet allows the retailer to access a wide range of potential customers across the globe. While this is potentially a valuable source of revenue and may lead to vastly increased sales it may also give rise to various legal liabilities. The rest of this chapter highlights some of these legal issues which have to be borne in mind as the European Commission, sports bodies and commercial organisations seek to take full advantage of the Internet age.

Domain Names and Cybersquatting

The first step for any business that wants to conduct its activities online will be to register a domain name. However, many words and names have already been registered as domain names, either by others who have a legitimate right to the name for their own business or personal homepage, or by those who hope to make money by selling them. Therefore a company that tries to register its own name or trademark may find that someone has got there first. For example, earlier this year Manchester United discovered that the names of several of its players had been registered as domain names and put up for auction on the Internet.[52]

The registration of trademarks as domain names creates difficulties because while the scope of a trademark is limited by territory or by the type of product, the scope of a domain name is not restricted in this way. Therefore while trademarks of the same name can co-exist in different locations and for different products, when this name is registered as a domain name there is potential for confusion.

Domain names are accessible worldwide and there are only limited forms in which a particular name can be registered. It may be an international level name, for example nike.com, or a geographical domain of a particular country, such as nike.co.uk. Either way, if the name is a fairly common name or the company's brand name or trademark is well known someone may have already registered the name as a domain name. It is clear that not all sports personalities will have registered their name as a trademark and in these cases an action for passing off may be brought. Passing off involves an attempt by one party to take advantage of the goodwill owned by another in relation to goods or services provided by him. Several years ago Nike brought an action against Spanish manufacturers of 'Nike' cosmetics that had been imported into the UK. The court held that there

---

[52] The names registered included those of Ryan Giggs, Roy Keane and Andy Cole. For further details see Lee D, 'Protecting brand names on the Internet makes the offside rule look simple' *The Times*, March 14, 2000.

had been passing off even though the defendants owned the Spanish trademark for Nike and the plaintiff had no intention to sell cosmetics. The decision was reached on the basis of evidence showing that consumers were actually deceived as to the source.

The intention of the person registering the domain name may be a critical factor in determining whether or not a party's rights have been infringed. Registering another's trademark or brand name with the intention of selling it to the trademark holder (cybersquatting) has been the subject of several court battles in Europe. In the United Kingdom the courts have relied on trademark law and the law of passing off to prevent dealers from registering and selling domain names, which comprise brand names of well known companies.[54] In the US legislation has been introduced to combat the practice of cybersquatting.[55]

A practical and increasingly popular alternative to litigation in disputes over domain names is the World Intellectual Property Organisation's Arbitration and Mediation Centre.[56] The WIPO Centre hears disputes over domain names and applies the Internet Corporation for Assigned Names and Number's (ICANN) dispute policy.[57] Where it considers that a name has been registered in bad faith it will order the transfer of the name to the other party.[58] The first dispute to be resolved was over the registration of the domain name 'worldwrestlingfederation. com' by Michael Bosman. The World Wrestling Federation Entertainment Inc. (WWF) submitted a complaint to the WIPO Centre at the end of 1999. Bosman had registered the domain name in October 1999. Three days later he contacted WWF to notify them of the registration and to state that the purpose of the registration was to sell or otherwise transfer the domain name to the complainant for a valuable consideration. In a later *e*-mail Bosman offered to sell the domain name to the WWF for $1000. The respondent had not developed a website using the domain name or made any other use of the name. The panel concluded that registration was in breach of the dispute resolution policy and ordered the transfer of the domain name to the World Wrestling Federation Entertainment Inc.

In addition to being far cheaper than court action, the WIPO process costs around $1000 (by coincidence the same amount as Bosman offered to sell the name for), the process is also much speedier as the target for resolving a dispute is 6 weeks.

Under the ICANN policy, before a domain name can be transferred the complainant must prove the following:

---

[54] In British Telecommunications plc and another v One in a Million Ltd and others and other actions Court of Appeal [1998] 4 All ER 476.

[55] Anticybersquatting Consumer Protection Act 1999.

[56] For more information see http://arbiter.wipo.int.

[57] This dispute policy has been incorporated by reference in all registration agreements with domain name registrars.

[58] The WIPO Centre has already settled over 350 disputes since it was set up at the beginning of 2000.

- that the domain name registered by the respondent is identical or confusingly similar to a trademark over which the complainant has rights; and
- the respondent has no legitimate interests in the domain name; and
- the domain name has been registered and used in bad faith.

The ICANN dispute resolution policy has also been applied to the registration of names of famous people as well as (in)famous organisations like the WWF. In March 2000 the author Jeanette Winterson discovered that a Cambridge academic had registered her name, along with the names of 129 other well-known writers, as a domain name. He offered the domain names to the authors in return for 3% of their gross book earnings for 1999. She filed a claim under the ICANN dispute procedures, and it was held that the names had been registered in bad faith. The tribunal ordered that the domain name should be transferred to her.

This decision makes it clear that the WIPO Centre is not limited to considering disputes relating to registered trademarks which have been registered as domain names. Names that have not been registered as trademarks may also be considered. Therefore this may be particularly useful for resolving disputes involving the names of sporting personalities. It has also already been used successfully by Nike over the use of the domain name 'niketown.com' and by Fifa over the domain name 'fifa-world-cup.com'.[59]

However, the WIPO Centre will not be able to resolve all disputes. It can only be used where the other party has no legitimate interest in the domain name therefore in cases where two parties are both entitled to use a particular name a satisfactory remedy will be hard to come by. This means that those businesses which have taken longer to acknowledge the potential value of the Internet are likely to find it more difficult to register the name they want.

Meta-tags

The success of a website will depend to a great degree on the steps, which are taken to market the name, from registering it with search engines to including meta-tags in the webpage. Meta-tags usually include keywords relating to the contents of the webpage; they are used by search engines to create lists of websites relevant to a user's request. Therefore by incorporating keywords into the meta-tags in a webpage the website owner can ensure that search engines will list their site when these keywords are selected by users. For example by including 'Reebok' as a meta-tag in a webpage this will ensure that the search engines list that webpage when a user searches for websites relating to 'Reebok'.

However some companies in an attempt to boost visits to their website have started to use competitors' brand names and trademarks in their meta-tags. This

---

[59] The WIPO Centre ordered the transfer of these names to Nike and Fifa respectively. Further details can be found on http://arbiter.wipo.int/center/index.html.

practice has been condemned by the courts. In a recent decision in the UK,[60] it was made clear that use of another parties' brand name or trademark in a meta-tag infringes that parties' rights. This is also clear in the US where several judges have reached similar conclusions.[61]

Commercial *e*-Mails and Spam

Another way of attracting potential customers to a website is by sending advertising by *e*-mail. An individual or business can send thousands of *e*-mails at little more than the cost of sending one. At present, the cost of unsolicited *e*-mails falls on the consumer when he or she downloads them rather than the sender, and consequently there has been widespread criticism of this practice. It would be anathema to the people at WK because it typifies the unsophisticated approach to marketing that they have sought to avoid in their relationship with Nike; those responsible for marketing sports organisations or apparel would do well to reject such a strategy.

At present most of the countries in Europe allow the sending of unsolicited commercial *e*-mail (spam) but have developed opt-out registers which individuals can join to avoid receiving it.[62] However, a proposal for a new Data Protection Directive published on the 12th of July 2000[63] proposes that unsolicited commercial *e*-mails must not be sent to potential customers without their prior consent. This proposal would in effect create an opt-in system whereby individuals would be required to expressly choose to receive unsolicited commercial *e*-mails as is currently the system with commercial faxes.

Sporting organisation and businesses intending to use this form of advertising should bear in mind the Electronic Commerce Directive which stipulates that where unsolicited commercial communications are sent they should be clearly identifiable as commercial communications as soon as they are received thus enabling individuals to use filtering mechanisms.

Webpage Contents and Copyright

The next step is developing the contents of the website. A webpage may contain various items such as text, images and databases. Each of these can be protected

---

[60] Roadtech Computer Systems Limited v Mandata (Management and Data Services) Limited, High Court, Chancery Division, 25th May 2000.

[61] Niton Corporation v Radiation Monitoring Devices Inc. 98-11629-REK , 18/11/98.

[62] In Europe four of the Member States have already adopted an opt-in system while the others have, at present, opt out systems. The Direct Marketing Association runs such a scheme. Further details can be found at www.dma.org.uk.

[63] Proposal for a Directive of the European Parliament and of the Council concerning the processing of personal data and the protection of privacy in the electronic communications sector, COM (2000) 385.

by copyright as literary, dramatic or musical works,[64] separately or collectively. Therefore if someone else copies images of a product or text from a website, perhaps to put on their own webpage, this would infringe copyright.

Infringement of copyright is a particular problem because of the ease of copying and reproduction online. In fact copying is a necessary part of online transmission. Each time a webpage is viewed or a document downloaded a copy is made. According to current UK copyright legislation even this 'transient and incidental' copying theoretically infringes copyright, although it is unlikely anyone would sue over it.[65] The proposed European Copyright Directive[66] would make reproduction – which is an essential prerequisite to the transmission – exempt from infringing copyright.

Elsewhere in Europe the courts have had to deal with the question of whether or not Internet Service Providers (ISP) can be held liable for hosting websites which link to other websites containing copyright infringing material. In Belgium, an injunction was granted against an Internet service provider which hosted websites that contained links to illegally copied musical works in MP3 format.[67]

When the Electronic Commerce Directive[68] is implemented in the Member States the position of ISPs will be clarified. The Directive provides that an ISP will not be liable for hosting information where it does not have 'actual knowledge of illegal activity or information' and upon becoming aware 'acts expeditiously to remove or to disable access to the information'.[69] The Directive also provides immunity from liability for intermediaries when they perform a passive role in the transmission of information or provide a 'caching' service.[70] There is no general obligation to monitor information.[71]

Advertising Online

By creating a website to advertise goods or services a business is effectively permitting consumers across the world to access its product information. While a sports retailer may takes steps to ensure that the information contained on a webpage complies with his or her own national law the method and form of advertising online could potentially infringe the national laws in those countries

---

[64] Copyright, Designs and Patents Act (CDPA) 1988.

[65] s17(6) CDPA It has been suggested that by setting up the website the owner has impliedly consented to the incidental copying required in order to view the contents of the webpages.

[66] Proposal for a Directive on Copyright and Related Rights in the Information Society, COM (1999) 0250, 21st May 2000.

[67] IFPI ASBL and Polygram Records SA v Belgacom Skynet SA Tribunal de commerce de Bruxelles, 2 November 1999.

[68] Directive on Certain Legal Aspects of Electronic Commerce in the Internal Market, OJ L178, 17 July 2000.

[69] Article 14.

[70] Articles 12 and 13.

[71] Article 15.

where the website can be accessed. National consumer protection regulations differ even within Europe, for example, while two for one offers are legal in some European countries they infringe national regulations in others such as Germany. An example of the possible problems can be seen in the recent decision of the Tribunal de Grande Instance de Paris.[72] The court held that Yahoo.com must take steps to prevent nazi paraphernalia, available on their auction website in the US, from being accessible in France. Although the material on the website complied with the law in the country in which it was hosted, US law, it was held to infringe the law of France in which it was accessible. This raises the important question on the extent to which one country's court can attempt to control access to materials emanating from another country. In this case the French courts asserted jurisdiction over activities which had taken place in the US because the effects of them could be felt in France.

There may also be general requirements on the form of websites and the information that must be contained therein. In Europe for example the Directive on Electronic Commerce[73] which must be implemented in the Member States by early 2002 requires service providers to provide certain information to potential buyers. The name, the geographical location where the service provider is established and contact details, including an email address must be made accessible to the recipient. The purpose of such provisions is to provide those purchasing goods and services online with some security in an online environment where little is known of the parties to a transaction. Although this Directive is, of course, only applicable within the European Union other countries are introducing their own measures to ensure protection of consumers.

In a 1999 decision by a US court it was held that a New York court had jurisdiction over online sports betting services offered by an Antiguan corporation.[74] Even though the company had not accepted customers who said they were resident in New York, where it is illegal to offer gambling services without authorisation, they had not carried out any checks to ascertain the true location of the customer.[75] This year a US company brought an action against UK defendants in the US for trademark infringement.[76] The case was however dismissed for lack of personal jurisdiction. The defendants' only presence in the state was through a website and the court concluded that this was not sufficient for it to assert jurisdiction.

---

[72] UEJF and LICRA v Yahoo! Inc and Yahoo France, Tribunal de Grande Instance de Paris, 22 May 2000.

[73] Directive on Certain Legal Aspects of Electronic Commerce in the Internal Market, OJ L178, 17 July 2000.

[74] People v World Interactive Gambling Corp et al, QDS 22310325 (Sup. Ct . N.Y.Co.)24 July 1999.

[75] In this case the Antiguan company had its Headquarters in New York.

[76] Ty Inc v Clark United States District Court, N.D. Illinois, Eastern Division, No.99 C5532, 14 January 2000.

Two particular concerns for businesses subject to action in a foreign jurisdiction are first the ability of the party to defend an action taking place in a foreign forum and secondly the manner in which a foreign judgment can be enforced. A defendant against whom proceedings are brought may try to challenge the jurisdiction of that court. However if unsuccessful the action will proceed irrespective of the defendant's presence. In many cases costs will prove a disincentive if not an obstacle to defending an action and the action may proceed undefended. Where this happens and the plaintiff is successful the next concern is the enforcement of this judgment on the defendant in his own jurisdiction.

Foreign judgments are not automatically enforceable in England. This is because the judgments of a court are territorially limited and therefore will not be enforced in foreign countries unless the foreign court agrees to enforce them. In the UK enforcement of a foreign judgment may be sought at common law or under statute and this will depend upon the country where the judgement was reached. As regards US judgments, due to the lack of any treaty between the US and the UK on the reciprocal enforcement and recognition of judgments enforcement must be sought at common law.

Security of Online Transactions

Although in practical terms the credit card is well suited to payment online as card details can be typed easily into an online payment form, there are security concerns over their transmission and storage. Concerns over third party interception of credit card details or their misuse by the retailer have led to the development of various technologies to protect the card details. The Secure Socket Layer Protocol (SSL) is integral in most browsers and allows a secure connection to be set up between the customer and the retailer for the transmission of the payment messages. This reduces the potential for messages to be intercepted while in transit.

However misuse of the credit card details by the retailer or employee is not eliminated by such technology. The recent security breaches have occurred because of unauthorised access to customer details including credit card information stored on the retailer's server. Companies are storing customer data (with the customer's consent) in order to speed up the process of online purchasing. For example, Amazon's 1-click technology enables frequent customers simply to type in a password which will bring up all of their purchasing information rather than having to retype this information every time a purchase is made. As such information is particularly valuable and must be stored securely in order to avoid unauthorised access. Where a breach of security occurs this will not only knock consumer confidence but may also result in breach of the Data Protection Regulations.[77]

---

[77] Directive 1995/46/EC of the European Parliament and of the Council of 24 October 1995 on

To prevent misuse of credit card details by a third party or wrongful repudiation by the consumer the Secure Electronic Transaction Standard (SET) has been developed.[78] This uses public key encryption to ensure the secure transmission of the credit card details directly to the retailer's bank without being revealed to the retailer. The use of digital signatures also affirms that the consumer has authorised the payment and ensures the payment messages have not been changed during transmission. As a result of using this system, retailers and banks are protected from unauthorised purchases and consumers are protected from illegitimate use of their cards. However the system has not yet been fully exploited in business to consumer transactions.

Consumers using credit cards online are provided with a fairly high degree of protection. In the UK, if a credit card is used fraudulently then the consumer is liable only for the first £50 of loss before notifying the issuer (unless he or she has been grossly negligent);[79] it is the credit card company which pays for any further loss. In many instances the consumer may avoid paying even the first £50 as various online retailers such as Amazon offer to pay this amount if a consumer's card is fraudulently used as a result of using their web site. The EU Distance Selling Directive,[80] which is due to be implemented in the UK at the end of October 2000, will provide even greater protection. Where payment cards have been fraudulently used in a distance sale then the customer will be able to request cancellation of the payment and have all sums refunded. Therefore the consumer will not even be liable for the first £50. Consumers are given further protection in the UK under the Consumer Credit Act 1974, but it is not clear whether this protection applies to purchases from overseas retailers.

However although consumers are protected when using a credit card online the retailer may suffer loss where there is a fraudulent payment. In Europe credit card issuers often place the risk for 'cardholder not present' transactions with the retailer which means that they will lose the value of the payment if it is disputed by the customer. Although credit cards are currently the most popular method of online payment developing electronic cash technologies which minimise the risk for both retailers and customers may well take over in the future.

Retailers in the process of receiving payment online will be involved in the collection of certain data from a consumer. When collecting personal data with a view to processing it, the data protection regulations[81] will apply. These regula-

---

the protection of individuals with regard to the processing of personal data and on the free movement of such data. These have been implemented in the UK in the Data Protection Regulations 1998.

[78] This standard has been developed by Visa and MasterCard, in conjunction with Netscape.

[79] The Consumer Credit Act 1974.

[80] Directive on the Protection of Consumers in Respect of Distance Contracts, OJ L144, 4th June 1997.

[81] Directive 1995/46/EC of the European Parliament and of the Council of 24 October 1995 on the protection of individuals with regard to the processing of personal data and on the free movement of such data.

tions place certain restrictions on those processing data. The data collected must be adequate, relevant and not excessive in relation to the purposes for which it is collected. The person who collects the data is also required to register with the Data Protection Commissioner and specify the purposes for which the data is held.

The retailer must also comply with provisions in the Distance Selling Directive[82] on the delivery of goods or services to the customer. The Directive provides that performance of the contract must take place within 30 days. Even after the conclusion of the contract the Directive gives the consumer the right to withdraw from a contract within seven days without giving a reason and without incurring any penalty.[83] It is therefore clear that a business has to develop a policy to deal with returned goods.

As more and more business is taking place on the Internet and more consumers are using the Internet any business with a presence on the web is at a competitive advantage. By doing business online a retailer has access to a wider customer base at a lower cost. However access to a wider range of consumers on an international level may also give rise to a wider range of potential legal actions. As a result, although the Internet provides many advantages for businesses it also raises new legal difficulties, many of which have not yet been resolved. For this reason it is necessary for businesses to keep up to date with legal developments. If doing business in an international arena, a retailer needs to not only be aware of legal issues on a national level or within the European Union but also of the international aspect and the impact of policies such as ICANN.

Conclusion

Although this chapter has concentrated upon the impact of, and the legal issues surrounding, the use of the Internet by the sports apparel industry there are, of course, plenty of businesses that are not directly involved in sport but which seek to push their products through the creation of connections with the sports sector. Any company involved in sport sponsorship in this way would surely want to use the Internet to push their endorsements of sports and of particular athletes in the way that Nike, Reebok and the others have. Accordingly, it is not only those companies that are directly involved in the sports business that need to be aware of the relationship between sport, e-commerce and the law – and it is not only the issues that have been discussed in some detail here that they need to be aware of. For example, product endorsements are as much a source of potential income for the endorsing athletes themselves as they are for the company that makes them, and care has to be taken to ensure that the athletes' rights are not infringed. In the

---

[82] This will be implemented in the UK at the end of October.
[83] Article 6.

United States, the unauthorised commercial use of individuals' images (which decreases the revenue potential of their authorised endorsements) has led some celebrities to seek legal redress under US privacy laws. However, the US courts have determined that protecting an athlete's right to publicity does not necessarily take precedence over competing concerns, such as the public interest in the free flow of information via the news media

That said, the US courts have been willing to protect manifestations of athletes' identities other than their names or photographs, particularly when there is no 'public interest' defence that can legitimately be raised. In *Motschenbacher*,[84] the Ninth Circuit Court of Appeals held a cigarette commercial featuring the racing car of a well-known driver amounted to misappropriation of the driver, for it gave the impression that he endorsed that particular brand: the Court ruled that the car was, effectively, an extension of his identity. Similarly, in *Hirsch*,[85] a famous grid-iron football player with the nickname 'Crazylegs' sought to prevent a manufacturer of women's shaving gel from promoting 'Crazylegs Shaving Gel' on the ground that is was an appropriation of his image. The trial judge found against the player, but the Wisconsin Supreme Court held the fact that 'Crazylegs' was merely a nickname did not preclude a cause of action: 'all that is required is that the name clearly identifies the wronged person'.[86]

Despite the potential pitfalls of the company/athlete relationship and the other legal complexities alluded to in this chapter, and notwithstanding the relative tardiness of EU companies to embrace the World Wide Web, businesses in all sectors of the European Union economy have become *e*-businesses. Inevitably, innumerable companies with no obvious connection to sports have indeed sought to cash in on the marketing and sponsorship opportunities that sport affords, and they have sought to increase the product value of those links by way of an Internet presence. If businesses concerned with marketing and selling in long-established sectors such as sports apparel have benefited from this putative economic revolution, then firms in (for example) the tobacco, toiletries, brewing and insurance industries will appreciate that plugging their sports sponsorship on the Internet could contribute to their commercial success too. The demographics make sense, the European Commission is keen to facilitate electronic commerce and, gradually, a suitable legal framework is being put in place.

Finally, it should be pointed out that so far as the European Commission is concerned the Internet is merely 'a commodity that allows companies to compete – that is, to offer, sell, buy and (sometimes) distribute goods and services – in a different way.'[87] The concepts of electronic commerce and electronic business fa-

---

[84] Motschenbacher v RJ Reynolds Tobacco 489 F. 2d 821.
[85] Hirsch v S.C. Johnson & Son Ltd 90 NW 2d 379.
[86] Ibid. at 397.
[87] Urrutia B, *Internet and its effects on Competition* (2000), Paper delivered to the UIMP Workshop 10 July: http://europa.eu.int/comm/competition/speeches/text/sp2000_011_en.pdf.

cilitate those companies' attempts to make the most of that commodity, and this has brought about a parallel market – the virtual market – that operates in tandem with the traditional market. It should also be mentioned that, for the purposes of competition law, 'the Internet leads to the creation of two segments (i.e. physical and online) that belong to the same market.'[88] The Internet commercial sector is not a separate market in its own right.

---

[88] Ibid. at 3. Consider also the Commission's authorisation on April 23, 2000 of a joint venture between Amadeus and Terra, reported at http://www.cc.cec/rapid.

Part Three:
The Re-regulation of Football:
A Quest for Order

THE BATTLE FOR TV RIGHTS IN PROFESSIONAL FOOTBALL

Paul Spink and Philip Morris

INTRODUCTION

It has been said that professional sport is the new Hollywood. Both media darling and marketers' dream, sport has emerged as a powerful commercial force in its own right. Now a fully-fledged billion-pound industry, hitherto unchallenged practices are falling subject to serious legal scrutiny for the first time. In this chapter we examine the law relating to the sale of television rights for English Premier League football matches. The 1999 Office of Fair Trading challenge to the Premiership's exclusive BSkyB/BBC television deal[1] is critically assessed against the backdrop of domestic and European legal regimes and other recent developments in this fast-evolving sphere.

Phenomenal growth in the popularity of sport is a defining feature of the twentieth century. One consequence of this dramatic increase in participation and popular support has been the commercialisation of elite sport. Fuelled by the marketing budgets of corporate giants eager to exploit the burgeoning public interest in sport and in turn feeding a voracious mass media, which has itself undergone unprecedented growth in recent times, this sector is one of the fastest expanding in the commercial world. Moreover, one need only consider the spectacle of government-led campaigns waged for some distant right to host the Olympic Games or World Cup to appreciate that, even on the global socio-political stage, sport has become an important player.

Major sporting events and leading tournaments regularly unite millions of spectators through the medium of television. Attracting audiences of such magnitude and conferring all the prestige and positive associations of elite sport, first-rank events present unrivalled commercial opportunities, both for broadcasters and for those wishing to showcase brands or products.[2] The introduction of cable

---

[1] Re F.A. Premier League Ltd. Agreement Relating to the Supply of Services Facilitating the Broadcast of Premier League Football Matches, (Restrictive Practices Court, 28 July 1999).

[2] In particular, professional football attracts the young male viewer – a notoriously difficult consumer to isolate for marketing purposes.

A. Caiger and S. Gardiner (Eds), Professional Sport in the EU: Regulation and Re-regulation
© *2000, T.M.C.Asser Press, The Hague, The Netherlands*

and satellite services has increased the televised coverage of sporting events by more than 600% over the period 1988 to 1999. Sports programming now accounts for in excess of 13,000 hours of television output per year. Accordingly, it can come as no surprise that top sportsmen and women are among the highest paid and highest profile figures in the world. Formula One drivers can earn £20 million per year and boxers have won almost that much for a single fight. Star footballers trade for eight-figure sums and command wages of over £40,000 per week, win or lose, play or not. Tennis players and golfers alike may earn an average lifetime's salary for winning one competition, while international athletes compete for diamonds and gold bars.

All this is to say nothing of the lucrative sponsorship and endorsement contracts underpinned by television exposure. Michael Jordan was paid $3.9 million for playing basketball in 1995, but he earned ten times more for putting his name to commercial products.[3] In 1997 Tiger Woods closed marketing deals worth around $100m, putting his name to an array of consumer products, including sports apparel, luxury watches and soft drinks.[4] Those, who like Jordan and Woods, have achieved excellence in the pursuit of a mainstream sport, are far from representative of the wider industry; but it is indicative of the financial power of sport, or rather its new bedfellows, that such rewards can be lavished on star performers. Promoted by a symbiotic circle of commercial and media interests, the sports industry now accounts for around 3% of gross global product, and has already achieved broad parity with the oil and motor industries.

FOOTBALL: THE PRICE OF COMMERCIAL SUCCESS

In Europe, the greatest beneficiary of this socio-economic phenomenon has been professional football. The elite game has reaped vast riches in recent years, but there has been a price to pay. The growing commercial significance of professional football has ensured the unwelcome attention and intervention of the law. As in other spheres in which legal regulation has encroached on hitherto untrammelled social fields, the juridification of sport has attracted considerable academic comment in recent years.[5] The celebrated *Bosman* case is a good example.[6] In this 1995 ruling, the wider ramifications of which still appear to elude many involved with the game, players were found to enjoy the right of free

---

[3] In the same year Jack Nicklaus earned $0.6 million for playing golf, but was paid over $14 million for endorsements.

[4] Nation's top-name marketers have golf's Tiger fixed in their sights *The Detroit News*, April 15, 1997.

[5] Gardiner S et al., *Sports Law* (1998) London, Cavendish, 67-70.

[6] Case C-415/93 URBSFA v Jean-Marc Bosman [1996] All ER (EC) 97. See Morris, Spink and Morrow, EC Law and Professional Football: *Bosman* and its Implications (1996) 59 *Modern Law Review* 893.

movement accorded to all European Union workers by the Treaty of Rome. The European Court of Justice ruled that professional footballers, their clubs, and national and international football associations should be treated as ordinary economic actors, subject to the full protection and discipline of EC law.

From a virtual standing start in the mid-1990s, by 1999 the European Commission had opened investigations into more than 60 sport-related cases. Most of these cases involve football and most were triggered by complaints over television broadcasting rights. In April 1999, in what is perhaps the most widely publicised case of its kind, the nascent UK Competition Commission intervened to disallow British Sky Broadcasting plc's ('BSkyB's') bid for Manchester United on competition grounds.[7] In another recent, high profile decision the Office of Fair Trading ordered football clubs and manufacturers to refrain from imposing minimum resale prices on replica football kits.[8]

Nowhere has commercial pressure and legal scrutiny been more keenly felt than in the boardrooms of English FA Premier League football clubs. One of the most important and contentious issues to confront the domestic game in recent years has been the mechanism governing the distribution of the rights to televise matches. Indeed, the FA Premiership was born out of the desire of leading clubs to achieve a more lucrative exploitation of television rights. The prospect of greatly enhanced revenues from television contracts was a major inducement; probably *the* single most important factor, in persuading clubs in the old first division of the Football League to sign up to the new Premier League.[9] The market for television rights was transformed by the emergence of satellite broadcasters in the late 1980s. Whereas the broadcasting rights in respect of live league football for the 1987-88 season were sold for £3.1 million, in 1996 BSkyB and the BBC signed a four-year deal worth a combined £743 million.[10] Season for season, the 1996 contract is worth sixty times more than the 1987/88 settlement. By the 1997/98 season, the earnings generated by television coverage accounted for approximately 26% of the total income of the Premiership.[11] The sale of television rights now delivers a revenue stream second only in importance to gate income, the significance of which is in relative decline despite attendance growth and spiralling ticket prices.[12] Given that an increasing number of fans, especially family

---

[7] Detailed discussion of this bid features below.

[8] 6 August 1999: http://www.oft.gov.uk/html/rsearch/press-no/pn30-99.htm.

[9] See *Re F.A. Premier League Ltd.*, supra n. 1. para 21.

[10] Sky paid £670 million for the rights to broadcast live matches and the BBC paid £73 million for the rights to broadcast recorded higlights.

[11] Boon G (ed), *England's Premier Clubs, A Review of 1998 results* (1998) Manchester, Deloitte & Touche, 12.

[12] Attendances grew by 2.3% and ticket prices by 12.5% over the 1997/98 season. Some clubs have dramatically increased prices – a Chelsea FC season ticket has increased in price by 200 per cent in the last three years: 'Supporters face hike in prices at Chelsea', *Electronic Telegraph*, February 17, 1998.

groups, are being priced out of stadia, the full exploitation of the television market will inevitably take on even greater significance.[13]

Television money has fuelled the growth of the Premier League throughout the 1990s and far from abating, it seems that the advent of Pay-per-View ('PPV') TV will further, and possibly greatly enhance the profitability of broadcast rights. Moreover, this is only one of a number of ways in which the medium makes a contribution to the game's 'bottom line'. By increasing the public profile of football and the accessibility of matches, television coverage facilitates the maintenance of a widely dispersed fan-base[14] and underpins other important revenue streams feeding the game, including commercial sponsorship, merchandising, and ground advertising.

Whether or not recent attempts by major broadcasters to build themselves share portfolios in leading clubs ultimately come to fruition,[15] the commercial interests of the Premiership and its television paymasters are already inextricably linked. Broadcasters, and BSkyB in particular, have repackaged and rebuilt the Premier League brand. Television has injected the capital that has attracted 'star' players from overseas and financed ground development, making the Premier League product the envy of the world. The sport now benefits from high quality, innovative coverage that is commensurate with its new-found status and market appeal. However, this is not philanthropic endeavour on the part of the media: its investment has been handsomely repaid. As Griffith-Jones puts it: 'this marriage between sport and television is one made in heaven.'[16] It has long been recognised that the ability to offer premium sports channels is essential to the development of a successful pay-TV business. On the formation of the Premier League in 1992, Rupert Murdoch's BSkyB paid £191.5 million to secure the exclusive rights to screen live Premiership matches for five seasons.[17] It later emerged that Murdoch was prepared to pay almost twice that vast sum, and this is indicative of the importance he placed on the deal.[18] In his 1996 report on BSkyB's position in the pay-TV market, the Director General of Fair Trading concluded that premium sports programming is a main driver of subscription to pay-TV.[19] In the same year, in his address to the AGM of News Corporation,

---

[13] 'FSA blame greed as gates drop,' *Electronic Telegraph*, September 2, 1999.

[14] Half of Manchester United's 200+ supporters' clubs are located overseas. They are based as far afield as Mauritius, Japan and New Zealand. *United*, the club's monthly publication, reportedly sells around 40,000 copies per issue in Thailand (in Thai): *BSkyB's bid for Manchester United: Potential impact on competition*, Independent Manchester United Supporters Association, September 29, 1998: http://www.imusa.org/libraryc/ oftsub2.htm.

[15] BSkyB aims to get onside with football clubs, *The Times*, August 11, 1999.

[16] Griffith-Jones D, *Law and the Business of Sport* (1997) London: Butterworths, 289.

[17] The BBC paid £22 million for the rights to show highlights over the same period.

[18] Conn D, *The Football Business: Fair Game in the '90s?* (1997) Edinburgh, Mainstream Publishing, 21.

[19] The Director General's Review of BSkyB's Position in the Wholesale Pay TV Market, (Office of Fair Trading, December 1996).

which is the major shareholder in BSkyB, Murdoch himself confirmed this finding. He stated:

> 'We have the long term rights in most countries to major sporting events and we will be doing in Asia what we intend to elsewhere in the world – that is use sports as a "battering ram" and a lead offering in all our pay television operations.'[20]

BSkyB's profitability was transformed after it acquired the rights to Premiership football. The satellite broadcaster turned a £47 million loss in 1992 into profits of £62 million in 1993, £170 million in 1994, £237 million in 1995, £315 million in 1996 and £374 million in 1997. Over the same period an increase in turnover of more than 300% was achieved.[21] Although a number of factors were instrumental in producing this impressive performance (including in particular BSkyB's near monopoly in major film premiers), it is clear that the 'pulling-power' of its premium sports channel substantially contributed to the company's success.

The BSkyB/BBC Deal

In August 1992 the Premier League granted BSkyB the exclusive rights to televise Premier League matches during the seasons 1992/93 to 1996/97. The BBC secured the exclusive rights to televise recorded highlights of Premier League matches (up to 35 minutes per game) over the same period. In 1996 new agreements extended these arrangements in similar terms to the end of the 2000/01 season. In this matter the Board of the Premier League is empowered to negotiate and contract on behalf of its member clubs by virtue of rules contained in its constitution. Two aspects of these arrangements are *prima facie* anti-competitive:

– *Exclusivity*: the grant of exclusive rights is restrictive of competition. Such agreements, particularly those extending over a long period or wide area, are typically prohibited unless rigorous criteria are satisfied.
– *Collectivity*: a cartel exists where competing firms substitute co-operation for independent competitive action. By presenting a collective face to broadcasters, Premier League clubs engage in behaviour that may fall into this category.

Negotiating TV Rights: The Legal Environment

Competition law, which not so very long ago comprised a fairly unobtrusive and low profile regulatory sector, has risen to prominence in recent years. In the 1990s this period of rapid growth coincided with the deeper and wider commercialisation of sport. As a consequence, although not quite *terra incognita*

---

[20] BSkyB's bid for Manchester United: Potential impact on competition, supra n. 8.
[21] See Conn, supra n. 18, 21.

for competition lawyers,[22] professional football began to attract the close attention of enforcement agencies at home and abroad for the first time. There is an
argument to the effect that professional sport is a quasi-commercial activity,
which incorporates important socio-cultural elements, and that as such it should
be exempt from competition law and indeed from certain other aspects of economic regulation, including the free movement provisions of the Treaty of Rome.

In the past, similar calls have attracted little political or judicial support. The
protestations of football's governing bodies seem, in today's climate, a little
jaded. A certain 'hard-nosed' commercial cynicism has infected the professional
game and the indications are that sympathy for those eager to plead a special case
for football is evaporating fast. In addition to the UK challenge featured below,
across Europe a number of national competition authorities are currently examining football and the sale of TV rights. In the context of this discussion it is therefore pertinent to consider the basic legal frameworks within which any TV deal
must be struck.

The United Kingdom Competition Framework

The United Kingdom competition regime has recently undergone extensive reform. Under the old system, ostensibly anti-competitive agreements are policed
under procedures established by the Restrictive Trade Practices Act 1976
(RTPA), while monopolistic abuses are subject to investigation under the Fair
Trading Act 1973 and the Competition Act 1980. It is necessary to register agreements falling within the RTPA at the Office of Fair Trading ('OFT').[23] The Director General of Fair Trading ('DGFT') is empowered to refer *prima facie* anti-
competitive agreements to the Restrictive Practices Court ('RPC'), which can
strike down any agreement held to be contrary to the public interest. It is important to stress that a balanced view is taken and socio-economic factors are influential. A 'rule of reason' US-style approach is adopted in this regard. Even where
anti-competitive behaviour is manifest, if it can be shown that the public interest
is best served by acquiescence, due perhaps to the existence of some significant
advantage or benefit exclusively associated with the agreement's survival, no
prohibitive action will be taken.

For many years this system had been criticised as impotent and unwieldy. In
response to these concerns, the Competition Act 1998 introduced a much sharper
anti-restrictive practices mechanism, bringing domestic competition law into
alignment with the existing European Union regime.[24] The Act, the main provisions of which came into force on 1 March 2000, contains cogent, 'effects-based'
prohibitions on anti-competitive agreements and abuses of market dominance.

---

[22] See Eastham v Newcastle United FC [1963] 3 All ER 139.
[23] Maintained under section 1(2) RTPA 1976.
[24] See Frazer T, The Competition Bill in the House of Lords (1998) 3 *Amicus Curiae* 7.

Most of the old law is repealed by the 1998 Act, although certain key elements of the Fair Trading Act 1973 have been retained. The 1998 Act also establishes the Competition Commission. This body assumed the role and functions of the Monopolies and Mergers Commission on 1 April 1999. It will also hear appeals against decisions made by the DGFT under the prohibition provisions of the new Act. Under the 1998 Act, as from 1 March 2000, it will be in the gift of the Director General to impose fines not exceeding 10% of the turnover of the undertaking in question in the preceding business year.[25] The new system is discussed in more detail below.

The EC Competition Framework

It is difficult to overstate the importance of the competition provisions of the Treaty of Rome in the legal order of the European Union. Competition law played a lead role in the early days of the Community and grew in significance as a key component of the Single Market project during the 1980s and 1990s. The guardian and enforcer of EU competition policy is the European Commission, specifically Directorate General IV (DG IV). DG IV is, *inter alia*, entrusted with the application of Article 81 of the Treaty of Rome, which prohibits anti-competitive agreements, and Article 82, which bans abuse of market dominance.[26] Both prohibitions are generally drawn and purposively applied. However in each case it is necessary to demonstrate that an agreement has the potential to affect trade between Member States.

At first sight, the latter requirement appears to exclude the Commission from interference in the domestic sale of English Premiership TV rights. Moreover, the doctrine of subsidiarity, which is set out in Article 5 of the Treaty,[27] dictates that the EU must refrain from taking action where the objectives of that action can be sufficiently achieved by the Member State itself. This appears to lend further support to the conclusion that the Commission is unlikely to intervene in the domestic distribution of Premiership TV rights, especially in light of the UK's new Competition Act, which implements in all material aspects, the Community regime and cures the relative deficiencies of the previous system.

However, the agreements under review impact upon both the United Kingdom and the Republic of Ireland, where there is substantial demand for television coverage of Premiership matches. Given that the key provisions of the agreement encompass two Member States, and thus an element of inter-state commerce, it is, in theory at least, easy to justify Commission intervention. The agreements also provide for the Premier League to market its television rights overseas. There is considerable interest in the Premier League on the continent of Europe and sev-

---

[25] Section 36(8) Competition Act 1998.
[26] Renumbered by the Amsterdam Treaty (ex Arts 85 and 86).
[27] Ex Article 3b.

eral foreign broadcasters have secured exclusive contracts. These may also be referable to DG IV.

Even in the absence of this cross-border factor, if for example Ireland was written out of some future deal in an attempt to evade Article 81, in practice the requirement to show that an act may affect trade between Member States poses a relatively low hurdle. DG IV seldom needs to adduce much evidence to satisfy this condition and enforcement action is rarely hampered by the assertion that a case encompasses insufficient 'Community interest'.[28] Although *prima facie* confined, or largely confined, to a single Member State, commercially significant agreements and abuses of a dominant position may nevertheless qualify for prohibition where an indirect, 'ripple' effect on inter-state trade is evident, or even where a bare potential for disruption or distortion in normal intra-Community trade flows can be identified. The European Court has endorsed a purposive interpretation of this condition in a number of cases.[29] It is highly probable that collective negotiation for the exclusive distribution of Premiership TV rights produces the kind of cross-border effects on, or at least negative implications for, inter-state trade that might trigger enforcement action.

The other criteria that serve to qualify action for DG IV investigation also merit brief discussion. There is no difficulty in inferring that professional sport, and especially football, qualifies as a trade for the purposes of competition law. In this context, 'trade' is an expansively defined concept and it cannot be seriously disputed that professional clubs engage in economic activity.[30] Given that the television rights to Premiership football matches constitute a product, it is a short step to infer that a cartel may be formed by individual producers, or clubs, for the purposes of its exclusive distribution. This form of activity may qualify for prohibition under Article 81 or under Article 82 if collective dominance, or a complex monopoly is identified.[31] Indeed, exclusivity is in general terms offensive to competition policy *per se*. Most single-state agreements previously found to infringe Article 81 or 82 have concerned cooperatives or price-fixing schemes that have served to compartmentalise a national market.[32] There is no reason to believe that a collective deal over television rights would elude Commission scrutiny.

In passing, its worth noting that UEFA Statutes have made provision to regulate the showing of football matches on television in countries affiliated to UEFA. These regulations prohibit the cross-border transmission of football

---

[28] See, *inter alia*, Comm. Dec. 90/38 Bayo-n-ox [1990] 1 C.E.C 2066.

[29] Case 56/65 Société Technique Minière v Maschinenbau Ulm GmbH [1965] ECR 235.

[30] See Boon, n. 11 supra.

[31] Although fairly unusual in the scheme of things, it would be a short step to infer the existence of collective dominance in the circumstances of a professional football league: Commission Decision Re Italian Flat Glass [1989] OJ L33/44.

[32] See, *inter alia*, Case 8/72 Vereeniging van Cementhandelaren v Commission [1972] ECR 977; Case T-66/89 Publishers Association v Commission (No.2) [1992] ECR II-1995.

matches during weekly time windows in which fixtures are typically played (e.g. Saturday afternoons) in an attempt to ensure that broadcasts do not have an adverse effect on ground attendances.[33] The rules have been notified to DG IV in the hope of securing an exemption under Article 81; but at the time of writing the Commission has served a Statement of Objections on UEFA, which is the first step in what may become a formal challenge to their validity.

THE OFFICE OF FAIR TRADING CHALLENGE

The Office of Fair Trading began its investigation into the sale of Premiership TV rights in 1992 when it received particulars of the initial five-year BSkyB/ BBC deal (1992/93-1996/97), which was referable to the OFT under the provisions of the RTPA 1976. After lengthy consideration, much to the consternation of the overwhelming majority of those involved with the game, the Director General of Fair Trading referred the matter to the RPC in February 1996. This was not the first time the OFT intervened in the distribution of rights to broadcast football matches. In 1979 the OFT acted on competition grounds against a contract under which London Weekend Television secured exclusive rights to broadcast recorded highlights of all the then Football League matches. The matter was compromised by an agreement under which Independent Television ('ITV') and the BBC entered into a joint contract with the Football League. This arrangement survived in one form or another until ITV secured a unilateral four-year deal in 1988.

In regard to the 1992 and 1996 BSkyB/BBC deals, the key terms of which are similar in material respects, the DGFT argued that, by agreeing to sell their rights collectively, Premier League clubs are acting as a cartel. As a consequence, the Premiership has effectively eliminated price competition, restricted supply and consumer choice in a manner that would not be permitted in any other industry. One issue caused the OFT particular concern. The agreements provide that, of the 380 Premier League matches played per season, only 60 (about 16%) will actually be televised live on BSkyB. The rights granted to Sky give the broadcaster a free hand to select its matches from the entire Premier League programme, subject to certain stipulations. The BBC's broadcasting rights are restricted to recorded highlights of any Premier League match not chosen for live broadcasting by BSkyB. The programme *Match of the Day* typically features extended highlights (of 20 to 30 minutes' duration) of two selected matches, and limited highlights consisting of goals scored and notable incidents in the other games. The DGFT asserted that these arrangements result in much unsatisfied consumer demand and unreasonably prevent clubs from marketing untelevised games elsewhere. Moreover, it was submitted that the consequent restriction in supply al-

---

[33] Article 14/44 of the UEFA Statutes.

lows prices to be maintained at higher levels than might otherwise be achievable in a competitive market. The entailed prohibition on club participation in matches and competitions not authorised by the Premier League was deemed to restrict choice and stifle innovation to the further detriment of consumers. At the outset of the case Director General John Bridgeman said:

> 'Developments in broadcasting have intensified the importance of sport in the market for television programmes. Within that market the Premier League has a major, if not unique, position. By selling rights collectively and exclusively to the highest bidder it is acting as a cartel. The net effect of cartels is to inflate costs and prices. Any other business acting in this way would be subject to competition law and I see no reason why the selling of sports coverage should be treated differently.'[34]

These concerns were exacerbated by the fact that BSkyB was deemed to enjoy a dominant position in the supply of sports channels in the UK. BSkyB's monopoly over Premier League rights, coupled with the lack of other broadcasters in this important field, was thought likely to harm competition, prejudice consumers and damage the development of broadcasting generally. In this regard the introduction of digital television[35] and the arrival of PPV (which is more suited to cable than satellite) is set to revolutionise the market. The ownership of premium sports rights is likely to become an increasingly important factor in commercial success as these innovations entrench themselves. It is arguable that the intervening technological developments have both raised the stakes and to some extent shifted the goalposts of the OFT's seven-year investigation. The successful market entry of ONdigital has now diluted the power of BSkyB and will certainly have a dramatic impact on any future inquiry.

The RPC hearing commenced in January 1999. Over the course of the proceedings, which lasted six months, it was for the parties to the agreements to show that the restrictions they contained did not adversely affect the public interest. Confronted by a complex web of contracts and a large amount of documentary evidence, the presiding judge, Ferris J, deemed it appropriate to limit proceedings to a consideration of certain specific provisions of the registered agreements. Those conditions reserved for the scrutiny of the court are summarised below:

– The restriction by which member clubs confer on the Premier League the exclusive right to grant licences to broadcast on television the Premier League matches and accept an obligation not to grant licences for that purpose themselves;
– The restriction arising from the fact that the Premier League has granted to Sky until the end of the 2000/01 season the exclusive licence to broadcast sixty Premier League matches live during each season and has agreed not to

---

[34] 6 February 1996, see: http://www.oft.gov.uk/html/new/football.htm.
[35] First used by BSkyB in October 1998.

grant to any other person a licence to make live broadcasts of any other Premier League matches;

- The restriction arising from the fact that the Premier League has granted to the BBC until the end of the 2000/01 season the exclusive right to broadcast recorded highlights of Premier League matches and has agreed not to grant to any other person a licence to make any recorded broadcast of the Premier League matches;
- Certain supplemental restrictions affecting the freedom of the Premier League clubs to engage in competitions other than the Premier League competitions or friendly matches.

It was for the court to declare whether or not any of these restrictions are contrary to the public interest. In this regard its discretion is not unfettered. By section 19 of the RTPA 1976, all relevant restrictions[36] are to be deemed contrary to the public interest unless the court is satisfied both:

- that the restriction passes through one of a number of specified 'gateways'; and
- that the restriction is not unreasonable having regard to the balance between the circumstances which enable it to pass through a gateway and any detriment arising or likely to arise from the operation of the restriction.

Of the eight gateways specified in section 19, two were pivotal to the present case.[37] These are expressed in the following terms:

'(b) ... that removal of the restriction ... would deny to the public as users of any services... specific and substantial benefits or advantages ... enjoyed ... by virtue of the restriction or any arrangements or operations resulting therefrom.

(h) ... that the restriction does not directly or indirectly restrict or discourage competition to any material degree in any relevant trade or industry and is not likely to do so.'

Analysis of the Restrictive Clauses

The court proceeded to consider whether all or any of the alleged restrictions set out above were relevant restrictions for the purposes of the 1976 Act. Although subsequent TV deals are likely to be analysed under the regime established by the Competition Act 1998, the same key issues will require to be resolved and Ferris J's approach offers some useful pointers towards future judicial practice.

It was argued that the obligations incorporated in the BSkyB and BBC contracts could not be regarded as restrictions because, rather than denying any pre-existing freedom, their observance in fact facilitates the creation of new commer-

---

[36] See below.
[37] Gateways (b), (g) and (h).

cial opportunities.[38] The concept that an obligation must involve 'the closing of a door that was previously open' if it is to be regarded as a restriction first emerged in *Re Telephone Apparatus Manufacturers' Application*,[39] and has been applied consistently under the 1976 Act. The court upheld this principle, although it is questionable whether the rule would survive the purposive application of either Article 81 EC or the new UK regime modelled on it. However, on the facts, Ferris J was not convinced that any new opportunity had been created by compliance with the restrictions contained in the Premier League regulations. In the absence of the said restrictions, any two clubs could sell the television rights to a match played between them at a ground owned or controlled by one of them without the concurrence of any other party. This conclusion is somewhat tenuous, given that the marketability of the product is largely derived from its status as a Premier League match, but in the view of Ferris J:

> 'It would be strange if parties could, by forming an organisation governed by themselves, subject themselves to an anti-competitive regime prescribed by the rules of the organisation and then claim that they have not individually accepted restrictions because they are not entitled to trade within the area to which the regime applies except subject to the restrictive provisions of that regime.'[40]

Exclusivity

As to the question of the exclusive nature of the respective deals, it was argued in the abstract that the owner of TV rights will aim to sell them on an exclusive basis to maximise the price obtained and that broadcasters will naturally seek exclusive rights to maximise the audience they attract. It is clear that pay-TV companies, such as BSkyB, can only attract subscribers, who always have the option of free-to-air television, by offering a unique and attractive product. The need for broadcasters generally, and pay-TV companies in particular, to differentiate their programming in order to compete effectively arguably invalidates conventional economic thinking on the undesirability of exclusivity. It may be that exclusivity, and the certainties which result from the present system for the central selling of television rights, foster, rather than impede, competition between broadcasters. In this respect, the court invested considerable effort in the assessment of other scenarios, including the potential of multiple non-exclusive deals, and the tensions created by the competing interests of pay and free-to-air TV.

The current system generates various anomalies. Where a sports event is filmed by its organiser, the copyright in the film can be licensed to a broadcaster

---

[38] (1963) LR 3RP 462.

[39] See for example: Re Ravenself Properties Ltd's Application, [1978] 1QB52

[40] Re F.A. Premier League Ltd, supra n. 2, para 5.

on an exclusive basis. Furthermore, where an event is organised by a single promoter at a venue he controls it is permissible for the broadcaster to be given exclusive rights. Ferris J accepted the existence of aberrant legal principle, but was not persuaded that this justified the form of exclusivity under review *per se*, which restricts the conduct of multiple parties[41] and not merely individual undertakings. Generated by the technical, formalistic approach of the 1976 Act, these irregularities should be cured by the entry into force of the Competition Act 1998.

Given that an exclusive agreement is *prima facie* anti-competitive, it is important to ensure that all aspects are capable of justification and that none will be construed as excessive. Tactically, it is useful to be able to point to some dilution of exclusivity, and in this sense the participation of the BBC, which guarantees a minimum level of free-to-air terrestrial coverage, is an important element of the Premiership's current TV contracts. In *German Film Producers*,[42] the European Commission granted exemption under Article 85 EC,[43] in respect of an agreement giving a German television network exclusive access to MGM films for a period of 15 years, after provision for short periods of access by other broadcasters was built into the licence.

That said, it would be rash to conclude that an exclusive 15-year grant of sports rights would be 'nodded through' by the European authorities on the ground that some concessions on access had been agreed. Generally speaking, only exclusive licences of a short-term nature will be tolerated and it will often be necessary to show at least that the grant of exclusivity itself is the product of a free and competitive bidding system. While holding the post of EU Competition Commissioner,[44] Karel Van Miert indicated that a grant of exclusive television rights will not necessarily contravene Community competition rules given the special characteristics of the sports broadcasting market. He conceded that, 'exclusivity is normally an appropriate means of maintaining the value of television programmes in terms of viewing figures and advertising revenues which they can attract.'[45] However, Van Miert proceeded to stress that the competition regime would be applied to prohibit agreements on exclusive television rights, which are excessive in their scope or duration. This position was subsequently endorsed by the Commission in 1993 in *Eurovision*, which involved a collective of public broadcasters, and the European Court of Justice has indicated that the grant of single-state exclusivity is not objectionable *per se*.[46]

---

[41] See Re F.A. Premier League Ltd, supra n. 1, paras 177-182.
[42] OJ L284 3/10/89.
[43] Now Article 81 EC.
[44] From 1993 to 1999.
[45] OJ 1989 L284/36.
[46] Case 262/81 Coditel SA v. Ciné-Vog Films SA [1983] 1 CMLR 49.

In *Coditel*[47] the ECJ ruled that the national court is obliged to determine whether the exercise of an exclusive right creates artificial, unjustified barriers, having regard to the requirements of the television industry. The possibility of royalties exceeding a fair remuneration for the price paid made must also be taken into account. Moreover, the Court reiterated the fact that the central question is whether the duration and geographical scope of an exclusive right is excessive in the circumstances and in view of the overarching aim to preserve effective competition within the Community.[48] In Commissioner Van Miert's opinion, the four-year term of the current BSkyB/BBC deal is unwarranted.[49] He warned that any exclusive television contract of more than one year in duration would be scrutinised by DG IV, commenting that significantly longer periods of exclusivity could only be justified where the relevant sporting events take place at longer intervals, such as the Olympic Games. This approach is consonant with the line taken by the European Parliament in its 1996 resolution on the broadcasting of sports events.[50] As discussed below, in the domestic arena the OFT is bound to take its lead from this line of policy under the Competition Act 1998.

Collectivity of Rights

An important part of the case advanced by the OFT was that the Premier League acts as a cartel over the distribution of television rights, and that this produces anti-competitive effects contrary to the public interest. The Premier League's argument that its annual change in membership by virtue of the relegation/promotion system prevents its classification as a cartel can be dismissed at the outset as lacking any foundation in law. The relevant provisions of UK and EC competition law should comfortably accommodate the activities of a group with a fluctuating membership.[51] Given that there is no minimum temporal requirement necessary to define a cartel there is no reason why a single football season, over which membership would be static, should not suffice in any event. Moreover, it is certainly true that the Premier League rules convert the Premier League Board into a monopoly supplier of the rights and facilities necessary for the broadcast of League matches. Basic tenets of competition policy dictate that a monopolist may restrict output in order to maximise his profits, and that consumers will consequently pay more and receive less than they wish from a restricted choice. The Premier League has publicly stated that it seeks to 'secure the best price for rights' and 'maximise the value of the rights' and has acknowledged that without the collective sale of rights a lower price would be realised. The OFT highlighted these statements in arguing that the collective deal should therefore be deemed a

---

[47] Ibid.

[48] For an interesting commentary on these issues see Conn, supra n. 18.

[49] Blowing the whistle on sports deals, *BBC Online Network News*, February 25, 1999.

[50] OJ C166/109, 10/6/96.

[51] See Case 45/85 Verband der Sachversicherer v Commission [1987] ECR 405.

cartel designed to extract a higher price than would otherwise be obtainable under normal competitive conditions.

In broad terms these submissions are fundamentally sound, but it is interesting to put this analysis in a wider setting. In the aftermath of the Hillsborough disaster in 1989 the Taylor Report recommended a move to all-seater stadiums.[52] Mindful of the high cost of implementing this recommendation, Taylor LJ suggested:

'In particular I would expect the football authorities to seek the highest possible price for television rights ... The television companies know that football on the screen has a vast following. They should be expected to pay a substantial price for the rights to relay popular matches.'[53]

This amounts to a cogent public interest argument in defence of the current collective system, although it will hereafter diminish in significance because the requirements of the Taylor Report have now largely been met within the Premier League.[54] It could be said that the OFT's orthodox approach, which is based on the standard producer cartel, should not be invoked in the analysis of a collective licensing agreement. The OFT argument fails to take account of the fact that the Premier League's product, namely the league competition and matches that comprise it, is produced by the collective endeavour of its member clubs. In an ordinary producer cartel, involving individual producers of a homogenous product, co-operation typically removes the incentive to innovate or compete on price or quality. While such negative implications typically justify regulatory intervention in those particular circumstances, they have no bearing on the case in point. The value of the television rights in any particular match is largely dependent on the perceived value of, and interest in, the Premier League championship itself. In one sense, collective licensing is justified by the fact that it is a fully collective process that derives the product.

In a similar vein, the assertion that the Premier League is restricting output in a cynical attempt to maximise price is somewhat weak. BSkyB has made it clear that it would like to acquire the right to broadcast live more than the current limit of 60 matches. During negotiations for the 1997/2001 deal, a figure of 90 matches was proposed. It is obvious that BSkyB or any other broadcaster would be prepared to pay more for a larger number of matches. The average amount received per match may be lower, but the total amount received would be greater. Given that the extra cost to the Premier League in permitting additional access to

---

[52] *The Hillsborough Stadium Disaster*, Final Report of an Inquiry by the Rt. Hon Lord Justice Taylor, January 1990, Cm 962.

[53] Ibid. para 117.

[54] Over the period 1991/98 a total of £692 million was spent on improving stadia by English League clubs. This includes expenditure of £459 million by the Premier League: see Boon G (ed), *Deloitte & Touche Annual Review of Football Finance*, (1999) Manchester: Deloitte & Touche, 80.

the broadcaster is minimal, there is no apparent profit-motive in restricting supply. In rebuttal, the OFT might point to the fact that the League has capped the number of televised matches with a view to maximising ground attendances, in an effort to ensure an optimal balance between these two important revenue streams.

Televised Football and Attendance at Live Matches

There is a widespread belief, not substantiated with rigorous research however, that the showing of games on television diminishes attendance at live matches and from the Premiership's perspective, if collective selling were outlawed, there would be no means of controlling the number of matches shown on television. In terms of its impact on gate receipts, a significant increase in the number of matches televised would be likely to intensify the polarisation of wealth and consequently power within the game, damaging smaller, weaker clubs and favouring the best supported. The match atmosphere and wider appeal of the game may also be adversely affected if television coverage tempts a higher proportion of fans out of the stadia.[55]

Ferris J was presented with research indicating that just over 50% of the games covered by BSkyB delivered ground attendances lower than the average for the home club. At first glance this would seem to prove a strong effect, given that other than where BSkyB is forced to act in fulfilment of minimum contractual conditions,[56] most of the matches selected by the broadcaster constitute the pick of the weekly fixture list. However, it is submitted that the real factor at play in this instance is not that the match is *televised*, but that most of the matches selected for television are *rescheduled* to take place either on a Sunday afternoon or a Monday evening. Obviously, many fans organise their lives around the traditional Saturday afternoon fixture and Monday matches in particular are likely to see a fall in attendance due, for example, to the work commitments of fans and the logistics of away travel. It is pertinent to note that the wholesale introduction of PPV television could have a much more serious effect on gate receipts, and especially season ticket sales, than the occasional broadcasting of a club's matches made possible under the current arrangements. That said, the facility for 'electronic attendance' or the 'virtual season ticket' has the potential to address most of the problems identified above and should provide a new revenue stream that more than compensates for the loss of gate income sustained.

---

[55] When BBC Scotland first televised the Scottish Cup Final in 1955, transmission was subject to 80 per cent of the tickets having been sold: Boyle R and Haynes R, The Grand Old Game: Football, Media and Identity in Scotland (1996) 18 *Media Culture and Society* 549.

[56] Every club must feature in at least one televised match per season: see Re F.A. Premier League Ltd, supra n. 1, para 235.

The Distribution of Television Income

Of all the arguments raised in defence of collectivity, probably the most cogent, in both legal and practical terms, relates to the fact that the current system facilitates an efficient and equitable redistribution of funds. Under the existing arrangements, before any money is distributed to Premier League clubs, a 'top slice' of television income is taken to finance payments to various external organisations. In the 1997/8 season £5 million was paid to the Football League for youth development, £5 million was paid to the Football Trust for ground improvements and the Professional Footballers' Association received £7.5 million.[57] The rules also provide for 'parachute payments' to recently relegated clubs. These amounted to £7.5 million in the 1997/98 season.[58] The remainder of television income is allocated according to the following formula:

- 50% equally between member clubs;
- 25% between member clubs in shares calculated by reference to their final position in the Premier League competition; and
- 25% between the clubs whose matches are shown on television, home and away clubs receiving an equal share.

Over the 1997/98 season this formula resulted in total payments ranging between £9.71 million to Arsenal (who finished first, with 12 BSkyB and 14 BBC appearances) and £4.26 million to Barnsley (who finished nineteenth, with 3 BSkyB and 5 BBC appearances).[59] This system is more egalitarian than most currently operating in Europe. However, it should be remembered that until 1986 television income in England was shared equally among all member clubs of the Football League, and that a much stronger redistributive mechanism survived until the establishment of the Premiership in 1992.[60]

Evaluating the Benefits of Collective Selling and Exclusive Rights

The collective selling of television rights is likely to achieve a higher price than the individual selling of those rights. It is argued that central selling derives an additional financial benefit to clubs, which in turn may be invested in stadia, facilities, youth development programmes and better players, all to the advantage of the football 'consumer'. It is certainly true that broadcasters put a premium on the administrative certainties and simplicity entailed in a collective deal. There

---

[57] These external payments combined represent approximately 11.5 per cent of total domestic television income for the 1997/98 season.

[58] See Boon, supra n. 11, 14.

[59] For a complete breakdown of the distribution of television revenue for the 1997/98 season see Boon, supra n. 11, 14.

[60] Morrow S, *The New Business of Football: Accountability and Finance in Football* (1999) London, Macmillan Business, 17.

are many reasons for this. A broadcaster needs to be able to schedule matches to its preferred peak-time slots and, week on week, to maintain balance and regularity in its schedule. If clubs were required to make their own deals it is likely that four or five different pay-TV and free-to-air broadcasters would jostle to secure a portfolio of rights and the situation would be confused by multiple asymmetrical contracts. This would increase the risk of 'head to head' competing broadcasts and fixtures would be scattered across the week. This in turn would make it difficult for supporters to attend matches and fans might stay at home to watch a big game on television rather than turn out to support a less prestigious local match. Broadcasters would be unsure of the value to put on a particular club's matches because of uncertainty as to the club's future performance and hence its 'viewer appeal'. Often viewer interest in a particular match is dependent on its significance to the state of the league table (the collective product); but the freedom to 'cherry-pick' pivotal matches could only be guaranteed by a collective deal. Any future attempt by rival broadcasters to coordinate their behaviour to mitigate some of these problems may in itself fall foul of the competition regimes at home and abroad.

In the case under review Ferris J formed his conclusions on the BSkyB/BBC deal under the framework of the 1976 Act. First, the court applied the aforementioned gateway (b) criterion to the benefits associated with the restrictive agreements. It was accepted that collective selling is the best, albeit not the only means of providing television broadcasts representative of the Premier League championship as a whole, and that this objective is in the public interest. Ferris J also agreed that abrogation of either the collectivity or exclusivity clauses would result in a significant fall in income, which would in turn substantially impair the ability of clubs to improve the infrastructure and of the game to benefit to the public.

The RPC accepted that the preservation of competitive balance within the Premier League is in the public interest, and that this objective is better served by the present scheme for the redistribution of television revenue than by any contemplated alternative. In similar vein it was found that the premium yielded by the combination of central selling and exclusivity underpins the external grants made by the Premier League. Crucially, Ferris J agreed that rather than exercising a restrictive influence, in the special circumstances of the market in TV sports rights exclusivity is the very quality most sought after: namely it is that characteristic of the product that inspires and sustains competition. Submissions relating to other benefits allegedly connected to the survival of the present arrangements were considered but ultimately rejected by the court. Attempts to bring the restrictive aspects of the current deal within the requirements of gateway (h) were similarly dismissed. Although Ferris J accepted that the restrictions exert some positive influences on competition, in other respects the market is manifestly inhibited. Derived from the 1976 Act, it is appropriate to subject gateway (h) to a narrow construction, and in this sense a restriction will pass only if the court can be satisfied that it has no restricting or discouraging effect on competition at all.

The Office of Fair Trading's Case

While the court accepted that the currently operated restrictions result in the broadcasting of fewer Premier League matches than might otherwise be the case, it was not convinced that significant latent public demand to see more matches broadcast goes unsatisfied as a consequence. The court also acknowledged that both the choice of programmes and level of innovation are restricted by the present deals, especially in regard to the degree of exclusivity afforded to the BBC over recorded highlights. However, having considered in particular the option of accommodating additional deals alongside the pre-existing arrangements, Ferris J admitted that he could conceive of no viable alternative that would avoid a serious level of commercial uncertainty. These imponderables include the effect of a separate sale of PPV rights on the price obtainable for the principal package of rights, and the fact that compliance with the UEFA prohibition on Saturday afternoon broadcasts would cause extensive fixture rescheduling (something broadcasters may desire even in the absence of the UEFA regulation) and all the damaging consequences thereof. Similarly, Ferris J rejected theoretically sound argument to the effect that the exclusive ownership of TV rights constitutes a barrier to the market entry of new broadcasters in the absence of any satisfactory 'half-way house' and the undesirability of a 'free-for-all'.

The Judgment

Amid a welter of publicity, Ferris J handed down his judgment on 28 July 1999. He ruled that, although the Premiership's rules on collectivity and its exclusive contracts with BSkyB/BBC comprise restrictions on trade, these restrictions are in fact in the public interest. Welcoming his decision, the footballing fraternity claimed with one voice that to rule otherwise would have been to unleash damaging commercial forces that would have upset the delicate competitive equilibrium of the Premier League. The ensuing celebrations were premature and may prove short-lived. The fact is that Premier League and its associate broadcasters have scored only a pyrrhic victory. The real battle over the distribution of television rights is still to come.

THE NEW UK REGIME

Under the regime established by the Competition Act 1998, which came into force on 1st March 2000, the RPC will be taken out of the loop. An altogether sharper legal framework, underpinned by a schematic and teleological interpreta-

tive policy largely alien to domestic competition law, awaits implementation.[61]
Just in time to intervene in the next round of negotiations over television rights,
the Office of Fair Trading will assume responsibility for the enforcement of competition policy. The new regime, as stated earlier, is closely based on EU competition law. Under s.2 of the 1998 Act, (which echoes Art. 81(1)):

'(1) ... an agreement between undertakings, decisions by associations of undertakings
or concerted practices which may affect trade within the United Kingdom, and have as
their object or effect the prevention, restriction or distortion of competition within the
United Kingdom, are prohibited unless they are exempt in accordance with the provisions of this Part.'

Section 4 of the Act provides that the Director General may grant an exemption
from prohibition (in domestic law)[62] if a party to the relevant agreement makes a
request for an exemption[63] and the agreement meets the criteria laid out in section
9. Section 9 (which mirrors Art 81(3) EC) provides that an agreement must:

'(a) contribute to improving production or distribution or, promoting technical or economic progress, while allowing consumers a fair share of the resulting benefit; but
(b) does not impose on the undertakings concerned restrictions which are not indispensable to the attainment of those objectives; or afford the undertakings concerned
the possibility of eliminating competition in respect of a substantial part of the products in question.'

There is little doubt that the current arrangements, or any conceivable successor
contracts incorporating similar collective/exclusive terms, would qualify for prohibition under section 2. However, while a persuasive case can be made out in
fulfillment of the positive exemption criteria[64] along the lines described above,
the negative conditions, relating respectively to the proportionality of restrictions
and the elimination of competition, are typically narrowly construed and present
a more formidable obstacle. Given recent history it is unlikely the OFT will be
favourably disposed to any future attempt to emulate the 1996 contracts. Market
conditions are evolving fast, due largely to the technological drivers of digital
television and PPV in particular, and (while he has every legal right to do so) this
should give the Director General the political latitude to depart from the recent
RPC ruling if he so desires. On this point the OFT is already formulating the
ground rules for the next round of negotiations, which are due to start in 2000.

---

[61] Maitland-Walker J, The New UK Competition Regime [1999] 20 *European Competition Law
Review* 51-59.

[62] The European Commission has the exclusive power to grant exemption from the parallel
Community regime under Article 85(3).

[63] Unless a participant gives notice of the agreement no exemption can be granted. See art. 4,
Regulation 17/62/EEC (1959-62) OJ (Special Edition), 87.

[64] Section 9(a) (i) and (ii).

Political expediency aside, far from being obliged to accord due respect to the ruling of the RPC, the OFT is required by section 60 of the 1998 Act to ensure that matters arising are dealt with in a manner consistent with the treatment of corresponding provisions of EU competition law. In a field of policy that has occasionally suffered somewhat lacklustre implementation in the past, this mechanism should not only ensure UK conformity with the competition *acquis communautaire*, but also facilitate the maintenance of a dynamic harmony with European Court jurisprudence as it develops.

The European Perspective

If the OFT decides to refuse subsequent TV contracts the exemptions they will almost certainly require it will be open to the parties to apply to an Appeal Tribunal constituted by the Competition Commission. In hearing any such appeal the Tribunal will be subject to the same section 60 obligations as the OFT. It is difficult to predict precisely what impact the assimilation of EU policy will have on the way in which future domestic television deals are treated. On the question of exclusivity the established EU line is, as discussed, broadly permissive of short-term restriction in the sporting field.[65] This view may be criticised as unrealistic, in that it would afford the broadcaster little opportunity to promote its coverage and little incentive to contribute to the long-term profile, status and continuity of the competition. Adherence to this principle would also deny the seller the chance to enter into long-term financial planning.

Given the recent change of staff at the Commission, DGIV's attitude towards this issue may soften slightly. The new Commission was approved by the European Parliament on 15 September 1999. Karel Van Miert, who favoured a rather pedantic, doctrinal approach, has been replaced by the pragmatic Italian Mario Monti. While it would be dangerous to overstate this speculation, on the strength of his track record as a member of the Santer Commission (1995-1999),[66] Monti may well be inclined to strike a deal over the exclusive distribution of television rights. However, while he may ultimately take a more permissive line than his predecessor, it is likely the DG IV machine will exert considerable influence over the new generation of contracts before granting its approval.

The Community position on club collectivity is also difficult to discern. As stated in relation to section 2 of the Competition Act 1998, which recites Article 81(1), it is likely the Premiership's rules on central selling would fall comfortably within the prohibitive scope of the Community regime. The real question is

---

[65] The Commission has indicated that an exclusive contract of up to one year in duration would in principle be acceptable.

[66] In which as Commissioner he held the brief on the Internal market, financial services and financial integration, customs and taxation

whether the arrangements would qualify for exemption under the Article 81(3) mechanism. It is possible to construct a persuasive case as to the economic benefits of the deal, in terms of certainty and administrative simplicity for the broadcaster and increased revenues and exposure for the club, and to associate these with consumer benefits in the form of a better standard of football, improved stadia and the production of higher quality programming. Again, it seems the argument will turn on whether the Premier League can demonstrate that its regulations are indispensable to the attainment of its claimed benefits. The availability of less restrictive terms that would be equally effective in realising the economic gains associated with strict collectivity/exclusivity would be fatal to an application for exemption. This criterion is significant because it puts the Commission in a position to insist on the deletion or moderation of conditions before it will grant an exemption. Often these enforced revisions, carried out under the threat of automatic nullity, prove extensive.[67]

The final Article 81(3) criterion, namely that the agreement must not afford the parties the possibility of eliminating competition in respect of a substantial part of the product in question, requires the definition of the range of products competing with those affected by the contract. This establishes what is known as the 'relevant market'.[68] In the case of live Premiership football, it is arguable that no other product is interchangeable to the degree that it satisfies the same consumer demands, which is the determining factor, because of the nature of football support. A fan will not readily switch his allegiance to a club in a different league where different competitive conditions prevail, and it is difficult to countenance the notion that any other sport presents a direct alternative to the serious football supporter. It is probably safe to conclude that 'cross-elasticity of demand' is marginal. Typically, DG IV adopts a restrictive approach to the definition of a relevant market by insisting on a high degree of product interchangeability. Narrow market definition reduces the risk that anti-competitive effects will be diluted or disguised by peripheral or background factors, and makes the job of enforcement easier in certain other respects. The now defunct Monopolies and Mergers Commission certainly took this line in its investigation of BSkyB's bid for Manchester United. In this case the relevant market was found to be no wider than the Premiership despite the club's extensive involvement in other domestic and European competitions and its growing exposure to the Far East market. In similar vein, the OFT has previously found that the market for pay-TV is to be separated from that for television broadcasting in general.[69] Therefore, although this criterion rarely poses an obstacle, especially where the other conditions are fulfilled,

---

[67] See, eg Re Optical Fibres O.J. 1986 L236/30.

[68] See the European Commission Notice on the definition of the relevant for the purposes of Community competition law (1997) OJ C372/5.

[69] See The Director General's Review of BSkyB's Position in the Wholesale Pay TV Market, supra n. 19.

in the special circumstances of football broadcasting it may operate to defeat an exclusive contract. At the time of writing DG IV has embarked on consultation with the sporting world with a view to adopting guidelines on the application of competition rules to sport in the near future. On adoption, these guidelines will feed directly into the UK regime via section 60 of the 1998 Act.

In the meantime, regardless of the Director General's decision on future action, it is unlikely that DG IV will accept the RPC verdict without further investigation. The RPC has a limited brief and little room for manouevre in equivocal cases. The regime established by the RTPA 1976 does not permit the court to modify or otherwise interfere with agreements that come before it. The RPC is empowered only to impose a blanket prohibition on those restrictions found to be contrary to the public interest. Left with a stark choice between outright prohibition, which would have provoked an immediate media 'free-for-all' with far-reaching and unpredictable consequences, and preservation of the status quo, the UK court understandably opted to err on the side of caution.

The point is that DG IV operates under no such constraints. As stated, the application of EU competition law, which would override any domestic ruling in the event of conflict, confers on DG IV the power to insist that adjustment is made to any agreement that falls foul of Article 81. The Commission's discretion is essentially unfettered in this regard, subject only to the review of the European Court of First Instance.[70] It is submitted that DG IV will adopt a muscular stance on this high profile issue. The current contracts are likely to be subject to intense scrutiny and most unlikely to survive intact. If DG IV is called upon to consider the grant of an exemption it will almost certainly require that the existing arrangements undergo material amendment. Any such alteration will inevitably serve in some fashion to dilute the deal's central collective and exclusive conditions.

In the immediate aftermath of the Restrictive Practices Court ruling the Commission sent letters to every Premier League club asking for clarification of their part in the television deal and spelling out the EU competition regime. At the time of writing, two months after delivery of these letters, DG IV has received only one reply. This uncooperative attitude, which is so typical of the football industry's approach to Europe, is only likely to antagonise Brussels and increase the prospects of intervention and retributive action. DG IV is a far more formidable watchdog than the RPC and the Premier League should bear two points in mind. First, there is little doubt that the existing arrangements are *prima facie* in contravention of Article 81. Even the RPC acknowledged this fact. Secondly, if DG IV finds a breach of EU law the agreements may be rendered null and void. Fines could be imposed which, although possibly mitigated by the existence of the RPC ruling, could amount to up to ECU 1 million (£650,000) or possibly, especially for those central to the deal, larger sums not exceeding 10% of the

---

[70] Article 230 EC (formerly Art. 173).

turnover of the parties in the preceding business year. In recent years, especially after the groundbreaking *Volkswagen* decision,[71] which imposed a fine of ECU 102 million (£67 million) on the car maker, DG IV has often stated that it is intent on increasing the general level of fines. The Commission is particularly keen to stamp its authority on this important sphere of activity and, as stated, several other investigations into the distribution of TV rights to football have been initiated on the continent. DG IV may be intent on targeting the Premiership with a view to sending a warning shot across the bows of other transgressors in Europe.[72] All this bodes ill for those involved in the current Premier League deal. As matters stand and especially in the absence of due notification, both the Premier League, its member clubs and its partner broadcasters, are wide open to punitive sanction.

THE FOOTBALL TASK FORCE REPORT

In forming his judgment on the recent OFT challenge, Ferris J considered the findings of various reports published while the present case was pending. Of particular relevance was the report of the government-appointed Football Task Force ('FTF') under the chairmanship of David Mellor Q.C.. In particular the Report recommends that the Premier League should continue to reinvest a significant part of its income in developing football at the lower levels. The FTF concluded that the fabric of English football depends on the redistribution of income, and that its ability to invest in its own future is critically linked to the preservation of the current collective bargaining arrangements. In strong opposition to the OFT case, the FTF argued that the individual sale of TV rights by clubs would hinder attempts to collect resources centrally for reinvestment. Moreover, it was submitted that the financial viability of clubs in the lower divisions would be jeopardised by any attempt to prohibit the existing collective agreements, given that many clubs are heavily reliant on income derived from the central fund supported by the current system. In the view of the FTF the present BSkyB/BBC deal benefits both the national game and its supporters.

While the FTF report hints darkly at the prospect of 'severe damage', and 'far-reaching negative outcomes', its authors can hardly be accused of overplaying the argument in favour of the redistribution of income in their recommendations. Football thrives on healthy, well-balanced competition and on the unpredictability of results. While many factors play a part, few would deny that the raw material of success is money. The sustained achievements of wealthy

---

[71] Comm. Dec. 98/273/EC [1998] O.J. L124/60. See Spink P, Enforcing E.C. Competition Law: fixing the quantum of fines [1999] *Journal of Business Law* 219.

[72] See Spink P, Recent Guidance on Fining Policy [1999] 20 *European Competition Law Review* 101, 105.

clubs like Chelsea, Arsenal and Manchester United, and the spectacular rise of Blackburn Rovers in the mid-1990s, after heavy investment from multi-million-aire-owner, the late Jack Walker, provides ample testimony for this point. There has always been a pronounced gap between larger and smaller, or rather, richer and poorer clubs, and this has traditionally manifested itself in the difference between the Football League divisions. In recent times, in part as a consequence of escalating player salaries, the competitive gap between rich and poor clubs has become a chasm. Even the Premier League itself is now polarised. Most pundits would concede that only a handful of top clubs currently stand a realistic chance of winning the Premiership. The also-rans of the Premier League are left to make up the fixtures and fight to avoid relegation. Given this state of affairs it is only a matter of time before the wider game and the competition on which it thrives begins to suffer serious damage.

Logic dictates that the only way to preserve a reasonable level of competitive balance on the field is in fact to develop, rather than curtail, that off-field collective activity considered anti-competitive in strictly commercial terms. Although professional football is undeniably a business, it is a business which is probably unique in that it requires the robust co-existence of a number of competing firms. Market domination, in this context, is ultimately self-defeating. In the United States, the governing bodies of various professional sports have made strenuous and explicit efforts to equalise the playing strengths of competing clubs in the face of a stringent anti-trust regime. US competition regulators tolerate not only the implementation of mechanisms providing for the redistribution of television and even merchandising revenue, but also countenance the use of salary caps and player draft systems.[73] Unless the issue of income redistribution is addressed at home, the self-perpetuating circle of TV and sponsorship revenue following media exposure, following success, following wealth, which, even after the adjustment of the current system, fosters significant inequality, may ultimately create a situation in which domestic competition is so impaired as to lose popular and thereafter commercial support.

The polarisation of competitive strength has long been a feature of professional football, it is by no means a recent phenomenon. However, widely asymmetrical flows of TV income can only destabilise the fragile status quo to the detriment of the game. The astronomical wage inflation of recent years has further magnified these pressures to such an extent that UEFA has recently agreed to set up a task force to investigate the vexed issue of capping players' salaries in an attempt to ensure that smaller clubs can remain competitive.[74] The Scottish Premier League ('SPL') which suffers in many respects from the absolute domination of Glasgow Rangers F.C. and Glasgow Celtic F.C., offers us a glimpse of a

---

[73] For example, in professional basketball, the team wage bill is capped, not individual player salaries. See also Morrow, supra n. 60, 15.

[74] 'UEFA to target big spenders' *Electronic Telegraph*, September 19, 1999.

not so distant future that distinctly lacks appeal.[75] *Inter alia*, the failure of Scottish clubs in European competition is often blamed on the lack of sufficient sporting competition at national league level.[76] Although it is perhaps unfair to draw a direct comparison, while exclusive rights for the 1996/97 season of the SPL were secured for only £3.3m, £88.8 million was paid to the English Premiership.[77] In October 1999, Celtic called on Rangers to join them in mounting a breakaway from the SPL.[78] If first class domestic competition is undermined, the national game will suffer at every level. Those television-engineered 'super-clubs' that manage to profit from the media 'free-for-all' that would be provoked by the condemnation of central selling are likely to migrate to some European super-league in search of more glamorous competition and even bigger pay-days. The current extended Champions League may provide the blueprint for the future in this regard.

FOOTBALL LEAGUE RULES ON TV RIGHTS

It is pertinent to note that the Football League has long operated rules on the collective sale of TV rights that are in all material respects similar in substance to the Premiership rules challenged by the OFT. In short, no match in any competition conducted by the League may be televised without the written consent of the Football League Executive.[79] Moreover, in 1995 the Football League entered into an agreement with BSkyB under which the broadcaster obtained the exclusive rights to televise Football League matches live for five seasons (1996/7-2000/01). This contract is in all material respects modelled on the Premiership deal. Interestingly however, the OFT has declined to refer the Football League deal, for which BSkyB paid the not inconsiderable sum of £125 million, to the Restrictive Practices Court. Indeed in January 1994 the OFT made representations to the Secretary of State for Trade and Industry for the purpose of soliciting a direction under Section 21(2) of the RTPA 1976. This direction, subsequently granted in July 1994, discharged the Director General from his duty to take proceedings in the RPC in respect of the Football League Rules.

In its representations to the Secretary of State, the OFT acknowledged that there was 'scope for anti-competitive behaviour' in the existing arrangements.

---

[75] In a Radio 5 Live interview on September 1, 1999 Jocky Scott, Manager of Dundee FC, confessed that he harbours no serious ambition to win the Scottish Premier League and argued that the disproportionate financial power of the old firm clubs had seriously damaged competition within the League. He suggested that Scottish football would be better off without Celtic and Rangers.

[76] No Scottish club has reached a European final since 1983.

[77] See Morrow, supra n. 60, 150-151, note that the English Premiership comprises 20 clubs as compared to the Scottish Premiership's ten.

[78] *Electronic Telegraph*, October 6, 1999.

[79] Rules of the Football League: Rule 66.1a.

However, it was argued that the restrictions contained within the agreements did not have a significantly detrimental effect on competition in sport. Endorsing a line of argument redolent of the defence mounted by the Premier League, the OFT stated:

> 'In devising a framework of rules and regulations the management committees of football associations and leagues have created a specific product... competitions which attract revenue from spectators advertising sponsors and broadcasters. Clubs accept that it is in their commercial interests to work within this framework in spite of the curtailment of their own complete freedom of action which this entails.'

In its challenge to the Premiership deals, the OFT sought to justify its ostensibly paradoxical stance by arguing that the Premier League forms a distinct market at arms length from the Football League, and that arrangements concerning the former have a much greater economic effect than those concerning the latter. While this is may be true, a £125 million contract which applies between the dominant satellite broadcaster and the 72 clubs of the three divisions of the Football League can hardly be considered *de minimis*, and this is the only argument that might justify acquiescence.[80] In terms of competition law, the framework and analysis to be employed in respect of the Football League contracts is essentially the same as that applicable to the Premiership TV deal. It cannot have escaped Ferris J that, in the circumstances, condemnation of the Premier League would have produced an anomalous and probably untenable situation.

Presumably the OFT was prepared to accept collective bargaining by the Football League in deference to the fact that its member clubs, especially in Divisions 2 and 3, lack the profile and support base necessary to attract individual TV deals. Consider the marketability of Cheltenham Town or the allure of Torquay United. It is doubtful that any broadcaster would be interested in contracting on an individual basis with more than a tiny fraction of Division 1 clubs. In the absence of a collective deal, most clubs would be deprived of both TV revenue and media exposure.

This argument is strong, but it is submitted the same logic translates with equal force to the lower and less fashionable reaches of the Premiership itself. Ex-Manchester United Chairman, Martin Edwards, has stated that he would be happy for the club to breakaway from the Premier League deal and market its own matches following the expiry of the existing contract[81] and it is not difficult to see why. The club could expect to receive at least £50 million per year,[82] for

---

[80] See Commission Notice on Agreements of Minor Importance [1997] OJ C 372/1.

[81] Lee S, Bringing the game into disrepute? The BSkyB bid for Manchester United plc Conference Paper, *The Corporate Governance of Professional Football*, University of London, February 3, 1999.

[82] This level of return would put the club on a par with Juventus and Barcelona, who already sell their TV rights on an individual basis.

the rights to its matches – around five times its return for its successful 1998/99 season. The TV rights for Arsenal, Chelsea, Liverpool and the like would also be highly-prized, but what of Coventry, Southampton or Bradford City? It is instructive that the Premier League Board deemed it necessary to insist that each club was to be featured in at least one BSkyB televised match during each season.[83] Giving evidence in the OFT case, David Dein, vice-chairman of Arsenal, said:

> 'If television rights are not sold collectively there would be a free for all. There would only be about four or five clubs who would do extremely good financial deals with television broadcasters and there would be a great temptation for the whole thing to break apart. You would probably have 14 or 15 clubs with blood on their fingers trying to hang on to the other clubs, because they were selling their rights for the League independently.'[84]

RECENT DEVELOPMENTS: MEDIA ACQUISITIONS AND THE NEW TV DEAL

Although BSkyB's bid for Manchester United was ultimately rejected on competition grounds, it raised the curtain on a new era in football's relationship with the media. In the aftermath of BSkyB's failed bid, media company NTL Incorporated called off its plans to buy Newcastle United and Carlton Communications dropped its proposed takeover of Arsenal. It is unlikely that either bid would have faced the same degree of regulatory scrutiny or opposition, given that BSkyB's plans threatened a unique concentration of power. The prospect of the marriage of the dominant sports broadcaster with what is arguably the world's largest football club generated concerns for the fabric of competition in the market for TV rights that may not have manifested themselves if less influential parties had been involved. However, the Competition Commission ruling inspired a rethink that has apparently resulted in broadcasters opting instead to build strategic portfolios of minority stakes in leading clubs.

This is in conformity with the European model. On the continent, the vertical integration of football club and media company is now commonplace. In France, the broadcaster Canal+ holds controlling interests in Paris Saint Germain and Servette Geneva, M6 has a majority stake in Bordeaux and Pathé owns a large minority share in Olympique Lyonnais. The Italian media group Fininvest is the major shareholder in AC Milan, in Greece Netmed has recently secured control of AEK Athens and UFA has interests in Hamburg and Hertha Berlin. Mindful of the potential for conflicts of interest, in 1998 UEFA banned clubs under common ownership from participating in the same UEFA competition. British sports and leisure group ENIC plc, which holds major shareholdings in a number of top European clubs including a 25% stake in Glasgow Rangers, has challenged this

---

[83] See Re FA Premier League Ltd, supra n. 1, para 235.
[84] Ibid. para 235.

regulation in the Court of Arbitration for Sport.[85] The outcome of this case will have far-reaching consequences for European football.

In July 1999 the Granada Group paid £22 million for a 9.9% stake in Liverpool FC.[86] Granada, which owns the ITV franchise for the North West of England and is a partner in ONdigital and Manchester United's MUTV channel, will act as media and commercial consultant for the club. In particular, the media company is likely to assist in the establishment of a Liverpool TV channel. Although the deal does not afford Granada a special interest in the sale of Liverpool's television rights there is no doubt that the broadcaster will fully exploit its new influence during any future negotiations. In this regard Granada's association with ONdigital is highly significant. The digital broadcaster pulled off a coup when it secured a joint deal with ITV to televise the UEFA Champions League in 1999.[87] ONdigital's refusal to supply coverage to either the cable companies or BSkyB provoked a spat which resulted in BSkyB threatening to withhold the Ryder Cup from ONdigital. While additional competition is to be welcomed, it is likely that the broadcasters will ultimately have to shift into a more cooperative gear, dispensing with exclusivity in favour of a share of the spoils of future competitions.

BSkyB paid £13.8 million for a 9.9% stake in Leeds Sporting plc, the holding company of Leeds United FC, in August 1999. The significance of this sub-10% acquisition (which mirrors Granada's stake in Liverpool) is that, under Premier League rules, a company is permitted to hold a share of 10% or more in only one club, whereas shares of *up to* 10% can be held in an unlimited number of listed clubs.[88] Leeds Sporting shareholders ratified the deal by a landslide majority in early October 1999. Under the terms of the deal BSkyB is entitled to 30% of all TV rights money. Given that the television rights to Leeds games may be worth around £40 million per year by 2002/3 the broadcaster could recover its investment in one season. Scottish Media Group, the dominant Scottish free-to-air terrestrial broadcaster bought a 19.9% stake in Heart of Midlothian in September 1999. In addition, NTL retains a 6% share of Newcastle United FC and, at the time of writing[89] Carlton has reopened negotiations with Arsenal, BSkyB has been linked with Chelsea and Tottenham Hotspur and a clutch of media suitors are lining up to bid for a stake in Glasgow Celtic.[90] Conspiracy theorists may be tempted to dwell on the fact that it will only be necessary to sway six Premier League clubs in order to veto any subsequent collective deal. It could also be ar-

---

[85] Headquartered in Lausanne Switzerland.

[86] 'Granada in league with Liverpool FC' *The Times*, July 14, 1999.

[87] 'ONdigital subsciptions leapt by 100 per cent during the first week of the competition: UEFA's money-making machine wins' *The Times*, September 17, 1999.

[88] As a consequence of this investment BSkyB was required to reduce its 11.6% holding in Manchester United (which was secured during it failed takeover attempt) to a sub-10% level.

[89] September 27, 1999.

[90] 'Media Pack chases stake in Celtic' *The Guardian*, September 21, 1999.

gued that once broadcasters have influence in enough clubs they may be able to steer the price of TV rights downwards in the long term. The OFT will doubtless examine the 'fine print' of all such deals in due course.

On June 14, 2000 the Premier League concluded various agreements with broadcasters for rights to the seasons 2001-2002, 2002-2003 and 2003-2004. BSkyB secured the main package of rights, to broadcast 66 live matches per season (including the first and second choice of games each week), for £1.1 billion (the current four-season deal, which expires in 2001, cost £670 million). BSkyB will enjoy a free choice of matches for broadcast, subject to the proviso that each club features in at least three televised games per season. The broadcaster paid an additional £22.5 million for rights to Premiership e-commerce and other web and interactive TV services. On news of the deal shares in BSkyB rose by 7%. ITV paid £183 million for the highlights package over three years, outbidding the BBC (the current rights-holder) by some £60 million. To guarantee at least a degree of universal exposure and access, only terrestrial companies were permitted to bid for the latter package. The US-based cable company NTL, secured the right to screen 40 live games per season on a pay-per-view basis (on Sunday afternoons) to cable and satellite customers, including ONdigital subscribers, for £328 million.

Five percent of the income generated by the new deal is allocated to the Football Foundation, which will channel funds into the grass roots of the game. This is approximately equivalent to the proportion of income withheld for reinvestment under the 1996 deal. The winners in all this are, without question, the Premier League clubs, especially the newly promoted Charlton Athletic, Manchester City and Ipswich Town, who will enjoy a vast increase in revenue. In the past, television revenue has in part been diverted to pay for the ground improvements demanded by the Taylor Report, but these obligations have largely now been met. Consequently, the unprecedented flow of revenue underpinned by the new deal will flood into the game, almost certainly fuelling the transfer market and the further inflation of player's wages. It is equally easy to identify the armchair spectator as the main loser. It is inevitable that subscription rates for Sky Sports will escalate from September 2001, to recoup the enormous cost of the licence.

In the days following the Premiership deal, other broadcasting contracts were concluded. On 15 June the BBC, this time in partnership with BSkyB, won a 'consolation prize' for the loss of the Premiership highlights package by reclaiming the rights to the FA Cup and England's home internationals under a three year agreement. Then, on 16 June, ONdigital (as lead broadcaster) and ITV agreed a £315 million deal with the Football League for the rights to First, Second and Third Division games and the Worthington Cup. A share of pay-per-view revenues will also be payable to the League. In addition, the League settled a £65 million, five-year deal with NTL to provide an Internet portal for all 72 Nationwide clubs.

As anticipated, the new Premiership deal is restricted to a three-year period in contrast to the existing contract, which is four years in duration. This may, to some extent, mollify the competition authorities. In particular, in terms of Premiership coverage, the involvement of three broadcasters as opposed to the previous two and the relatively inclusive nature of the pay per view agreement may ease concerns over exclusivity. In the wider context of general football coverage, the fact that no fewer than five broadcasters now hold a significant stake in the game may also serve to deflect criticism over the concentration of Premiership rights. That said, the Premier League has clearly ignored OFT pressure to dispense with collective selling. As a consequence, it is not yet clear whether these new, looser arrangements will be sufficient to defeat another legal challenge.

CONCLUSION

Broadcasters need to fill an ever-increasing amount of airtime and at one level this trend towards vertical integration is merely aimed at the future acquisition of premium sporting content. The digitalisation of TV has made it possible for clubs to move into the broadcasting arena themselves and media companies are doubtless manoeuvering for a foothold in this emerging market too. Ultimately, those broadcasters that do manage to forge strong links with key clubs should at least guarantee themselves marginal influence over the distribution of TV rights in the new millennium, but with holdings restricted to sub-10% levels, this leverage will usually be dislocated from direct control. That said however, extensive cross-investment is likely to produce a somewhat incestuous market and enforcement agencies at home and abroad will need to be convinced that competition has not been compromised. Both DG IV and a revitalised OFT are now active in this field: broadcasters and clubs alike must proceed with caution.

There is little chance the current arrangements will survive to be replicated in any future deal. It will hereafter be necessary to opt for less restrictive and looser forms of commercial association and cooperation. Every step into the legal minefield that now confronts those intent on marketing football's TV rights must be capable of unambiguous reconciliation with the criteria necessary to secure exemption from prohibition under the new domestic and EU competition regimes. Guidelines are expected from the OFT in 2000 and it is only a matter of time before DG IV produces dedicated regulations to police this increasingly important sphere, but the conditions set out in Article 81(3) will remain the benchmark. For the present, the early intervention of DG IV remains a distinct possibility. Despite the recent acquiescence of the RPC, the current Premiership contracts remain pregnable to the threat of nullity and financial sanction. The Premier League and its partner broadcasters would be well advised to adopt a positive and cooperative stance in their future dealings with the competition regulators at home and abroad. At the very least, all existing agreements and proposals for future deals must be notified at the earliest opportunity. There is no sense in provoking a fight that cannot be won.

THE END OF THE AFFAIR[*]: THE '*ANELKA* DOCTRINE' – THE PROBLEM OF CONTRACT STABILITY IN ENGLISH PROFESSIONAL FOOTBALL

Andrew Caiger and John O'Leary

INTRODUCTION

In July 1999 an exciting debate broke in the English press. A talented young French footballer – Nicolas Anelka – decided that he no longer wanted to play for his English football club – Arsenal. He wanted to transfer to another club on the continent and there was no shortage of interest – first, Lazio, then AC Milan and eventually – Real Madrid vied for his services.[1] The problem was that Anelka was bound by contract to Arsenal who bought him for a modest sum and were unwilling to sell one of their most valuable assets. This frustrated Anelka's ambitions leading him to declare ultimately that he would never play for Arsenal again.

Lazio was happy to pay a considerable transfer fee for his move from Arsenal. However, Lazio was not prepared to wait for an unlimited period and insisted that unless the transfer was completed by a certain date the deal would fall through. Arsenal resisted the transfer.

Anelka's move was no doubt motivated by the promise of an enhanced contract. His frustration was temporarily assuaged by Jean-Louis Dupont, Bosman's lawyer, who then entered the debate by suggesting that Anelka could leave Arsenal provided he pay compensation to the club.[2] Lawyers retained by clubs and sports bodies hotly contested this interpretation of the legal position.

The consensus of opinion within the game is that a player is bound by his contract unless both club and player agree that the contract can be terminated and the player transferred to another club for an agreed transfer fee. Further, should the player breach his contract by leaving the club he will be prevented from joining another club because of the registration system which requires the player's registration to be transferred from one club to another. This view of the *Anelka* situa-

---

[*] The title was inspired by Graham Greene, *The end of the affair*.
[1] From March to September 1999 the Anelka saga was followed and reported by *BBC Online*. See especially August 2, 1999 for the chronology of the Anelka affair.
[2] See *BBC Online* July 22, 1999, Anelka case 'threatens clubs'.

A. Caiger and S. Gardiner (Eds), Professional Sport in the EU: Regulation and Re-regulation
© 2000, T.M.C. Asser Press, The Hague, The Netherlands

tion is based on the belief that the *Bosman* ruling does not apply to players under contract. The *Bosman* ruling, it is believed, only applies to players who have reached the end of their contracts. Our disagreement with the latter view hinges on one issue: when does a professional football contract end?

The opinion of Jean-Louis Dupont accords with the view that in English law a player can walk away from his football contract but will have to offer compensation to the club with which he is in breach of contract – but the contract will effectively be at an end.[3] If this is the case then the player is entitled to a free transfer under the *Bosman* ruling.

However, the '*Anelka* doctrine' has caused disquiet amongst the football fraternity and therefore requires closer investigation. One of the problems that the doctrine highlights is the relationship between professional football contracts and the registration and transfer system which, operates in professional football. Three other related problems also emerge:

– Firstly, the 'doctrine' may encourage contractual breaches since these may be perceived as more advantageous for players and leave the mid-contractual transfer in tatters. But, it is our contention that mid-contract transfers fall foul of the EU Competition rules and subvert the *Bosman* ruling.
– Secondly, we contend that the purpose of the transfer system has changed little since it was first established: – to control players rather than promote competition in the game through 'uncertainty of outcome'. Also it has not been proved that the income derived from the transfer system is an efficient vehicle for encouraging new talent.
– Thirdly, should we be correct in our view that the current operation of the transfer system in England is contrary to EU law – the question arises whether players' contracts alone can provide stability and serve the legitimate expectations of both club and player. In this regard – what enforceable restraint may future football contracts contain?

This chapter investigates the relationship between players' contracts and the transfer and registration system. Our argument is that both contract and transfer and registration system are part of the control mechanism of management over players. The debate about both contract and transfer system is essentially one that concerns a 'frontier of control'.[4] It is about the ability of player power to move this frontier of control to accord with legal norms consistent in the European

---

[3] The orthodox view is that where one party repudiates the contract the other party must accept in order for the contract to come to an end. It would thus appear that Arsenal could refuse Anelka's repudiation, however courts will not allow one party to uphold the contract indefinitely. See Bojo v Lambeth London Borough Council [1994] ICR 727 CA. Furthermore, for all practical purposes the contract will be at an end since no English Court will order a player to play or grant a negative injunction. See Warren v Mendy [1989] ICR 525.

[4] The term 'frontier of control' is a term of industrial relations first used by Richard Hyman. See Hyman R, *Strikes*, (1972) Fontana.

Union. This player power has been asserted through legal challenge in the courts – both at national and European level and in the 'shadow of the law'[5] through more traditional forms of negotiation. Players have been assisted through the interest shown in the area of sport by the European Commission – especially in the field of competition. The ineptness of governance in sport – especially football – has also served to shift power to players.

The implications of relying exclusively on contracts as the basis of the business relationship between player and club is also considered. In particular we consider the remedies available in English law for breach of a football contract and compare these with those available in the Netherlands and Belgium.

Finally, possible contractual solution that may promote the stability that is so desirable in players' contracts is considered. It is maintained that any restraint must comply with the norms applicable to the restraint of trade rules and domestic and EU competition rules.

In the next section the relationship between the transfer/registration system and players' contracts is considered.

The Transfer and Registration System

All professional football players are contracted to play for a club while the latter holds their registration. The registration is transferred from one club to another for a fee. The nature of this transaction is mired in custom and practice and myth.[6] Yet it is the transfer and registration system that exercises significant control over the freedom of contract of football players. The system operated as a regulatory mechanism, which serves clubs better than it does players.

Hard Times

From the earliest days of professional football the main concern of clubs was to control the movement of players and their wages. In its nascent years players were engaged for a year at a time. Players could change clubs at the end of the season irrespective of their clubs wishes. They were not allowed to change clubs mid-season unless they had the permission of their present clubs. It was the English Football League in 1888 which, set about imposing more stringent limitations on the movement of players. The effect of these new restrictions was to prevent a player moving to another club at the *end* of his contract unless his present club gave permission. This formed the basis of the 'transfer and retain' system,

---

[5] This term is used by Mnookin R and Kornhauser L, Bargaining in the shadow of law: the case of divorce, (1979) *Yale LJ* 88 950 – 997.

[6] O'Leary J and Caiger A, The Re-regulation of football and its impact on Employment contracts in Collins H *et al*, *The Re-regulation of the Employment Relation*, (2000) The Hague, Kluwer. Also see Young P M, *A History of British Football* (1969) London, Sportsmans Book Club.

which severely affected the rights of players to move from one club to another.

This system blighted many careers. Players who did not want to accept their old club's offer could effectively be prevented from playing football. There were many such cases and some of the stories tend to be anecdotal. One such player was Wilf Mannion, an England international, who was compelled to re-sign for Middlesbrough in the 1950's. At the end of his contract he applied to go on the transfer list. The club wanted to retain him and so pitched the transfer price too high. As a result he was unable to transfer and left the club for a few months to sell chicken coops in Oldham.[7]

Eastham and the Retain and Transfer System

This transfer system operated for the best part of seventy years until it was challenged in the *Eastham* case.[8] This case was brought after a long campaign by the PFA (Professional Footballers' Association) to bring about changes in the relationship between players and clubs. In 1960 the PFA campaigned for the abolition of the maximum wage; the right of players to a proportion of any transfer fee; a new retaining system and a new form of contract. By 1961 the Football League appeared to offer concessions including longer playing contracts; the abolition of the maximum wage and a minimum wage for retaining a player. The League ultimately rejected these concessions later in the same year – it was not prepared to alter the 'retain and transfer system'.[9]

The *Eastham* case swept aside the old 'retain and transfer' system and the maximum wage limits were abolished. Under the old system the player found himself in the following position:

– The player could reregister for the same club at any time between April 1st and the first Saturday in May. In effect, the contract was simply renewed.
– The club could retain the player on less favourable terms by serving notice between 1st May and 1st June giving details of the terms it was offering. If the Football Association considered the offer to be too low it could refuse the retention, but if it felt the terms were reasonable, the player could not sign for any other club. Players were allowed to petition the FA with their reasons for wanting to move to another club, but if the Association refused to intervene clubs could retain a player indefinitely.
– The player could be placed on a transfer list at a fee fixed by the club.
– If the club did not want to keep the player and did not seek a fee for him, it could release him and he would be free to conduct negotiations with other clubs at any time from the end of June.[10]

---

[7] *Evening Gazette*, Special Edition, Saturday, April 22 2000.
[8] Eastham v Newcastle Football Club Ltd (1963) 3 All ER 139; (1964) ChD 413.
[9] Harding J, *For the good of the game*, (1991) London, Robson Books 276.
[10] Osborne G and Greenfield S, *Contract and control in the Entertainment Industry*, (1998) Aldershot, Dartmouth Press, at 35.

Lord Wilberforce was moved to comment:

> 'The transfer system has been stigmatised by the plaintiff's counsel as a relic from the Middle Ages, involving the buying and selling of human being as chattels; and indeed to anyone not hardened to acceptance of the practice it would seem incongruous to the spirit of a national sport. One must not forget that the consent of the player to the transfer is necessary but on the other hand the player has little security since he cannot get a long term contract and while he is on the transfer list awaiting an offer, his feelings and anxieties as to who his next employer is to be may not be very pleasant'.[11]

The *Eastham* decision merely confirmed a view held by many players that 'the transfer system was slavery. Well paid slavery perhaps, but slavery nonetheless'.[12] The decision led to a modification of the 'retain and transfer' system. Players now had to be paid while being retained and their club had to offer them the same or better terms than before. If the player still wanted to leave then the agreed transfer fee would have to be paid and if there was no agreement about this fee then the matter went to arbitration. Should the club offer a contract worse than the current one then the player could move on a free transfer.

It is ironic that had Bosman played for an English club he would have been entitled to a free transfer. Clearly the Belgian football rules were even more oppressive than those obtaining in England. However, despite the *Eastham* case the 'retain and transfer' rules – although improved and less oppressive – remained in place as a restriction on the movement of football players in England. The *Bosman* ruling finally abolished the 'retain and transfer' rule when players were at the end of their contracts. *Bosman* has not brought the transfer system to an end. In fact the system has flourished and players are now on longer contracts which, is something they have always wanted, and are now being transferred in mid-contract.

During the earliest period of English professional football there were at least two leagues – the English league and the Southern league – in which players could ply their skills. Even after 1888 a player could move to another league should he be unable to make a satisfactory transfer. This freedom was also squashed once reciprocal agreements were made between the leagues respecting each other's rules.[13]

---

[11] Eastham v Newcastle United FC supra at 145. See further Gardiner et al, *Sports Law*, (1998) Cavendish, 357 *et seq*.

[12] *Evening Gazette*, supra 14. The special edition deals with the life and death of Middlesbrough footballer Wilf Mannion.

[13] See McArdle D, 'One hundred years of servitude: Contractual conflict in English professional football before Bosman', [2000] 2 *Web Journal*, 1 for a detailed account of this early history.

What Grounds for Justification?

Our argument is that the registration and transfer system has always and primarily been used to assert power and control over players' ability to ply their skills freely. In this regard it has always represented a serious deviation from the normal principles governing restraints of trade – whether these be at common law or European law.

However, two grounds have been offered as a justification for the transfer and registration system:

– Compensation for costs of training and player development and
– Maintaining a competitive balance to ensure uncertainty of outcome.[14]

As regards the second ground – it is unproven and not persuasive. Ross points out:

> 'A snapshot of competition in the English Premier League illustrates both that free agency does not hurt competitive balance and how it can actually improve such balance'.[15]

The ECJ agreed that the transfer rules were inadequate to maintain the competitive balance:

> '... Mr Bosman has rightly pointed out that the application of the transfer rules is not an adequate means of maintaining a financial and competitive balance in the world of football. Those rules neither preclude the richest clubs from securing the services of the best players nor prevent the availability of financial resources from being a decisive factor in competitive sport, thus considerably altering the balance between clubs'.[16]

Advocate General Lenz addressed the question of compensation. He noted:

> 'The transfer fees cannot be regarded as compensation for possible costs of training, if only for the simple reason that their amount is linked not to those costs but to the player's earnings. Nor can it seriously be argued that a player, for example, who is transferred for a fee of one million ECU caused his previous club to incur training costs amounting to that vast sum...

---

[14] Will D, The Federation's viewpoint on the new transfer rules in Jeanrenaud C and Kesenne S, *Competition Policy in Professional Sports: Europe after the Bosman Case*, (1999) International Centre for Sports Studies, University of Neuchâtel, Standaard Editions Ltd, Belgium.

[15] Ross S F, Restraints on player competition that facilitate competitive balance and player development and their legality in the United States and in Europe, *Competition Policy in Professional Sports* (supra).

[16] Case C-415/93 ASBL Union Royale Belge des Societes de Football Association and Others v Jean-Marc Bosman [1996] 1 CMLR 645 para 107 of the judgement.

A second argument against regarding transfer fees as a reimbursement of the training costs which have been incurred is the fact that such fees – and in many cases extraordinarily large sums – are demanded even when experienced professional players change clubs. Here there can no longer be any question of 'training' and reimbursement of the expense of such training. Nor does it make any difference that in such cases it is often 'compensation for development' (not compensation for training) which is spoken of. Any reasonable club will certainly provide its players with all the development necessary. But that is expenditure which is in the club's own interest and which the player recompenses with his performance. It is not evident why such a club should be entitled to claim a transfer fee on that basis'.[17]

Although the legitimate interests of the club and football were recognised, the justifications offered for the maintenance of the transfer system (at the end of the footballer's contract) could not be defended. There was no compliance with the principle of proportionality. The objective of redistribution of income among clubs could be better achieved if the authorities set up a system of redistribution.[18] Other writers have also supported this position.[19] The ECJ also did not accept the argument put forward by UEFA and others regarding the incentives provided by transfer fees:

'... the argument that the rules in question are necessary to compensate clubs for expenses which they have had to incur in paying fees on recruiting their players cannot be accepted, since it seeks to justify the maintenance of obstacles to freedom of movement for workers simply on the ground that such obstacles were able to exist in the past'.[20]

While it is admitted that assessing compensation for training and development of players is difficult, the football fraternity in several EU countries have ignored the opinion of Advocate General Lenz and the ruling of the ECJ. In too many footballing nations the transfer fee is still accepted as the rough and ready method of 'compensating' clubs when their players move to the new club. It appears that the football authorities are impervious to the criticisms of the transfer system and the fact that their claims cannot be proved. This is a defiant cultural statement that the transfer system is part and parcel of a *lex sportiva*. Clubs are not interested in debating the question of compensation since they are quite happy with the system – this is in spite of the fact that in England, for example, the transfer

---

[17] Ibid. para. 237 of the Opinion. Also see Gardiner S and Welch R, The winds of change in professional football: the impact of the Bosman ruling, [1998] *Contemporary Issues in Law* 289; Caiger A and O'Leary J, A new rainbow? The promise of change in professional football, [1998] *Contemporary Issues in Law*, 313.

[18] Bosman, supra, para. 227 and 133 of Opinion. Also see Gardiner and Welch, supra, 292.

[19] See Ross, supra and Moorhouse H F, Football Post-Bosman: the real issues, *Competition Policy in Professional Sports*, supra, 161.

[20] Bosman, supra, para. 113 of the judgement.

fees obtained in the Premier league were circulated amongst the top clubs in England and Europe.[21]

While the football authorities may be uncritical of the transfer system – players are clearly aware of the anomalies of 'compensation'. A former Ajax player commented:

> 'The footballer acquires his skill on the streets, the school playground or in the park. There the youngster, at a tender age, develops control over the ball. There is no youth-trainer or talent scout. The future football player with all his qualities and shortcomings is developed here before and after school either with friends, but sometimes alone. After the technical basis of his game is developed on the street the youth of 8 – 10 years of age joins as a youth-player at the local amateur club. He may then play in football matches as club member as well as member of the sports association to which he pays a membership fee. He is trained by an enthusiast or an underpaid football coach. When at the age of 14 to 16 the scouts arrive from the professional clubs, mostly unpaid enthusiasts, who strip the amateur football fields looking for talent. These are then enticed by the professional clubs to undergo youth training. In my time Ajax obtained the services of Van Basten and Vanenburg having enticed them at the age of 16 from Elinkwijk and 15 at Blaau Wit respectively. At this stage most of the footballer's game has been formed. The cost of training is between zero and a minimal sum and bears no relation to the income generated by that footballer'.[22]

There is also evidence of player dissatisfaction with the 'compensation' aspects of transfers. Molenaar relates one example of the Dutch experience: Sparta, a lower division football club used the transfer system to play one club off against another when offering a player's transfer. It was also aware that Ajax was in a position to pay more and that few players are able to resist an offer from Ajax. Thus Sparta allowed the clubs to bargain against each other for the player. In one such transfer Sparta received fl 2.2 million from Ajax for the player Winston Bogarde. This sum was sufficient to sustain Sparta's youth training programme for the next 25 years. Bogarde was entitled to receive 10% of the fee but had to take the matter to arbitration at the Dutch Football Association (KNVB). According to Sparta the sum paid by Ajax was partly for compensation and partly for buying-off the contract.[23]

Avoiding the *Bosman* Ruling: Longer Contracts and Mid-contract Transfers

Research[24] into the affects of the *Bosman* ruling in East Anglia revealed that clubs in the higher league divisions wrote longer contracts: usually between three

---

[21] Szymanski S, The market for soccer players in England after Bosman: Winners and losers, in *Competition Policy in Professional Sports*, supra 133 at 145.

[22] Molenaar C I M, De nieuwe status van de profvoetballer, (1996) in Siekmann R C R and Giltay Veth N J P (ed), *Sport en Recht*, T.M.C. Asser Instituut, De Vrieseborch Haarlem.

[23] Ibid. 75.

[24] See Caiger A and O'Leary J, 'Towards a Paradigm Shift in Professional Football: The Chang-

and five years. Clubs then employed a system of rolling contracts offering to extend a players contract while he was still in mid-contract. The reason for rolling contracts was not necessarily the desire to keep players – but rather a desire to retain some transfer value – when and if the club required this. Longer contracts have been one of the benefits of the *Bosman* ruling since these provide players with greater security – on the face of it. But we found that when new managers were appointed at clubs they often change the composition of the team which, meant that some players would be transferred. On the whole we found that longer contracts were about retaining the possibilities of a transfer fee and seldom an intention to retain the players for the length of the contract. In fact players who have sat out their contracts and gone on a free transfer (a *Bosman* as it is colloquially called) are notable since very few players do this. Some players[25] are now using the threat of a free transfer as a bargaining lever against their clubs as well.[26]

A recent example of this 'bargaining lever' can be seen in the proposed transfer of Ugo Ehiogu from Aston Villa to Middlesbrough. Ehiogu has been offered inducements to agree to the transfer – a quarter of the proposed £8 million transfer fee. While this practice is not uncommon – we think that the level of the inducement is significant. Perhaps a factor in the level of the inducement reflects the concern amongst Premiership clubs that the abolition of the transfer fee is immanent.[27]

In smaller clubs there has been less evidence of longer contracts. Contracts in the second and third divisions of English football are seldom for more than two or three years. This 'inefficient' contract writing is due to financial constraints faced by these clubs.

Blanpain[28] has argued that mid-contract transfers is strong evidence of the circumvention of the *Bosman* ruling. The ruling specified that there had to be a free transfer at the end of the football contract when a player moved between Member State football clubs. The ECJ confined itself to the free mobility of workers pro-

ing Contours of Business Relationships in English Football', (1999) 2 *Sport and the Law Journal*, 44.

[25] Szymanski, supra.

[26] Notably Marc Bosnic, Manchester United's goalkeeper.

[27] www.teamtalk.com. 12 October 2000. 'Fresh reports suggest that Middlesbrough are to sign Aston Villa's Ugo Ehiogu, after a apparent breakthrough in the long running saga. The Villa centre-half looks set to move to the Riverside outfit in an £8 million deal, after weeks of trying by Bryan Robson. Villa are reportedly prepared to give the player up to £2 million to leave now, rather than the end of the season, when he'll be available on a Bosman free transfer. The player initially rejected an earlier move to Boro, because he thought a better offer from someone else may be forthcoming if the transfer system is scrapped.Villa are likewise interested in the outcome of the EC ruling on the system later this month, but for different reasons of course, to the former West Brom player. It now seems the final decision is with Ehiogu, as to whether he wants to move to Teesside'.

[28] Blanpain R, *Mensenhandel in de Sport*, Press conference 4 December 1998. Also see Blanpain R, Vrijheid en gebondenheid in de sport: De CAO van 12 juni 1998. *De Balog Case*, (1998) Leuven, Peeters Publishers.

visions of the Treaty and not the restraints on competition issues.[29] However the EU Competition Commissioner Mario Monti recently expressed his views as regards the transfer system thus:

'International transfer systems based on arbitrarily calculated fees that bear no relation to training costs should be prohibited, regardless of the nationality of the player *and whether the transfer takes place during or at the end of the contractual period ...*' (*our italics*)

While FIFA was obliged to amend certain transfer rules in the light of *Bosman*, it has continued to apply its international transfer rules to situations not addressed by the ruling. In a statement of objections addressed to FIFA in December 1998, the Commission took the view that certain transfer rules violate EU competition rules:

'FIFA, UEFA and FIFPRO are currently preparing new transfer rules, and proposals of a very general character have been discussed with them at an informal level. In the absence of any structured and clear proposals from FIFA for new regulations bringing the transfer rules into line with Article 81, a negative decision will be prepared. At the same time we will continue to collaborate with FIFA in the search for a new system which is compatible with the rules of the Treaty. Here, to mix my sporting metaphors, the ball is in FIFA's court'.[30]

It is clear that the current transfer system is unsustainable and has come into conflict with the normative system of EU law. It is expected that this view will be maintained by the ECJ in due course when the *Balog* case is heard in November 2000.

In view of the above the legal issues surrounding breach of football playing contracts – the '*Anelka* doctrine' becomes pertinent both from a theoretical and a practical point of view.

EMPLOYMENT AND FOOTBALL CONTRACTS

It has already been argued that if a footballer breaks his contract by walking out and joining another club and offers the deserted club damages, then his old club will be compelled to transfer his registration without the usual transfer fee. The old club can only insist that the player pay damages. Whether it is the player in breach or his new club that pays the damages is no matter – as long as it is paid.

Naturally this view of the law is alarming for any football club. There are several issues that require clarification:

– When does a contract come to an end?

---

[29] Article 39 (previously Article 48) of the EU Treaty.

[30] Monti M, Sport and Competition, Excerpts of a speech given at a Commission-organised conference on sports, Brussels, 17 April 2000.

- Can the old club insist on contractual performance?
- What would constitute damages in English law (as well as other systems)?
- If the transfer system cannot be relied on: can a contract – which is apparently so easy to break – be relied on and how?
- How can a club be compensated for developing the player?

When Does a Contract Come to an End?

Our views in this regard have already been mentioned above. When a party unilaterally repudiates the contract the innocent party, in theory, has two options. First – to abide by the contract and insist on contractual performance and sue for damages for non-compliance. The second option is to accept repudiation and sue for damages. In the first case the contract is said to subsist, whereas in the second it does not. However, in practice where one party refuses to observe the contract it is difficult to see how it can subsist in the long or medium term. This is especially true in the employment context where courts will find circumstances from which it will be inferred that the innocent party has accepted the repudiation.[31] While this scenario usually occurs in the case where an employee has been dismissed – there is no reason why the approach of the court should not apply to the employer as well. This, we argue, is especially the case in football contracts. This argument is further strengthened by the fact that no English court will grant a football club either an injunction or an order of specific performance against the player (as indicated below).

If one applies the *Bosman* ruling one observes that it also relevant to contracts that are broken during the term of the football contract. It is therefore contended that a footballer breaking his contract before completion cannot be lawfully transferred in terms of the *Bosman* ruling. Clubs are merely entitled to compensation for breach of contract.

Can the Old Club Insist on Contractual Performance?

Ultimately, a club wishing to hold a player to his contract may need to resort to legal measures. In English law the remedies available are those common law remedies that are applicable to contracts generally. However English law has long recognised those remedies, which enforce the contract of employment, may amount to contractual slavery. Courts therefore, have been reluctant to apply remedies other than damages except in the rarest of instances.[32] Additionally Parliament has explicitly forbidden the use of the order of specific performance to enforce the contract of employment against employees.[33]

---

[31] See *Boyo* (supra).

[32] See Warren v Mendy (supra) that deals with a boxing contract. In that case the court refused to grant an injunction preventing a boxer contracting with a new manager.

[33] S.236 Trade Union and Labour Relations (Consolidation) Act 1992.

The only contractual remedy that may be of relevance is the injunction. In its negative form it would be possible theoretically for a football club to apply to the courts for an injunction which, rather than force the player to play for the club, would prevent the player from playing for another club. The distinction is a fine one but the injunction, it could be argued, does not tie the player to the club and, therefore, does not amount to slavery. In *Warner Bros. v Nelson* the actress, Bette Davis was prevented successfully from breaching her contract with Warner Brothers. By the granting of an injunction, which rather than force her to complete her contract with Warner Brothers, prevented her from contracting with any other film studio, Davis was effectively forced to see out her contract.[34]

This approach has been utilised effectively in the United States to force employee sportsmen to honour their contracts. U.S. courts appear comfortable with the idea that a sportsman wishing to jump contract can either honour the deal or work in another line of business. English courts have not adopted this approach taking perhaps the more realistic view that a sportsman cannot be prevented from following his chosen profession simply because he is in breach of contract.[35]

If the object of the club is to prevent the footballer joining a rival club (not something that could be established easily if the player moves to another country) then football clubs may consider the use of garden leave. The idea of this concept is to draft the contract of employment with a long notice period. English courts have been prepared to grant injunctions preventing employees working for rival employers in breach of the notice arrangements in their contracts. However, assuming that English courts felt such an order was suitable in the context of professional football, it is questionable whether a limited extension of a player's availability is really what a club would desire.

Ultimately, it is very unlikely under English law that football clubs to prevent a player jumping contract and playing for another club could use the law. Anelka was eventually allowed to leave Arsenal to join Real Madrid for £22 million. Arsenal was ultimately unwilling to retain a player unwilling to play for it, nor did it want the court to pronounce on the law in this situation.

The *Anelka* scenario would have been dealt with differently in the past. Players under the old retain and transfer system before *Eastham* who were in conflict with their club over transfers to another club would rather leave the game than be forced to play. Equally there are numerous examples of players such as Eric Cantona who have retired mid-contract.[36] It would seem that clubs are particularly upset where a player wants to leave mid-contract to play for another club, rather than retire.

---

[34] Warner Bros. Inc v Nelson [1937] 1 KB 209.

[35] McCutcheon P, Negative enforcement of employment contracts in the sports' industries, (1997) *Legal Studies* 65.

[36] See the remarks of Martin Edwards in Cantona E, *The complete Cantona*, (1997) London, Headline Book Publishing, 188.

The Netherlands provides an interesting example of the use of contract to retain the services of players for a certain period. Frank and Ronald de Boer contracted in 1997 to play for Ajax till 2004. Their contracts contained a clause that they would remain with Ajax till July 2001. They were not allowed to entertain other offers during the period 1997 to 1 July 2001. In 1998 both brothers desired a move to Barcelona realising that Ajax could not match the salaries and international competition provided by the new club. Ajax resisted their request and the matter went to arbitration by the Dutch Football Association [KNVB]. The arbitration went in favour of Ajax. The arbitration Commission held that the brothers were legally represented when the contracts were entered into and the offer from Barcelona did not constitute a serious reason for bringing the employment relationship between Ajax and the brothers to an end. Nevertheless soon after this decision Ajax thought better of it and agreed to transfer the brothers for a hefty sum to Barcelona.

Mid-contract breaches impacts adversely on the competitiveness of smaller clubs and also on the top club whom play in smaller leagues in the smaller European Member States.[37]

What Would Constitute Damages in English Law (As Well as Other Systems)?

The football contract is a contract of employment rather than a contract for services. Where a breach has occurred in a contract for services the estimation of damages may be relatively easily calculated. Damages would be in respect of defective performance, which may involve the need to find another contractor to complete the work. In employment contracts damages are rarely sought on the basis of contractual breach. At best the claim is usually in respect of the notice period. Fixed term contracts – such as three-year football contracts – are subject to the same rules as period of notice constituting the measure by which damages are assessed. In most fixed term contracts a notice period is usually fixed and in high-income jobs the notice period is often longer than in ordinary employment or fixed term contracts.

In a football contract there is usually no notice period. This has not been necessary in the past (in England) due to the fact that players were transferred at the end of their contracts or mid-contract. Since the *Bosman* ruling the transfers have occurred mid-contract and the sums involved have increased dramatically. We maintain that these transfers have occurred contrary to the *Bosman* ruling and are therefore unlawful. The question remains – if these transfers are unlawful – what

---

[37] Van Staveren H, Arbeidsverhoudingen in de Beroeps(voetbal) sport na het Bosman-Arrest. Paper delivered at a roundtable seminar at the T.M.C. Asser Institute, The Hague, 19th March 1999. Also see: Siekmann R, 'Transfercode' in zaak – de Boers door Ajax doorbroken, (1998) 3 *Sportzaken*, 9 and commentary by professors Abas and Blanpain in the same edition.

damages may clubs rightfully expect to recover for mid-contract breaches? It is submitted that it is difficult to establish the measure of damages.

Damages may include compensation for the loss of the player such as an amount representing the outstanding period of the contract – at best. This might be based on the salary earned by the player. It may also include wasted costs of publicity such as football strips and other types of club merchandising. There may be other losses such as gate money and the like – but these losses would be difficult to justify as foreseeable damages directly flowing from the breach.

It is suggested that damages would not include transfer costs or losses because these are external to the contract or unlawful in terms of the *Bosman* ruling.

There is a popular view that the cost of obtaining the services of a replacement player is also recoverable. Tsatsas argues:

'In an employment context the basic measure of damages is the cost to the employer of arranging for another person to carry out the work less what it would have cost to continue employing Anelka through the remainder of his contract. ... Thus the damages due to Arsenal would amount to the cost to the club to replace Anelka with a comparable striker'.[38]

The writers do not share this view. It appears that the employment contract has been confused with a contract for services i.e. the type where an independent contractor has walked off the job. It is argued that the cost of Anelka's replacement is not recoverable – rather the criteria specified above i.e. damages based on the level of his wages and the length of his outstanding contract minus the duty to mitigate. This means that if the striker is replaced after two months – then the damages caused by the walk out is reduced proportionally.

Ross argues that contract damages include the value of the transfer fee and argues further: '... the courts would also enforce a liquidated damage clause in the contract that approximated the transfer fee'.[39] This may represent the position in the United States – but it is clearly incorrect in England where damage clauses need to represent a genuine attempt to calculate damages in contracts ahead of its occurrence.

One wonders why the player should be saddled with damages for the transfer fee when the latter (which we argue is unlawful) is as a consequence of an arrangement between two clubs and has nothing or little to do with the contract that the club has with the player.

The Netherlands provides an interesting example of where the measure of damages for breach of contract is estimated on the basis of the player's transfer value. Van Staveren mentions the case of Laseroms and the Sparta Rotterdam

---

[38] Tsatsas N, Anelka's costly walk-out case has a hole in it, in *The Guardian/The Observer* on line July 23, 1999.
[39] See Ross (supra) 106.

football club. The district judge in Rotterdam determined that the compensation due to Sparta from Laseroms for terminating his contract was equal to his transfer value at the time. Van Staveren notes that this case (of 1967) set a precedent for the inter-relation between the transfer system and the player's contract. All football contracts in the Netherlands are governed by the Dutch Civil Code (Burgerlijke Wetboek). Football contracts are therefore governed – like all other fixed term employment contracts – by Dutch labour law. Football contracts can only be terminated by consent or by the court. In the case of football, the arbitration commission of the Dutch Football Association [KNVB] arbitrates contractual terminations.[40]

What is clear in Dutch law is that a player may terminate his contract against the wishes of his club provided he can show good cause – which may include a change of circumstances.

In Belgium similar mid-contract terminations are effected by a court under the Belgian Civil Code. However, in Belgium the damages are fixed at the equivalent of six months salary.[41]

The Dutch example represents a unique approach to this particular problem. In fact, the essence of the transfer system appears to be retained in the application of domestic labour law in the instance of football. It is far from clear to what extent, if any, the principles of the EU Treaty may affect Dutch labour law. In practice – using the contract as a basis for fixing a 'transfer' may be unavoidable.

If the Transfer System Cannot be Relied On: Can a Contract – Which is Apparently so Easy to Break – Be Relied On and How?

The football authorities in Europe notably UEFA and FIFA have been given till December 2000 to propose a compensation system when players move from one club to another. Various options are being considered including at what age compensation should stop. One proposal suggests that compensation should stop at the age of 18, another that the age of 21 would be appropriate. It seems clear that no firm decision has yet been reached. Any agreement will have to comply with the basic requirements of the EU Treaty, more particularly, competition law principles. These principles include the ability of players to move freely in the EU and contracts that are equitable. Where contracts are restrictive such restrictions should satisfy the following criteria:

– They must be restrictions which are necessary for the game;
– They must comply with the principle of proportionality: balancing the interests of the players, the clubs and the sport as a whole.

---

[40] See Van Staveren (supra).
[41] Interview with Luc Silance, Advocate at the Brussels Bar, June 2000.

The nature of the football industry suggests that it will be very difficult to draft a breach-proof contract – nor is this desirable. Bearing the above mentioned criteria in mind we suggest that contracts be drafted with the intention of promoting labour stability. Clauses such as those mentioned in connection with the *de Boer* case are clearly problematic since they try to retain the resale value of the player. In the *de Boer* case the 'loyalty' clause arguably also infringed the Dutch civil code.[42]

Failing a satisfactory outcome of the negotiations between the Commission and the European football authorities – an incentives-based contract might achieve a degree of stability. This would involve the loading of benefits and bonuses towards the end of the contractual period. While this approach would be consistent with the principles of proportionality and necessity referred to above, it would not prevent a club luring away a player with a promise to make good the contractual rewards of completing the contract. Therefore mid-contract breaches cannot be prevented but there may be other remedies available, which might discourage contractual breaches by players.

Where such mid-contract breaches occur, the new club is paying the old club for the player. Less clear is what – in legal terms – the payment is for. In some cases this 'buy-off' – as it is termed – is for buying-off the obligations owed by the player to his old club under that contract. In other cases it serves also as compensation for training. Some have suggested that the sum paid is for the assignment of the contract.[43]

Assignment clauses may be inserted into contracts and this practice is becoming more common. The original intention of such clauses was to provide a means whereby players could escape the confines of their contract should a new club offer an amount of money to the old club which was equal to or in excess of a figure prescribed in the contract. However it has been argued that this 'assignment' figure could form the basis of a quantifiable measure of damages should the player leave the club mid-contract.[44] This is only possible where a genuine estimation is made of the old club's contractual losses. Say, for example that the Anelka contract with Arsenal contained an assignment clause specifying that on assignment the club would be entitled to £22 million. Such a clause would clearly be illegal and unenforceable since it does not represent a genuine estimation of Arsenal's losses under the contract.

The term assignment is a misnomer in this instance. A contract which, is assigned is one where the contract remains in force and one party assigns their rights and obligations under it to another. This is not what happens when a player changes clubs. There, the old contract is terminated through the novation of the

---

[42] See Siekmann R, 1998(3) Sportzaken 9 and Van Staveren (supra).
[43] See Ross, supra; Van Staveren supra.
[44] Jeanrenaud C and Kesenne S, *Competition Policy in Professional Sports*, supra.

new contract.[45] In practice therefore, the 'assignment' clause is a buy-out clause – a buy-out of the player's obligations to the old club. The assignment clause cannot be used as a substitute for a transfer fee where an unrealistic amount is specified. Where there is no assignment in the player's contract the legal position remains the same – but the new club may offer the old club a substantial sum (unrestricted in value) for the services of the player. This would be a genuine buy-out of the obligations of the player under the old contract. The old contract will cease through the process of novation.

It is clear that there is little within the contract to ensure stability. Perhaps therefore, stability of football contracts can be assured by means outside of the contract. It has long been recognised that interference with contractual performance is a tort (delict).[46] A club attempting to induce a player away from his current club could commit this tort. The inducement would be liable in tort even if the inducement was made indirectly by, say, an agent.[47] Courts are prepared to award substantial sums in damages for losses to a business arising from such liability. This is important because the measure of damages could be in excess of the damages for breach flowing from the contract. Indeed, with the development of economic torts to include imposing liability for behaviour short of breach,[48] action may well lie if a club merely contacts a player, if such contact results in diminished performances. The effect of pursuing these actions will be to force courts to consider the wider ramifications of financial loss and dissuade clubs from destabilising existing contractual relationships. This would probably be the most effective way of ensuring contractual stability should a club want to hold on to its player. A similar remedy would be available on the continent either in contract or delict since continental legal systems are more inclined to insist on contractual performance – *pacta sunt servanda* – than is the case in England and Wales.

How Can a Club Be Compensated for Developing the Player?

If the transfer system can no longer be used as a vehicle for transferring money between clubs, is it possible for the smaller clubs in particular to receive some form of 'compensation' in its widest meaning for the costs involved in training a player? Further, it is possible for a system to be established to achieve what Ad-

---

[45] Note: In English law the assignment of personal contracts is usually not possible unless the employee agrees. The exception is provided by statute – The Transfer of Undertakings (Protection of Employment) Regulations 1981 – which places an obligation on the new employer. Usually the benefit of this will be to protect continuity of employment. Also see Beatson J, *Anson's Law of Contract*, (1998) Oxford, OUP, 460.

[46] Lumley v Gye [1852] 2 E&B 216.

[47] J T Stratford & Son Ltd v Lindley [1965] AC 269, [1964] 3 All ER 102, HL and Torquay Hotel Co Ltd v Cousins [1969] 2 Ch 106, [1969] 1 All ER 522.

[48] Merkur Island Shipping Corpn v Laughton [1983] ICR 490, [1983] IRLR 218, HL.

vocate General Lenz thought that the transfer system did not: namely to redistribute wealth to lower clubs.

It is clear that the transfer system does not achieve this worthy ambition and lower division clubs have, in general, become more creative in establishing alternative revenue streams.[49] Of course there is a simple alternative: larger clubs could give money to smaller clubs. However giving smaller clubs gifts will not, in itself, encourage them to develop their own players. A more sophisticated system is required to distribute the gift according to the number and quality of players lost to each club. Perhaps a central fund could be established to which the richer clubs make a contribution. Compensation could be paid to smaller clubs in accordance with an agreed formula. It would not be beyond the abilities of football authorities to devise a formula for the distribution of money from the rich man's table that would accurately reflect the smaller club's contribution to the game.

Conclusion

The transfer system as it currently exists is insupportable because it cannot be justified and it is unlawful in terms of European Law. The nature of the football contract has been examined and it was suggested how stability might be brought about through means additional to contract. Ultimately the use of transfer fees to maintain a system of control and buttress lower clubs against financial hardship cannot be maintained. The contract offers limited legal means of ensuring stability in the relationship between player and club and clubs as a last resort may be forced to consider action based on tort rather that contract.

In the future the relationship between a player and his club will only be contractual. Yet contract will not entirely eradicate the high prices paid for the services of football players – but the obligations of football players will rest on contract rather than the additional arbitrary, extraneous and feudal relationship as represented in the transfer system. This represents a vital paradigm shift in football from a dominant regulatory regime to one based on the reasonable expectations of the individual.

In one respect it is a pity that Anelka did not have recourse to the law since it would have highlighted the problematic nature of the transfer system and precipitated an unprecedented upheaval. On the other hand it is not surprising that the *Anelka* case did not reach the courts since neither the club nor the football authorities would want this matter to be adjudicated upon.

---

[49] See Caiger A and O'Leary J 'A New Rainbow? supra; 'Towards a Paradigm Shift in Professional Football: The Changing Contours of Business Relationships in English Football' supra; The re-regulation of football and its impact on employment contracts, in Collins H et al, *The Re-regulation of the Employment Relation*, supra.

A player *still under contract* can move from one club in one country to another (and even perhaps in the same country) without the agreement of his present club. The example of the *Anelka* conundrum illustrates this proposition.

The recent negotiations between the football authorities and the EU Commission represent a positive development in the field of sport. The process has encouraged the sport to come to terms with the clash between its own traditions and the dominant legal norms of the EU. Sports administrators can measure their proposals against EU law and reformulate their rules themselves. This process supports the tradition of self-regulation while ensuring that this occurs within acceptable parameters. In so doing a clear frontier of control is established between the interests of sport and the legitimate interventions of the law. In short a form of supervised self-regulation.

The role competition law might play in the re-regulation of the football contracts and a compensation system has not been considered here. The reason for this is that it appears that the Commission is eager to see whether or not football, and for that matter other sports authorities, might be able to effect the necessary changes themselves. This 'hands-off' approach is one that sports authorities should embrace with alacrity. It gives sport a chance to establish a more accountable and transparent order itself – which may ultimately be more satisfactory and cheaper to administer.

THE EFFECTIVENESS OF THE CORPORATE FORM AS A REGULATORY TOOL IN EUROPEAN SPORT: REAL OR ILLUSORY?

Tom Mortimer and Ian Pearl

INTRODUCTION

This chapter will consider two aspects of the regulatory impact of the corporate form upon English football. The first aspect to be considered will be that long-lived and influential rule of the Football Association, Rule 34. The second aspect will be the availability of potential alternatives to the 'English' corporate form within the European Union. As will be seen, both areas clearly demonstrate the persistent difficulty attending any would-be holistic assessment of the corporate regulation of sport: namely how to meaningfully accommodate the 'X-Factors' informing the regulatory goals within the relatively narrow confines of the enquiry. It is a matter of common knowledge that there is an increasing divide between the game of football and the business of football yet this divide was not always so obvious and thus it is to a brief consideration of its development that this chapter will now turn.

In a number of respects the histories of the limited liability company and association football may be regarded as having developed from the same socio-political milieu. Both can trace their origins to the access-widening reforms of mid-nineteenth century English social and business conditions: each may be regarded as representing what was then thought to amount to an appropriate regulatory structure for its would-be participants. That these regulatory forms have subsequently developed at different rates should occasion little surprise. However, the present enquiry is based around the comparatively sudden impact of exclusive broadcasting contracts upon the regulatory equilibrium of English football.

Writing today, the ability of a fan to spectate upon sporting activity has never been greater. Technological advances within broadcasting have allowed an almost undreamt of delivery of sporting events direct to the fan's television set. Such technological advances have seemed to hold out the prospect of similarly impressive opportunities for the generation of profits to those concerned in the delivery of the sporting events. Recently the UK's broadcasting organisations agreed to pay an unprecedented £2.36 billion for the right to show football on

A. Caiger and S. Gardiner (Eds), Professional Sport in the EU: Regulation and Re-regulation
© *2000, T.M.C.Asser Press, The Hague, The Netherlands*

television for three years from 2001.[1] The consequences associated with this, and other, influxes of money have not been universally greeted with delight.

A common complaint, aimed at the English football regulators, is that the sheer scale of the monetary inflows are destroying the foundations upon which the game was built. This criticism comes in the form of a two-pronged attack, firstly directed at the escalating costs of players' salaries and secondly directed at the cost to the ordinary fan of remaining an active spectator. The most recent figures do appear to show that players' salaries represent a percentage of income that would be unheard of in most other businesses, contributing to the waning of the Plc clubs' star on the stock market. For example, the ratio of wages to income in 1998-99 at Liverpool was 79%, while at Arsenal it was a slightly more modest 54%.[2] It has been suggested that already over half of all Premiership clubs' total wages and salaries bills exceed 50% of turnover[3] and according to Deloitte and Touche 'at least one Premiership club's wage and salary bill is currently equal to, if not greater than, its annual turnover'.[4]

At the same time, the Football Task Force has been created to examine among other issues the escalating financial burden that the clubs are placing upon the fan. Moreover, it is seeking to redress the balance against wholesale commercialism currently dominating the corporate culture and also to re-inject a community spirit into the game. The Football Task Force is searching for a 'third way', beyond the community and beyond the market place: the stakeholder concept may eventually supply this. But before turning to this consideration this chapter will attempt to examine the underlying regulatory structure of the clubs and the English Football Association (the FA).

THE REGULATOR

The FA is the governing body of English football. It provides a rulebook for the nature of play and for the construction of the leagues. It oversees both the amateur and professional games. The FA's rules still display something of the culture which prevailed at the inception of the English game. For example, Rule 34[5] which specifies that no club should have directors on salaries and goes further by capping any dividend payment beyond a minimal amount.[6] The rule was in-

---

[1] Snoddy R, 'BBC loses again in football play-offs', *The Times*, June 17, 2000.

[2] *The Times*, August 12, 2000.

[3] Garland J, et al (eds) *The Future of Football – Challenges for the Twenty-First Century*, (2000), London, Frank Cass.

[4] Deloitte and Touche, *Deloitte and Touche Annual Review of Football Finance*, (2000) Manchester, Deloitte and Touche.

[5] A full description of the role of the FA was given in the judgement handed down by the Restrictive Practices Court. Re F.A. Premier League Ltd. Agreement Relating to the Supply of Services Facilitating the Broadcast of Premier League Football Matches (Restrictive Practices Court, 28 July 1999).

[6] See Hamil S, Michie J and Oughton C, (eds.) *Football in the Digital Age: Whose Game is it Anyway* (2000) Edinburgh, Mainstream.

tended to protect clubs from either asset stripping or from simply failing to re-invest club profits.

However, Rule 34 has not been enforced against clubs who chose the Plc sta-tus, these clubs are thus open to the charge that their business management lacks a real interest in the game and are merely concerned with financial return. This charge may in fact be true but the unrealistic nature of the rule itself could cor-rectly be blamed for creating an environment in which some sort of reaction was inevitable. The persistent cries of dissatisfaction from the terraces over the fre-quent mismanagement of non-Plc club finances may be a direct result of the pro-hibitions imposed under Rule 34.

While there have long been a few clubs[7] that have enjoyed financial stability the vast majority of football clubs have struggled through the years in an environ-ment with continually escalating labour costs. Indeed, today even in the Premier League only a few clubs reap much of a reward when considered from their profit and loss accounts. While many externalities can be offered in explanation, a lack of professional business management must be ranked as a significant rea-son for these financial difficulties.[8] The FA's Rule 34 has ensured that effective management remains unavailable unless the club opts to become a Plc.

At present, the official regulator of the game, the FA, in failing to alter this rule appears so enchanted with the nostalgic notion of maintaining the traditions of football that it has failed to notice that the Plc clubs have left it standing by the side of the highway. In suggesting that the FA has effectively resigned its regula-tory role in the face of financial power, the question arises as to why the regulator should behave in such a fashion? The answer appears to lie in a realisation by all the parties of the financial position of modern football. The upper echelons of the Premier League contain the 'product' that 'anchors' the media money now driv-ing the industry. Indeed it is ironic that only those clubs with a professional fi-nancial management team and executive directors are realistically able to run what would now be considered a sizeable business in any industry. In this changed environment the regulator has become the regulated.

The first obvious manifestation of this shift of power occurred with the advent of the Premier League itself, established in 1992. The disenchantment by the ma-jor clubs may be attributed to the poor treatment meted out to football by the ter-restrial broadcast media then able to exploit a monopsonistic position. However, with the emergence of a competitor to terrestrial broadcasting in the form of sat-ellite technology in the late 1980's the true value of the broadcast rights swiftly became obvious. It was only when the major clubs of the old first division of-

---

[7] Szymanski S, and Kuypers T, *Winners and Losers – The Business Strategy of Football*, (1999), London, Viking .

[8] This notion has been borne out by Barrie Pierpoint in his essay on business strategies in foot-ball. Supra, n.4.

fered something akin to an ultimatum that the FA sanctioned the creation of the new Premier League.

This process has been described as 'regulatory capture' and is one of the dangers that have been identified as existing within self-regulatory regimes.[9] In justifying self-regulation, one of the benefits is that it is a less costly method than public regulation. However, one should only cautiously assume that self-regulation to reflect exclusively altruistic intentions. Anthony Ogus has suggested that '...private interests which are threatened by regulation may gain considerable benefits if they are allowed themselves to formulate and enforce the relevant controls'.[10] As an example of this acquiescence, upon ticket price structuring, the FA continually submitted to the claims of clubs that they are independent bodies. This argument, however valid, nevertheless ignores the regulatory *raison d'être* of the FA.

It appears ever more clearly that with the new found confidence of the major clubs the FA has lost its role as a regulator in the core areas of the management of football's infrastructure. When a self-interested element of an organisation is able to avoid the 'conventional constitutional channels'[11] and usurp power by financial force the regulation imposed by modern corporatism is seen in a poor light. The response has been the summoning forth of the Football Taskforce (which has received all party Parliamentary support). Quite unusually, this government-sponsored project has also been welcomed at a grass roots level. This reaction demonstrates the feeling of impotence experienced by the core supporters of the game in the face of the rampant commercialisation of modern football.

THE APPROPRIATE LEGAL ENTITY

While many football clubs are plagued with accusations of greed and self-indulgence, it is worth examining the legal framework under which they operate. In so doing, certain ethical issues may be adduced that, go some way towards mitigating the actions of the clubs.

Almost all professional football clubs operate as limited companies. Many were incorporated in the latter part of the nineteenth century or at the beginning of the twentieth century. This was at a time when notions of stakeholding were almost heretical. Late Victorian England was in favour of private property and the Entrepreneur. The limited liability company was thus to emerge as the favoured vehicle for all businesses. However, in a sporting environment one is forced to question the necessity for a limited company, or more accurately to enquire whether an alternative legal entity would be a more appropriate vehicle.

---

[9] Ogus A, Rethinking Self-Regulation, (1995) *Oxford Journal of Legal Studies*, 375.
[10] Ibid.
[11] Ibid.

The qualities offered by incorporating as a limited liability company are the minimising of risk to the individual members and greater capital raising powers. It would appear that during the period when the game was becoming established the owners of clubs feared the effects that failure might produce. While there can be no ill intent founded upon the simple utilisation of a valid statutory procedure, its use may have assisted in producing the 'them and us' atmosphere that currently divides the boardroom from the fans.

In making their clubs assume the form of private limited companies, the owners effectively segregated themselves from the other elements that make up any football club, successful or otherwise. One of the greatest assets of English clubs lies in the cultural ties that have developed in the area in which the club is situated. In the greater metropolitan areas this can be readily recognised by the loyalty towards a particular team being determined by which side of Stanley Park one is born in Liverpool or which side of a road one is born in North London.

One of the benefits of Rule 34 was to eliminate the risk of the franchise system that operates in the United States. Under such conditions teams can not only be bought and sold but also transplanted to a different area where no links remain from the place of its creation. In England, the club remains geographically attached to its birthplace, yet spiritually and culturally its links to its locality are being increasingly subsumed by the owners' desire to maximise their investment.

When one examines the football club as a business, the conflict can be seen to exist between the goals of the owners: profit maximisation or the winning of trophies. While in the past many owners/chairman were re-living schoolboy fantasies, the reality of financial control of an asset will almost always produce the desire to maximise the gains from the interest held.

Advocates of those clubs floating on the Stock Exchange would state that by raising capital on the open market they are increasing the opportunity for success of their core supporters. The conflict once again re-emerges in that a new dimension is added to the equation, that being the shareholder. While the loyal fan may hold some shares, it will be the institutional shareholders who determine whether a proposed dividend will be enough to satisfy the shareholders' requirements. Thus, the Board of Directors may be driven into selling a valued player with the effect of squandering future footballing success for more immediate financial reward or stability.

The 1990's fashion for predominantly Premier League clubs seeking to raise capital in the open market has had varied results. In effect, the quite unique nature of football as a business activity has been seen in all its glory. Public investment in the stock market is normally driven by a desire to maximise capital. When football clubs offer their shares, fans have sought to buy them as they would many of the clubs other merchandising products. However, a company's share price is governed amongst other factors, by growth. Only a very few clubs will have the ability to turn their fans' wishes into reality.

The greatest success story is Manchester United, which has seen its name become a brand image throughout the world. With the continuing advancement of technology on the internet, it appears that their financial status as the Goliath of the game is guaranteed for many years to come. This becomes even more apparent when one is given to understand that the Manchester United web site receives eight million hits per month.[12] Such a success rate becomes even more enviable to other dot-com companies since the web site is not currently showing live links to their games. Once this capability is in place the appetite of their purported multi-million-fan base will become even more profitably satisfied.

However, even while the success of Manchester United appears to be supreme both on the pitch as well as on the stock market, there is unrest on the terraces. While the potential for unprecedented investment was available with the BSkyB offer, the fans were unequivocal in their distaste for the proposed merger. In pure financial terms such a reaction is irrational. Even at Old Trafford where the voracious appetite for success is no less sought than at any other club in the country, there exists a desire to retain those intangible links between supporter and club. These links are the very qualities that commercialisation appears to challenge.

With the escalating commercialism driven by the effects of broadcasting and the increase in labour costs brought about by *Bosman*, many of the clubs that have sought a stock market listing are no longer considered to be such viable investments. While corporate accountability can be seen as being advantageous in any business, the football club's susceptibility to a take-over only increases the alienation experienced by its fan base. The reason being that the rescuer's motives are unlikely to be philanthropic. However, given the current commercial realities of the football business why would anyone wish to purchase an interest in any but the most successful club?

THE EFFECT OF BROADCASTING

There have been two high profile rulings affecting football: one was the consideration of the Monopolies and Mergers Commission (now the Commission for Competition) the other was brought by the Director General of Fair Trading in the Restrictive Trade Practices Court. In the former case the attempted take-over by BSkyB of Manchester United Plc was adjudged to be against the public interest. In the second case the collective sale of the Premier League broadcasting rights was held to be anti-competitive but yet to be in 'the public interest'.

These two results appear contradictory at first glance, one adopting a more rigid approach to classic competition policy, the other having a high regard for the particular industry and nature of the relevant market. While these rulings appeared to forestall the advancing influence of the broadcasting companies, the pot

---

[12] Blackshaw I, BSkyB aims to hit the Net, *The Times,* April 18, 2000.

of gold at the end of the rainbow was too great an incentive for these companies to resist. The attempt to purchase the biggest club in the world was motivated by the conclusion that the collective sales agreement of the Premier League would be ruled anti-competitive. Had the bid been successful, Mr Murdoch's company would have been actively supporting the efforts of the Director General of Fair Trading. In the event, its holding had to be reduced yet the collective sales agreement remained lawful.

The broadcasting companies have now adopted a new approach in order to maximise their efforts in capturing this highly profitable market. The various competitors within this advancing technological industry are purchasing *significant* interests in football clubs as if on a supermarket sweep. The only limitation in their activity is contained in Rule S:4 of the Premier League rules, which imposes a 10% threshold of an interest in more than one club. However, a 9.9% interest in Manchester United or Chelsea could be described as a significant holding, if not by the League or FA, certainly by the Stock Exchange.

More recently, with the advent of digital broadcasting as a new technology, further companies have entered into the market. Significantly, Granada has purchased an interest in Liverpool FC. In a joint venture with Carlton, Granada owns On-Digital. It is pointless to attempt to list the current roll call of media companies purchases since the current state of the market will result in this information inevitably being out of date within a matter of weeks. What is more relevant is the reason why such a buying frenzy is occurring.

The American-owned media company, NTL has stated internally that it 'is interested in gaining a seat at the negotiating table when it comes to television rights'.[13] Such a statement is evidence enough of the motives for the actions of these companies. Thus, as far as the clubs are concerned, the effect of the rulings mentioned above is to generate a cash bonanza across the entire spectrum of the Premier League as opposed to a few exclusive clubs. However, what is the true cost to the game?

While the value of the purchases has been restricted by the 10% rule, the level of intervention below 10% may be creating a breach of other rules of the League. Within the same section as the 10% limitation, exists an outright exclusion of any involvement of more than one club in the administration or influence of another.[14] While there is a caveat that such activity may be authorised by agreement, the most recent purchase by BSkyB of Manchester City shares has been said to have occurred without prior consent.[15]

While the above scenario may have repercussions in respect of competition law, it should not be forgotten that the Premier League is operating as a limited company and thus subject to the rights and duties that are invoked by the Compa-

---

[13] The £2 billion Ball Game, *Panorama* BBC TV, May 15, 2000.
[14] FA Premier League Rules, Section S: (Miscellaneous) ss. 2.3 and 2.4.
[15] Broome E, and Szczepanil N, 'Putting Themselves About', *The Times*, June 6, 2000.

nies Act 1985. While an interest may be declared and authorised retroactively, the composition of three or four cliques within a particular media company's interest acting as a unifying bond has the potential to generate the risk of minority shareholder actions. Such a scenario is not unrealistic when BSkyB has an interest in at least five Premier League clubs.

The constitutional framework of the Premier League Ltd as contained within the articles of association seeks to preserve the democratic legitimacy of the body by allotting one share to each club within the league, regardless of size or wealth. However, a consequence of the level of financial investment by broadcasting groups into the game has had the effect of severely restricting such equality. As the richer clubs proceed to enjoy even greater wealth, driven from the proceeds of the European competitions, so the Premier League itself has now been said to contain three divisions. One is fighting for the title, one for the right to play European football and finally one for the right to remain within the league. The possible ramifications of this state of affairs will be examined below.

An Alternative Entity

It has been submitted that the use of the limited liability company and more recently the Plc has been instrumental in channelling large amounts of funds into a few shareholders or ex-shareholders pockets. Moreover, the creation of anonymous Plcs where control can shift easily from one company to another has further eroded the relationship between club and supporter. While it is easy to identify the problems, it is more constructive to at least seek to offer an alternative.

The stakeholder concept has been referred to earlier. It requires that the interests of the club should be drawn from a broader notion of what are the clubs assets and its aspirations. Ideally such an approach will allow the natural links that are present between community and club to be utilised rather than squandered, while at the same time fostering a real opportunity for footballing success.

From a corporate legal perspective this would require a change in the club's ownership structure. No longer would there be an individual or company in control but rather a more Corinthian spirit would permeate the club. This idea is not as idealistic as it may sound. Michie gives the account of the NFL team, the Green Bay Packers, 'who have maintained local fan and community ownership whilst becoming one of the most successful teams in American football history'.[16] The concept of mutualism can be expressed in varying degrees of orthodoxy, however, the ultimate goal is that 'in every case the structure is giving the supporter a form of ownership which matches his or her sense of the relationship with the club'.[17]

---

[16] Michie J, *'New Mutualism – A Golden Goal?'* (1999) London, The Co-operative Party.

[17] Jaquiss K, Football, fans and fat cats: whose football club is it anyway? in Hamil S, et al (eds) *Football in the Digital Age – Whose Game is it Anyway?*, (2000), Mainstream, Edinburgh.

In order for such a co-operative system to come into existence, the present shareholders would have to be bought out. Given the current value of clubs in the Premier League alone, such a financial restructuring would bring with it grave financial risks. However, as already stated such a purist notion of mutuality is not the only option. Indeed, at Northampton Town FC a supporters trust was set up for the purposes of advancing the interests of the many, rather than just the few. By obtaining two seats on the board of directors, the fans had secured themselves a true say in the boardroom. However, it should be stated that these seats were offered by the administrator of the club and not voted upon at an annual general meeting. While the above theory may be *feasible* in the lower divisions, in the current environment of the Premier League reality would deem such an occurrence highly unlikely.

ADVANCING FROM THE PREMIERSHIP

The difference in wealth that exists as between clubs in the Premier League may be one of the main causes of its own demise. Ultimately, the league could resemble the grocery industry where the supermarkets have virtually eliminated the small corner shop. The dichotomy, is that within sport, a team does not wish to eliminate its competitor, merely beat it. This is known as the uncertainty of outcome theory and is one reason proffered for sports special status within competition policy.

Beyond competition law, which is outside the terms of this chapter, it can be shown that employment law within sport displays anti-competitive behaviour that is not countenanced in any other areas of the economy.[18] The ability of a club to enforce its property rights over an employee has been the well from which the traditionally poorer clubs have drawn. However, the right of any club to demand a transfer fee even when a player seeks to move before the completion of his contract is about to be challenged before the ECJ.

In such a situation the effects will not be felt on the terraces. Home supporters are loyal of necessity, however, those spectators paying broadcasters annual subscriptions have no compelling reason to demonstrate such loyalty in the long run. In recent years, the European Champion's League has been expanded in an attempt to prevent the formation of a European super league. While such a league would re-establish the uncertainty of outcome it may also give rise to altogether different regulatory problems. In an attempt to identify some of these problems this chapter will now move to consider the impact of the EU upon the corporate forms available to European Football Teams.

---

[18] Gratton C, The Peculiar Economics of English Football, in Garland J, et al (eds) *The Future of Football – Challenges for the Twenty-first Century*, (2000) London, Frank Cass.

THE CORPORATE FORM IN EUROPE

The question to be addressed in the remainder of this chapter is the extent to which the development of a European super league will impact upon the fundamental freedom established in the Treaty of Rome. The right given to freedom of movement of persons established in Article 39 extends a similar facility to companies by virtue of Article 43. These provisions require each Member State to adjust their laws progressively so that foreign nationals and foreign companies will be treated in the same way as domestic individuals and domestic companies when they wish to establish themselves across national frontiers. The immediate purpose of this freedom was identified as being to remove the barriers at national frontiers set to the entrepreneurial and organisational skills of the nationals and companies of each Member State.[19] In a broader context this freedom is also intended to enhance and develop the objectives of a more effective utilization of available resources in the Single Market. The issue is whether this freedom provides a threat or an opportunity for the future regulation of football and the development of a European superleague. Before reaching a conclusion this chapter will offer a brief sketch of the freedom of establishment which will then be followed by an analysis of relevant decisions by the European Court of Justice.

The Components of Freedom of Establishment

The freedom of establishment has two components:[20]

– Freedom of non-discriminatory access to and exercise of non-salaried activities, and
– Freedom to organize and manage, without discrimination, enterprises and in particular companies as this term is defined in the Treaty.[21]

The freedom within the Treaty is an absolute freedom and has direct applicability.[22] The obligation that the Member State has assumed is an obligation to assure 'national treatment'. It is important to remember that the design is to equalise the competitive conditions in the Community arena. In order to take advantage of this freedom a national who wishes to organize an agency branch or subsidiary in another Member State must first himself be established in the Common Market.[23]

---

[19] EEC Commission Action Programmes of the Community for the second stage at 17 para. 19 (Brussels October 24, 1962) and First General Report on the Activities of the Community at 58 (September 1958).

[20] Article 43.

[21] Ibid.

[22] See Case 2/74 Reyners v Belgium [1974] ECR 631. See also Case 270/83 Commission v France [1986] ECR 273, Case 143/87 Stanton v INASTI [1988] ECR 3877 and Case 81/87 Crown v HM Treasury and Commissioners of the Inland Revenue, Ex parte Daily Mail and General Trust plc [1988] ECR 5483.

[23] Article 43(1) EC.

That is he must have a recognised economic base or link in one of the Common Market countries.

Companies were and are intended to benefit from this freedom of movement in the same way as natural persons.[24] The implementation of this goal has posed problems. It is inherent in the nature of companies as legal persons that they cannot in reality or in law exercise freedom of establishment in the same manner as natural persons. In order to attempt to resolve this problem, Article 48 provides that rather than considering the 'nationality' of the company, its management or its shareholders all companies can benefit from this freedom as long as they possess a specified link with the Member State.

Article 48 provides that this link should be that the company has its registered office, central administration or principal place of business within the Community. These criteria are often referred to as the 'connecting factors' and are now understood to be alternative rather than cumulative.[25] However this alternative approach fails to take into account differences in the underlying philosophies of the jurisdictions.

Such differences of approach can be seen for example in the various attitudes to the recognition of a corporate form registered in another jurisdiction. Thus, whilst the UK, Netherlands and Ireland adhere to 'the incorporation theory' the other Member States regard a company as a national of the particular State in which it has its 'real seat' (*siege social*, *siege real*) that is its central administration, its 'brain or nerve centre'.[26] One consequence of this difference of approach could be that while a company which maintains only a registered office in the UK or the Netherlands would be considered as validly incorporated and organized by the English and Dutch courts, it might not be so recognised by the courts of the other Member States. Therefore such a company could be denied recognition as a legal person with resultant potential personal liability for its officers or at the very least the company could be held to be subject to the Company law of the state in which its 'real seat' is deemed to be located.

In the establishment context, Article 48 should mean that this potential has been restricted if not excluded. Indeed the general suitability of such an ambiguous approach must be questioned in an increasingly trans-national market. If, as it appears the rationale for retaining this difference of approach is to prevent organizational decisions being made other than on the basis of normal business considerations[27] would not a greater approximation of national laws be a more obvious answer to this dilemma?

---

[24] Articles 43(2) and 48 EC.

[25] See for example the comments of the ECJ in Case 270/83 Commission v France, supra and Frommel, EEC Companies and migration: A setback for Europe? *Intertax*, December 1987 413-414.

[26] Latty P, Pseudo Foreign Corporations, (1965) *Yale Law Journal* 137 at 167.

[27] The often expressed fear (see Case 81/87 *Daily Mail* supra) is of a 'Delaware effect' that is that companies would base their decisions to relocate on the opportunity to obtain greater legal freedom as is afforded by, for example, Dutch law as compared to German Company law.

In the context of the development of a European superleague this difference of approach is clearly a fundamental issue. It strikes at the ability for effective regulation either through the football league of an individual country or through the regulators of the European arena.

The Impact of the European Court of Justice

The case law of the ECJ concerning Articles 43 and 48 is of relatively recent origin. The first decision emerged in the mid-1980's.[28] As we have seen, there is a cultural distinction between the 'real seat theory' and the 'incorporation theory'. In *Commission v France* the ECJ had its first opportunity to consider the right of establishment created by Articles 43 and 48. It had to decide whether a German Insurance company which invested on the Paris Stock Exchange through a French Branch Office and a French insurance company which also invested on the same exchange through a branch should be entitled to the French Imputation Credit *(avoir fiscal).*[29] Although both were taxed in the same way in respect of dividend income, only the French company received the imputation credit. The question before the ECJ was: did this amount to discrimination? The ECJ's answer was yes! The ECJ argued this difference in treatment deterred companies registered in other Member States from setting up agencies or branches since they were placed at a disadvantage vis a vis French companies.[30]

The effect of this judgement was clear and simple. Insurance companies from other Member States are free to choose whether to do business through an agency or a branch on the one hand, or through a subsidiary registered in France on the other. But which ever is chosen – no tax disadvantage must result.

---

[28] See Commission v France supra n.23.

[29] Article 158 of the *Code Generale des Impots (CGI)* provides for an imputation credit designated as *avoir fiscal,* which is granted to shareholders receiving dividends distributed by French corporations. This is equal to half the amount actually distributed by those corporations. This credit may be off-set against the income tax due by the shareholder receiving the dividend. If the credit exceeds the shareholders income tax liability individual shareholders may request a refund of the excess amount. Corporate shareholders are not entitled to such a refund. Art. 158 goes on to provide that the imputation credit is only granted to persons who have their actual domicile or registered office in France. In other words the imputation credit is only available to resident shareholders.

[30] The Commission put forward two submissions to show that the contested French rules were contrary to Art. 43(2) EC: 1. Those rules discriminate between insurance companies resident in France and non-resident insurance companies established in other Member States. The French tax system prevents such branches and agencies from holding shares and thus places them at a disadvantage. 2. Since the French tax provisions are unfavourable to insurance companies established in other EC states they indirectly restrict the freedom of insurance companies to establish themselves in France. The provisions constitute an inducement to establish a subsidiary in order to avoid the disadvantage resulting from the fact that the benefits would not otherwise be available.

In practical effect this decision may be contrasted with the *Daily Mail* case.[31] This case raised fundamental questions about the scope of Articles 43 and 48. The principal question addressed by the ECJ was: could a company incorporated in England – as was the *Daily Mail* – move its central management and control to another Member State – here the Netherlands – in order to avoid paying English Capital Gains tax on its investment portfolio.[32]

The UK Treasury was prepared to grant permission to this transfer only if the *Daily Mail* sold at least part of its assets prior to the transfer of residence. Such a sale would have given rise to the CGT the transfer was designed to avoid. This was unacceptable to the *Daily Mail* and they sought a declaration from the High Court that Article 43 allowed a transfer without Treasury consent. The High Court sought a preliminary ruling from the ECJ.

The *Daily Mail's* argument was that Articles 43 and 48 granted to both natural and legal persons a right to freely exit one Member State and a corresponding freedom to enter another Member States for the purposes of establishment. They also contended that the motive for the transfer of the company under Article 43 was irrelevant.[33] Finally, the *Daily Mail* asserted that to seek Treasury consent was incompatible with the supremacy of EC law as it subjects Community law to national law. This subjugation had already been rejected by the ECJ in the areas of free movement of goods[34] and free movement of persons.[35]

The judgement of the ECJ started well for the *Daily Mail* and was consistent with previous decisions:

> '... freedom of establishment constitutes one of the fundamental principles of the Community ... The provisions of the Treaty guaranteeing that freedom have been directly applicable since the end of the transitional period ... Those provisions secure the right of establishment in another Member State not merely for Community nationals but also for companies.'[36]

However, the remainder of the decision fails to accord with the very clear stance towards mobility previously taken by the ECJ:

---

[31] Case 81/87 supra. For a more detailed discussion of this case an its implications see Van Thiel, Tax planning and the right of establishment, (1988) *European Taxation*, November, 357.

[32] The *Daily Mail* wished to sell a significant part of its non-permanent assets and to use the proceeds to buy its own shares. If the *Daily Mail* did so in the UK it would be subject to CGT and Advance Corporation tax under UK Tax law. In the Netherlands the *Daily Mail* would become taxable as a resident which does include taxation of capital gains but only for accruals *after* the transfer of residence. To avoid this tax liability – and it was common ground that this was the reason for the application for consent.

[33] This accords with the ECJ decision referred to above.

[34] See, for example, Case 130/80 Kelderman [1981] ECR at 527 and joined cases 41-44/70 International Fruit Co. [1971] ECR at 411.

[35] Case 157/79 Pieck [1980] ECR at 2171.

[36] Case 270/83 [1986] ECR 273 at para. 15.

'In defining in Article 48 the companies that enjoy the right of establishment the Treaty places on the same footing as connecting factors the registered office, central administration and principle place of business. Moreover, Article 220 of the Treaty provides for the conclusion, so far as is necessary, of agreements between the Member States with a view to securing *inter alia* the retention of legal personality in the event of transfer of the registered office of companies from one country to another. No convention in this area has yet come into force.'[37]

The ECJ thus concluded:

'It must therefore be held that the Treaty regards the differences in national legislation concerning the required connecting factor and the question whether – and if so how – the registered office or real head office of a company incorporated under national law may be transferred from one Member State to another as problems which are not resolved by the rules concerning the right of establishment but must be dealt with by future legislation or convention.'[38]

This decision has been roundly condemned by leading academics and judges.[39] It is submitted that this decision severely limits the 'fundamental' right of establishment laid down in Articles 43 and 48 and reintroduces barriers to corporate mobility. However, from certain perspectives within the context of the development of a European Champions League this decision may actually be welcomed. It restricts the ability of football clubs to take advantage of the so called *Delaware effect*[40] and preserves the appearance of domestic control. Such a climate of uncertainty affords a further opportunity for national regulatory control of football clubs. We still have no clear indication as to the extent to which a football club operating through the vehicle of the corporate form is to be regulated purely at a national level or whether Community interests are to be considered.

The *Centros* Case

This recent decision of the ECJ may be understood to allow the revelation of a modicum of clarity concerning the appropriate approach to be adopted in considering these corporate issues.

A decision delivered by the ECJ in 1999 has raised again the question of the extent to which Articles 43 and 48 provide real freedom of establishment for

---

[37] See para. 21.

[38] See para. 23.

[39] See, for example, Frommel 'EEC Companies and Migration: a set back for Europe' *Intertax* December 1998 at 409 and Van Thiel 'Tax Planning and the Right of Establishment' (1988) *European Taxation*, 357.

[40] This is the notion that companies would base their decision to relocate on the opportunity to obtain greater legal freedom as afforded by, for example, UK and Dutch company law as compared, for instance, with the stricter company law of France and Germany.

companies. The *Centros* case[41] concerned, Centros Ltd., which was registered on the 18th May 1992 at Companies House in England. Its initial unpaid share capital was £100. The shares were owned by two Danish nationals resident in Denmark. One shareholder was the director of the company and the company's registered office was the home of a friend of a shareholders and situated in the UK. The company never traded since its formation. In 1992 the company requested that the Danish Trade and Companies Board (DTCB) register a branch of Centros Ltd in Denmark.

According to Danish company law private limited companies and foreign companies having a similar legal form which are established in one Member State of the EU may do business in Denmark through a branch.

However, the DTCB refused to register a branch on the grounds *inter alia* that Centros was in fact seeking to establish a principal establishment and not a branch. The DTCB believed that Centros was attempting to avoid Danish national rules relating to the formation of a company and in particular trying to avoid paying the minimum initial capital in Denmark which was then set at approximately £11,000. Indeed the Shareholders confirmed that they had formed the company in the UK precisely for the purpose of avoiding the Danish requirements with regard to minimum paid up share capital.

The DTCB did not in any way deny that a private limited company with its registered office in another Member State might carry on business through a branch. Indeed they argued that if Centros had conducted *any* business in the UK they would have agreed to register the branch in Denmark.

Centros argued that having been incorporated in the UK it was entitled by virtue of Articles 43 and 48 to set up a branch in Denmark and that such a refusal on the part of the DTCB amounted to a breach of this fundamental principle. The Danish Supreme Court referred the matter to the ECJ.

The observations of the Danish government as to why Centros should be refused the right to establish a branch included the following:

– The situation was purely internal to Denmark and did not amount to a relevant external element in the light of Community law and that the sole purpose of the request was an avoidance of the application of Danish legislation.
– That the Danish shareholders could not rely on Articles 43 and 48 since the sole purpose of the formation amounted to an abuse to freedom of establishment and that Denmark could take steps to prevent such abuse.
– That the minimum capital requirement was in compliance with the principal of proportionality because it (1) provided for the protection of public creditors who were unable to secure their debts by means of guarantees and (2) provided protection from the risk of undercapitalised companies.

---

[41] Case 212/97 *Centros* judgement.

The ECJ response was to say that it was irrelevant that a company was formed in one Member State solely for the purpose of establishing itself in a second Member State. Further that 'shopping between jurisdictions' in order to form the company in the least restrictive jurisdiction and then to form a secondary establishment elsewhere is not in itself an abuse of the right of establishment. Finally the arguments relating to the safeguarding of creditors were found not to be within the ambit of Article 46 or indeed did not fulfil the conditions set out on the ECJ's case law on imperative requirements in the general interest. Also, Community law measures relating to, for example, annual accounts and disclosure requirements provided protection for creditors.

It has been asserted that this decision is going to be to a companies right of establishment what *Cassis de Dijon* was to free movement of goods.[42] That European law is now a major consideration within the context of sports regulation can be seen from the above discussion and also from other chapters included in this work.[43] That sport is subject to Community law insofar as it constitutes an economic activity within the meaning of Article 2 of the EU Treaty is now beyond question.[44] As we have seen this requires non discrimination on the grounds of nationality and is clearly reflected by the most recent case of the ECJ.[45] This issue has recently arisen in relation to the activities of English side Wimbledon (at the time in the Premiership) and Scottish League side Clydebank. Both clubs were reported to be planning to announce their intention to move to Dublin in the Republic of Ireland. Their intention was to continue to play in the Premiership and Scottish league respectively. This plan was against the FIFA, UEFA and national association rules which prohibit this form of cross border move. It is important to note here that no such objection exists in Scotland. This activity is similar to the attempt by Belgian football club Excelsior Mouscron who whilst not wanting to permanently locate did want to play the home league of a UEFA cup tie in a larger stadium across the border at Lille in France. This proposal was also blocked by UEFA on the basis that the home and away structure of its games required protection. In the light of the *Centros* case[46] these proposals would now be within the spirit of Articles 43 and 48. It is interesting to note that the Commission had the opportunity to consider this proposal in relation to Excelsior Mouscron and the Commission rejected the suggestion that such restraint by UEFA was in contravention of Article 48. This approach is not altogether surprising particularly when compared with the Commission approach in the *Daily Mail*

---

[42] See, for example, the comments of Danish professor Erik Werlauff.

[43] Also see Parrish R, 'Reconciling conflicting approaches to sport in the European Union' (1998) *Sports Law Bulletin*, 10.

[44] See, for example, Case 36/74 Walrave and Koch v Union Cycliste International and also Case 13/76 Dona v Mantero.

[45] Centros case, supra.

[46] Ibid.

case.[47] This approach is reflective of the tension between national and European regulation and indeed of the tension between the approach adopted by different institutions within the EU itself. However, in the wake of the *Centros* case this tension must be addressed. The most effective way of balancing such competing regulatory requirements is for the regulators to recognize and adopt the spirit of the Treaty of Rome and it is upon this issue that this chapter will conclude.

CONCLUSION: BACK TO THE FUTURE?

This chapter has sought to demonstrate that there are significant problems associated with the rigid and unyielding national regulation of football clubs. The actions of the English FA were seen to have amounted to an effective regulatory abdication which forced many clubs to adopt the Plc status. Allusion was also made to the difficulties of maintaining even a semblance of regulatory control, after the abdication, with the dawning of the Premiership. It is in this context that the emergence or otherwise of a European Super League must be considered. Assuming the *Centros* case to be of general application it now appears that the football clubs of Europe may legitimately plan their corporate location in a Member State other than that in which their fan base has been traditionally located. However, how will the various regulators respond to the coming challenge?

It is hoped that the regulators will not choose to repeat their earlier mistakes, the distinctive regulatory challenges presented by mass spectator sports require an inclusive appreciation of the legitimate concerns of a wide constituency. The example of the FA and Rule 34 demonstrates the regulatory danger. If the various national regulators in the Member States of the EU do not actively address the issue of corporate mobility they will be marginalised and those they are intended to protect may have to suffer a sports industry governed only by short-term financial considerations. Although this is necessarily a matter of speculation, a European Regulation may be able to clarify the appropriate use and abuse of the newly portable European corporate form.

---

[47] Supra n. 31.

Part Four:
Comparative Perspectives:
Localisation and Specificity

LEGISLATION ON SPORTS IN POLAND

Andrzej J. Szwarc

Introduction

Poland has a similar regulatory structure to countries such as France, Belgium and Greece, where certain issues involved in sport are regulated by law. However the present regime is different from the highly regulated communist framework which existed before 1989. That was the year that the well-known political, social and economic changes took place and Poland has been essentially a democratic country ever since with a free-market economy. The changes affected sport as well, which will be discussed later in this chapter.

Despite the fall of communism the State regulation of Polish sport has, however, endured in certain areas. Physical culture and sport fall within the jurisdiction of one of the government administrative departments and includes physical culture, popular sports, professional sport and sport involving the disabled.[1] The government administrative agency for these matters is the President of State Physical Culture and Sports Administration,[2] currently reporting to the Minister of National Education.

Certain issues in sport are governed by the Physical Culture Act of January 18, 1996[3] and other legislation discussed below. This legislation governs diverse issues relating to sport such as: the legal status of Polish sports clubs and unions, the legal status of athletes, professional sport, arbitration courts for sport, disciplinary liability in sport, doping, safety in sport including safety at sports events. In addition other general legislative provisions apply to sport because they have come to govern the relationships that occur in sport.

The law of the European Union does not yet apply in Poland as Poland has yet to become an EU Member State, however, Polish efforts prior to full membership have resulted in an EU association treaty. Under this Treaty Poland must meet a

---

[1] Art. 15.1 of the Government Administration Divisions Act of September 4, 1997 (consolidated in *Dziennik Ustaw* of 1999, No. 82, item 928, as amended). *Dziennik Ustaw (Dz. U.)* and *Monitor Polski (M.P.)* are names of Polish official journals for promulgation of laws and regulations.

[2] This agency was enabled by the Physical Culture and Sports Administration (Enablement) Act dated January 25, 1991 (Dz. U. No. 16, item 74, as amended).

[3] Dz. U. No. 25, item 113, as amended.

A. Caiger and S. Gardiner (Eds), Professional Sport in the EU: Regulation and Re-regulation
© 2000, T.M.C.Asser Press, The Hague, The Netherlands

number of conditions before accession takes place. The fundamental condition is harmonisation of Polish law with that of the EU, which is now ongoing. Regulations applicable to sports are being harmonised accordingly, including free movement of employees, freedom of pursuing a business, free movement of services, free movement of capital and payments, competition and anti-monopoly laws. Poland has already achieved significant compliance with EU law.

THE CONSTITUTION OF THE REPUBLIC OF POLAND

The Polish Constitution April 2, 1997,[4] only makes one reference to physical culture, the concept inclusive of, inter alia, sport. In Article 68(5) it is provided that: 'Public authorities shall promote the development of physical culture, particularly among children and adolescents.' There are also other provisions of the Constitution that implicitly refer to sport. The most important are:
- Article 12, which ensures, inter alia, freedom to establish and operate associations;[5]
- Article 57[6] and 58,[7] which ensure freedom of assembly and association;
- Article 65(1),[8] which ensures freedom to choose and pursue one's occupation;
- the aforementioned Article 68,[9] which lays down, among others, the right to have one's health protected.

PRESIDENT OF STATE PHYSICAL CULTURE AND SPORTS ADMINISTRATION

A special central agency has been established within the framework of the Polish state administration to implement state policy regarding recreation, rehabilitation and sports. The agency is the President of State Physical Culture and Sports Ad-

---

[4] Dz. U. No. 78, item 483.

[5] Art. 12: The Republic of Poland shall ensure the freedom to establish and operate trade unions, farmers' social and professional organisations, associations, citizen movements, and other non-compulsory organisations and foundations.

[6] Art. 57: Every one shall have the freedom to organise and participate in peaceful assemblies. Such freedom may only be restricted by statute.

[7] Art. 58: 1. Every one shall have the freedom to associate; 2. Associations whose purpose or activities contravene the Constitution or a statute shall be prohibited. The power to refuse to register or to prohibit an association shall be vested in the court; 3. The types of associations subject to registration by the court, the procedures for such registration and supervision over such associations shall be set out by statute.

[8] Art. 65.1: Every one shall have the freedom to choose and pursue one's occupation and place of work. Exceptions shall be set out by statute.

[9] Art. 68: 1. Every one has the right to have one's health protected; 2. The public authorities shall ensure that citizens, regardless of their wealth, shall have equal access to publicly funded health services. The terms and conditions as well as the scope of such services shall be laid down in a statute (...).

ministration. This agency operates under the regime of the Physical Culture and Sports Administration (Enablement) Act of the January 25, 1991. Article 1(4) of the Act provides that the Prime Minister shall have the power to appoint and dismiss the President of State Physical Culture and Sports Administration on application of the Minister competent for physical culture and sports, now the Minister of National Education. This Minister supervises the President of the State Physical Culture and Sports Administration. Article 3 of the Act sets out in detail the agency's tasks and how they should be implemented, while Article 4 lays down that state funds earmarked for physical culture, tourism and leisure, be available to the agency. The Physical Culture and Sports Administration operates under statutes granted by the Prime Minister.

The agency of the President of the State Physical Culture and Tourism Administration has certain powers. Such agencies operated before entry into force of the aforementioned act of January 25, 1991. The legal basis for their operations was provided by statutes previously in force, and their status and scope of tasks were differently defined. For this reason, the names of these agencies have also changed.

LEGISLATION APPLICABLE TO SPORT

The Physical Culture Act

Sports are governed by many different statutes. The most important of these is the Physical Culture Act of January 18, 1996, which replaced the earlier Act dated July 3, 1984.[10] The Physical Culture Act currently in force is a comprehensive statute composed of 67 articles, laying down rules for the activities in the field of physical culture as well as specifying tasks of government administration and territorial self-government agencies, physical culture associations, their unions and other entities the aim of which is to ensure the correct process of physical education, exercise of sports, active leisure and rehabilitation. Hence the Act is not focused on sport issues exclusively.

Changes may soon be made to the Act, and it may possibly even be replaced, as some of its provisions have come under criticism. There are proposals to regulate certain matters in a different way and to add certain new regulations. Still, it is difficult to say if, when and how such proposals will be incorporated.

---

[10] Dz. U. No. 34, item 181, as amended.

Other Statutes Applicable to Sport

Sport issues are also referred to in the Horseracing Act of April 19, 1950[11] and the Safety of Public Events Act of August 22, 1997.[12] There has been a more detailed regulation of sport by way of secondary legislation. In this regard the Physical Culture Act (1996) and the Safety of Public Events Act (1997) are enabling statutes. This secondary legislation ranks as regulations (ordinances) of the Council of Ministers (the Government) or individual ministers, or the President of the State Physical Culture and Sports Administration. The most important of this secondary legislation are detailed in the appendix.

International Conventions

A number of international conventions/treaties concerning sports have been signed or ratified by Poland:

- Nairobi Treaty on Protection of the Olympic Symbol, adopted in Nairobi on September 26, 1981,[13] which upon its ratification entered into force in the Republic of Poland on November 22, 1996;[14]
- International Convention against Apartheid in Sports, adopted by the General Assembly of the United Nations Organisation on December 10, 1985,[15] which upon its ratification entered into force in the Republic of Poland on April 3, 1988;[16]
- European Convention on violence and excesses of spectators during sports events, football matches in particular, adopted in Strasbourg on August 19, 1985,[17] which upon its ratification entered into force in the Republic of Poland on June 1, 1995;[18]
- European Anti-Doping Convention No. 135 dated November 16, 1989, which upon its ratification entered into force in the Republic of Poland on November 1, 1990.

---

[11] Dz. U. No. 20, item 173, as amended.

[12] Dz. U. No. 106, item 680, as amended.

[13] Dz. U. of 1997, No. 34, item 201.

[14] See Government's Declaration of December 12, 1996 on ratification by the Republic of Poland of the Nairobi Treaty on protection of the Olympic symbol, adopted in Nairobi on September 26, 1981 – Dz. U. of 1997, No. 34, item 202.

[15] Dz. U. of 1988, No. 14, item 100.

[16] See Government's Declaration of April 30, 1988 on ratification by the Polish People's Republic of the International Convention against Apartheid in Sports, adopted by the General Assembly of the United Nations Organisation on December 10, 1985 – D. U. No. 14, item 101.

[17] Dz. U. No. 129, item 626.

[18] See Government's Declaration of May 31, 1995 on ratification by the Republic of Poland of the European Convention on violence and excesses of spectators during sports events, football matches in particular, adopted in Strasbourg on August 19, 1985 – Dz. U. No. 129, item 626.

There are various statutes that although having no specific reference to sport, regulate legal relations that are valid in sport. These include: the Associations Law Act of April 7, 1989;[19] the Labour Code Act of June 26, 1974;[20] decree of the President of the Republic of Poland of June 27, 1934 – Commercial Code;[21] the Personal Income Tax Act of July 26, 1991;[22] the Corporate Income Tax Act of February 15, 1992;[23] the Traffic Law Act of June 20, 1997;[24] and many others. As in other countries, sport is governed by these general legislative rules of law.

LEGAL STATUS OF POLISH SPORTS CLUBS AND UNIONS

The legal status of sport clubs and unions in Poland is an issue to be discussed in a wider context, namely that of the status of all entities functioning in sport. Apart from sports clubs and unions, there are other sport entities: public entities, such as the state administration agencies (particularly the President of the State Physical Culture and Sports Administration), the territorial self-government agencies as well as private entities. This latter category includes various organisational entities (sport clubs and unions, Polish Olympic Committee, Olympic Foundation, Foundation for Development of Physical Culture, etc.) as well as natural persons, e.g. athletes, coaches, instructors, sport doctors and other medical staff, sports clubs and unions officials, clubs, unions and sport facilities administrative and technical staff, sport managers and agents.

An issue of major importance concerns the status of sports clubs and unions, which are the basic organisational entities in sport. Legal status is an important issue not only for the clubs and unions, but also for their members or entities functioning within their framework. The Physical Culture Act (1996) has introduced substantial changes to the legal status of sports clubs and unions. To help evaluate the scope of the changes that have been introduced to legal regulations concerning the status of sports clubs and unions in Poland, let us outline the regulations that were previously in force.

The Physical Culture Act's predecessor (1984) provided that when sport was practised in physical culture associations and their unions, their legal status was that of an 'association' or a 'union of associations'. Also sport could be exercised in other organisational entities that ran sport activities. In practice, before the advent of the 1996 Act, sports clubs functioned almost exclusively as 'associa-

---

[19] Dz. U. No. 20, item 104 as amended.
[20] Dz. U. No. 24, item 141, as amended.
[21] Dz. U. No. 57, item 502 as amended.
[22] Consolidated in Dz. U. of 2000 No. 14, item 176.
[23] Dz. U. No. of 1993 106, item 482, as amended.
[24] Dz. U. No. 98, item 602, as amended.

tions', while sports unions as 'unions of associations'.[25] More recently, before the 1996 Act, few clubs were registered under new legal forms, for instance a joint-stock company or a foundation.

With the advent of the Physical Culture Act (1996), the legal status of sports clubs and unions were re-regulated by a number of statutes.[26]

Naturally, the status of sport clubs and unions is also subject to self-regulation by their internal statutes and rules of procedure. The new Physical Culture Act (1996) distinguishes between two types of sport clubs:

– clubs participating in sport competition, and
– clubs not participating in sport competition.

Another type of sports club provided for in the Act are school sports club. School students, teachers and parents are examples of persons entitled to join in. As regards sports clubs not participating in sport competition, the Act in principle provides that their legal form should be an association, but at the same time it does not exclude other legal forms (nor does it specify them *expressis verbis*). Inevitably, questions soon arise: what are these legal forms? Should such clubs function as legal persons only or are organisations without legal personality also permissible? But in practice such questions are not important as there are relatively few sports clubs that do not participate in any sports competition.

Clubs Participating in Sport Competition

In this regard the Act identifies two modes of club competition:

---

[25] Before coming into force on April 6, 1996 of the Physical Culture Act of January 18, 1996, the legal status of sports clubs and unions in Poland was regulated by the Physical Culture Act of July 3, 1984 and the Associations Law Act of April 7, 1989. In the former act, the legal status of sports clubs and unions was regulated by Art. 15, sec. 2 and Arts. 58-74. The provisions of the law on associations applied on the basis of Art. 59 of the Physical Culture Act as amended by Arts. 58-74 of the Physical Culture Act.

[26] The Physical Culture Act of January 18, 1996, in particular Arts. 6-11, 13-18, 29-36 and 62-64; the Associations Law Act of April 7, 1989; ordinance of the President of the Republic of Poland of June 27, 1934 – Commercial Code; provisions of the code concerning joint-stock companies (Arts. 307-490) provide the basis for the functioning of sport companies pursuant to Art. 31, sec. 2 of the Physical Culture Act, as amended by this act; ordinance of the Minister of Justice of June 19, 1996 on standard form and maintenance of register of physical culture associations and sports unions; ordinance of the Council of Ministers of January 24, 1997 on detailed conditions, rules and procedures for licensing professional sports and licence fee; order of the President of the State Physical Culture and Tourism Administration of September 17, 1996 on sport disciplines and fields of sport with regard to which Polish sports unions may carry out activities, as well as specific terms and procedure of granting permits to establish Polish sports unions; order of the President of the State Physical Culture and Tourism Administration of January 8, 1997 on granting and withdrawing licences to participate in certain sport disciplines; order of the President of the State Physical Culture and Tourism Administration of February 18, 1997 on requirements, rules and procedures for granting and withdrawing a licence of sport referee.

– amateur sport competition, and
– professional sport competition.

Sports clubs participating in amateur sport competitions are considered to be associations by the Act and this is their obligatory and exclusive legal form, whereas sports clubs participating in professional sport competitions must be sports joint-stock companies.

Sports clubs functioning as associations are governed by the provisions of the Associations Law Act as amended by the Physical Culture Act (1996).[27] The Act provides, inter alia, that sports clubs functioning as associations register with the circuit court appropriate for the club's registered office, and be supervised by the competent regional head of their county. National sports clubs register with Warsaw Circuit Court and are supervised by the President of State Physical Culture and Tourism Administration. School sports clubs do not have to be formally registered but must be listed instead by the head of county appropriate for the club's registered office.

In any case, sports clubs functioning within the framework of associations are non-profit, self-governing organisations governed by the Associations Law. They are independent in setting their objects, strategies, policies and organisational structures. They are also empowered to make their own regulations. Being an association, the club relies on voluntary work of its members, but may hire employees to manage its affairs. Sports clubs may be established as associations by Polish nationals of full legal capacity. Non-Polish nationals may also become members if the statutes of the association so provide.

Minors between 16 and 18 years of age, with limited contractual capacity may join sports clubs and associations and vote and be elected, but the majority of the club's management must be conducted by persons of full contractual capacity. On the other hand, minors under 16 years of age may join the clubs if their guardians consent and the club's statutes so allow. They may not vote at general meetings of members nor enjoy any other voting rights (including the right to be elected), unless the club's membership is limited to minors only.

The procedure to set up a sports club in the form of an association is as follows: Founders (of whom there must be at least 15) lay down the statutes and select the founders' committee. The statutes determine such things as: the name, the territory, the registered office, the objects and how they are to be attained, the membership procedures, the rights and obligations of members, the governing bodies, electoral procedures, how vacancies are to be filled, the bodies' competencies and authority to represent the club and to borrow to its credit, the validity requirements for resolutions, the methods of financing, the provisions for mem-

---

[27] The modifications concern, for instance, different registration of sports clubs as well as their supervision, which is vested in government administration and provides authority to control the clubs.

bership dues, the procedures for change of statutes and dissolution of the club. The supreme club's authority is derived from the general meeting of members or representatives. The club must have its management and an internal control organ.

The founders' committee applies to a court to register the club, its statutes, and a list of founders. After the court is satisfied that the statutes and the founders meet all legal requirements, it orders registration of the club. Once final, this order converts the club into a separate legal entity and it is then registered in the register of associations. Such status may also be granted to school sports clubs.

Sports clubs participating in professional sport competitions are now obliged to function as sport joint-stock companies pursuant to the provisions of the Commercial Code, as modified by the Physical Culture Act. A sports joint-stock company may be formed by a minimum of three persons (promoters) who sign the articles of association, which must be notarised to be valid. The articles should, among other things, set out the name of the club and its registered office, the objects, the amount of share capital and methods to subscribe for shares, the nominal value and the number of shares, an indication whether shares are registered or bearer, the names and surnames (or business names) and addresses of promoters, the organisation of governing and supervisory bodies, the number and kinds of instruments entitling their holders to participate in profits or distribution of assets and rights attached thereto, any duties to provide consideration to the company as attached to shares, the requirements and procedures to redeem shares. The shares may be paid up on in cash or by transfer of non-cash assets. The management may but does not have to consist of shareholders. The company should also have a supervisory board or an audit committee.

After an organisational meeting, the management file for registration of the company. Commercial Code requires certain documents to be filed on this occasion and sets out the notifiable data to be registered. On registration the company starts as a separate legal entity. To carry on the business of professional sports, the company must be licensed by the President of the State Physical Culture and Tourism Administration. The licence requirements, the licensing rules and procedures and the license fee are governed by the Physical Culture Act and the ordinance of the Council of Ministers of January 24, 1997 on detailed conditions, rules and procedures for licensing professional sports and the licence fee.

Clubs participating in sport competitions (whether as associations or joint-stock companies) may establish unions of clubs, called 'sports unions'. There must be at least three such clubs to form a union. Supporting members of a sports union may be sports clubs that do not participate in sport competitions or other organisations or legal persons who have as their objects activity in the field of physical culture.

The fundamental tasks of sports unions are set out in the Physical Culture Act:

– to carry on activities in the field of sports and recreation,
– to organise sports and recreational events and competitions,

– to educate in and promote physical culture,
– to train coaches and instructors and improve their skills,
– to support school sports clubs.

The legal status of a sport union is – as it previously was – a union of associations. Sports unions are governed by the Associations Law Act as modified by the Physical Culture Act. A special type of sports union are 'Polish sports unions', which operate nation-wide in just one discipline or field of sports. Only one Polish sports union may be responsible for a particular discipline or field of sport. Such union must be established on permission of the President of the State Physical Culture and Tourism Administration, who approves its statute and amendments to it. As enabled by the Physical Culture Act, the disciplines and fields of sports, detailed rules and procedures for granting permissions to establish a Polish sports union are regulated by the order of the President of the State Physical Culture and Tourism Administration of September 17, 1996.

The fundamental tasks of Polish sports unions are set out in the Physical Culture Act:

– to organise and implement sports competitions,
– to licence sports clubs to participate in sports competitions,
– to represent Polish sports (subject to authority vested in the Polish Olympic Committee) in international sports organisations and to enable participation in international sports competitions,
– to prepare national teams to participate in international sports competitions.

A local sports union, other than a Polish sports union, is registered in the circuit court appropriate for its registered office and is supervised by the head of the local county. Polish sports unions and other national unions are registered in the Warsaw Circuit Court and are supervised by the President of the State Physical Culture and Tourism Administration. Sports unions become separate legal entities once the court registration order becomes final.

Under the Physical Culture Act, if the activities of a sports club or union are in breach of the law or the unions' statutes the supervisory authority may:

– demand that this situation be remedied within a prescribed time,
– warn the governing bodies of the club or union,
– suspend individual members of the club's or union's governing bodies, or
– apply to court to order appropriate remedies.

The remedies that the court may order are the following:

– the court may suspend execution of a resolution or decision that is in breach of the law, or may demand that it is repealed, and if not repealed in a prescribed time, the court may repeal it,
– the court may suspend the governing bodies and appoint a curator until new governing bodies are elected,

– the court may suspend the whole club or union, but for no longer than one year, or
– the court may dissolve the club or union, if it grossly breaches the law or its own statutes, and strike it off the register.

LEGAL STATUS OF OTHER SPORTS ENTITIES IN POLAND

The Physical Culture Act of January 18, 1996 specifies also the legal status, objectives and tasks of the Polish Olympic Committee (Art. 11) and the Polish Paraolympic Committee (Art. 12).

The Polish Olympic Committee is a union of associations and other legal persons, governed by the Associations Law Act. The main objectives of the Committee, as set out by the Physical Culture Act, are to ensure participation of the national team in the Olympics, to promote Olympic principles, to represent Polish sports in International Olympic Committee and before national Olympic committees and other international organisations, and to draft athletes to the national team for the Olympics.

Granting the Polish Olympic Committee an exclusive right to use the Olympic symbols as defined in the Olympic Card and the names 'the Olympics' and the 'Olympic Committee' (Art. 11, sec. 3), the Physical Culture Act provides liability for unauthorised use of Olympic symbols and names specified in the act (Art. 57, sec. 1). As mentioned earlier in this paper, in accordance with the Government's Declaration of December 12, 1996, the Nairobi Treaty on protection of the Olympic symbol, adopted in Nairobi on September 26, 1981 and ratified by the Republic of Poland, entered into force in Poland on November 22, 1996.

The Physical Culture Act enables the setting up of the Polish Paraolympic Committee, which however has yet to be established. The statutory objectives of this Committee will be to organise, promote and support the development sports for the disabled, to ensure participation of the Polish national team of disabled athletes in the Paraolympics and to represent Poland in the International Paraolympic Committee.

A special organisational structure provided for by the act is a professional league (Art. 36, sec. 1). The act provides that a professional league may be established by a Polish sports union that holds a licence to carry out activities in professional sports. The principles of functioning of a professional league are established by means of agreement between a competent Polish sports union and clubs that function as sport joint-stock companies and are members of a professional league (Art. 36, sec. 3 of the Act). Such agreement should guarantee that the union is able to meet its national and international commitments and that it has disciplinary authority. The Act does not provide what the legal form of the professional league should be.

The only professional league set up so far is men's basketball. It is a joint-stock company whose shareholders are the Polish Basketball Union and the clubs making up the league, joint-stock companies themselves. Preparations are underway to organise professional leagues in football, volley-ball and speedway.

There are also other organisations involved in sports, other than sports clubs or unions. The law does not impose any restrictions on the legal form these may take. Accordingly, we have various sports associations (e.g. the Society for Promotion of Physical Culture) or foundations (e.g. Foundation for Development of Physical Culture and the Olympic Foundation).

STATUS OF ATHLETES

Naturally, the aforementioned regulations and diversification in the status of sport clubs have an impact on the status of athletes, which depends, among other factors, on the membership in a club participating or not participating in sports competitions, on the club's participation in amateur sport competitions or professional sport competitions, on the club's status as an association or a sport joint-stock company. Legal relations between athletes and sports clubs, national unions and international sports federations are, therefore, diversified.The Physical Culture Act includes few provisions that directly refer to the status of athletes, since this is left to be determined by their parent Polish sports unions.

The act provides that professional competitors exercise sports pursuant to employment contracts (contracts under the Labour Code) or on a free agent basis (contracts under the Civil Code) and receive remuneration therefore (Art. 22, sec. 2 of the Act), whereas amateur competitors may only receive endowments (Art. 22, sec. 3 of the Act).

Such endowments are usually made by sports clubs or unions. The law does not regulate the granting, withholding, cancelling or amounts of such endowments. The only administrative intervention in this area is that, as enabled by the Act, the minister competent for labour matters will, concurrently with the President of the State Physical Culture and Tourism Administration, lay down the rules and procedure for the endowment periods to be included in employment history of an athlete.

On the other hand, national or olympic team athletes may be awarded endowments from the government budget. The Act authorises the President of the State Physical Culture and Tourism Administration to lay down the rules and procedures for such endowments, which he did in the above-mentioned order of December 18, 1996. The order provides that such endowments will vary between the amount of the average national pay to even three times this amount, depending on the particular discipline/field of sport and on whether the athlete is a member of the national or of the olympic team.

Moreover, the act provides that competitors, i.e. athletes participating in sports competitions, whether professional or amateur, must hold licences to practice their sports disciplines, granted by the competent Polish sports union (Art. 24, secs. 1 and 2 of the Act). Pursuant to Art. 24, sec. 3 of the Act, the principles of granting and withdrawing licences are specified in the order issued by the President of the State Physical Culture and Tourism Administration on prior consultation with competent Polish sports unions (cf. order of the President of the State Physical Culture and Tourism Administration of January 8, 1997).The Physical Culture Act also regulates such issues as competitive exercise of sports by minors (who may only compete with the consent of their legal guardians) the obligations of competitors, and matters of status concerning athletes appointed to the national team or in military service.

The Physical Culture Act was amended at the end of 1999 to introduce a special monthly endowment out of governmental funds for national team members who have been awarded at least one olympic medal. To obtain such an endowment, the athlete must be under 36 years of age, not compete professionally, be a Polish national, have permanent residence in Poland and a clean criminal record (intentional crimes only). The endowment is awarded by the President of the State Physical Culture and Tourism Administration and amounts to the average national pay as officially calculated for the prior calendar year.

PROFESSIONAL SPORTS

As explained in this chapter, the current Physical Culture Act, unlike the previous one, provides an explicit regulation of a professional exercise of sports. The regulations in question, as mentioned above, are those providing that sports clubs participating in professional sport competition must function as sport joint-stock companies and that professional competitors exercise sports pursuant to the employment contract or on a free agent basis, and receive remuneration therefore; finally, those related to the functioning of a professional league. Similarly, Art. 29 of the Act provides that the clubs functioning as sport joint-stock companies and Polish sports unions are required to obtain a licence of the President of the State Physical Culture and Tourism Administration to carry out activities in the field of professional sports. Pursuant to Art. 30, sec. 4 of the Act, specific terms, principles and procedures of granting licences and the amount of licence fee were provided in the ordinance of the Council of Ministers of January 24, 1997. Art. 57, sec. 2 of the Act imposes criminal liability for unauthorised activities in the field of professional sports.

Professional sports law is now being implemented in Poland. Sports clubs are being formed as joint-stock companies and professional leagues are being set up. The clubs and Polish sports unions are applying for licences. The status of amateur and professional athletes is being put in order.

For various reasons these processes are not as quick as originally projected. For example, promoters have difficulties in raising enough capital to set up joint-stock company sports clubs or professional leagues. Developing joint-stock companies associations from clubs may generate numerous problems, for example, what assets and liabilities are to be divested, including athletes or even whole teams? A bone of contention is often the legal and sports succession (league ranking!) of the new joint-stock company. At times problems are caused by lack of experience or insufficient qualifications, including legal ones, of officials implementing the changes in sports clubs or unions.

ARBITRATION COURTS AND TRIBUNALS FOR SPORTS

The Physical Culture Act provides a possibility of arbitrating property disputes arising in connection with sports activities. The Act provides that sports unions may establish permanent courts of arbitration and that the Arbitration Tribunal for Sports will be established with the Polish Olympic Committee. Therefore, there is a statutory background for courts of arbitration for sports in Poland, such as the Football Arbitration Court with the Polish Football Association (since 1993) and the Arbitration Tribunal for Sports with the Polish Olympic Committee (since 1994).

The Arbitration Tribunal for Sports with the Polish Olympic Committee consists of 21 arbiters. Each of the following bodies appoints 7 arbiters: the President of the State Physical Culture and Tourism Administration, the Executive Board of the Polish Olympic Committee and the Executive Board of the Association of Polish Sports Unions. The Tribunal serves three functions:

The Tribunal has the power to determine property disputes (both Polish and foreign) arising in connection with organisation, participation in and development of amateur and professional sports, as put under the Tribunal's jurisdiction pursuant to contractual arbitration clauses. Parties before the Tribunal may, regardless of where they are based or resident, be sports clubs and unions (federations), natural persons participating in or promoting or organising sports, businesses engaged in sports and all other legal persons.

The Tribunal has the power to determine disputes relating to such matters as:

- legal relations (including the ones that are derived from relations of membership) between athletes, clubs, unions and other sports organisations,
- legal and economic status of amateur and professional athletes,
- legal aspects of granting, withholding or cancelling licenses to athletes, clubs, coaches, referees and other participants in sports,
- changes of club membership and transfer fees,
- contracts (for specific work or for services) with sports coaches and instructors and other persons engaged in sports,

- sponsoring, management and advertising contracts,
- broadcasting, advertising and promotion rights pooling agreements (between media rights sellers and organisers of sports events),
- all contracts involved in organisation of sports events,
- equipment contracts by persons engaged in sports.

Under the Physical Culture Act, the Arbitration Tribunal for Sports with the Polish Olympic Committee is the highest court of appeals against disciplinary and internal decisions of Polish sports unions. Following the procedures set out in the statutes of Polish sports unions, the Tribunal may be appealed to in the following matters:

- exclusion or deregistration of an athlete, coach or sports official from a sports club, union or organisation,
- lifetime disqualification of such persons,
- stripping an athlete or a sports team of the title of national champion or Polish Cup winner,
- transferring a sports club to a lower league, and
- ban on representing Polish sports in international competitions or international cup events.

A party may appeal to the Tribunal even notwithstanding any provisions of the union's statutes, if the contested determination was made union-internally such that:

- it was in breach of law or sports regulations, or
- the party was deprived of due process rights.

The Arbitration Tribunal for Sports with the Polish Olympic Committee may also be consulted on legal aspects of organisation, participation in and development and practice of sports, unless such matters are within exclusive powers of administrative agencies.

Disciplinary Liability in Sports

The Physical Culture Act provides legal premises for disciplinary liability in sport but has no further regulation in that field. The Act enables, however, the Polish sports unions to provide for these matters in their statutes; the matters include: disciplinary bodies and their competencies, disciplinary procedures and disciplinary penalties. Only two disciplinary issues are governed directly by the Act.

Firstly, according to the Act, some disciplinary decisions made by the competent organs of Polish sports unions may be appealed against to the Arbitration Tribunal for Sports with the Polish Olympic Committee in accordance with the rules laid down in the statutes of Polish sports unions. But for some of such decisions, the appeal lies, the statutes notwithstanding.

Secondly, the act expressly imposes disciplinary liability for doping. This liability is not only on athletes, but also on coaches, officials and other persons found in breach of doping regulations. It is governed by order of the President of the State Physical Culture and Tourism Administration of July 21, 1997 on rules of disciplinary liability for breach of anti-doping regulations, which order is statutorily enabled.

DOPING

Anti-doping measures are an important part of the Physical Culture Act. It is said that Polish doping regulations are the most sophisticated among the countries of Eastern and Central Europe.

A definition of doping in sports is provided in art. 47, sec. 1, while art. 48 authorises the Committee to Combat Doping in Sports, financed out of government funds and appointed by the President of the State Physical Culture and Tourism Administration concurrently with the Minister of Health and Welfare. The current Committee was appointed by order of the President of the State Physical Culture and Tourism Administration of May 8, 1997 on appointment of Committee to Combat Doping in Sports.

The Act sets out the tasks of the Committee. Accordingly, the Committee should develop and enforce anti-doping regulations and programmes, organise doping check tests, provide education against doping and lay down a list of proscribed substances and methods that are considered doping, to be approved by the President of the State Physical Culture and Tourism Administration concurrently with the Minister of Health and Welfare. The current list is provided by order of the President of the State Physical Culture and Tourism Administration of June 20, 1997 on approval of list of prohibited substances and methods considered doping.

Under the Act, athletes must undergo doping checks (tests) and it provides for disciplinary liability of athletes, coaches, officials and others for beach of anti-doping regulations. The liability is governed by order of the President of the State Physical Culture and Tourism Administration of July 21, 1997. Concurrently with the Minister of Health and Welfare, the State Physical Culture and Tourism Administration drafted a list of institutions responsible for anti-doping analyses and methods, rules and procedures of payments for doping checks.

Neither the Physical Culture Act nor the Polish Criminal Code or any other criminal law provides for criminal liability for doping. However, on certain conditions such liability may sometimes be enforced under Criminal Code[28] provi-

---

[28] The Criminal Code Act of June 6, 1997 (Dz. U. No. 88, item 553, as amended).

sions on liability for crimes against life and health (particularly arts. 148, 155-157 and 160) and on fraud (art. 286) as well as under the Drug Addiction (Combating) Act of April 24, 1997.[29]

Anybody who directly gives a doping substance to an athlete may be held criminally liable under Criminal Code provisions on crimes against life and health. Detriment to health or death need not actually occur, as direct exposure to such a threat is sufficient to establish guilt. These provisions do not make the athletes themselves liable for using doping substances, because death or detriment to health must be caused (or threatened to be caused) to another. Moreover, whoever persuades the athletes to take or assists them in taking doping drugs will escape punishment as aiding and abetting are punishable only when committed in relation to crimes. The taking of proscribed substances by the athletes themselves is not a crime, as noted above.

An accusation of fraud may perhaps be made against a person who is engaged in doping practices, i.e. the athletes themselves or other persons, but on condition that the persons engaged committed the crime for profit by deceiving another and thereby causing that other person property loss.

The Drug Addiction (Combating) Act affords more instruments to punish doping practices. The act provides for liability for many various practices involving drugs such as: producing, processing, transforming, importing, exporting, trafficking, selling/purchasing, giving to another, persuading another to take, and even mere possession. But all this may be punished only if the substance involved is found to be a so-called 'stupefacient'. But not all doping substances are stupefacients.

SAFETY IN SPORTS

The Physical Culture Act does not omit safety in physical culture. Arts. 50-56 impose liability of legal persons and individuals who are engaged in physical culture for safety, order and health at sports events and a duty to ensure safe and healthy conditions for practising sports. Other matters provided for are: medical care, safety of sports facilities, athletes' accident insurance, safety measures in particularly dangerous sports disciplines/fields of sport, safety of mountain walkers, swimmers, bathers and persons doing water sports, and life saving by Mountain Life-Saving Teams and Water Life-Saving Teams. Art. 57, sec. 2 imposes criminal liability for breach of those regulations.

The Safety of Public Events Act of August 22, 1997 determines in detail the duties of organisers of sports events. Although its purpose was to regulate mass events in general, it obviously governs also sports events. The matters provided for include: permits to organise an event, liability of organisers for damage suf-

---

[29] Dz. U. No. 57, item 468, as amended.

fered during an event and for breach of the law. The duties of security personnel were set out in detail in the ordinance of the Council of Ministers of March 10, 1998.

Pursuant to the Act, each organiser of a mass event which charges an admission fee must be insured against liability for damage/loss to participants. These requirements were laid down in the ordinance of the Minister of Finance of August 4, 1998 on determination of detailed rules for setting out minimum sums for liability insurance of organisers of mass events against losses to participants of such events, if an admission fee is charged.

CONCLUSION: POPULARISATION OF SPORTS LAW IN POLAND

In light of so many regulations governing sports directly, not to mention those that apply to sports although not having been legislated for such purpose, there is an increasing need to promote knowledge of such regulations, particularly in the sports environment.[30] To this end it may be appreciated that, from a Polish per-

---

[30] The following efforts are being made to this end: 1) university level education syllabuses feature a course in sports law (like at Poznan Academy of Physical Education) or in organisation and management of physical culture (other academies of physical education); 2) a sports law collection has been published ('Sports law. Legal Acts'. ed. by Andrzej J. Szwarc, collected and developed by Piotr Paluch. Poznan 1999. Published by: Ars boni et aequi); 3) Polish Association of Sports Law, a scholarly association focused on sports law issues, has been in existence for some time now.

The Polish Association of Sports Law was set up in 1990 in Poznan. The seat of the Association is also in Poznan. The aim of the Association is to formulate, discuss and solve legal problems connected with practising sport. This objective is realised mainly by the organisation of scientific conferences focusing on the above problems, and using the proceedings from those conferences to publish a series of the Association entitled 'Sport i prawo' ('*Sport and Law*') with English, French and German abstracts.

The following conferences have been held so far, with all the proceedings published in that series (the latest conference proceedings will appear in print later in 2000): 1) Prawne problemy transferu w pilce noznej w Polsce i Republice Federalnej Niemiec (Legal problems of transfers of football players between clubs in Poland and Germany), Poznan, 13-15 September 1990. The conference was organised in conjunction with a German association of sports law (Konstanzer Arbeitskreis für Sportrecht); 2) Prawne problemy dopingu w sporcie (Legal aspects of doping in sport), Poznan, 12-13 December 1991; 3) Prawne problemy sportu zawodowego (Legal problems of professional sport), Zajaczkowo/Pniewy, 1-3 October 1993; 4) Naruszenia porzadku towarzyszace imprezom sportowym (Disturbance of the public order related to sports events), Zabrze, 15-17 April 1994; 5) Ubezpieczenia w sporcie (Insurance in sport), Bydgoszcz, 7-9 October 1994; 6) Sport i media – problemy prawne (Sport and the News Media – Legal Problems), Leszno, 1-3 February 1996; 7) Status prawny polskich klubów i zwiazków sportowych (Legal status of Polish sports clubs and unions), Swieradów Zdrój, 16-18 January 1998; 8) Status prawny sportowców (Legal status of sportsman), Poznan, 3-4 September 1999.

The next conference will be held in Warsaw between 23 and 24 November 2000, under the title 'Odpowiedzialnosc dyscyplinarna w sporcie' (Disciplinary liability in sports). The subsequent conferences are projected to focus on such issues as: Sports conflicts – Justice ordinaire – Justice sportive – Arbitration, Sponsoring in sport – Legal problems, Swindles in sport and others.

spective, there is a pressing need to encourage the wider appreciation of sports law and its underlying regulatory issues. A fuller appreciation of the regulatory issues may even allow for a simplification of the formidable body of legal regulation alluded to in the course of this chapter. To a significant extent the apparent 'density' of the Polish regulation is attributable to the combination of an officialdom partly conditioned by the earlier Communist regime and partly by the keen desire of any 'new' political entity to make a good job of their 'new' regulatory tasks. It is to be hoped that the less helpful aspects of this combination prove to be 'bio-degradable' over the medium-term. The wider study of sports law should facilitate this process.

APPENDIX

Ordinances of the Council of Ministers:

- ordinance of the Council of Ministers of March 14, 1983 on working time of coaches and sports, physiotherapy and biological renewal instructors employed in physical culture organisations;[31]
- ordinance of the Council of Ministers of January 24, 1997 on detailed conditions, rules and procedures for licensing professional sports and the licence fee;[32]
- ordinance of the Council of Ministers of May 6, 1997 on determination of safety requirements for mountain walkers, swimmers, bath takers and persons doing water sports;[33]
- ordinance of the Council of Ministers of June 10, 1997 on rules and procedures to approve compliance of sports facilities and equipment designs with requirements of health and safety and use by the disabled;[34]
- ordinance of the Council of Ministers of September 12, 1997 on yachting;[35]
- ordinance of the Council of Ministers of March 10, 1998 on detailed requirements for and proceedings of security personnel of organisers of sports events;[36]
- ordinance of the President of the Council of Ministers of November 19, 1998 on determination of sports and recreational facilities under the management of provincial governors to be transferred to provincial home-rule authorities to be used for tasks prescribed them by statute, sports and recreational facilities under the management of ministers and directors of central governmental agen-

---

[31] Dz. U. No. 20, item 88.
[32] Dz. U. No. 8, item 39.
[33] Dz. U. No. 57, item 358.
[34] Dz. U. No. 63, item 395.
[35] Dz. U. No. 112, item 729.
[36] Dz. U. No. 32, item 169.

cies to be transferred to counties or municipal counties, and sports and recreational facilities under the management of ministers and directors of central governmental agencies not to be transferred to local home-rule authorities due to country-wide nature of purposes such facilities are used for;[37]

Ordinances of individual ministers:

- ordinance of the Minister of Finance of April 25, 1997 on detailed rules of financial support for sports investment projects out of funds coming from surcharges on gambling, procedure for filing applications, transferring the funds and accounting for them;[38]
- ordinance of the Minister of Finance of August 4, 1998 on determination of detailed rules for setting out minimum sum insured for liability insurance of organisers of mass events against losses to participants of such events, if admission fee is charged;[39]
- ordinance of the Minister of Finance of November 9, 1999 on determination of list of sports plant and equipment and physiotherapy and biological renewal means and apparatus appropriated for the purposes of national and olympic teams and for the purposes of life saving, exempted from custom duties, as imported by nation-wide physical culture organisations and associations;[40]
- ordinance of the Minister of National Defence of January 22, 1998 on requirements for sports training and preparations of national team athletes who have been drafted to do active military service;[41]
- ordinance of the Minister of Agriculture and Rural Development of January 20, 2000 on sea fishing for sports and recreation purposes;[42]
- ordinance of the Minister of Justice of June 19, 1996 on standard form and maintenance of register of physical culture associations and sports unions;[43]
- ordinance of the Minister of Justice of April 29 1998 on detailed rules and procedures for making entries in register of final injunctions ordering not to enter mass events and final injunctions ordering not to be on such places where mass events are held (such register maintained by the Chief Police Inspector), and on ways to maintain such register;[44]
- ordinance of the Minister of Internal Affairs and Administration of March 15, 2000 on standard-form regulations for shooting grounds;[45]

---

[37] Dz. U. No. 143, item 919, as amended.
[38] Dz. U. No. 46, item 293, as amended.
[39] Dz. U. No. 105, item 665.
[40] Dz. U. No. 93, item 1076.
[41] Dz. U. No. 22, item 115.
[42] Dz. U. No. 6, item 81.
[43] Dz. U. No. 71, item 342.
[44] Dz. U. No. 62, item 397.
[45] Dz. U. No. 18, item 234.

– ordinance of the Minister of Internal Affairs and Administration of April 3, 2000 on safekeeping, carrying and registering firearms and ammunition;[46]
– ordinance of the Minister of the Environment of April 4, 2000 on environmental protection requirements for construction and operation of shooting grounds facilities;[47]
– ordinance of the Minister of Health and Welfare of April 26, 1982 on rules for providing health services by public health centres to athletes receiving sports endowments;[48]
– ordinance of the Minister of Maritime Affairs of July 12, 1968 on safety of sports sea vessels;[49]

Orders of individual ministers:

– order of the Minister of National Education of February 12, 1997 on detailed rules for sports schools and classes and sports excellence schools;[50]
– order of the Minister of Transport of February 22, 1963 on determination of emblem, flag and banner of Aviation Club of the People's Republic of Poland;[51]
– order of the Minister of Transport of July 20, 1964 on technical requirements for airworthy gliders and their parts;[52]
– order of the Minister of Transport of October 30, 1965 on signalling glider flights, standard and size of signals in gliding, and making and analysing reports of aircraft crash danger;[53]
– order of the Minister of State Farms of July 31, 1951 on horseracing rules;[54]
– order of the Minister of State Farms of December 11, 1951 on staffing and by-laws of Horseracing Commission;[55]

Orders of the President of the State Physical Culture and Sports Administration (or equivalent earlier agency):

– order of the President of Central State Physical Culture and Tourism Committee of September 15, 1965 on sailing in inland water routes in tourist and sports vessels;[56]

---

[46] Dz. U. No. 27, item 343.
[47] Dz. U. No. 27, item 341.
[48] Dz. U. No. 13, item 110.
[49] Dz. U. No. 30, item 202, as amended.
[50] M. P. No. 13, item 107.
[51] M. P. No. 27, item 140.
[52] M. P. of August 1, 1964.
[53] M. P. of December 14, 1965.
[54] M. P. No. A-84, item 1157, as amended.
[55] M. P. No. A-105, item 1542.
[56] M. P. No. 53, item 279.

- order of the President of the State Physical Culture and Tourism Administration of July 19, 1996 on standard physical education syllabus for organisations subordinate to the Minister of National Defence, the Minister of Internal Affairs and Head of National Civic Guard;[57]
- order of the President of the State Physical Culture and Tourism Administration of September 17, 1996 on sport disciplines and fields of sports with regard to which Polish sports unions may carry out their activities, as well as specific terms and procedure of granting permits to establish Polish sports unions;[58]
- order of the President of the State Physical Culture and Tourism Administration of November 7, 1996 on types of distinctions and sums awarded for good sports results in international and national competition, and on rules and procedures for granting such distinctions and awards;[59]
- order of the President of the State Physical Culture and Tourism Administration of December 11, 1996 on rules and procedure for making awards and awarding distinctions and medals to persons who stand out in physical culture in terms of pro-active attitude or outstanding achievements;[60]
- order of the President of the State Physical Culture and Tourism Administration of December 18, 1996 on rules and procedures for granting, withholding, cancelling and amounts of sports endowments for members of national and olympic teams;[61]
- order of the President of the State Physical Culture and Tourism Administration of January 8, 1997 on granting and withdrawing licences to participate in certain sport disciplines;[62]
- order of the President of the State Physical Culture and Tourism Administration of February 18, 1997 on requirements, rules and procedures for granting and withdrawing a licence of sport referee;[63]
- order of the President of the State Physical Culture and Tourism Administration of May 8, 1997 on appointment of Committee to Combat Doping in Sports;[64]
- order of the President of the State Physical Culture and Tourism Administration of June 20, 1997 on approval of list of prohibited pharmaceuticals and methods considered doping;[65]

---

[57] M. P. No. 55, item 514.
[58] M. P. No. 59, item 556.
[59] M. P. No. 76, item 699.
[60] M. P. of 1997 No. 4, item 30.
[61] M. P. No. 85, item 761.
[62] M. P. No. 4, item 31.
[63] M. P. No. 13, item 109.
[64] M. P. No. 34, item 330.
[65] M. P. No. 44, item 432.

– order of the President of the State Physical Culture and Tourism Administration of July 15, 1997 on physical culture qualifications, degrees and professional titles and rules and procedures for granting them;[66]
– order of the President of the State Physical Culture and Tourism Administration of July 17, 1997 on determining institutions responsible for anti-doping analyses and methods, rules and procedures of payments for doping checks;[67]
– order of the President of the State Physical Culture and Tourism Administration of July 21, 1997 on rules of disciplinary liability for breach of anti-doping regulations;[68]
– order of the President of the State Physical Culture and Tourism Administration of October 9, 1997 on physical culture reporting duties;[69]
– order of the President of the State Physical Culture and Tourism Administration of October 10, 1997 on responsibilities and proceedings of Committee to Combat Doping in Sports.[70]

[66] M. P. No. 45, item 445.
[67] M. P. No. 59, item 571.
[68] M. P. No. 46, item 452.
[69] M. P. No. 77, item 733.
[70] M. P. No. 76, item 721.

THE REGULATION OF SPORTS ACTIVITIES IN GREECE

Dimitrios Panagiotopoulos and Gregory Ioannidis

INTRODUCTION

Sport has always been part of the Greek psyche and was one of the first aspects of cultural life to be protected in the Hellenic Constitution of 1974. Sport falls under the auspices of the government with regard to its organisation and operation. The government is responsible for the finance of sport and supervises it through the General Secretariat for Sport, which is a subdivision of the Ministry of Culture. The question here for sports law is whether the constitutional protection relates to sporting activity as a whole or whether it relates to either amateur and/or professional sport. The legislator at the time did not intend to make a distinction between amateur and professional sport. The new law has made this distinction.[1]

The recent successes of Greek athletes in the international sphere has sparked greater interest in sport and the regulation thereof. This enthusiasm resulted in the realisation that sport is the cornerstone of Greek society and culture and therefore merits special protection by the law.

LEGAL REGULATION OF SPORT AND ITS PROTECTION BY THE CONSTITUTION

Only a year after the creation of the Hellenic Constitution, the legislature prioritised sport in the change to a new Greek society. These developments took place after the end of the military dictatorship, which lasted, from 1967 until 1974. The intention of the legislator was obvious, as it placed sport under the immediate protection of the State, creating for the latter a highly interventionist regime. Article 16(9) states:

'Athletics shall fall under the protection and supervision of the State. The State shall make grants to and shall control all types of athletic associations, as specified by law.

---

[1] Law No. 2725/99.

A. Caiger and S. Gardiner (Eds), Professional Sport in the EU: Regulation and Re-regulation
© 2000, T.M.C.Asser Press, The Hague, The Netherlands

The use of grants in accordance with the purpose of the associations receiving them shall also be specified by law.'[2]

It is not clear whether the law covered both amateur and professional sport. The legislator did not distinguish between the two and the problem for the study of sports law is whether such a distinction needs to be made. Theoretically, one would argue that such a distinction should not be made since the protection of sport by the Constitution can be characterised as a 'social right', and as such, applied to both amateur and professional sport. The jurisprudence in this area offers little help, and therefore any suggestions would be inconclusive.

THE NEW SPORT LAW

In 1999 a new sports law came into operation in Greece. This created a new era in the development of sport and its governance.[3] Sport, as an individual and collective pursuit, is considered as an influential factor in life since it produces healthy personal development and qualities within societies. These factors are recognised in the Preamble to the new Law.

The international success of Greek athletes during the 1980s and 1990s created a source of national pride and popularised sport, leading to higher levels of participation in recreational activity. However, while there was an increase in the international status of Greek sporting achievements, there has also been an increase in corruption, bribery and violence. This downside also effected dispute mechanisms in sport proving the latter to be ineffective and subject to delays and injustice. The inadequacy of sports governance led to demands for a radical reform of the Sport statute. This led to the enactment of the new 2725/99 Sport Law.

The new Sport Law addresses the inadequacies of the old statute. It distinguishes between professional and amateur sport and provides improved dispute mechanisms for the resolution of offences and disputing connected to sport. It also placed professional athletes on the same footing as employees under Greek employment law.

The new law deals with the following issues:

– creation of regulatory bodies to organise sporting activities;
– the independence of sporting organisations;
– it separates the amateur sporting activity from the professional activity and regulates sporting entertainment;

---

[2] Article 16(9) of the Constitution of Greece. The Sixth Revisionary Parliament of the Hellenes.
[3] 2725/99.

- rules that establish a transparency in the organisation of the game and the adjudicatory process with the intention of benefiting athletes and clubs;
- rules to expedite judgements;
- recognition of the idea of 'sport for all' as a fundamental right of the citizens and as an obligation of the State;
- guaranteeing participation by the disabled in sporting activities;
- the recognition of commercial activity in sport;
- the protection of athletes' rights in employment and contract law.

The new law will be considered under four headings. The first relates to amateur sport, the second to professional sport, the third to sports justice, and the fourth supplementary provisions.

Amateur Sport

The New Law re-regulates amateur sport and provides a framework within which it can be carried out.[4] Amateur sport in Greece is organised in the familiar pyramid structure, the base being formed by the clubs, the next level the unions of the 54 municipalities (including the islands). At the apex are the national associations. The State is responsible for the financial support of amateur clubs, allowing them autonomy in making their own rules and their internal organisation.[5] The New Law seeks to eliminate bureaucracy in relation to the registration of athletes, and encourages transparency amongst sports administrators. In addition, people who have been convicted of criminal offences and breaches of the civil law are prohibited from involvement in sports governance. There are provisions for transparent accounting.[6] Clubs have to apply to the Court of First Instance for recognition of legal personality.[7]

Chapter 2 relates to Sporting Unions who are responsible for the organisation of their sports at local level (Arts. 10-17).

Chapter 3 contains provisions for the governance of national sporting organisations. The provisions suggest that the administration of the sporting organisations should have tenure in office for 4 years. New office bearers should be elected after each Olympic Games, in order to assess their competence. In addition, this Chapter allows for the election of office bearers of the national associations. The presence of legal representatives during the elections is mandatory in order to ensure 'free and fair elections'. All national associations are accountable to the Minister for Sport for their budgetary affairs.[8]

---

[4] Chapter A of Part A refers to sporting clubs.
[5] Articles 4 and 5.
[6] Article 6.
[7] Article 8.
[8] Article 25.

Chapter 5 relates to amateur athletes. These provisions are radical in that they allow amateur athletes to conclude and benefit from commercial agreements. This includes sponsorship agreements and the advertisement of brand names as long as these agreements do not break the rules of the sporting organisations and the rules of the International Olympic Committee. While the law says nothing about the impact of EU law on amateur athletes, the fact that these athletes may participate in commercial activities to a limited extent, means that EU law must be taken into consideration. The question is whether this commercial activity involves EU law in the governance of amateur sport. This part of the New Law is silent on the issue. However it is considered that where amateur athletes are engaged in economic activity which may have implications for inter-state trade, EU law would apply.

Professional Sport

The New Law regulates professional sport.[9] Chapter A provides that No State aid is available to athletes' unions[10] (the so-called 'Departments of Remunerated Athletes'). This measure is consistent with EU law and represents a radical departure with the past. Under the Old Law these unions were subsidised by the State. Chapter B refers to clubs that are registered as limited liability companies. Article 69 takes consideration of the European law and states that nationals of the European Union will be entitled to participate in the share capital as long as this participation does not exceed 25%. This shows an attempt of Greek law to be consistent with EU law, but there must be some doubt as to the limitations placed on the participation of other EU Member State nationals.

Chapter 4 contains the most important provisions, which cover the relationship between athletes and clubs registered as limited liability companies. The *Bosman* ruling was the catalyst for the restructuring of the employment relations between professional athletes and their employers. It allowed the Greek law to take cognisance of the fact that Bosman was a worker in terms of EU law. Athletes can now take advantage of the provisions of the Greek employment law. Under the previous dispensation professional athletes did not fall under the Greek employment laws. In this field, the legislative intervention was necessary in order to align the national law with European law's concept of 'worker'.[11] Previous legislation and more specifically, law No. 1958/1991, created interpretative

---

[9] Part B.

[10] Τμήματα Αμοιβομένων Αθλητών.

[11] As the ECJ held in Levin v Staatssecretaris van Justitie (case 53/81), the concept of 'worker' is a Community concept, not dependent for its meaning on the laws of Member States. In Lawrie-Blum v Land Baden-Wurttemberg (case 66/85), the ECJ suggested that the 'essential characteristic' of a worker is that during a certain period of time he performs services for and under the direction of another in return for remuneration. See Steiner J and Woods L (1999) *Textbook on EC Law* London, Blackstone.

doubts about the employment relations between athletes and their employers. For the first time, it is clear that the provisions of employment law will govern the relationship between athletes and their employers. This puts a stop to the interpretative anomalies, and now disputes between athletes and their employers can be dealt with in the normal manner.

Specific provisions state that the monthly salary of athletes should, under no circumstances, be less than the minimum wage, recognising at the same time the inequalities of the bargaining and financial power between athletes and their employers.

Moreover, any written agreement between an athlete and a new club before the commencement of the transfer period from his old club will be invalid.[12] This creates more options for the athletes, because they will not be bound by any agreements during the transfer period and in that case they will be able to negotiate better deals. Clubs with financial difficulties should not sign any agreements with athletes, unless they clear their debts first and they should not promise increased salaries to athletes without financial backing.[13]

Finally, the legislator intended to avoid the unnecessary involvement of the courts in financial disputes between athletes and their employers. The relevant provisions state that the relations between athletes and their employers are governed now by the provisions of employment law. As a result financial disputes should not be allowed to be referred to arbitration, but should be referred to the Committee of the relevant sporting organisations who is obliged to reach a decision within 30 days.[14] The reason behind this provision is a fast dispute resolution mechanism. The argument here, of course, is whether a mechanism like this will work in practice and whether justice will be served. The provisions also state that the athletes will not be deprived of their right to seek redress in the relevant courts.

Sporting Justice

This Third Part of the new legislation creates changes that are fundamental. Before the new legislation came into force, the restructuring of sports justice was considered imperative. It is hoped that with the new provisions a greater credibility for the sporting justice will be achieved.

The main, and most important, change however, concerns the personnel to hear sporting disputes. All disputes will be heard by judges of the ordinary courts. It is submitted that this is a credible and objective way of the award of sporting justice. It is not clear whether this includes employment disputes but will include other disputes such as the expulsion of the athlete from the game or deci-

---

[12] Article 92.
[13] Article 93.
[14] Article 867 of the Code of Civil Procedure.

sions of misconduct. This process will guarantee the objectivity and fairness of the decisions.

The new legislation offers new powers to the Supreme Council of Sports Disputes Settlement. For the first time decentralisation is taking place on two levels. Apart from Athens, the Supreme Council will also operate in Thessaloniki, the country's second largest city, hopefully increasing efficiency in the operation of justice and the reduction of expenses.

EUROPEAN UNION AND SPORTING ACTIVITY

It is important to consider whether the recent Greek Sport Law has its origins in European law. To a certain extent, it has been argued that the Greek legislator intended to harmonise the national legislation with European law. It is appropriate to consider the areas in which possible conflicts may arise.

Athletes' Contracts in Greece

The rapid development of professionalism in sports during the last few years increased both the social and the economic impact on sports law relations.[15] As a result their regulation could only be achieved through legislative intervention. The first systematic intervention in the field of professional sports was effectuated with the introduction of Law 879/1979 and exclusively referred to professional football.

The Law 1958/1991 supplemented the 1979 provisions and provided additional rules for governance and development of professionalism in sports. This intervention was indeed necessary since professionalism in sport and especially in football was already a reality at the international level. This international practice can be seen, for instance, in Italy, in France as well as in a large number of laws and decrees in other European countries. As we have seen, the New Law 2725/1999 re-regulates *de novo* amateur and professional sports.

Athletes' Contracts After the *Bosman* Case and the Current Situation in Greece

The EU provisions for free movement of workers does not apply to domestic situations of a Member State, unless this movement is between at least two Member States.[16]

---

[15] See Panagiotopoulos D, Field of application and effects of the European Community Law on Sports Activities in *Sports & European Community Law – International Implications* (1998) Proceedings of 5th International Congress, Athens, IALS.

[16] C-415-93. As far as the athletes' transfers among the Member States are concerned, the European Court decided that the regulations on transfers constitute obstacles in the free movement of

The *Bosman* ruling does not allow for covert payments to be made between two clubs in different Member States when an athlete transfers from his old to the new club at the end of his contract. Such covert or transfer payments have been ruled illegal and constitute a barrier to free movement of persons.

Greek legislation on the sports sectors of Basketball and Volleyball extended the limits of free movement of athletes within and outside Greece after the end of the contractual duration of their contract,[17] rendering invalid the prior quasi-hostage status of athletes. The contracts signed in Greece between Greek clubs and Greek athletes before the *Bosman* ruling are not affected by this ruling. Where transfer fees where agreed these remained binding until 1996. Any transfer fees specified in contracts signed after 1996 are not valid for any athlete regardless their nationality.

Today, the remuneration and profit constitute major objectives for the people involved in sports and especially in occupational activities. In Greece, the occupational sports activity is governed by complicated legislation regulating issues of sports services provision, the contracts' content, and the professional, semi-professional and remunerated athletes' employment. The situation in Greece until the *Bosman* ruling, was generating excessive restrictions for sports activity. Provisions restricting the occupational athletes' freedom have been *de facto* gradually abolished. Contracts drawn in Greece regarding sports services should be clear and accurate and they should include terms ensuring uniformity in the free movement of athletes (transfer, abolition of valuable consideration, contract formation) within and outside Greece.

CONCLUSION

The new legislation has created radical changes recognising not only a changing society, but also the new dynamics in professional sport. The legislator, for the first time, has produced a comprehensive legal structure for the operation of sport. What is important in this legislation is the fact that professional athletes are being recognised as employees and are being dealt with in a consistent manner with the exception of financial disputes between clubs and athletes. These must be settled at first instance by the relevant sports association. Their rights and their obligations are also being recognised.

One major concern, however, relates to the application of EU law. It appears from certain provisions that the intention of the legislator is to follow the spirit of

---

workers since the professional athlete can not exercise his or her activity within a club registered in another Member State, if this club has not paid to the aforementioned a transfer compensation, the amount of which was agreed upon by the two clubs or was set according to the sports federations' rules.

[17] Ministerial Decree 20904/1995 and 20907/1996.

EU law. In certain circumstances, as we have seen, it achieves this by making the appropriate amendments. There are issues, however, that still need further clarification. For example, the State provides aid for professional clubs but not athletes' unions. This may contravene the EU State aid rules. The New Law has not been put to the test yet and we can only speculate as to its consequences. It is highly likely that there will be challenges from the EU authorities in the future. This is an area where further legislation is needed.

Another area where possible challenges may arise is the area of doping. The European Convention on Human Rights plays an important role and the legislator does not appear to have considered this dimension. Given the fact that Greece has criminalised doping (Law No. 1646/1986), changes also need to be made in this area. The legislation on doping remains intact and there are certainly issues that need to be addressed such as lack of enforcement by the appropriate sporting organisations. Human Rights and doping are elements, which may trigger challenges in court. The relevant issues here are connected with the rights of privacy[18] (against urine and blood testing) and fair hearings by sporting governing bodies. It is outside the scope of this article to consider 'urinalysis' (in relation to privacy), which produces a major and fundamental distinction between the athletic activity and the athlete's private life, and which is an issue for the philosophy of sports competition. It is speculative to suggest that the New Law will produce grounds for legal challenges in this area, nevertheless, it is submitted, that amendments need to be made. Prevention is always better than cure!

Overall, the new legislation is a positive step forward and it produces greater certainty and efficiency in many areas of sport. There are aspects, however, that need clarification, and for the reasons explained above, the need for further change is imperative.

---

[18] Ioannidis G and Grayson E, Drugs, Health and Sporting Values, in O'Leary J (ed), *Drugs and Doping in Sport: Socio-Legal Perspectives* (2000) London, Cavendish.

THE APPROACH TO SPORTS POLICY IN BELGIUM

Luc Silance

INTRODUCTION

Belgium is a small kingdom in the north western corner of Europe with a population of ten million inhabitants, and better known as the site of the capital of the European Union together with Strasbourg, and for its political and linguistic divisions, rather than for sport and the unifying virtues of sport. The population is not very sports-minded, and there are few well-known Belgian sportsmen: the athletes Aston Reiff, Gaston Roelants, Emile Puttemans, the swimmer Frederic Debuggraeve are a few examples.

Beyond Brussels, the seat of the European Commission, and the second capital of the European Parliament, little is known about Belgium. What is Belgian sports policy? What influence has the European Union on sport in Belgium?

BELGIAN SPORTS POLICY

To define Belgian sports policy and the juridical structures of sport in Belgium one must clarify, or attempt to clarify, a certain number of problems relating to the very organisation of sport in the country. In fact, the organisation of sport in Belgium is *not* the same as its political organisation. Sports policy is made, not only by public bodies, but also through the organisation of sport itself. The political organisation of Belgium is complex and trying to explain it is like trying to square the circle. From both a constitutional and an administrative point of view, even a lawyer who specialises in constitutional law cannot describe it easily.

A united kingdom since 1830, Belgium has been a federal state since 1970. The King only ratifies the legislation voted by the Parliament. The Federal State is headed by a parliament and a senate, elected by universal suffrage, from within which is elected a government which, together with the King, holds executive power. The Kingdom is divided into regions and communities. The communities, respectively French, Flemish and German speaking, were created by a constitutional modification in 1970.

A. Caiger and S. Gardiner (Eds), Professional Sport in the EU: Regulation and Re-regulation
© *2000, T.M.C.Asser Press, The Hague, The Netherlands*

The Organisation of Sport in Belgium

By virtue of the dispositions of the constitution, cultural activities lie within the authority of the communities. These activities, as defined by the Law of 21 July 1971, comprise notably, amongst a great many other activities, physical education, sport and outdoor activities. This means that a cultural council, like parliaments, which are also elected by universal suffrage, heads each of the communities. They have the authority to regulate by decree the cultural activities (notably sports activities). A national institute of physical education and sport was set up in 1956. In 1963 this became the administration of physical education, sports and outdoor activities (A.D.E.P.S.).

In 1971 it was divided; each part was attributed to one of the communities and a third was created for the German community in the east of the country. These civil services, composed of civil servants, are charged not only with setting up an infrastructure, that is to say building sports centres, but also, under the direction of the relevant Minister, with the management of the activities within their sphere of competence, amongst which are physical education, sport and outdoor life in general.

Let there be no mistake, however, sport does not exist in Belgium (any more than in other European countries) by virtue of the creation of a civil administration. Besides, it is not the civil servants that govern sport. Sport has been organised on a voluntary basis, in the form of clubs since the second half of the 19th century. These clubs or circles are grouped within the regional federations, which form the national federations for each sport. A national federation, considered as the sole authority, is recognised by an international federation governing the sport in question worldwide.

The National Olympic Committee (the Belgian Olympic Committee, which became the Belgian Olympic and Interfederal Committee) which is recognised by the International Olympic Committee, is made up of these national federations.

Each of the communities having decided by decree in 1977 to allocate subventions to sport and outdoor activities has the right, by these decrees, to decide on the manner in which the subventions should be distributed. To this end, they demanded that in order to receive subventions the federations should be organised regionally, and administered in the language of the region.

The boards have practically forced the federations to be constituted by region because of the bias of two decrees: a Flemish decree of 2 March 1977, and a French decree of 22 December 1977. The federations are, therefore, set up on a geographic and linguistic basis. Most Belgian federations, even if they have to become *national* in order to be recognised, on the one hand by the relevant international federation, and on the other by the Olympic Committee, have had to allow themselves to be set up in two wings, one French speaking, the other Flemish speaking, under the aegis of the national federation (which does not however 'head' them).

Only two large federations have resisted this pressure: the Royal Belgian Union of Football Associations, and the Belgian Cycling league. They remain single bodies, although the former has decided to split in 2000.

From a political point of view, each community has its own options. Each puts emphasis on different elements. These options have more to do with politics than sport. They are decided on the one hand by the Flemish community and on the other by the French speaking community.

Since the best known and world class sportsmen and women are mostly Flemish, the French speaking community has concentrated on the development of top class athletes. The Flemish community has built installations, sports centres and swimming pools for the propagation of sport over the geographic area reserved to it. The sports federations, often less well off, have lost a lot of time and energy and even money in organising this division. It is not at all certain that the subventions have covered the costs of these operations.

REGULATING DOPING

An example of the complexity of sport and the difficulty of defining it, above all of managing it from a juridical point of view, lies in the phenomenon of doping and its suppression.

Belgium was the first country to adopt legislation in this domain: the Law of 2 April 1965 forbade the use of drugs during sports competitions and during training and preparation. Belgium was followed a few months later by France, with the Law of 1st June 1965. This legislation closely follows the recommendations of the Council of Europe following the European colloquium held on 26th and 27th January 1963 at which 'doping' was defined. The Belgian law of 2nd April 1965, forbids the use of drugs, and defines that use, but has been difficult to apply in the courts of law, since infractions were difficult to check.

The Flemish community decided by a decree of 27th March 1991, relating to the practice of sport in respect to the imperatives of good health, to approve different measures, consisting of a series of additional obligations imposed on federations and sports clubs whose headquarters were situated in that community.

In the Flemish community, the sports federations were charged by this decree with the task of supervising and administering drug testing in collaboration with the Board. They were obliged to communicate the results derived from the doctors who carry out the tests, those doctors who supervise the samples after the competition and those technicians who test the samples in laboratories. Doping does not carry a penal sanction but an administrative one.

In a country the size of Belgium the complexity of systems which differ according to region can only be imagined.

To sum up the situation, it must be concluded that the only sports policy in Belgium lies with the sports federations and the Olympic Committee.

THE DIVISION OF SPORTS POLICY

The federations are in effect, divided and as a consequence do not have sufficient power to impose a true sports policy on the whole country. The civil service can only do this in the community, except for sport in schools and even there such a policy is not practicable, nor is 'Sport for All'. The civil administration can only intervene in the federations to attribute subventions to the linguistically divided federations and to give general directions. In fact, general sports policy lies with the Belgian Olympic Committee.

A distinction must be made, however, between 'Sport for All' (that is to say the sport practised by the greatest number, wholly outside competitions), the clubs and federations which govern the sport, and competitive sport as practised within these clubs and federations. The federations also govern top level sport and professional sport. At this level, the influence of sports agents themselves, and the power of sponsors, that is to say those who pay the sportsmen and women to wear their colours and the brand names of their products, is such that one can no longer speak of sports policy, but financial investment.

THE INFLUENCE OF THE EUROPEAN UNION ON SPORT AND THE POSSIBLE EFFECT OF UNIFICATION

If one seeks a trend and a political sense in European terms it must not be forgotten that within the European Union, since the Treaty of Rome on 25 March 1957, the question of sport arises only episodically. Neither culture nor sport are highlighted in the Rome treaties which set up the Common Market, the Community of Coal and Steel (CECA) and the Atomic accords (EURATOM), nor in subsequent treaties. There is no question anywhere of culture, not to mention sport. The Treaties of Maastricht and Amsterdam, did not fundamentally modify this situation.

While the Treaties of Maastricht and Amsterdam modified the competences, notably those of the European Parliament, in matters of sport nothing was changed. As a result, it is evident that the problem of sport, or rather the question of physical education and sport, which are cultural matters in Belgium, has not been touched or modified by the more or less recent dispositions in Europe.

The Director General of Culture (formerly DGX), has authority in sports matters, but only in a marginal way. The important decisions which concern sport and which touch on it, did not come from the Commission, but from the Court of Justice of the European Community in Luxembourg, firstly by the ruling on the case of *Walrave and Koch v UCI*,[1] then *Donà v Mantero* of 14 July 1976,[2] but

---

[1] Case 36/74 Walrave & Koch v Union Cycliste Internationale [1974] ECR 1405.
[2] Case 13/76 Donà v Mantero [1976] ECR 1333.

above all the *Bosman* ruling[3] against URBSFA and Football club Liège, of 15 December 1995.

These cases have affected the practice of sport. Uniquely from an economic point of view, they identify whether or not the Treaty of Rome, covers the professional sportsman or woman and his or her professional environment as much for freedom of establishment, with regard to freedom of movement and with competition as an appendage.

In my view these are only ancillary elements in sport, which besides, concern only the professionals, and not the sports organisation itself. They have nothing to do with 'Sport for All'. Nothing to do with physical education. Nothing to do with sport outside professional sport.

The Treaty of Rome in Europe after 31 December 1992, provided a 'space without internal barriers' which has brought four essential elements to the future development of the Community:

– A modified decision making mechanism, since a majority voting replaces unanimity, except in three instances;
– Solidarity between rich and poor regions;
– The reinforcement of the role of the European Parliament;
– The mutual recognition of national rules.

None of this affects sport, except in a distant and episodic manner. The European Commission is only interested in it on a cultural basis, above all as propaganda.

The Parliament only does it by questions to which not very positive responses have been made. Sport only becomes affected when it constitutes a professional activity.

Only the European Court of Justice has, by four rulings, taken a precise attitude since neither the Commission nor the Parliament have powers to do so.

THE ECJ AND THE 'SPORTS CASES'

More than twenty years ago (in two cases, *Walgrave and Koch* and *Donà*) the Court of Justice of the European Community in Luxembourg decided that the Treaty of Rome applies to professional sportsmen and women, at least in as far as the fundamental principles, in particular the banning of discrimination on grounds of nationality, the right of establishment and the right to carry out a profession. The two rulings apply of course to those who have made sport a profession.

---

[3] C-415/93 Union Royale Belge des Sociétés de Football Association ASBL v Jean-Marc Bosman [1995] ECR I-4921.

Given the objectives of the European Community, the exercise of sport relates to community law in as much as it constitutes an economic activity in the sense of Article 2 of the Treaty. This is in the case of the activity of professional or semi-professional players, footballers or cyclists, since they exercise a paid occupation or are remunerated for services rendered. When these players or athletes are nationals of a Member State, they benefit, like all Member States, from community arrangements in matters of free circulation of persons and services (articles 39 and 40, 57 et seq.).

The fourth ruling, and the best known, *Bosman*, completes the first two. The Court of Justice went further in its analysis of the consequences of the dispositions of the Treaty of Rome on contracts made between footballers and the clubs which employ them than in the first two rulings.

The Court decided that Article 39[4] of the Treaty of Rome was opposed to the application of rules made by sports associations by which a professional footballer, a national of a Member State, may not on the expiry of his contract with the club be employed by a club in another Member State unless the latter paid the club of origin a transfer, training or promotional fee.[5]

Article 39 of the Treaty also opposes the application of rules made by sports associations whereby, during competitive matches, organised by them, the football clubs may only line up a limited number of professionals who are nationals of other Member States.

However, the Court refused to go further in its analysis, and to rule in particular regarding the infractions of which the Belgian Union of Football, the Football Club of Liége and UEFA had been accused, concerning the violation of articles 81 and 82 regarding competition and the abuse of dominant economic power.

The consequences of the *Bosman* ruling have obviously been extremely important for professional sport.

CONCLUSION

Sport is not governed by the European Union. It remains subject to management by national and international sports federations and by Olympic Committees. Professional sport is practised by those who escape from the world of sport (and the European Union) but it is the media who hold the purse strings.

Legal dispositions are applicable in each country. Only professional sport, that is to say the most important fringe of sport, is affected by some European directives and decisions but even then only in regard to money and the fame of individuals and teams.

---

[4] Formerly Article 48.
[5] See Richard Parrish's and Ken Foster's contributions to this book.

A good example can be found in the attitude of the European Union to doping. When the world conference on doping in sport was held on 4th February 1999 in Lausanne, Switzerland, different European countries were represented, as well as the European Union itself. They did not take any particular view at Lausanne.

Certain European countries came to a decision in mid-October 1999. This decision comes in fact from the Ministries of Sport, within whose authority sport lies. They decided together to participate in the setting up of a world agency to combat doping (October 1999 in Finland).[6] This important decision will have repercussions in the different countries that took part, through the European Union, in the fight against doping. In reality, the decision is taken by ministries rather than by the European Union itself.

Finally, the role of the Council of Europe cannot be overlooked; the European Sports Charter emanates from the Council of Europe. The first studies into doping came from the Council of Europe. Even if it does not possess a coercive power, it plays an important role, at least in the evolution of ideas.

The harmonisation of Europe does not yet cover sport. Each nation remains master of its own legislation in this domain. The international sports federations (and equally the continental federations) which have each created their juridical order, each still govern their own sport. Professional sport is clearly moving towards greater autonomy, towards separate management, but there is no sign of intervention here by public authorities, except in limited areas, such as tobacco or alcohol advertising.

---

[6] Commission of the European Communities, *Report from the Commission to the European Council with a View to safeguarding Sports Structures and Maintaining the Social Significance of Sport Within the Community Framework (the Helsinki Report on Sport)*, Com (1999) 644.

REGULATION OF SPORTS LEAGUES, TEAMS, ATHLETES AND AGENTS IN THE UNITED STATES

James T. Gray

INTRODUCTION

In the United States, the law has been applied to professional sports in order to achieve two goals: firstly, to define the parameters of power and influence among all stakeholders, and secondly, to divide the significant influx of money generated by professional sports among these stakeholders. For instance, the National Football League has steadily increased its national television revenues from US$142 million in 1981 to US$1.1 billion in 1998. Similarly, Major League Baseball salaries increased from an average salary of US$19,000 in 1967 to an average salary of US$1,378,506 in 1998. In 1999, the United States General Accounting Office noted that between 1994 and 1998 average player salaries in the National Football League, Major League Baseball, National Basketball Association and the National Hockey League increased between 14 per cent and 64 per cent. In 1996, Financial World magazine estimated that the Dallas Cowboys earned US$39.8 million in sports facility related revenues at their home Texas Stadium. Further, almost every National Football League team within the next ten years will have either a new or refurbished sports facility in order to maximize stadia related revenues such as luxury suites, club seats, naming rights, concessions and parking.

In 1967, a thirty second television advertisement for Super Bowl I sold for US$40,000, as compared to 1996 when an identical advertisement for Super Bowl XXX sold for US$1.2 million. As the American sports industry delves into the realm of the World Wide Web, there are those who estimate that billions of dollars can be earned with this emerging technology. For example, according to the Internet commerce research firm, Jupiter Communications, American consumers are expected to spend approximately US$3 billion in sporting goods, apparel, footwear and tickets via the Internet by 2003. Similarly, Forrester Research estimated that more than 22% of North American households actively follow sports on the Internet and that by 2004 Internet related sports advertising is expected to reach US$2.4 billion, with sports related e-commerce increasing to US$4.7 billion.

A. Caiger and S. Gardiner (Eds), Professional Sport in the EU: Regulation and Re-regulation
© 2000, T.M.C.Asser Press, The Hague, The Netherlands

In order to further define the relationship between the various stakeholders of American professional sports, American antitrust law and labor law have been used as the primary methods to decide almost all sports related power and revenue sharing issues.

OVERVIEW OF THE AMERICAN ANTITRUST LAW

Two sections of the United States Sherman Act apply to American professional sports. Section 1 prohibits contracts or agreements in restraint of trade. Section 2 prohibits monopolization or attempts to monopolize. When American courts review sports related antitrust claims, they apply two analyses:

– Rule of Reason – all of the circumstances surrounding combinations, such as mergers and joint ventures, are reviewed by the courts to judge whether their market power and market structure unreasonably restricts competitive conditions in violation of American antitrust law.
– Per se Illegality – certain activities or agreements, such as horizontal price fixing, group boycotts and market allocation, are so inherently anti-competitive that each is deemed to be in violation of American antitrust law without a court inquiry into the harm it has actually caused.

Once a violation of the Sherman Act is established, the Clayton Antitrust Act allows the plaintiff to recover treble damages against the defendant who has violated the antitrust laws. The Clayton Act states in the pertinent part:

> 'Any person who shall be injured in his business or property by reason of anything forbidden in the antitrust laws may sue therefore in any district court of the United States in the district in which the defendant resides or is found or has an agent, without respect to the amount in controversy, and shall recover threefold the damages by him sustained, and the cost of suit, including reasonable fees.'

When American antitrust law is applied to professional sports, players specifically allege in their lawsuits that owners and leagues violate the Sherman Act because restraints such as the player reserve clause, the player draft and player salary caps are in restraint of trade, and as a result, prevent players from obtaining the maximum salary that the market will allow.

The Major League Baseball Antitrust Exemption

One of the first cases to examine the application of antitrust law to professional sports was *Federal Baseball Club of Baltimore, Inc. v. National League of Professional Baseball Clubs*.[1] In this case, the United States Supreme Court held that

---

[1] 259 U.S. 200 (1922).

professional baseball leagues and teams were not engaged in interstate commerce and therefore not subject to antitrust law. The Court found that in order to give the exhibitions in another state the Leagues must induce free persons to cross state lines and must arrange and pay for their doing so. This is not enough to change the character of the business.[2] For example, the Court pointed out that a firm of lawyers sending out a member to argue a case, or the Chautauqua lecture bureau sending out lecturers, does not engage in such commerce because the lawyer or lecturer goes to another State.[3] As a result, the Court found that the business of professional baseball was exempt from American antitrust law.

In *Toolson v. New York Yankees*,[4] the United States Supreme Court reviewed its holding in Federal Baseball, as well as the application of antitrust law to Major League Baseball's reserve clause. The reserve clause is contained in the standard player contract. It is the means by which a team can maintain exclusive control over the players they employ by placing the name of a player on a 'reserve list' which is then distributed to other league clubs. A player on the reserve list cannot play for or negotiate with any other league club until his contract has been assigned or the player has been released. In other words, a player under the reserve system cannot leave his team unless he is traded, cut, waived or otherwise terminated from his team or the player has died.

'The Court held that the business of providing public baseball games for profit between clubs of professional baseball players was not within the scope of the federal antitrust laws. Congress has had the ruling under consideration but has not seen fit to bring such business under these laws by legislation having prospective effect. The business has thus been left for thirty years to develop, on the understanding that it was not subject to existing antitrust legislation.'[5]

The United States Supreme Court believed that the only way that American antitrust law would be applied to Major League Baseball was in the event that the United States Congress would specifically include baseball in the law's purview.

In *Flood v. Kuhn*,[6] the business of baseball and its antitrust exemption was again reviewed by the United States Supreme Court. In this case, the plaintiff argued that the reserve clause violated antitrust law. The Court reviewed its holdings in *Federal Baseball* and *Toolson* and provided four reasons for affirming its previous rulings that baseball was exempt from antitrust laws, as follows:

'(a) Congressional awareness for three decades of the Court's ruling in *Federal Baseball*, coupled with congressional inaction; (b) The fact that baseball was left alone to develop for that period upon the understanding that the reserve system was not subject

---

[2] Ibid. at 208 (1922).
[3] Ibid. at 208-209.
[4] 346 U.S. 356 (1953).
[5] Ibid. at 357.
[6] 407 U.S. 258 (1972).

to existing federal antitrust laws; (c) A reluctance to overrule *Federal Baseball* with consequent retroactive effect; (d) A professed desire that any needed remedy be provided by legislation rather than by court decree. The emphasis in *Toolson* was on the determination . . . that Congress had no intention to include baseball within the reach of the federal antitrust laws.'[7]

While the Flood decision reaffirmed Major League Baseball's antitrust exemption, this exemption could be somewhat eroded by a federal district court decision. For example, in *Piazza v. Major League Baseball*,[8] the issue was whether a Major League Baseball team could move to another location without the permission of the league. The court reviewed the United States Supreme Court opinions in *Federal Baseball, Toolson* and *Flood* and found that baseball's antitrust exemption was confined to the context of the player reserve clause.[9] Moreover, the court found that *Flood* invalidated the rule *stare decisis* of *Federal Baseball* and *Toolson* and left only the result *stare decisis* which meant under the facts of the case, Major League Baseball's antitrust exemption applied only to the player reserve system.

However, there may be reluctance among judges to adopt or extend the *Piazza* decision. For instance, the Minnesota Supreme Court was the first court to examine Major League Baseball's antitrust exemption after the *Piazza* decision. In *Minnesota Twins Partnership et. al. v. State of Minnesota*,[10] the court reviewed whether the Minnesota Twins had to comply with civil investigative demands (CIDs) issued by the Minnesota Attorney General's Office. The CIDs were requested in connection with the proposed sale and relocation of the Twins to North Carolina and a potential boycott of Minnesota by Major League Baseball in violation of state antitrust laws.[11] The Twins argued that their conduct was exempt from Minnesota's antitrust laws because the United States Supreme Court had held in *Federal Baseball, Toolson* and *Flood* that the business of professional baseball is exempt from compliance with federal or state antitrust laws.[12]

The Minnesota Supreme Court said that the issue was the scope of professional baseball's exemption from Minnesota's antitrust laws.[13] The Court reviewed several United States Supreme Court cases where it was made clear that professional baseball's exemption rested on a narrow application of the rule of *stare decisis* applicable to baseball.[14] The Court also examined the *Piazza* deci-

---

[7] Ibid. 278.
[8] 831 F. Supp. 420 (1993).
[9] Piazza v Major League Baseball, 831 F. Supp. 420 (1993).
[10] 592 N.W. 2d 847; 1999 Minn. LEXIS 249; 1999-1 Trade Cas. (CCH) P72,507 (1999).
[11] Ibid. at 849.
[12] Ibid.
[13] Ibid. at 850.
[14] The cases reviewed by the Court included Federal Baseball Club of Baltimore v National League of Professional Baseball Clubs, Inc., 259 U.S. 200, 66 L. Ed. 898, 42 S. Ct. 465 (1922); Toolson v New York Yankees, Inc., 346 U.S. 356, 98 L. Ed. 64, 74 S. Ct. 78 (1953); United States v

sion, where that court concluded that the United States Supreme Court's statement in *Flood* that baseball was a business engaged in interstate commerce as limiting the scope of the exemption to the reserve clause at issue in *Flood* and *Toolson*.[15]

While the Court agreed that the *Piazza* opinion was a skillful attempt to make sense of the Supreme Court's refusal to overrule *Federal Baseball*, it ignores what is clear about *Flood* that the Supreme Court had no intention of overruling *Federal Baseball* or *Toolson* despite acknowledging that professional baseball involves interstate commerce.[16] The Court, in holding in favor of the Minnesota Twins, concluded its opinion as follows:

'We choose to follow the lead of those courts that conclude the business of professional baseball is exempt from federal antitrust laws. Further, we conclude that the sale and relocation of a baseball franchise, like the reserve clause discussed in *Flood*, is an integral part of the business of professional baseball and falls within the exemption. . . Accordingly, we hold that the conduct of the Twins being investigated by the Attorney General is exempt from Minnesota, as well as federal antitrust laws. Enforcement of the CIDs against the Twins is therefore outside the scope of the Attorney General's authority because no enforcement action could follow.'[17]

AMERICAN ANTITRUST LAW APPLIED TO ALL OTHER PROFESSIONAL SPORTS LEAGUES

While professional baseball enjoys an exemption from antitrust law, American courts have declared that other professional sports leagues do not. For instance, in *Radovich v. National Football League*,[18] a professional football player argued that the NFL reserve clause as contained in the standard player contract was in violation of antitrust law. The NFL believed that the holding of *Federal Baseball* regarding baseball's antitrust exemption applied to other professional sports as well. The United States Supreme Court held that baseball's antitrust exemption was limited to the business of baseball and did not extend to professional football.[19] Further, the Court held that the nature of interstate business involved in organized professional football places it within the auspices of antitrust law. Similarly, in *Robertson v. National Basketball Ass'n*,[20] National Basketball Asso-

---

Shubert, 348 U.S. 222, 230, 99 L. Ed. 279, 75 S. Ct. 277 (1955); Radovich v National Football League, 352 U.S. 445, 451-52, 1 L. Ed. 2d 456, 77 S. Ct. 390 (1957); and Flood v Kuhn, 407 U.S. 258, 32 L. Ed. 2d 728, 92 S. Ct. 2099 (1972).

[15] Piazza v Major League Baseball, 831 F. Supp. 420 (E.D. Pa. 1993).

[16] Supra n.10 Minnesota Twins at 855-856.

[17] Ibid. at 856.

[18] 352 U.S. 445 (1957).

[19] Radovich v National Football League, 352 U.S. 445, 452 (1957).

[20] 389 F. Supp. 867, 884-95 (S.D.N.Y. 1975).

ciation players filed a lawsuit to prevent the proposed NBA-ABA merger. Further, the players argued that the player draft, the reserve clause and the NBA-ABA merger proposal were all in violation of antitrust law. In ruling for the players, the judge held in *Robertson* that:

> 'I must confess that it is difficult for me to conceive of any theory or set of circumstances pursuant to which the college draft, blacklisting, boycotts and refusals to deal could be saved from Sherman Act condemnation, even if defendants were able to prove at trial their highly dubious contention that these restraints were adopted at the behest of the players association.'

Likewise, in *Denver Rockets v. All-Pro Mgt., Inc.*[21] a professional basketball player argued that the eligibility requirements of the NBA draft were in violation of antitrust law. The court held that all professional sports, with the exception of professional baseball, were governed by antitrust laws and held that the NBA's draft eligibility requirements were illegal.

A NEW APPROACH TO LEAGUE REGULATION AND STRUCTURE – THE SINGLE ENTITY THEORY

In *Fraser v. Major League Soccer*,[22] a group of professional soccer players claimed that Major League Soccer (MLS) violated section 1 of the Sherman Antitrust Act. The players argued that by contracting for their services centrally through MLS, member teams were prevented from competing for players on an individual and direct basis. As a result, the plaintiffs maintained that individual player salaries are lower when directly contracted by MLS. In comparison, players could have the opportunity to obtain higher salaries if they were permitted to negotiate their player contracts directly with each MLS team and have more than one team bid for their services simultaneously.

The court found, however, that there are limits to antitrust law. For example, one critical limitation for the purposes of this case is that the statute does not prohibit single economic entities from acting unilaterally in ways that may, in some manner, decrease competition.[23] Further, the court held that there can be no section 1 claim based on concerted action among a corporation and its officers, nor among officers themselves, so long as the officers are not acting to promote an interest, from which they would directly benefit, that is independent from the corporation's success.[24] In examining the players' antitrust claims, the court found that:

---

[21] 325 F. Supp. 1049 (C.D. Cal. 1971).
[22] 97 F. Supp. 2d 130 (2000).
[23] 97 F. Supp. 2d 130 at para. 13.
[24] Ibid. at para. 16.

'On balance, the business organization of MLS is quite centralized. The league owns the teams themselves; disgruntled operators may not simply 'take their ball and go home' by withdrawing the teams they operate and forming or joining a rival league. MLS also owns all intellectual property related to the teams. It contracts for local level services through its operators, who act on its behalf as agents. Operators risk losing their rights to operate their teams if they breach the governing Agreement. The Management Committee exercises supervisory authority over most of the league's activities. It may reject, without cause, any operator's individual attempt to assign the rights to operate a team.'[25]

As a result, the court concluded that the MLS:

'As a single entity, it cannot conspire or combine with its investors in violation of section 1, and its investors do not combine or conspire with each other in pursuing the economic interests of the entity, MLS's policy of contracting centrally for player services is unilateral activity of a single firm. Since section 1 does not apply to unilateral activity ... even unilateral activity that tends to restrain trade ... the claim [regarding MLS policy of centrally contracting all players through the league as compared to individual teams being in violation of section 1] cannot succeed as a matter of law.'[26]

The practical result of this case is that American sports leagues can implement the single entity model in order to avoid costly player salaries and antitrust lawsuits.

OVERVIEW OF LABOR LAW – THE REGULATION OF THE EMPLOYER/EMPLOYEE RELATIONSHIP IN PROFESSIONAL SPORTS

Statutory Labor Exemption Section 6 of the Clayton Act

The statutory labor exemption to antitrust law is found in section 6 of the Clayton Act. The Clayton Act states that: the labor of a human being is not a commodity or article of commerce. Nothing contained in the antitrust laws shall be construed to forbid the existence and operation of labor ... organizations from lawfully carrying out the legitimate objects thereof; nor shall such organizations, or the members thereof, be held or construed to be illegal combinations or conspiracies in restraint of trade under antitrust laws. [27]

Non-statutory Labor Exemption

In *NBA v. Williams*,[28] the court succinctly described the non-statutory labor exemption as follows:

---

[25] Fraser v MLS, 97 F. Supp. 130 at para. 22.
[26] Ibid. at para. 31.
[27] 15 U.S.C. 17.
[28] 857 F. Supp. 1069, 1076.

'The non-statutory exemption was created by the [United States] Supreme Court to reconcile the conflicting policies between antitrust and labor laws. We have two declared congressional policies which it is our responsibility to try to reconcile. The one seeks to preserve a competitive business economy: the other to preserve the rights of labor to organize to better its conditions through the agency of collective bargaining. We must determine here how far Congress intended activities under one of these policies to neutralize the results envisioned by the other.'

In *Mackey v. National Football League*,[29] the court established the following three-pronged test for when the non-statutory labor exemption could be invoked by the league:

- labor policy of collective bargaining may be favored over antitrust where 'the restraint on trade primarily affects only the parties to the collective bargaining agreement',
- federal labor policy will prevail only where the agreement sought to be exempted concerns a mandatory subject of collective bargaining, and
- policy favoring collective bargaining will pre-empt antitrust application 'only where the agreement sought to be exempted is the product of arm's-length bargaining.'

In *Wood v. National Basketball Ass'n*[30] the court considered an antitrust challenge to the NBA's salary cap and college draft. The court in holding in favor of the defendant held that antitrust laws may not 'be used to subvert fundamental principles of our federal labor policy'. Thus, where a collective bargaining relationship exists, federal labor law, and not antitrust law, applies to the disputes that arise between the bargaining parties. Further, in *Bridgeman v. National Basketball Ass'n*,[31] the court examined the issue of whether professional sports leagues enjoyed continued antitrust immunity regarding restrictive practices such as the player draft and the player salary cap. The court decided that antitrust immunity survives so long as the employer continues to impose the restrictions unchanged, and reasonably believes that the challenged practice or a close variant of it will be incorporated in the next collective bargaining agreement.

In *Powell v. National Football League*,[32] the Eighth Circuit Court of Appeals held that the non-statutory labor exemption could be invoked after a collective bargaining agreement had expired. In this case, the court held that the non-statutory labor exemption extends beyond a mere impasse in negotiations and for as long as the labor relationship continues. The court reasoned that once a collective bargaining relationship is established, federal labor policies become pre-eminent.

---

[29] 543 F. 2d 606 (8th Cir. 1976).
[30] 809 F.2d 954, 963 (2d Cir. 1987).
[31] 675 F. Supp. 960, 967 (D.N.J. 1987).
[32] 930 F.2d 1293, 1302-04 (8th Cir.1989), cert. denied, 498 U.S. 1040, 112 L. Ed. 2d 700, 111 S. Ct. 711 (1991).

In conclusion, the court stated that antitrust immunity exists as long as a collective bargaining relationship exists and labor law remedies are available.

In *McNeil v. National Football League*,[33] the court concluded that the existence of a collective bargaining relationship depends upon whether a majority of employees in a bargaining unit support a particular union as their representative. Since the National Football League Players Association decertified as a labor union, the National Football League could no longer enjoy the protections of the non-statutory labor exemption. As a result, the NFL player draft and the reserve clause were held to be in violation of American antitrust law.

The United States Supreme Court, in *Brown v. Pro Football, Inc.*[34] reviewed the application of the non-statutory labor exemption to the issue of player free agency relative to first year players. The NFL owners proposed a plan where up to six first year players, who as free agents, failed to secure a position on a regular team roster were placed on a 'developmental squad.' The owners desired to pay all of the players a $1,000.00 weekly salary. The players union wanted the players to be able to negotiate their own salaries and receive the same benefits as regular players. The collective bargaining agreement negotiations between the owners and players on this issue reached an impasse.

After impasse, the owners unilaterally implemented their restrictions regarding first year players membership on the developmental squad. The Court ruled in favor of the owners and held that the non-statutory labor exemption applied to this case and afforded the NFL antitrust protection while implementing its developmental squad procedures because the:

> 'conduct took place during and immediately after a collective bargaining negotiation. It grew out of, and was directly related to the lawful operation of the bargaining process. It involved a matter that the parties were required to negotiate collectively. And it concerned only the parties to the collective bargaining relationship.'

COLLECTIVE BARGAINING IN PROFESSIONAL SPORTS

With the influx of money generated by television, licensing, sports facility, and now Internet revenues, players and owners have also turned to collective bargaining agreements in order to decide how these revenues will be distributed among themselves. Some of the more significant issues that collective bargaining agreements have addressed regarding the distribution of sports related revenues are player free agency, the implementation of player salary caps and the regulation of player agents.

---

[33] 764 F. Supp. 1351 (D. Minn. 1991).
[34] 116 S.Ct. 2116 (1996).

Arbitration

In the major professional sports leagues of the NFL, NBA, NHL and MLB, owners and players have established binding arbitration as the mechanism to resolve
disputes stemming from their collective bargaining agreements. The authority to
use arbitration is contractually agreed by the parties and is found in both the
league's collective bargaining agreement as well as the league's standard player
contract. The parties bound by arbitration are typically owners, players and
agents. For example, the NFL collective bargaining agreement under Article IX
states, under non-injury grievance, as follows:

> 'Any dispute (hereinafter referred to as a 'grievance') arising after the execution of this
> Agreement and involving the interpretation of, application of, or compliance with, any
> provision of this Agreement, the NFL Player Contract, or any applicable provision of
> the NFL Constitution and Bylaws pertaining to terms and conditions of employment of
> NFL players, will be resolved exclusively in accordance with the procedure set forth in
> this Article, except wherever another method of dispute resolution is set forth else-
> where in this Agreement, and except wherever the Settlement Agreement provides that
> the Special Master, Impartial Arbitrator, the Federal District Court or the Accountants
> shall resolve a dispute.'[35]

The advantages of arbitration are many. First, arbitration is viewed as a relatively
speedy way to resolve disputes. The American court system is notoriously slow
in reaching a decision. Second, the arbitration process is informal because there is
a reduced emphasis on procedural and evidentiary issues as compared to a formal
court hearing. Third, since American professional sports generates significant
publicity and interest from the media and general public, both owners and players
have a vested interest in resolving their disputes which may have a negative public perception in private binding arbitration as compared to a public forum such
as a court.

Major League Baseball and the Fall of the Reserve System

In 1975, the most significant sports related arbitration decision occurred in Major
League Baseball as it pertained to the player reserve system. As discussed previously, Major League Baseball since 1922 was able maintain its reserve clause
system because it was exempt from the purview of antitrust law as decided by the
United States Supreme Court in *Federal Baseball, Toolson* and *Flood*. While unsuccessful with antitrust law and the federal court system in challenging
baseball's player reserve system, the Major League Baseball Players Association

---

[35] NFL Collective Bargaining Agreement, 1993-2003, as amended June 6, 1996 at 20.

instituted an arbitration proceeding known as the *Arbitration of Messersmith-McNally.*[36]

In this case, Andy Messersmith was a Los Angeles Dodgers pitcher who signed a one year contract in 1974 for US$90,000.00. A dispute arose between Messersmith and the Dodgers over a new contract. Messersmith wanted a no trade guarantee in his contract, or, alternatively, he desired to have the right to approve any trade involving him. The Dodgers refused to agree to add this clause in his player contract. During the 1975 baseball season, Messersmith played without a baseball contract. Similarly, Dave McNally, a pitcher, also had a contract dispute with his team, the Montreal Expos. Messersmith and McNally declared themselves free agents where they argued that the reserve clause was effective for only one year after the expiration of their contracts. On the other hand, the Dodgers and Expos pointed out that the reserve clause was perpetual and both players were bound by their 1974 contracts whether their contracts had expired or not.

The Major League Baseball Players Association filed a grievance before an arbitrator pursuant to the terms of their collective bargaining agreement with the owners. The arbitrator held that the reserve clause permitted baseball teams to reserve players for only one additional year after his contract had expired. The arbitrator did not find an express provision in baseball's standard player contract which created a perpetual player contract. As a result, the arbitrator ruled that Messersmith and McNally were free agents at the conclusion of the 1975 baseball season.

The owners appealed the arbitrator's decision in *Kansas City Royals Baseball Corp. v. Major League Baseball Players Ass'n,*[37] The court in rejecting the owners' appeal of the arbitration decision held that:

'the question of interpretation of the collective bargaining agreement is a question for the arbitrator ... because it was the arbitrator's construction which was bargained for [and] that the arbitrator only interpreted provisions of the Agreement as it was authorized to do.'

Major League Baseball Salary Collusion Cases

The second most important arbitration decision involved Article XVIII of Major League Baseball's collective bargaining agreement. This article provided that:

'The utilization or non-utilization of rights under the Article XVIII is an individual matter to be determined solely by each player and each club for his or its own benefit. Players shall not act in concert with other Players and Clubs shall not act in concert with other Clubs.'

---

[36] Grievance No. 75-27, Dec. No. 29 (1975).
[37] 532 F. 2d 615 (8th Cir. 1976).

The players filed three grievances regarding the owners' alleged collusive behavior. In 1986, 1987 and 1988 the Major League Baseball Players Association argued that the owners had violated Article XVIII of their collective bargaining agreement by engaging in collusion in the market for free agent services after the 1985, 1986 and 1987 baseball seasons. For example, the players alleged that the owners had a common understanding that no team would bid on the services of a free agent until his former team no longer wanted to sign him. Furthermore, the players alleged that the owners had violated Article XVIII when they established an 'information bank' where they could exchange final salary offers they made to their own players with other teams. As a result, very few player free agents were signed by other teams from 1985 to 1987.

All of the arbitrators who heard the baseball collusion cases found that the owners had engaged in collusion and caused extensive damage to numerous free agent players. In 1990, the owners and the players entered into a Global Settlement Agreement to resolve all collusion grievances. Pursuant to this Agreement the owners established a fund of US$280 million to be distributed to the damaged free agent baseball players.

Professional Sports League Salary Caps

Over the last twenty years, American sports leagues have introduced the use of player salary caps. The benefits of a salary cap is the cost certainty of player salaries and related costs such as employee benefits. On the other hand, traditional player personnel moves by teams are no longer solely based upon individual talent and team chemistry. Presently, many American professional sports teams now must take into account salary cap considerations in attracting new players and keeping current players on their rosters.

For instance, in 1983, the National Basketball Association was the first American sports league to introduce a player salary cap. At the time, the NBA contended that a salary cap was necessary because the majority of league teams were losing money due in large part to rising player salaries and benefits. The players responded by filing an antitrust lawsuit claiming that the salary cap was unlawful.[38] In order to hear the *Lanier* salary cap lawsuit a special master was appointed to determine if the owners proposed salary cap violated the terms of their *Robertson* lawsuit settlement agreement with the players. In other words, could the owners impose a player salary cap without the players consent. In the meantime, the players and owners ultimately collectively bargained an initial salary cap scheme that started in 1983 and concluded at the end of the 1986-87 NBA season. The 1983 salary cap designated a fixed percentage of league revenues devoted to player salaries. Further, teams could sign their own free agents to an un-

---

[38] See Lanier v. National Basketball Ass'n, 82 Civ. 4935 (S.D.N.Y.).

limited amount of salary, known as the 'Bird exception,' while a maximum amount of team revenue was allocated to each club in order to sign another team's free agent.

Presently, the new salary cap, negotiated between the owners and players at the conclusion of the NBA 1998-99 lockout, includes the following provisions: No fixed number of league revenues allotted to player salaries during the first three years of the NBA collective bargaining agreement. In year 4, 55% of NBA revenues are devoted to player salaries, in years 5 and 6 of the agreement, 57% of NBA revenues are devoted to player salaries and 57% in year 7 if the owners exercise an option to extend the current collective bargaining agreement.[39]

Similarly, during the 1990s, the National Football League had adopted a salary cap. In this case, the players and owners agreed to a concept known as 'Defined Gross Revenue' which is approximately 85% of the total revenues which the NFL generates. Of this amount, 63% is designated for player salaries. This means that, for the 2000-01 NFL season, each team will allocate approximately $62 million for player salaries.

Regulation of Agents Who Represent Professional Athletes

With the advent of multi-million dollar American professional athlete salaries, problems have occurred regarding the handling and investment of these significant sums of money. Some athletes encountered financial problems because their agents were dishonest. Others have experienced problems because they do not possess the requisite business or negotiations skills necessary to protect their personal and business financial interests from their advisors and other business partners. Over the last twenty years, American athletes have lost their sports related fortunes while investing in highly speculative business ventures such as gas, oil, music groups and restaurants.

---

[39] Other important aspects of the new NBA collective bargaining agreement are as follows:

Maximum NBA Salary: NBA service 0-5 years: US$9 million; NBA service 6-9 years: US$11 million; NBA service 10-plus years: US$14 million. Rookie Salaries: Four year scale with right of first refusal for fifth year. Maximum Annual Raises: 12% for Bird exception players, 10% for others. The Bird exception is a loophole that enables a team to resign one of its own free agents for whatever price it wants up to a maximum 12 % annual raise. Cost Certainty: Escrow tax of 10 % withheld from players paychecks if percentage of income devoted to salaries exceeds triggers of 55 % in years 4-7, with the players deciding who among them must pay the 10 % escrow tax. Backup dollar for dollar tax charged to highest spending teams if escrow account does not make up entire coverage. Minimum Salaries: In year 1: Rookies: US$287,500. One year: US$350,000. Two years: US$425,000. Three years: US$450,000. Four years: US$475,000. Five years: US$537,000. Six years: US$600,000. Seven years: US$662.500. Eight years: US$725,000. Nine years: US$850,000. 10 years: US$1 million. Additional Issues: End to opt-out clauses in the first five years of all contracts. Performance bonuses limited to 25 % of the value of a contract. Union's group licensing revenue guarantee dropped to US$20 million during 1998-99 season, then restored to US$25 million during the 1999-00 season.

In order to protect professional athletes from financial ruin and from unscrupulous agents and advisors, a number of regulatory schemes have been developed. For example, those American states that have big time college football and men's basketball passed athlete agent registration laws.[40] The authority of states to enact athlete agent registration laws is through the states' 'police power.' In the past, the states have used their police power to regulate the professional conduct of lawyers and doctors. Typically, these laws require a player agent to complete a state athlete agent registration application, pay a registration fee, file a surety bond, obtain state approval of agent/athlete contract forms, establish a maximum agent fee, and prohibit inducing college athletes with prospective professional careers to sign athlete-agent contracts which result in making these athletes ineligible for National Collegiate Athletic Association competition.

Likewise, professional athletes who are represented by a union have established an agent certification and regulation program. The player unions authority to regulate agents is found in the National Labor Relations Act (NLRA). The NLRA provides the player unions with the authority to ensure that every agent is certified by them before the agent can negotiate an employment contract with any unionized team. Under the NLRA the player unions have the power to be the exclusive representative for all employees in such a unit.[41] As the exclusive representative of players, the union can then delegate individual contract negotiations to certified player agents.

The exclusive use of union certified player agents is addressed in the league's collective bargaining agreements. For example, the NFL Collective Bargaining agreement under Article VI states that both the owners and players recognize that the union regulates the conduct of all agents who negotiate contracts for players with NFL teams. Under no circumstances can a non-certified agent negotiate an employment player contract with a team. If this rule is violated the NFL shall impose a US$10,000 fine on a club who negotiates a player contract with a non-certified agent.

In general, the requirement for union certification of player agents includes the completion of an application which requests information regarding an agent's education, professional and employment background. In order to maintain certification, the payment of an annual union fee is required along with annual attendance of a union-sponsored continuing education seminar concerning player contract negotiations and collective bargaining interpretations made by leagues, unions, and arbitrators.

Prohibited agent activities include the offering of money in order to induce an athlete to become a client of an agent, providing false information on the union's

---

[40] The states which passed athlete agent registration laws include: Alabama, Arkansas, California, Florida, Georgia, Indiana, Iowa, Kentucky, Louisiana, Maryland, Michigan, Minnesota, Mississippi, Nevada, North Carolina, Ohio, Oklahoma, Pennsylvania, Tennessee, and Texas.

[41] See 29 U.S.C. 159(a)-(e) (1982).

agent certification form, and charging in excess of the union's established contract negotiation fees. All disputes between athletes and agents are to be settled by the arbitration system, as established by the unions.

CONCLUSION

It is clear from the aforementioned that there is a tension between the use of anti-trust and labor law in American sport. This tension is exacerbated by the large sums of money coming into professional sport. For example, the spectacular rise of player employment salaries and athlete licensing revenues in the 1960s directly coincided with the formation of player labor unions during this time. With this large source of money made available to professional athletes, they were able to employ lawyers, accountants, business managers, public relations and media personnel, as well as professional labor negotiators to ensure that their economic interests were protected and maximized. This tension between the use of anti-trust and labor laws has been used by players and their unions to improve the financial power of players in the game. Both player labor unions and team owners have utilized a cadre of lawyers, economist and accountants to represent their respective interests during collective bargaining negotiations as well as antitrust litigation regarding player free agency.

The usual way in which this tension between antitrust law and labor law developed in the United States is as follows. First, a professional sports league is created by a group of team owners. The owners usually refuse to conduct any meaningful collective bargaining agreement negotiations with their labor force, the players or athletes. The players have two options to improve their position. First, they could either file an antitrust lawsuit to declare free agency limitations, salary caps, and the player draft as in violation of American antitrust laws. These lawsuits are expensive and players need money to pay their lawyers for at least several years.

Second, if the players win their antitrust lawsuits against the owners, they will possess greater leverage in negotiating a collective bargaining agreement with their employers. If the players should lose their lawsuits, the owners are not interested in negotiating a collective bargaining agreement. Instead, the owners present the players with a 'take it leave it' standard player contract which is drafted in their favor and completely protects the owners' financial interests.

Third, with the 'Single Entity Theory' winning approval in a Boston Federal District Court, antitrust lawsuits may not be as effective for the players as in the past. However, the final legal assessment of this issue has not been reviewed by a Federal Court of Appeals or the United States Supreme Court. Further, older professional sports leagues such as the NFL, NHL and NBA are not single entity leagues for antitrust purposes and, therefore, the single entity theory is not applicable. For those players who find themselves in single entity leagues, the only option left is a players strike. However, the smaller the financial resources available to players the less likely players are to win a strike.

Lastly, team owners and leagues enjoy all of the initial leverage because they usually have access to money. Players, however, have little or no leverage until they win their antitrust lawsuits or commence collective bargaining agreement negotiations with the league and their owners.

The American antitrust and labor law experience pertaining to professional sports can serve as a harbinger for European sports law practitioners and academics considering this issue in the following respects: significant sources of revenues generated by European sports leagues, will foster antitrust and labor law litigation and case decisions will soon follow. For example, the *Bosman* decision has permitted European based athletes to auction their services to the highest bidder. As a result, the traditional notions of 'sports business' such as the use of player transfer fees as well as strong and long identification between player, team and host city are being challenged, modified or entirely eliminated.

Second, certain aspects of the American sports model are manifesting itself in Europe. For instance, salary caps are being utilized in a number of team sports including professional rugby, ice hockey and basketball (salary caps are also under consideration by UEFA). Using the American sports industry model as a guide, there are several scenarios which may adopted by European professional sports stakeholders as it relates to competition law and professional sports.

Sports leagues are using their lobbying efforts to provide a 'sports exemption' to the European Union competition rules. There will be an increase in antitrust law litigation to define the scope and parameters of owner-player relations pertaining to salary, free agency, as well as player trades and transfers. European leagues may evolve into rich or 'super' leagues and poor or 'farm' leagues. In the United States, farm leagues are located in smaller cities and towns where player talent is groomed and trained for competition in the rich or super leagues such as the National Football League, National Basketball Association, National Hockey League and Major League Baseball. Further, the rich leagues are usually located in large American cities. As a result, the relegation system as European sports fans know it may come to the end.

In comparison to the United States, European professional leagues have a surplus of teams within the league and within close proximity to one another. In order to remain competitive or to ensure their own economic survival teams may merge. For example, in English football, Portsmouth and Southampton may become one team while Manchester United may reach a player development or 'farm' agreement with Blackpool. Alternatively, teams across Europe may simply fold.

POSTSCRIPT: LEGAL INTERVENTION AND THE POSSIBILITY OF ENLIGHTENED GOVERNANCE

Andrew Caiger and Simon Gardiner

INTRODUCTION

The purpose of this book is to encourage and contribute to a debate about the future of professional sport in the EU as far as it relates to governance and, more particularly, to explore the possibilities for the re-regulation of sport. This is a timely intervention in the debate in view of the fast changing milieu of professional sport. Professional sport is driven by money and new technologies especially in broadcasting. European sport now reaches audiences far beyond the boundaries of the European Union. Money and new technologies have accelerated and contributed to the globalisation of sport.

Globalisation is difficult to define precisely because it is a contested concept. Giddens provides a useful definition:

> 'Globalisation can be defined as the intensification of world-wide social relations which link distant localities in such a way that local happenings are shaped by events occurring many miles away and vice-versa. This is a dialectical process because such local happenings may move in an obverse direction from the very distanced relations that shape them. Local transformations is as much a part of globalisation as the lateral extension of social connections across time and space'.[1]

This process of globalisation is clearly evident in sport especially since the advent of satellite television in the early 1990's. An example of this significance can be seen in the United Kingdom where the price paid by BSkyB for broadcasting football matches of the English Premiership increased exponentially.[2] The combined effect of money and technology has been most evident in football – the global sport. But the effect has not only been confined to football. Other sports such as rugby, golf and tennis, to name a few, have come in for similar treatment.

---

[1] Giddens A, as cited in Waters M, *Globalisation Key Ideas*, (1990) London, Routledge; also see: De Knop P, Globalization, Americanization and Localization in Sport, (2000) *International Sports Law Journal*, Issue 2, 20.

[2] See Spink and Morris, in this book.

A. Caiger and S. Gardiner (Eds), Professional Sport in the EU: Regulation and Re-regulation
© 2000, T.M.C.Asser Press, The Hague, The Netherlands

Money and technology have attracted new actors to the growing sports industry. Sports organisations, whose previous role was the management and governance of the sport, now find themselves thrust into a far more activist economic role for which they were not designed. As a consequence sports associations have increasingly tried to consolidate a monopoly in the economic fortunes of their respective sports. It is because of their economic involvement in sport that sports associations have found themselves challenged where they thought they wouldn't be challenged – in the running of their own sport. Evidence of this arrogance is clearly illustrated in the events leading up to and subsequent to the *Bosman* case. The football authorities had been warned early on – both by the EU Commission and EU case law in the *Walrave* and *Dona* decisions – that they had to be mindful of EU Treaty provisions. This warning has up until recently been ignored. The *Bosman* ruling acted as a catalyst in a world that was already changing. Sports men and women as well as clubs have in recent years challenged the rules of their respective sports associations – primarily because of a lack of transparency, questionable decisions and the economic impact of these decisions.

Perhaps the most important issue – which has not been addressed – is the contribution made by certain sports organisations to undermining the social aspects of sport, to wit solidarity. Their claims to entitlements clearly indicated that these organisations were not concerned in promoting solidarity in sport. The *Bosman* ruling clearly illustrates how incapable the football authorities were of justifying the restrictive rules of their game with regard to the transfer fee. The comments of Advocate-General Lenz are worth repeating:

'The transfer fees cannot be regarded as compensation for possible costs of training, if only for the simple reason that their amount is linked not to those costs but to the player's earnings. Nor can it be seriously argued that a player, for example, who is transferred for a fee of one million ECU caused his previous club to incur training costs amounting to that vast sum.

A second argument against regarding transfer fees as a reimbursement of the training costs which have been incurred is the fact that such fees – and in many cases extraordinarily large sums – are demanded even when experienced professional players change clubs. Here there can be no longer any question of 'training' and reimbursement of the expense of such training. Nor does it make any difference that in such cases it is often 'compensation for development' (not compensation for training) which is spoken of. Any reasonable club will certainly provide its players with all the development necessary. But that is expenditure which is in the club's own interest and which the player recompenses with his performance. It is not evident why such a club should be entitled to claim a transfer fee on that basis'.[3]

---

[3] Case C-415/93 ASBL Union Royale Belge des Sociétés de Football Association and others v Jean-Marc Bosman [1996] 1 CMLR 645 para. 237.

It is at the juncture between the rules necessary for playing the game and economic activities that the sports associations find themselves in greatest peril. The EU Commission for Competition has made it plain that the Treaty – especially the mobility and competition rules – apply where sport is engaged in an economic activity. It is often difficult from an organisational point of view to decide when a particular rule supports the game and when it has economic significance. It is because of this conundrum that sports associations find themselves exposed to the threat of legal intervention, which will undermine their regulatory credibility.

But it is not only the danger of 'rule exposure' that is problematic. Sports organisation rules and governance have not kept pace with the times. The introduction of money into the game has also coincided with several legal challenges to the authority of sports bodies on the part of various actors. Sportsmen and women and clubs have challenged the rules – successfully in many cases. Where the rules have not been challenged there has been considerable dissatisfaction and frustration with the manner of governance. In football in particular, there has been dissatisfaction between players and clubs and between clubs and the national sports authorities. An example of the latter is the growing dissatisfaction regarding the division of broadcasting revenue amongst football clubs. In the Netherlands Feyenoord recently won a case against the Dutch Football Association entitling the club to keep revenues generated by broadcasting from their football ground. The basis for this decision was that the club had to bear the risk of staging the event and was therefore entitled to the income from the game. As regards players – they are demanding greater mobility as is their entitlement under European law. They have used the law in some cases to strengthen their bargaining position against their old clubs and some of these clubs – unprepared for legal challenges – have acceded to these requests.

There are many other examples of crises in sports governance – many of which have been dealt with in this book. But this crisis in sports governance raises the important question as to whether we could safely leave the issues of solidarity to sports organisations alone? The answer is clearly indicated in this book: no!

While the courts – both domestic and the ECJ – have had to wrestle with sports governance in particular cases developing a casuistic approach to the subject, both national governments and the Commission have shown concern for the consequences of commercialisation of sport.

In the case of the EU Commission a meeting was held at Olympia, Greece, in May 1999 where a debate was initiated about the *European Model of Sport*. Several major sports organisations were not present although invited. There was a concern about the effects of drugs and commercialisation on sport generally. However, the meeting set an important precedent: the need for a dialogue. The impression was gained that the Commission did not want to be responsible for running a European sports policy – but rather discover what it was that the actors were concerned about.

The European Competition Commission has also given a clear indication that it is only the economic activities of sport that will fall to be scrutinised. Clear indications have been given about how competition policy is likely to be applied to sport. The ECJ has given guidelines in the recent *Deliège* and *Lehtonen* cases on how the rules of a sport association can be justified with regard to selection for national competitions.

It has been pointed out that the distinction between rules relating to the organisation of sport and those, which have an economic bearing is artificial and that a human rights approach may resolve this conundrum.[4]

THE DANGER OF COMMERCIALISATION: RECENT INTERVENTIONS

The meeting at Olympia, Greece, clearly indicated that the commercialisation of sport was of great concern to many sports organisations. It threatened social cohesion and those Corinthian values of fairness and sportsmanship, which are of so much value to society at large. Commercialisation might not only corrupt these values, but is increasingly affecting access to the enjoyment of sport by all those who enjoy actual or visual participation.

The Dutch Report[5]

The Dutch Ministry of Health Welfare and Sport commissioned a report on how a balance could be achieved between sport and money. This report entitled 'The Balance Between the Game and the Money'[6] investigated the social and commercial aspects of sport. It considered the legal issues of the sports market and the application of the EU competition rules. A special study was made of the role of the media, especially broadcasting, and the application of EU and domestic competition rules.

The Report identifies the role of the national government in promoting mass sport. The government wants to exploit positive social values of sport by:

– Safeguarding and where necessary improving the quality of playing sport;
– Improving the quality of the sports infrastructure;

---

[4] See Foster, in this book.

[5] The Dutch report on sport, European competition and the media ('The balance between the game and the money') was prepared by a research group of KPMG, CMS Derks Star Busmann Hanotiau and the T.M.C. Asser Institute for International Law at the request of the Netherlands Ministry of Health, Welfare and Sport in order to be submitted by the Netherlands government to the EU Summit in Helsinki in December 1999. The text which is a translation of the original Dutch version of the report on behalf of the Ministry, is published as an Appendix to this book with the Ministry's permission.

[6] Project 2720, 16 March 2000, The Hague.

– Improving the cohesion of the policy relating to sport.[7]

The Dutch government is also concerned to promote a positive climate for top-class professional sport.

While commercialisation may promote optimal efficiencies in the sports market, these efficiencies need to be considered in a wider context. The traditional way in which sports are organised sits uncomfortably with market efficiencies – a factor already identified. But it would appear that smaller countries like the Netherlands are affected adversely by the interaction of the market and old-style sports organisations. The national sports market is small and the competitions available within these limited markets attract less money than is the case with other national competitions. This is probably the reason why there is such enthusiasm for the Atlantic League amongst smaller European states. In short, smaller countries are losing out. Money ensures that the best players from the smaller countries are leaving to pursue their professional careers elsewhere.

The Dutch report canvasses various solutions at EU level rather than the national level. It considers four possibilities, which may establish a balance between the game and money:

– the extension of the declaration on sport;
– revision of the EU Treaty;
– Rule of Reason approach;
– exemption/discharge because of the task of general economic importance.[8]

The Report favours an extension of the Declaration on Sport because the other options are too problematic. The revision of the Treaty is most unlikely and all Member States would have to agree to such an amendment at a future IGC. An exception to Article 39 – on free mobility – to favour sport is highly unlikely. The most promising exemption may be under the competition rules. Full exemption for sport from the competition rules is unrealistic. A partial exemption in terms of Article 81(3) also seems problematic since the conditions for such an exemption must be met cumulatively.

The 'Rule of Reason' approach with the aid of group (block) exemptions is attractive. But the Report notes that the Commission only uses group exemptions when it has gained sufficient experience with certain types of agreement, yet a group exemption for sport would be attractive and provide positive guidance. In the meantime a Notice as to how to deal with agreements in sport might be a very useful interim measure. [9]

The Dutch Report favours a much higher political profile for sport in a new Declaration on Sport. In the meantime it advocates certain practical measures to

---

[7] Supra 17.
[8] Supra 54.
[9] Supra 53.

alleviate existing horizontal and vertical solidarity issues identified in the Report. These include:

- the threat of a few European football clubs to leave the national competitions and set up a commercial Superleague;
- the threat that Dutch football will lose its link with the European elite competition and the resultant call by the top Dutch clubs for a 'more lopsided' redistribution of income from TV rights;
- the remarkable distribution of income in the Champions League that just makes the gap between the 'haves' and 'have-nots' all the greater;
- the discussion about the events list;
- the rapidly increasing inter-penetration between sport and media;
- the growing number of sports dossiers with the Dutch Competition Authority, NMa.[10]

While the issues listed above relate specifically to the Dutch sporting scene some of these issues resonate elsewhere as well. The difficulty is to identify who is responsible to bring about practical changes.

The Report recommends that the Dutch government provide positive incentives to reward associations promoting sport solidarity. It is not clear how this redistribution is to be encouraged when Dutch clubs own and may sell their TV rights individually. Another vexed question is the unequal income distribution rules of UEFA. The example given in the Report is that if Ajax beats Barcelona it receives a smaller payment than if the reverse were the case. Apparently these rules were agreed to by UEFA at the instance of pressure exerted by a few elite European Clubs. These rules are clearly discriminatory and negative and increase the gap between the rich and poor clubs. It also discriminates between clubs on the basis of country of origin – and this is contrary to the Treaty. Yet the Report is far from clear what is to be done and by whom. This is yet another example of an area susceptible to regulation. UEFA have to revise this rule on income distribution and should be flexible about the creation of new leagues. It seems highly problematic that such discriminatory behaviour can be brought about by threats.

The Report advocates three further areas for immediate action:

- The deduction of a solidarity levy by participants in lucrative European competitions. This would bolster vertical solidarity and will promote both mass sport and encourage a competitive balance (horizontal solidarity). Again, the Report does not say how this is to be achieved.
- Drawing up rules for cross-ownership. Again, it is not indicated how this will be achieved and by whom.
- Application of American measures to promote the competitive balance. The tools used to manage this in American professional sport are advocated – but it

---

[10] Supra

is far from evident that these rules have actually been effective in maintaining or restoring a competitive balance.[11]

The Dutch Report is an interesting intervention in this debate. While it identifies the general problems of the interface between sport and law in various areas, it is of more particular interest as far as it relates to the negative effects of the market and regulatory measures on Dutch sport, in particular football. However, while there is a identification as to what is to be done – it is far from clear as to the most effective means of achieving these goals. The Report advocates a new Declaration on Sport and a Notice on sports agreements. This approach is rather minimilistic – but allows for a casuistic development of the relationship between sport and the law.

The English Football Taskforce

British sport can be characterised as essentially a self-regulatory environment where sports national governing bodies are autonomous. This has been the hallmark of sports governance for a period of over one hundred years. This has become increasingly incongruous within the expanding commercialised and sophisticated contemporary sports world. In 1996, the then England rugby union captain Will Carling famously described the committee of the English Rugby Union as '57 silly old farts'. This epitomised the failure of sports governance to reconcile the traditional amateur and Corinthian ideal with the dynamics of the 'real sports world'.

Football is the English national game and despite continued failure of the national team, the professional game supports 92 clubs. These include long established clubs such as Preston North End to the new-boys of the league, Kidderminster Harriers; from the superstar cosmopolitanism of Chelsea to the small-town based, fan-owned club such as AFC Bournemouth. The corporatism – the acute awareness of the mutuality required for a common existence – between the clubs in the last century, has been replaced by individual self-interest. While there may be coalescence around particular issues, the football landscape in the early twenty-first century is characterised by accelerating financial divisions and the emergence of the 'haves' and 'have-nots'.

Football, essentially a working class game both in terms of players and fans, has in the last ten years been transmuted into a game for the bourgeoisie middle class and the armchair spectator. The top players are multi-millionaires and the lesser players earning far in excess of the average working wage. Many football fans have become marginalised, unable to regularly attend matches or afford the subscription to gain access to live TV transmissions. The response has been calls for a greater recognition from the football authorities of 'fan equity' in the cul-

---

[11] Supra 55.

tural ownership of the game. In 1997, soon after coming into power, the Labour government appointed a Taskforce comprising different interest groups in football. Their fourth and main report was published in early 1999 and focussed on commercial issues, how football should best be governed in the future and how the interests of the governing bodies, clubs and supporters be reconciled.

The Taskforce produced two conflicting reports: one representing the perceptions of football fan groups, the other from the football establishment – the FA and the Premier and Football Leagues.

The Majority Report that represented the fan groups perspective supported a radical interventionist approach with support for the creation of a permanent standing body, the *Football Audit Commission* (FAC), and the establishment of a new consumers' voice for football, the *Ombudsfan*. Supporters' groups would have formal involvement in the FAC. In addition, where a club intended to float on the Stock Exchange, the long-term interests of the club ought to be considered.

The Minority Report from the football authorities perspective was significantly more conservative. It argued that increased regulation was not needed for what is 'not an under-governed sport'. They recommended the emphasis should be on self-regulation but found merit in supporting an advisory body, the Independent Scrutiny Panel (ISP) to provide assessment of the quality of regulation, best practice and governance found within individual clubs. This body would merely provide advice and no powers to intervene.

The two Reports, although sharing some areas of commonality, seem far apart particularly on the issues of governance and accountability. The highly interventionist FAC is a very different form of regulation than that of the ISP. Presently, the Reports are now under consideration by the Minister for Sport. The new regulatory framework that emerges is likely to be a compromise between the two approaches. The football authorities seemed to have heavily influenced the development of what will be an essentially 'soft-touch' independent monitoring body. Whether this new body together and the existing framework of the FA, the Premier and Football Leagues will bring more representative and accountable governance concerning English football is open to question.

How Should Sport Be Re-regulated?

The chapters in this book all highlight various aspects of the problem when sports rules and governance clash with the normative legal framework of Member States and the EU. The result of such clashes produces uncertainty – not only for sports organisations but also for the law in Member States. Where Member States adopt different approaches to the same problems different results often emerge. If we consider the approach of the courts to collective sales of broadcasting rights, we find different result. Collective sales are allowed in France and Germany because of national legislation, but not in the Netherlands because it is prohibited under the competition rules. The same can be said for cross-ownership of clubs. In Italy and France it is allowed, but not in the UK and the Netherlands.

What is however clear from the debate presented in this book is that this is a time of fluidity in sports regulation. This is fuelled by money and new technology and by the process of globalisation. European sport is watched all over the world and there is more sport available for viewing in the homes of sports enthusiasts than was ever the case before. Globalisation provides new challenges to governance and legal regulation. Many of these challenges have been examined in considerable detail in this book, but the focus has fallen on issues of policy and legal responses to the regulatory problems in sport. The debate is about the complexities and the extent of the re-regulatory intervention of the EU and, perhaps to a lesser extent, Member States.

Both Parrish and Foster deal with policy choices in sport. While Parrish provides an incisive analysis of the recent history of sports policy in the EU, Foster analyses the careful approach of the ECJ in the *Lehtonen* and *Deliége* cases in which he shows that there is certainly an appreciation and sensitivity towards rules made for promoting competition in sport. He favours re-regulation via supervised autonomy of sports governance by the Commission as this offers 'a legally independent protection of the widest consituencies'. Parrish considers, without deciding, which regulatory approach might be tenable for the EU to adopt with regard to sport. He argues that there is precedent for agreeing a protocol for sport – but this would require the agreement of all Member States at an IGC.

Boyes considers the issues of improved technology and globalisation and the effect this has had on commodifying sport. Sport with the involvement of the media and big money contribute a significant share of economic activity in the world. The usual cautious approach to legal intervention in sport which, is so much part of the English legal tradition is probably quite inappropriate to deal with global regulation. Europe can play a significant role in the process of the re-regulation of sport – but Boyes does not prescribe how this might be achieved.

Vieweg's analysis concentrates on trying to demarcate the space within which sport should operate autonomously. He argues that sporting associations should first and foremost revise their rules and regulations to be consistent with European legal principles, especially those regarding freedom of mobility and competition. He also recommends exploring the possibility of engaging the EU Competition authorities in the possibility of a group exemption. This dialogue or constructive engagement between the sports organisations and the EU Commission authorities is considered by Vieweg to be vital to the future re-regulation of sport. A similar argument is made by Caiger and O'Leary in their treatment of the transfer system in professional football. They argue that the recent discussion between FIFA and the Competition Commission represent a positive move towards re-regulating football and argue that this is supportive of a tradition of self-regulation. They agree with Vieweg that sporting organisations should revise their rules to bring about consistency between sports and the legal norms of the EU. Foster argues that the *Lehtonen* case strongly suggests that this revision of rules is likely to have a mandatory effect – sports organisations must comply with the normative rules of the EU – and if they do not, then be able to justify this on some objective basis.

Mortimer and Pearl argue that sports associations have shown themselves inflexible and incapable to regulate their sports effectively or equitably. The advent of the Premiership football competition in England can be related to 'regulatory abdication' on the part of the FA. Again, financial muscle and threats compromised the regulatory function. The example cited in the Dutch Report concerning the UEFA income distribution rules resonate in England as well. They argue that the football rules regarding the mobility of clubs will need to be addressed urgently as these are clearly contrary to the EU rules on freedom of establishment.

Spink and Morris see an active role for the competition authorities both in the EU and the UK in regulating sports broadcasting. They expect that this area of sports activity might be regulated by Article 81(3) of the Treaty prior to any dedicated group exemption. They advocate a co-operative attitude between the Premier League and the competition authorities both at national and EU level.

McCutcheon investigates the national eligibility rules after *Bosman*. He sees two distinct forces at play: the need and attraction for national identity and globalisation – which appears to militate against national identity. While localisation is the other side of the globalisation coin, reality dictates a more subtle approach to national eligibility rules. This is necessary because sportsmen and women have such diverse backgrounds and there is so much more movement between countries than there used to be.

Gardiner and Welch deal with the migration of professional sportsmen in the EU. They argue that the arrival of third country sportsmen and women in Europe is one of the positive aspects of globalisation yet they suffer from the disadvantage of requiring a work permit in any EU country they work in. This tends to fragment sportsmen and women relegating third country athletes to limited mobility. The mobility of these athletes should be enhanced. Unfortunately these issues are still determined by national rules for the foreseeable future. There is a move afoot to encourage free movement within the EU even of third country citizens.

Edgar and McArdle deal with the problems presented by *e*-commerce with reference to the sports industry. This is an area whose regulation is either limited or fragmentary. The authors present the problematic without prescribing any particular mode of regulation.

The final section of the book concentrates on the sports regulatory regimes in various countries. In most there is a framework of regulation through statute. In the case of Greece the New Law responds to a certain extent to some of the issues raised with regard to commercialisation. There a national regime within which sport is regulated. On the other hand Gray's chapter on the US indicates a considerable clash between two separate branches of law: labour law and antitrust. The law is far more intrusive and dominant in US sports. It almost appears to be a deterministic approach. Scwarz and Silance deal with the regulatory dimensions of sport in Poland and Belgium respectively. In the case of the former the new regime since the fall of the Iron Curtain is detailed, while Silance shows how the unique political dispensation in Belgium intrudes into the regulatory regime of sport.

CONCLUSION

The chapters of this book indicate that the regulatory aspects affecting sport is multi-dimensional and require a variety of responses. It is not possible to make a consistent distinction between rules affecting the organisation of sport and those having an economic impact. This distinction is artificial, but probably necessary for the EU competition authorities. The issues of migration of sportsmen and women cannot be dealt with in the same manner as broadcasting for example. But is there a theoretical approach to regulation that can be of assistance to the world of sport?[12] Up till now sport and sports associations have enjoyed a measure of autonomy in rule making and enforcing. Various national laws to a greater or lesser extent have regulated only issues concerning employment. In some cases, the custom of the sport has been more forceful in regulating employment relationships than has been any labour law regime. In short sport has enjoyed relative autonomy.

This relative autonomy in sport is perhaps most closely mirrored by the *Lex Mercatoria*. The application of the *Lex Mercatoria* to the area of sport must be selective. There are two discernible approaches that may indicate a starting point for the re-regulation of professional sport in the EU:

'The "autonomist" approach conceives of an anational, autonomous, self-generating system of laws articulated by the international commercial community to regulate its activities. Its practices, usages and customs, supplemented by the general principles of law recognised by commercial nations form a – not yet fully developed – normative order that exists independent of any national system of law. On the other hand the "positivist" position views the *Lex Mercatoria* as having transnational origins, but only by virtue of states giving effect to conventions and uniform laws by ratification

---

[12] See Black J, Constitutionalising Self-Regulation, 1996 *Modern Law Review,* 24; Ogus A, Rethinking Self-Regulation, 1995 *Oxford Journal of Legal Studies,* 97; Sun J-M and Pelkmans J, Regulatory Competition in the Single Market in Baldwin R, Scott and Hood, *Reader on Regulation,* (1998) Oxford University Press, 443; Baldwin R, Scott and Hood, Introduction, in Baldwin *et al* (supra). These texts provide a good general insight into regulation, but none of these, with the exception of Black, proved useful for our purposes.

into municipal codes, and by trade usages that are articulated by international agencies.'[13]

This formulation explains much of what is now occurring in sports governance. When sports rules and governance are challenged – whether from a competition point of view or from a mobility point of view – the national court, or the Commission or ECJ is asked to recognise or validate the sports usage as represented in the rules of a particular sporting association. These institutions and courts must decide to what extent they are prepared to recognise these rules, customs and usages. This in fact is what has happened with every legal challenge thus far. This interaction between the sports world and the normative order is helping to build, redefine and establish a distinct *Lex Sportiva*. For the purposes of this analogy it is not essential to decide which of the two approaches may be the most appropriate.

This analogy with the *Lex Mercatoria* allows sports law to develop distinctiveness and an incremental formation. It encourages sports organisations to reconsider their own rules and mode of governance in the light of the dominant legal norms. This process of acculturation allows and promotes a convergence between the *Lex Sportiva* and the dominant legal norms.

This book has suggested various solutions to particular problems of the sports governance interface with dominant legal norms. If one considers the Dutch Report, for a moment, it becomes clear that the drafters of that Report found it difficult to prescribe a particular means through which sport could be re-regulated. The Football Taskforce also found agreement difficult when it came to English football. Certain solutions may be appropriate for particular problems e.g. with regard to broadcasting the competition authorities both national and at EU level may be able to provide a sufficient mode of regulation. When we consider questions of eligibility rules or migration of third country players – it is clear that the solution at present lies with Member States and that the most the EU can achieve is co-operation between them.

In view of these considerations the re-regulation of sport may best be undertaken in a casuistic fashion allowing the solutions to present themselves to solve particular problems. This does not advocate passivity, rather it is a plea for realism. Sports organisations are encouraged and should undertake the revision of their rules to bring them into line with the basic principles underlying the EU Treaty. The criteria of proportionality, transparency and fairness should permeate any new dispensation. The first encouraging signs are to be found in UEFA's recent notifications since January 1999.[14]

---

[13] Wiener J, *Globalization and the Harmonization of Law*, (1999) London, Pinter, 161.

[14] See OJ C 363, 17.12.1999: Communication made pursuant to Article 19(3) of Council Regulation No 17 concerning request for negative clearance or for exemption pursuant to Article 81(3) of the EC Treaty (Case No 37.632 – UEFA rule on 'integrity of the UEFA club competitions: independence of clubs'); OJ C 70, 13.3.1999, Case No IV/37.400 – Project Gandalf: Notification of a num-

Sport is and will continue to be regulated at different levels of governance. The processes of globalisation challenge each level. The question is whether globalisation will dictate sports governance or whether sport organisations, Member States and the EU will determine the new regulatory regime? Giddens suggests that the forces of globalisation can be arrested by co-operation between these rule-making entities.[15] What is required is a positive sense of purpose between sporting associations and Member States and the EU. Convergence of rules between these entities is essential for the future of sport and for the good of the game.

---

ber of agreements concerning the European Football League, 5; OJ C 6, 9.1.1999, Case No IV/37.214 – DFB: Central marketing of TV and radio broadcasting rights for certain football competitions in Germany, 10-11; OJ C 99, 10.4.1999, Case No IV/37.398 – UEFA Central marketing of the commercial rights to the UEFA Champions League, 23-24.

[15] See Giddens A, *1999 Reith Lectures*, (1999) London, BBC Publications. Also see Giddens A, *Runaway World: How Globalization is Reshaping Our Lives* (2000) London, Routledge.

APPENDIX
THE BALANCE BETWEEN THE GAME AND THE MONEY

FINAL REPORT

Study commissioned by:
The Netherlands' Ministry of Health, Welfare and Sport
Sports Directorate

Prepared by:
KPMG Bureau voor Economische Argumentatie
CMS Derks Star Busmann Hanotiau
T.M.C. Asser Instituut

Members of the Research Team:
Mark Minkman and Pieter Verhoogt (KPMG BE)
Dolf Segaar (CMS Derks Star Busmann Hanotiau)
Rob Siekmann, Ingrid Nitsche and Marjan Olfers (T.M.C. Asser Instituut)

Hoofddorp, 16 March 2000

A. Caiger and S. Gardiner (Eds), Professional Sport in the EU: Regulation and Re-regulation

Table of Contents

SUMMARY

The subject of the commercialisation of sport has long been on the European agenda. On occasion the special significance of sport is stressed in a European context (Amsterdam, Vienna). To arrive at a well-founded opinion on this question, the Sports Directorate of the Ministry of Health, Welfare and Sport has had a study carried out into the problems in the field of sport, competition and media and the related questions. This study was carried out by KPMG Bureau voor Economische Argumentatie together with the T.M.C. Asser Instituut and CMS Derks Star Busmann Hanotiau. This summary contains the main findings of the study.

Sport – and certainly top-class sport – is developing more and more into a 'normal' business. Top level sporting activities are generating more and more money. That offers individual sportsmen and women and associations opportunities to lift the level of sport to a higher plane. It also offers the government opportunities for an even better expression of the social function of sport. Richard Krajicek, who hits a ball around with the children in Schilderswijk in The Hague and in this way passes on standards and values such as tolerance and fair play, is perhaps an excellent example of the way in which society can profit from the commercialisation of sport.

The commercialisation of (top-class) sport is however also under threat. The effect of economic forces does not always square with a number of elementary characteristics of sport. For example, financially strong sponsors focus primarily on the sportsmen and women operating at top-class level. Vertical solidarity cannot be taken for granted. Marianne Timmer once learned skating at an ice club that could only exist thanks to the dedication of many volunteers and the facilities and support of the skating association and the regional association structure. In top-class sport that is increasingly governed by economic forces, horizontal solidarity can also not be taken for granted. If football clubs can individually exploit their broadcasting rights, the revenue from these will not automatically be redistributed between them. This makes the most popular clubs economically stronger and the less popular clubs economically weaker.

On a 'normal' economic market that is a fact. The producer who offers the best product will ultimately gain the biggest market share. In sport things are different. An essential characteristic of the product that sports clubs offer, is sports competition between the clubs. This characteristic exists by the grace of an equilibrium in sports relations between the clubs. These come under pressure when the most popular clubs become economically stronger, for in the long term they will also become stronger in a sporting sense.

In addition as a result of economic forces there is also an increasing interpenetration between sport and media. The relationship between sportsmen and women, clubs and media companies is therefore changing. Television broadcasters invest in clubs or clubs set up their own television broadcaster. As a result the supplier of broadcasting rights (club) becomes one with the demander on the market (the media company). That makes this specific market very different and in the long term this will be bound to affect the character of sport as 'the people's game' (fairness, accessibility to everyone).

The question is what the government can (or must) do to emphasise the social function of sport, to make the most of the opportunities that commercialisation offers and as far as possible to turn the threats into opportunities. In other words, to keep the balance between the game and the money in equilibrium. As far as keeping major sports events accessible to the general (and not financially strong) public, the government has existing tools available. These tools aim to give shape to the social significance of sport. On the basis of the European Directive Television without frontiers, national governments can designate sports events that must be accessible to all viewers on a public network (at no extra cost).

Clubs, sportsmen and women and associations are more and more frequently carrying out activities in the commercialised environment that are of a purely economic nature. As a result they are operating as businesses. In principle European competition law applies in full to these activities. The heart of this law is free competition, which has from way back been the great benefit of European integration. A 'general pardon' for sport within competition legislation is therefore unlikely. At the same time the action of economic forces clearly injures the specific nature of sport and something must therefore be done.

The report pays attention to the possible tools for giving the special features and the social significance of sport a more specific place in Community law. After weighing up the various possibilities, the conclusion is that at present the most obvious thing is to aim for the agreement of a (new) European Declaration on Sport. The text of this could run:

'The EU stresses the social significance of sport as laid down in the Treaty of Amsterdam. The EU recognises that because of the specific nature of sport there may in certain circumstances (solidarity, transparency) be justification for granting exemptions from Community law for economic activities within the sports sector, where the economic activities in question in accordance with objective criteria fully or substantially target or benefit (the organisation of) sport and/or are aimed at maintaining or reinforcing the competitive balance within sport.'

1. INTRODUCTION

1.1. **Background**

Sport is rapidly developing into a real business. Particularly in top-class (inter)national football, so much money is now involved that playing the game seems to take second place to the money. National and international football associations are also expressing their concern about the threat that commercialisation is creating for the status of football as 'the people's game'. In other sports too economic forces from the media and the sports world itself are making their stamp on the way European consumers can experience the performance of their sports heroes.

Where economic forces lead to an increase in scale and concentrations of power, the specific nature of sport (fair competition, accessible to everyone) is coming under pressure. The question of *competition in sport* is therefore coming urgently onto the political agenda. During the European Summit in Helsinki last December, the European Commission presented the European government leaders with a report on the significance of sport for Europe[1]. To prepare for this report ('The Helsinki Report on Sport') Directorate General X of the European Commission (Culture, media and sport) drew up a consultation document[2]. At the first European Union Conference on Sport in Olympia (May 1999) this document was discussed in detail. In an internal working document that the Commission had prepared for this conference, one of the biggest challenges for European sport at this time was seen to be 'avoiding the pitfalls of excessive commercialisation'. In February 1999 DG IV (competition) had also drawn up a preliminary working document which focussed on the specific characteristics of sport and their possible significance for the application of competition policy.

To arrive at a well-founded opinion on this question, the Ministries of Health, Welfare and Sport (VWS), Education, Culture and Science (OC&W) and Economic Affairs (EZ) need a clear picture of the questions in the field of sport and competition and the related opportunities and threats. The Sports Directorate of the Ministry of Health, Welfare and Sport has asked KPMG Bureau voor Economische Argumentatie, the T.M.C. Asser Instituut and CMS Derks Star Busmann Hanotiau to carry out this study jointly.

1.2. **Study assignment**

The three ministries involved, each with their own approach, have a range of questions about sport and competition. Sometimes these questions follow from one another, but sometimes they differ widely. The aim of the study is on the basis of a clear (economic) analysis to chart the background to the many questions relating to sport and competition. The aim of the study is not to give a cut-and-dried answer to the many relevant questions. That would not only be very difficult and time-consuming, but sometimes also impossible as the relevant jurisprudence is still lacking. The study assignment can be described as follows:

---

[1] In the concluding document of the European Summit in Vienna (December 1998) the desirable contents of this Helsinki report were described as: 'to safeguard the current sport structures and maintain the social function or sport within the Community framework'.

[2] This consultative document focuses on the European model of sport.

> Outline the best possible picture of the problems in the field of sport and competition
> and the related questions. Use this to produce building blocks and recommendations
> for the view of the government on this subject.

1.3. Layout of the report

This report is laid out as follows. In section two we present a (theoretical) analysis framework. We analyse the essential characteristics of the two central themes of this study: the
sports market and competition law. In addition, both economic and legal approaches are
discussed. The analysis framework aims to give a clear understanding of the complex relationship between sport and 'the market'. In section three we then describe a number of
questions posed in the field of sport, media and competition. We do this using practical
examples (case studies). This practical approach, combined with the insights from section
two makes the problems of sport and competition tangible and understandable. In the
fourth and last section we present our recommendations and we a give number of considerations for (inter)national governments, associations and clubs/players for maintaining
and/or restoring the equilibrium in the field of influence.

2.   THE ANALYSIS

2.1. Introduction

The effect of the commercialisation of sport covers several policy fields. Many questions
exist both in the field of sport and that of media and competition. These questions are articulated in the introductory memorandum that the Sports Directorate of the Ministry of
Health, Welfare and Sport (VWS) has drawn up for this study in consultation with the
other Ministries involved. We have decided in our approach to look at the problems from
a broadly economically slanted perspective. We do not start here by answering the
(largely legal) questions from the introductory memorandum. We did this intentionally.
We think that it is relevant to first give a picture of the main lines of the problems. This
picture will show the relationship between the different questions posed at the start of the
study and a knowledge of this relationship will in our view give us good points of departure for counteracting the threats resulting from the commercialisation of sport and for
turning them into opportunities. In this way the questions discussed in the introductory
memorandum will of themselves come back into the picture.

Layout of section
Paragraph 2.2 explains the special significance of sport compared with ordinary businesses. Then paragraph 2.3 discusses the specific characteristics of the sports market. We
describe a number of the relevant markets and indicate which specific characteristics from
an economic point of view characterise these markets. Thirdly we discuss the significance
of Community law and competition legislation for sport. After all, once activities within
sport are described as economic activities, Community law and competition legislation
come into play. We discuss some relevant jurisprudence (2.4). Then at the end of this section we state more specifically the significance on the one hand of the social role of sport

and on the other the economic aspects of the sports markets for competition legislation in sport (2.5).

2.2. The special significance of sport

Compared with ordinary businesses sport occupies a separate position. On a European and national level the specific characteristics of sport are recognised and there is an understanding that these characteristics must be respected if sport does not want to lose its specific nature. The European Commission, Directorate-General X, has in a working document of 29 September 1998 again described the specific nature of sport on the basis of 5 functions of sport, namely:
- the educational function;
- the health function;
- the social function;
- the cultural function;
- the games function[3].

In the Netherlands the Ministry of Health, Welfare and Sport emphasises in various policy memoranda the social significance of sport and at the same time draws attention to its economic aspects.[4] The government has therefore entrusted NOC*NSF and national sports associations with the task of ensuring that sport is properly organised particularly at amateur level and for the benefit of young people.

The national government also recognises that the local sports sector deserves support in order to exploit to the full the social values of mass sport. These social values of mass sport are attributable to what the European Commission also sees as the specific characteristics of sport. The policy memorandum of the Secretary of State of Health, Welfare and Sport dated 18 June 1999 on mass sport flags up key financial problems that the sports sector has to cope with at local level. These key problems are in particular caused by local sports clubs not being sufficiently able to generate their own financial resources. The Secretary of State remarks in its memorandum that the national sports associations in addition to organising competitions and promoting their branch of sport have important functions in supporting the clubs. This concerns in any case matters specific to sport, but because of their social responsibility other topics such as anti-discrimination, the integration of the disabled and the promotion of tolerance and fair play are on the agenda.

Helsinki Report on Sport
To prepare for the meeting of European Council of Ministers in December 1999 in Helsinki the European Commission wrote a report with the working title 'The Helsinki Report on Sport' (hereinafter also called: the Helsinki report). This report was written as a result of the declaration on sport in the Treaty of Amsterdam and was commissioned by the Council of Ministers meeting in December 1998 in Vienna. The commission given to

---

[3] Working document of the European Commission, Directorate-General X dated 29 September 1998, 'Development and prospects of Community action in the field of sport', Page 5.

[4] An example of this is the memorandum 'Opportunities for Top-class sport, the Government's policy on top-class sport dated 23 February 1999, Ministry of Health, Welfare and Sport (VWS) and the memorandum 'Mass sport' dated 18 June, TK 1998-1999, 26632, No.1.

the European Commission was to write a report with a view to safeguarding current sports structures and maintaining the social function of sport within the Community framework.

The European Commission comes to the conclusion in the Helsinki report that the European Union is gradually changing its approach to sport among other things because of the increase in the number of people doing and watching sport, the internationalisation of sport, the increase in the value of TV rights to sports events, the increase in sponsoring etc. The European Commission sees in addition to the advantages of growth and increasing commerce in sport – such as the increase in jobs in the sports sector – a considerable number of dangers as well. The overloading of sporting calendars and the need to produce results for sponsors for example increase the risk of using doping.

The Helsinki report then confirms that the emphasis placed on the commercial aspects of sport involves the danger that as a result sporting principles are lost from sight. Commerce also involves the risk that horizontal and vertical solidarity within sport are lost. It seems attractive to start one's own sports organisations if in this way large sums of money can be divided between a small number of participants.

The Helsinki report finally refers to the possibilities that Community law and European competition law offer for maintaining European sports structures and the specific significance of sport. In paragraphs 2.4 and 4.6 we take a further look at these possibilities.

2.3. **Sports market**

We use a number of approaches to consider the sports market. In the first place we describe the most important sub-markets that can be identified within 'the sports market'. Secondly we present a few specific organisational characteristics of the sports market. Thirdly we describe the specific economic characteristics of the sports market. The present competition questions are largely based on these economic characteristics of the sports market.

Sub-markets
It is in fact not possible to talk about 'the sports market'. Within the sports world there are various areas to which economic laws apply and where we can then talk of markets. Different parties are always active in these sub-markets. From an economic point of view the three main sub-markets of the sports world are:
– the market for players;
– the market for sponsoring;
– the market for broadcasting rights.

The market for players
The players are of prime importance in this market. Because of their specific qualities they are coveted by clubs (in the case of team sports) or tournaments (for example in the case of tennis tournaments or cycling criteria). Players sign a contract for a certain period. In the football world the clubs were until recently allowed – even after the end of a contract – to demand a transfer sum when a player left to go to another club. The Bosman judgement has in any case put an end to this for EU players. Transfer sums are now only permitted if a contract is broken prematurely. A result of this pronouncement is that clubs must reach deeper into their pockets to hold onto players. The salaries for (top-class) foot-

ball players have increased considerably since the Bosman judgement. In addition to players and clubs there are also various agents active on the players market who in return for payment bring supply and demand together.

The market for sponsoring
On the sponsor market business is done by clubs, associations or sportsmen and women on the one hand and the business community on the other. The business community aims via sponsoring to profit from the exposure of the sponsored party. The sports world in this case derives great benefit from the great media attention to sport in general and top-class sport in particular. Compared with the purchase of regular visual advertising in broadcasting, sponsoring of much-watched sportsmen and women or teams can be an efficient way to spend advertising money. On this market there is a certain tension between sportsmen and women on the one hand and associations and clubs on the other about the question of who makes money out of the exposure of the sportsman or woman: the sportsman or woman, the club or association or both parties together? Agents are also active on this market.

The market for broadcasting rights
The market for broadcasting rights is economically very important. Televised sport is so popular that the prices on the broadcasting rights market have leapt up in recent years. In addition to the popularity of sport (and above all football) the market structure was also one of the causes of prices being pushed up. The market for broadcasting rights was after all until recently a suppliers' market, in which the supply was combined into one collective contract. A growing number of authorised broadcasters bid against one another for the exclusive TV rights to live-broadcasts and highlights. Since the Dutch court ruled that the broadcasting rights were the property of the club playing at home, the most popular clubs tend to sign individual contracts with big media companies. In any case the legal judgement in question has put pressure on the negotiations and solidarity between the clubs. In the countries around us this question of collective or individual sales is dealt with in different ways. We will look at this further in the next section.

Organisational characteristics
Although the sports market shows more and more similarities with ordinary businesses, there are a few specific organisational characteristics that distinguish the sports market from other businesses. These characteristics are closely related with the way in which sport has long been organised in Europe. We talk about the European model of sport. Some of the characteristics of this European model of sport are:
– the 'Ein Platz Prinzip' (one place principle);
– promotion and relegation;
– horizontal and vertical solidarity.

The 'Ein Platz Prinzip': when do association regulations apply?
The 'Ein Platz Prinzip' means that only one association has exclusive competence for each discipline of sport in each country. The national associations are bound by the statutes, regulations and resolutions of the federations (worldwide, continental/regional) that represent their sport at international level. The same applies at European level. The monopoly position of the international sports federations is guaranteed because in their stat-

utes they prohibit their members from joining other, competing international sports associations or because they make the membership of such an association dependent on their
approval. The national associations that are members of a federation are also prohibited
from allowing their clubs to play matches against clubs of national associations that do
not belong to the federation without the approval of the federation. For example Article 9,
paragraph 4 (e), of the FIFA Statutes provides that it is one of the rights and obligations of
the confederations (the continental/regional associations), such as UEFA:

*'to ensure that international leagues or any other such combination of clubs or leagues
shall not be formed without its consent and the approval of FIFA'.*

At national level the monopoly position of national associations is equally protected.
For example in Article 7, paragraph 4 of the FIFA Statutes:

*'Leagues or any other groups of clubs at association level shall only be permitted with the
association's express consent and shall be subordinate to it. The association's statutes
shall define the powers apportioned to any such group as well as its rights and obligations. The regulations of any such group shall be subject to the approval of the association.'*

Promotion and relegation
The European model of sport is also characterised from an operational point of view by a
pyramid structure. Promotion and relegation regulations give clubs and players the opportunity to be active at very different levels. Regional champions play against one another
for a national title. Amateur clubs can be promoted and compete in cup tournaments for
the highest honour. Winners of national competitions can compete in European competitions, etc. This 'open competition' in which clubs can be promoted and relegated differs
considerably from the more closed American sports system.

Horizontal and vertical solidarity
In the European sports world the sports associations are trying to bring about and monitor
horizontal and vertical solidarity. Horizontal solidarity involves keeping the differences
between one another limited within one competition. An example of horizontal solidarity
is the redistribution of the income from the sales of television rights by the Premier
League, Eredivisie NV. Vertical solidarity involves supporting the base of the pyramid
(mass sport) with income from the top of the pyramid. There is after all a link between
competitions at different levels. Top-class sport is dependent on new talent from amateur
sport. The KNSB and the KNWU[5] for example use part of the money that they receive
from their sponsors (respectively Aegon/Deloitte & Touche and Rabobank) for creating
facilities for junior and amateur sportsmen and women.

These characteristics of the European model of sport are essential in our analysis. They
partly explain the views that associations take in the field of influence on the different
sub-markets. In addition it is obvious in advance that the monopolistic nature of the 'Ein
Platz Prinzip' may directly or indirectly lead to questions regarding the abuse of power
and/or competition.

---

[5] Koninklijke Nederlandse Schaatsenrijders Bond (Royal Dutch Skating Association) and
Koninklijke Nederlands Wieler-Unie (Royal Dutch Cycling Union).

Economic characteristics

The reason for this study is the increasing commercialisation of the sports market. It seems that on all the previously described sub-markets, the economic forces are continually increasing. The suction effect can largely be explained by a few economic characteristics that have already long been present in sport. We then go into the following aspects:

- the inter-dependency of clubs;
- the competitive balance;
- the winner-take-all principle;
- increasing interpenetration between sport and media.

The inter-dependency of clubs

An important characteristic that distinguishes the sports market from ordinary businesses is the inter-dependence of clubs in offering their product. Clubs cannot function – and also have no product to sell – without one another's opposition in matches and competitions. In other words, it is not sensible in sports world to try and 'work the competition out of the market'. Clubs and sportsmen and women are jointly responsible for the quality of their product. Making agreements about the optimum exploitation of that product – without thereby influencing the sports contest – is then an obvious thing. To ignore this existing solidarity in sport in the long term constitutes a threat to sport.

The competitive balance

The economic value of sports events (tournaments, competitions or a single competition) is in the first place determined by the popularity of sport and the absolute quality of the supply. Secondly the difference in strength between the participating parties has an important role. A competition in which one top-class club dominates is not as interesting as one with several equal opponents. The more excitement, the more attractive the product. This emphatically distinguishes the sports market from other 'normal' economic markets. In the sports market the suppliers not only need competition (after all, no opponent no competition). From an economic viewpoint, they also benefit from strong competition of the same quality. The indicator for the equilibrium in a competition is the so-called *competitive balance*. The problem is however that the maintenance of a good competitive balance though economically desirable runs counter to the basic sporting principle of aiming for the greatest possible lead over the competition.

The winner-take-all principle

An important feature of the sports market is the winner-take-all principle. This means that in a market where different suppliers offer their products, the one with a slightly better or more popular product attracts all the attention. And 'all' the attention also means 'all' the income. This disproportionate distribution of profits occurs not only in the sport sector but also in the art and entertainment sector. Certain people, products or clubs have such unique characteristics that substitution is not possible or virtually impossible.

For winner-take-all markets there are high fixed but low (or no) variable costs. It costs a lot of money to acquire the rights to a football competition or an artist, but after acquiring them the costs of wider distribution of pictures or CDs are zero. This means that scaling up (growth of the sales market) intensifies the effects of the winner-take-all principle. Compared with the relatively low marginal costs there are after all considerable additional revenues. Developments in the media world (internationalisation, Internet, pay-per-view TV) make it possible to enter new markets and generate additional revenues at relatively low costs. The broadcasting of a football competition in an additional country after all does not cost much more, as the production costs for the competition have already been incurred. The additional revenues (paying viewers, advertising) are relatively high. In practice it is mainly these product suppliers that in relative terms are slightly better than their competitors who profit from these scale benefits.

The concentration of the demand for such absolute top-class players, top-class painters and top-class artistes causes an enormous upward pressure on prices. Broadcasters bid against one another for the broadcasting rights of a couple of (unique) top-class clubs. There is hardly any interest in the competitions of sub-top-class players, even though these broadcasting rights are considerably cheaper. As a result the (financial) gap between the 'haves' and 'have nots' is increasing all the time. The result of this is that the differences in (sporting) strength between the clubs also threatens to become bigger and bigger. This may be fatal for the national competition. After all for the majority of competitions everyone knows beforehand who will win. This reduces the excitement of the competition, and hence the interest of viewers and sponsors in the product. And the top-class clubs themselves have no interest in it. This emphatically raises the question of the mutual solidarity between clubs.

The winner-take-all principle has an enormous impact on the sports world because of its snowball effect. The strong become stronger, the weak become weaker. This not only works between *clubs*, but also between *sports* (football grabs all the attention, other sports hardly get a look in) and between *countries* (traditionally strong football countries like Spain, Italy and England attract all the good players and as a result in turn sign the most lucrative TV contracts; the Netherlands hardly has a chance).

This is clearly one of the key problems that we have to tackle. The economic laws irreversibly lead to a bigger gap between the top-class clubs or top-class countries and the rest, while a more even relationship of strength is desirable for a balanced (sports) competition (and in the long term the best operation!)[6].

Increasing interpenetration between sport and media
Sport is not only fun to do, but also fun to watch. When at the end of the year the list is drawn up of the most popular television programmes, the top of the ranking is always dominated by sports broadcasts. Sport is entertainment. With the arrival of radio and TV interest in sport has increased considerably and so has the (sponsorship) income. The arrival of more (commercial) television broadcasters[7] has drastically changed the previously languid relationship between the sports world and the media. The increase in the number of inquirers has ensured that parties are at present bidding against one another for the broadcasting rights of sports events. The possession of broadcasting rights to football competitions is considered of strategic importance when putting a new TV broadcaster onto the market. The amounts offered for these rights have long ceased to be justified by the potential advertising revenues generated around sports events.

Because of market effects, the relationship between sports clubs and TV broadcasters is subject to enormous movement. Television broadcasters invest in sports clubs[8], clubs

---

[6] See also above the section on horizontal solidarity.

[7] Ten years ago the ban on commercial television was lifted.

[8] For example BSkyB has investments in Manchester United, Manchester City and Leeds, Canal+ owns 100% of Paris Saint-Germain and Mediaset holds shares in AC Milan. Also the sponsoring of the German Telecom cycling team by the public network (ARD) is worth mentioning.

invest in television broadcasters[9] or start their own TV channel[10]. In America people have long been used to these forms of cross-ownership and the effect of the media on the sports world (see also the case study in section 3). The close relationship between sports organisations and media companies leads in each case to three essential questions:
- to what extent is the nature of sport injured by making the product suitable for television?
- what are the consequences for the objectivity of the news service?
- how is public tendering for TV rights affected? Does this involve restriction of competition, or even distortion of competition?

The first question is an interesting one. In a number of sports the influence of commercialisation is clearly present through an adjustment of the rules of the game. Recently the scoring system in volleyball has been adjusted to make matches more attractive for television broadcasts. In addition matches are now being played with brightly coloured balls. In tennis too the size of the ball is under discussion as a means of counteracting power tennis as a threat to this popular television sport. In the American basketball competition the coaches are obliged to wear a small microphone[11]. Also there is talk of hanging up cameras in the changing rooms. This is all in the interests of the viewing figures. In the Netherlands we still have to get used to the fact that the matches of the Amsterdam Admirals are halted when it is time for an advertising break in the direct TV transmission. Or that the qualification chances of our volleyball team are limited because the Japanese organisation of the pre-Olympic tournament decided that Spain would be considered for the only wild-card as the TV rights in that country will produce more than in the Netherlands. That however is the harsh reality. Top-class sport is in the hands of investors who see sport (which is very understandable) as an entertainment product on which a return must be made and this has the consequences described above.

The second question is difficult to answer and also falls outside the scope of this study. The third question emphatically comes up for discussion in the recent ban by the English Supreme Court on the take-over of Manchester United by BSkyB (see also the case study in section 3).

2.4. Competition law

After our explanation of various facets of 'the sports market', we now give a further description of competition law. We do this as far as possible from a sports approach. We first briefly describe the way in which sport is dealt with in the European legal system. Then we discuss the application criteria of competition law regarding activities in the sports world. We also dwell briefly on the phenomenon of the relevant market.

---

[9] Four Italian clubs have a joint interest of 24% in the media company Stream.

[10] Manchester United and Real Madrid have their own TV-stations, AC Milan has announced it is setting up its own TV station and in the Netherlands Heerenveen has recently started its own production company.

[11] This regulation has resulted in increasing conflicts between the National Basketball Association and a few coaches whom such an intrusion of their work does not suit.

Sport in Community law

Since Walrave-Koch[12] the principle is that sport falls under Community law once the activities are characterised as economic activities. This principle does not however detract from the fact that both the European Commission and the Court of Justice of the EU acknowledge the specific characteristics of sport and are prepared to take this into account when taking decisions about activities of sports associations and clubs. After studying different cases submitted to the European Commission or the Court of Justice of the EC the following picture emerges:

(1) the sports sector is dealt with by Community law like any other sector, where an economic activity in accordance with Article 2 of the EC Treaty is concerned;

(2) the European Commission and the Court of Justice of the EC acknowledge that in the application of Community law one must take into account the specific nature and the own identity of sport. In the Bosman judgment the Court of Justice of the EC for example states:

'In view of the great social significance of sport and in particular of football in the Community, it must be recognised that the maintenance of an equilibrium between the clubs by ensuring a certain equality of opportunities and the uncertainty of the results, and encouraging them to take on and train young players, are legitimate objectives.'[13];

(3) Community provisions offer wide scope for regulations that are justified by non-economic considerations that are related to the specific nature and framework of certain competitions. Such a restriction on the scope of action of Community law must however be limited to the actual aim and cannot be used to put any sporting activity outside the scope of action of the EC Treaty[14];

(4) regulations or practices other than those mentioned under (3), that can be considered as an economic activity, fall under Community law, but may be exempted if they contribute to or are necessary for the right equilibrium within sport;

(5) the above-mentioned basic principles lead to a casuistic approach to the applicability of Community law to activities in the sports sector.

Application criteria for competition law

In February 1999 the European Commission formulated four categories for its competition policy within the sports sector, to cover the rules, practice and organisation of sport. These categories can be used to establish whether an activity does or does not fall under competition law, or may be exempted from it:

(a) all the activities inherent in sport or which are aimed only at the organisation of sport fall outside the scope of competition law. For example selection standards, national quota, transfer periods and nationality requirements in case of national selections[15];

(b) competition law applies in full to the rules, practice and organisation of sport, if they prevent, limit or distort competition. One can think here of forms of transfer restric-

---

[12] CoJEC 12 December 1974, case 36/74, Walrave, jurispr. 1974, p. 1405, legal ground 4.

[13] CoJEC, 15 December 1995, case C-415/1993, jurispr. 1995, 'Bosman'.

[14] CoJEC 14 July 1976, case 13/76, Donà, jurispr. page 1333, legal ground 12 and conclusion Solicitor-General Cosmas, Deliège, dated18 May 1999, case C-51/96 and case C-1991/97.

[15] See for example the Deliège case.

tions, collective sales of TV rights, FIFA rules relating to caretaker managers, ticketing and conditional sales[16];

(c)   the European Commission is on the basis of Article 81 paragraph 3 of the EC Treaty prepared to grant exemptions for schemes and agreements to which competition law[17] applies, but which ensure the right equilibrium within the sports sector and/or contribute to the improvement of the organisation and the accessibility of sport. One can also think of rules aimed at maintaining the equilibrium between clubs, creating equal opportunities and uncertainty of the results and rules to promote the recruitment and training of young players. This also includes discouraging multi-ownership, or the ownership of several teams within the same discipline of sport by one owner[18];

(d)   abuse of a dominant position is also prohibited within the sports sector on the basis of Article 82 of the EC Treaty. The European Commission recognises that because of the European model of sport, dominant positions may arise in national and European sports associations, but the execution of activities may not lead to abuse. The European Commission names as examples of abuse the exclusion without objective reasons of a competing organiser of a sports event, the non-award of quality or safety certificates for products of a market participant who complies with all the quality or safety standards. Solicitor-General Cosmas takes the view in the matter of Deliège that no abuse of a dominant position is made if regulations of sports associations (here the Belgian Judo Association) find their justification in non-economic reasons derived from the specific nature of certain sports competitions and the specific requirements of sport in general.

The categories mentioned above can be applied equally to the Dutch situation, whereby in such a case Article 6, or Article 24 of the Competition Act will come into play.

Relevant market
The application of competition law in the above-mentioned categories does not simply lead to the conclusion that behaviour that may come under one of these categories relates to prohibited behaviour. It is important to establish that such behaviour is regarded as a competition restriction or as abuse of a dominant position. In both cases to establish a restriction or abuse, it is important to define the relevant market and to see whether the behaviour in question is noticeable on this market. With regard to sport at Community level and in the different Member States decisions have been made in which relevant markets for sport are defined (sponsoring, TV etc.). Both the study into relevant markets and into the noticeability requirement in the above-mentioned sense are mainly economic questions which demand a casuistic approach.

In this paragraph we have taken a further look at competition law and its application within the sports world. Assessment of the application of competition law is often an economic question and requires a casuistic approach.

---

[16] Bosman judgement, EC decisions relating to collective sales and pending action of the EC against FIFA regulations relating to the admissibility of caretaker managers.

[17] Article 81 paragraph 1 of EC Treaty.

[18] This was the case for AEK Athens.

2.5. **Significance of the above aspects for the sports market**

In the above paragraphs the specific characteristics of sport, the economics of the sports markets and the developments in the field of sport within competition legislation are described. In this paragraph we take these two aspects together and go into what the significance of the special economic characteristics of the sports market is in the light of competition legislation. We do that by looking at the degree to which the relationship between the different actors involved in sport is changing.

The different actors
A varying number of actors are involved in sport. We can identify five of them.
– associations;
– clubs and individual sportsmen and women;
– consumers/supporters;
– media companies;[19]
– the government.

These parties all have to deal with one another in the organisation and exploitation of sport. We first briefly discuss the role that the different actors play.

Associations
Sports associations organise the amateur and pro sports competitions. They have an interest in sport staying popular with the general public. If participation in amateur sport decreases, the continuity of the relevant sport is called into question. In addition to the organisational aspect associations increasingly carry out commercial activities. For example they sell television broadcasting rights and sign sponsorship contracts. The associations use the revenues from these activities to support the professional discipline of the sport in question, but also to help finance the organisation of their own competitions.

Clubs/sportsmen and women
Clubs and individual sportsmen and women participate in the competitions organised by the associations. They also increasingly develop economic activities (in professional sports). To be able to participate at a professional level, clubs need money to be able to pay good sportsmen and women. It is therefore very important for these clubs to exploit the commercial activities as far as possible. Individual sportsmen and women try to exploit their individual skills in such a way (for example via individual sponsoring) that they are able to play top-class sport at the highest possible level. Although some Dutch clubs do in fact operate on the market as professionals, a lot of volunteers are without exception active in these clubs, without which it would be impossible for the clubs to function as they now do.

Media
Media (and sponsor companies) need sport as a product to increase their market share. The exposure of the product plays an elementary role in this. The media try to gain possession of broadcasting rights for sport as sport is a relatively risk-free product in the total

---

[19] We include in this group the advertisers who play an important part in the media companies.

broadcasting package. A relatively large number of people watch certain sports, so it is tempting to invest in that type of product. In the case of an expensive game show one always has to wait and see if the investments are paid back. When buying broadcasting rights for football matches from the first division for example a broadcaster is assured of a certain market share without it running very much risk.

Consumers/supporters
Consumers, supporters and amateurs are in a certain sense the final piece in the whole story. For the media companies, and indirectly the clubs and sportsmen and women, they are of major importance as it is to them that the sportsmen and women are exposed. Without the consumers there is no attractive sport and without consumers there is in fact nothing to exploit. Consumers are increasingly faced with a higher price for continuing to consume top-class sport (entrance tickets, pay-per-view TV, etcetera).

Government[20]
It is one of the government's public functions to promote mass sport. The government wants to exploit the positive social value of sport to the optimum by:
– safeguarding and where necessary improving the quality of playing sport;
– improving the quality of the sports infrastructure;
– improving the cohesion of the policy relating to sport.

The government also pursues a policy aimed at promoting a top-class sports climate. The successful action of Dutch sportsmen and women on a world or European level has a positive effect on social cohesion within the Dutch community. Such sports success also has an indirect economic impact (Holland promotion).

In addition the government ensures that existing legislation is enforced, which in reality means that it is a government function to supervise balanced competition relationships. As far as media policy is concerned, the national government implements the Television Directive agreed in a European context. This directive means that the national governments make a proposal to the European Commission on the contents of a list of sports events that must be accessible to everyone when broadcast on television.

Changing relationships between actors: opportunities and threats
A number of the actors described above have in recent decades increasingly started to carry out economic activities. For example: a volleyball club that wants to sell the broadcasting rights of home matches individually to the regional radio, is operating as a supplier on an economic market. Or an individual sportsman or woman looking for finance for training facilities to gain a place for the Olympic Games, offers him- or herself to the market on which sponsors are trying to buy media exposure. On these markets the 'normal' economic principles of supply and demand apply. Another characteristic of the changing distribution of roles is that some parties increasingly focus on a bigger scale: from the national to the European scale if the European market is the relevant market for them.

---

[20] We realise that this brief description of the role of the government in the sports sector can hardly do justice to the actual efforts of the government in this area.

The result of this development is that money will increasingly dictate the action of parties in the sports world. Sports aspects play an ever smaller role. That is in fact the core of the commercialisation of sport. It is in this respect only understandable that Ajax is aiming at the top in Europe and that top-class skaters go for 'the big money'. This type of thing does not have to be a problem in itself. The market mechanism can ensure that financial resources are allocated (extremely) efficiently.

We can also argue in accordance with economic laws that the sponsor of a professional football club in long term has no (economic) interest in the individual broadcasting rights of the club falling to a network that will offer the matches via pay-per-view TV. That does after all mean less exposure for the club sponsors. And in the end the club is even worse off as in the long term it may become less popular as a result of which the value of the product that the club offers falls. The market can then do its work here.[21]

Commercialisation may then under certain circumstances ensure an efficient allocation, the operation of the market mechanism also has a reverse side. Tensions arise between actors who still operate in the 'old' world and parties who are more and more in a full market environment. By 'old' world we mean the closed (non-economic) world of pure amateur sport. Sport there is entertainment to be actively played, instead of entertainment to be watched. In addition tension arises between the economic motor driving the parties and the specific economic aspects of the sports market.

This tension between the two is expressed in a number of ways.
1. association regulations relate with difficulty to the market laws;
2. some actors operate more on a bigger scale (European level), others remain active at national level;
3. because of cross-ownership conflicts of interest may occur that may have consequences on sports relations;
4. the solidarity between clubs comes under pressure at national level.

1. Tension between regulations and competition legislation
The association regulations often originated at a time when there was no question of commercialisation and none of the activities carried out relating to sport were regarded as economic activity. Once parties do carry out economic activities, competition legislation automatically applies. And this legislation in principle prohibits agreements that restrict or distort the competition between parties. While the (old) association regulations for solidarity reasons often contain provisions that oblige the participating clubs to sell the television rights collectively or to make agreements in another way (association mentality).

---

[21] The practice in the countries that surround us does however show that this far from always happens. Sometimes the interests of the bigger companies (the media) in the end have more weight (and that is also understandable on the basis of the economic principle 'who pays (the most money), (in the end also) decides') than the interests of smaller sponsors. And the broadcasting rights disappear behind the decoder as a result of which the consumption of the product (watching a live football match) is available to fewer people and football drifts away from the status of 'the people's game'. It is also quite possible that the rights for top-class events such as the World Championship football will in the long term be so expensive for the Netherlands and so important for the other countries that the supplier of these rights does not consider it vital that the TV pictures can be seen in the Netherlands (and so is not prepared to let the price fall).

2. Scaling up

Clubs and sportsmen and women who are seeking to reach the top, aim their sights more at a higher level of exposure. Top-class Dutch clubs in the KPN-Telecompetition realise that their sporting and hence their commercial exposure will extend beyond national frontiers and so they aim at a European market as by increasing the market of their football product they will also generate more income. This development towards scaling up is in no way special to sport. It characterises just about all European economies. Companies are aiming increasingly for the European or even world markets. The result is that the attention that the clubs pay to national competitions is decreasing all the time. This is after all not where the big money is earned. The revenues from the television broadcasting rights of the Champions League may for a club like Feyenoord in the present season easily amount to ten or twenty times the revenues of the broadcasting rights from the national competition. As a result the attention paid to national interests fades. Also scaling up leads to a distortion of the fields of influence on the different sub-markets. Some parties see their strength increase via scaling up, other do less well from it. It is these changing relationships of strength that largely form the basis of the competition questions.

3. Cross-ownership and potential conflicts of interest

The motives of (big) companies for taking holdings in sport are usually of a purely economic nature. If it is strategic to take a holding in one or more football clubs, then this will be done. That a company may in the long term (partly) own two clubs that play one another in the same competition, is less important from an economic point of view. From the sporting point of view of a fair competition things are however different. If a media company owns a club, that may have consequences on relationships of strength on certain markets. The media company is at the same time demander for and supplier of the broadcasting rights of this club. That in itself may adversely affect the competition relationships on this market.

4. Solidarity between clubs at national level is coming under pressure

One of the important aspects of an exciting and interesting competition is that the relationships of strength between the clubs are more or less comparable, so that the differences in strength between them are not too great. For this a certain redistribution of the joint income is often agreed. Once the best clubs in a national competition set their sights more on the European level, the tendency in these clubs to redistribute income with a view to national differences in strength will be rather lost from sight. As a result the solidarity between them will come under pressure.

In conclusion

An important element of the changing relationships of strength is that some parties can operate more easily than others on a bigger scale and feel at home in circumstances more in line with the market. That applies for media companies, to a slightly lesser degree for clubs and individual sportsmen and women and even less for associations. As not all the parties succeed as well in this scaling up, the fragile fields of influence in the different sub-markets of the sports world are brutally disturbed. In some cases the differences in power give rise to the central questions in this study on competition and abuse of power.

Another important conclusion is that a completely free market may under certain circumstances result in certain basic principles of sport being suppressed. As the major threats for sport we can identify:

- reduced solidarity within one competition (horizontal solidarity), which is at the expense of the competitive balance and hence the excitement in the competition;
- reduced solidarity within one branch of sport (vertical solidarity), which is at the expense of the organisation of sport at amateur level and forms a threat to junior and disabled sport;
- passing on the increasing costs to the supporters (through higher entrance prices, pay-per-view TV, etcetera), which is at the expense of the accessibility of sport for the public ('the people's game');
- increasing influence of media companies in sport and its organisation, which may mean that the nature of sport is changed into an entertainment product.

We shall illustrate these general conclusions in section 3 by describing a number of practical examples.

3. SPORT, MEDIA AND COMPETITION: CASE STUDIES

3.1. Introduction

The previous section has in a general sense portrayed a number of key problems. These key problems have arisen as part of the sports sector is subject to economic forces. In this section we present a number of cases. They are practical examples from the Netherlands and abroad, in which questions at the interface of sport, media and competition are discussed. With this practical approach we want to demonstrate how current these problems are, how they appear in different forms and the way in which the questions in hand are dealt with. We discuss in succession:
- the collective sales of broadcasting rights. This involves the solidarity and importance of competitive balance within a competition;
- the judgement of the English Supreme Court on the attempt by Rupert Murdoch's BSkyB to take over Manchester United. This case centres on the issue of cross-ownership;
- the conflict between the Royal Dutch Skating Association, KNSB, and the commercial skating teams. This involves the possible abuse of a dominant position;
- the American model of sport. In this case we describe how in America the competitive balance in the sports world is 'managed'.

At the end of each case study is a brief commentary. In this we indicate how the example in question fits within our analysis from section two. We also identify where we can draw possible lessons for the future.

3.2. Collective sales of broadcasting rights

The collective or co-ordinated sales of broadcasting rights for football matches is in the spotlight at European level and in the individual countries. The market for broadcasting rights for big sports events is a prime example of a market in which the commercialisation of sport is manifested. Not only are the amounts paid in this market for broadcasting rights getting higher and higher, but there is also a continuing discussion of the question of how the co-ordinated or collective sale of broadcasting rights relates to competition law. This case study dwells on the collective (or co-ordinated) sale of broadcasting rights for national football competitions in Europe.

This paragraph is laid out as follows. First we discuss the nature of the question of the collective sale of broadcasting rights. We also deal with the situation in a number of European countries. Then we describe the economic aspects of the market for broadcasting rights and carry out an economic analysis of this market. Then we look at the importance of the competitive balance for the commercial value of a competition. At the end of the paragraph we formulate our conclusions.

Description of the question

The sale of the broadcasting rights for football matches from the national competition is emphatically on the agenda in the Netherlands. This is partly the result of a number of legal judgements. These make it clear that individual clubs must in a legal sense be regarded as the owner of the rights for their home matches and not the association as organiser of the competition. The reasoning followed here (and confirmed in the judgements) is that the home club is the one that runs the economic risk when it plays a competition match (see *inter alia* Arrondissementsrechtbank Rotterdam, 1999). The home club incurs costs to organise the match. If not a single spectator turned up, it is the home club and not the organising association that has a deficit. In this reasoning the clubs are in terms of competition law in principle individual suppliers of a product (namely the right to broadcast a home match). That has led to the question of to what extent clubs who sell their rights collectively or in co-ordination, hence as separate suppliers, harmonise their behaviour with one another, operate as a cartel and as a result restrict or distort competition.

Another important element of the question is the exclusivity of the broadcasting rights. In most cases the clubs (or the collective that represents them) jointly sell the broadcasting rights exclusively to one market party and this often involves multi-annual contracts. The result is that the market for broadcasting rights is closed to new entrants during the contract period. The question is how this relates to competition law, which does after all aim to create (and maintain) balanced competition conditions. Entry barriers resulting from long-term contracts directly affect the equilibrium of competition conditions.

The question in a number of European countries

In a number of the countries around us the question of the collective sales of broadcasting rights is also an issue. In Germany discussion has arisen about the rights following a judgement by the German Cartels Office, Bundeskartellamt. This declared that the German football association DFB was acting illegally by collectively selling the rights for home matches in European competitions in which German clubs were taking part. This judgement confirmed that the legal ownership of the broadcasting right lies with the home club. The role of the German association as central 'marketer' is of course to maintain the economic well-being of the combined clubs (and is not aimed at maximising profits), but the Bundeskartellamt considered that was not sufficient justification for an exemption from the competition act. A few years later at the initiative of the German football association an exception clause was included in the German competition legislation. This exception to competition makes the central sales of broadcasting rights for matches in the

Bundesliga (national competition) possible.[22] The 1961 American Sports Broadcasting Act served as a blueprint for this.

In England the Restrictive Practices Court (RPC) recently pronounced on the contract that the Premier League has signed with BSkyB and the BBC about respectively the broadcast of live matches and highlights of competition matches from the Premier League (RPC, 1999). The judgement goes at length into the view previously put forward by the Office of Fair Trading that the organisation of the Premier League must be regarded as a classic cartel. The judgement also focuses on the exclusivity of the contracts. For example BSkyB has the exclusive right to show 60 matches in a season directly via pay-per-view TV. The rights to the live broadcast of the other matches are by agreement with BSkyB not available for other networks. The RPC ruled that the agreements of the Premier League with both networks mentioned fall within the exemption clauses that the (old) English competition law contained. It is not clear whether this reasoning still applies now that English competition law has been changed.

In most European countries it is assumed that the exclusive right to exploit television rights lies with the individual clubs. In that respect the English judgement of the RPC is peculiar. This does in fact assume that the clubs do not have the exclusive right to do this (although the RPC does not deny the right of an individual club to decide which network has access to the stadium to provide broadcasts). That confirms (one of) the differences in jurisprudence between the different European countries.

In Spain the discussion is more about the exclusivity of the contracts than about the question of who is the beneficiary.[23] For example the Adiencia Nacional in 1998 confirmed a judgement of the Spanish competition authority that agreements about contracts are against the law. The exclusivity (among other things the length of the contracts) was too widely defined. The case is moreover still being dealt with by the High Court. In Italy the competition authority has banned the Italian football association from collectively selling the broadcasting rights for live matches. The association may on the other hand collectively sell the highlights. France differs most from the other European countries in a number of respects. In France the national football association is authorised by law as organiser of the national competitions as the sole body to sell the broadcasting rights to them. The restriction here is that the contracts must not cover a period of more than five years.

The essence of the situation in different European countries is that the sale of broadcasting rights for matches from the national competition is always tested against the national competition law. Although a number of Member States have found ways in their national legislation of bringing the collective sale of broadcasting rights into line with national competition law, the status of collective sale is not yet clear in the light of European competition law.[24] There are of course also questions relating to economic movement between Member States. And it is also clear that European law must form the touchstone.

---

[22] This clause has also been submitted to the European Commission for review.

[23] In Spain clubs sell the broadcasting rights individually: they do however all have an individual contract with the same networks (Forta for the live matches on the public network and Canal+ for matches broadcast via pay-per-view TV).

[24] A number of cases on collective sales are pending with the Commission (European Commission, 1999).

The economics of the broadcasting rights market

The broadcasting rights market differs in a number of respects from normal economic markets. We go systematically through the main aspects below:
- the interdependence of the suppliers;
- the time aspect plays a part as a component of the relevant market;
- the market shows characteristics of a winner-take-all market.

Co-ordination and interdependence of clubs
In order to offer the product of the clubs – the right to broadcast a football match – to the market, some form of cooperation between the clubs is necessary. Home matches largely derive their value from the competition context in which they are played. The suppliers cannot do without one another. In this respect there is a clear difference with a market in which two biscuit factories offer their goods, as they do not need one another to get their product on the supermarket shelves. A club playing at home as the supplier of broadcasting rights will on the other hand have to make arrangements with the visiting club about the date and time when they are going to play the match against one another. That means there will in any case have to be an independent third party who co-ordinates such aspects (for example the party who plans the competition matches).

The role of this co-ordinator affects the value of the rights the clubs are supplying. When a home club is hosting a commercially attractive opponent, then the value of the broadcasting rights for this match falls if the competition planner schedules another match that is of interest to the television public at the same time. As a result the competition match scheduler partly determines the value of the package of home matches that a club can offer. The result of this is that the home club does not have full control of the quality (and hence the value) of its product. That is a major difference from independent enterprises such as those present on most other markets.

Dependencies between clubs also distinguish them as joint operators of the television rights from a cartel in a normal economic sense. In the judgement of the Restrictive Practices Court in England already mentioned, Yamey made a comparison with a 'widgets cartel' and concluded that the clubs in the Premier League do not form a cartel (RPC, 1999 and Yamey, 1999). The agreements that enterprises make in a 'normal' cartel add nothing to the product that they are offering to the market. In the case of the clubs that is clearly different. An individual club on its own is not in a position to offer a product: two clubs are needed to create a product.

Time aspect of the relevant market
The European Commission makes a distinction in the concept of relevant market between the product market and the geographic market on which producers offer their goods and services. In the case of the market for broadcasting rights there is a further dimension: that of time. We shall discuss a number of aspects of this dimension.

When two networks supply television broadcasts, this involves absolute competition. Someone who watches one programme, cannot also watch the other. Programmes that networks broadcast at different times only compete with one another in a limited way. A viewer can see both programmes and will only weigh up whether to watch one programme or the other if he wants to put a limit on his total viewing time.

Another time aspect of the market for broadcasting rights is that rights to broadcast a match live are only worth money for a relatively short period. A day after a match has been played, a network will attract a lot less viewers than if the network broadcasts the match live. As a result the broadcasting right is worth less. Also the position in the competition affects the value of a match. A duel between numbers 1 and 2 in a competition is valuable when this takes place a couple of rounds before the end of the competition. Only towards the end of the competition is it known which two teams that is and whether in fact at this phase in the competition both can still win the championship. That aspect also makes the concept of relevant market for the broadcasting rights of football matches peculiar in an economic respect.

The market for broadcasting rights as a winner-take-all market
High fixed and low variable costs characterise a winner-take-all market.[25] An important feature of such a market is also that the value of the product depends on the relative quality of the product. The value of a product depends on the value of the other products and not so much on the absolute quality. The markets for information, communication and software apply increasingly as winner-take-all markets. As a result of technological developments the reproduction of products on these markets is increasingly cheaper. The development of a product thus involves high (fixed) costs, the reproduction (variable costs) are low. This combination of high fixed and low variable costs involves economies of scale during production. And these economies of scale do of course bring about a natural concentration trend. Because of the low marginal costs of offering an additional product, it is easy for a producer to serve an additional market segment.

The market for broadcasting rights is a market derived from the market for television broadcasts. And the market for television broadcasts shows characteristics of a winner-take-all market. The costs of a television broadcast are fixed costs; the marginal costs of an additional viewer are zero. An important feature of a winner-take-all market is that the relative quality of the product determines the preference of the consumer for one product over the other.

One of the reasons that the rights for broadcasting sports events are undergoing a price explosion, is that the market for broadcasting rights shows the characteristics of a winner-take-all market.[26] An important feature of such a market is high pricing. The product that is offered, for example the rights to broadcast the pictures of the football competition, can only be substituted by other products to a limited degree. For this reason the demander on such a market to less extent weighs up trading off the price and quality of what is offered against each other. The demanders on a winner-take-all market show the tendency only to consume products that are relatively speaking better than the other products.

Televised sport has such a great power of attraction for the television public that it is very attractive for a commercial network to have these rights. Networks are prepared to put (a lot) more money on the table for this than they can earn back in a direct sense from the exploitation of the advertising space around the matches. On the television broadcasting market the people who can exploit the football broadcasting rights are the winners on

---

[25] For a full description of the winner-take-all phenomenon in sport among other things and the related superstar economy: see among others Rosen, 1981, Frank and Cook, 1997 and Borghans and Groot, 1998.

[26] One of the other reasons is that a keener competition for these rights (in the form of more demanders on the market) also has the effect of increasing prices. That is confirmed by the empirical analysis of the value of broadcasting rights for European national competitions that we discuss further on.

the winner-take-all market. They have a product that is disproportionately more attractive for the consumer than other (television) products.

The same sort of reasoning applies for the market on which individual clubs offer their broadcasting rights. That is also a market with the characteristics of a winner-take-all market, though the winners on this market are the most attractive clubs. They will attract all the attention as relatively speaking they are just a bit more attractive than their sporting competitors. In the same way as Madonna attracts a disproportionately large part of the added value on the market on which female singers offer their CDs, that also applies for the most popular clubs. On the market where clubs individually offer the broadcasting rights for football matches, the attention (and the money) will go to the most attractive clubs. That will in the long term mean that these clubs will be able to generate more income and as a result become richer than less strong clubs. That has consequences for sporting balance, or the competitive balance, which we will go into below.

The importance of the competitive balance

In the United States the competitive balance of sport has for years attracted attention (see also the case study on sport in the United States). The competitive balance is very important if a certain equilibrium in sports relations means that a (random) match from a competition is exciting. It is not then certain beforehand who will win. The reasoning is that the excitement within a competition helps determine the commercial value of this competition. The competitive balance is a measure of the excitement within a competition.

Within (in particular American) econometric literature a number of objective criteria have been developed. These criteria indicate what the sports equilibrium is within a competition. There are already a number of empirical applications of these measures developed in America to European data.[27] These show that there is a clear difference in the competitive balance between the different national football competitions in Europe. Those in Germany, England and Spain are much more exciting than those in the Netherlands, Belgium and Portugal (which tracks well with the intuition of the neutral football fan). In the first countries mentioned it is much less certain beforehand who will win a match. For this reason these competitions are also more attractive from a commercial viewpoint than other competitions. That is also obvious from the fact that the amounts that networks pay for the broadcasting rights in these competitions are (much) higher.

That is not all however. The fact that higher amounts are handed over for such competitions may after all be due to other factors. The size of a country for example determines the potential number of television viewers and therefore presumably (also) affects the amount that networks are prepared to pay for the broadcasting rights. Furthermore the competition conditions in a country, for example the number of networks active in a country, may also push up prices.

An analysis of the value of broadcasting rights shows that the competitive balance plays an important part in the value of broadcasting rights, if an adjustment is made for other factors that cause differences between countries.[28] In addition to the competitive balance other factors play a part. The amounts paid for broadcasting rights are higher in

---

[27] We refer for the method *inter alia* to Neuman and Tamura, 1996 and for empirical applications to Dutch data to Koning, 1999. We have derived the empirical results that we discuss here from the article by Goeree and Minkman, 1999.

[28] For data, estimated results and model specification see Goeree and Minkman, 1999.

countries where more networks are active. And also the number of inhabitants is important. The bigger a country, the more potential TV viewers there are, the more a network can earn back from the sales of the advertising space and the more the network has left for broadcasting rights. Finally it also seems that the absolute level of a competition has an effect. The stronger a national competition (measured against the club results in European competitions), the more this competition is worth. The analysis to which we refer therefore confirms the importance of the competitive balance as a determinant factor in the commercial value of a competition. The maintenance of that equilibrium is ultimately also in the interest of the best (or commercially most attractive) clubs. For the product that they offer is in the long term less attractive if the excitement in the matches they play is less.

Ultimately the consumers are also better off with a competition in which a sports equilibrium remains more or less in balance. The maintenance of the competitive balance within a competition ensures that the quality of the product remains the optimum. An average competition match remains exciting to watch. A consumer does not get much out of a match for which the result is a foregone conclusion.

Lessons and conclusions

In a general sense competition law aims to create a level-playing-field on the market on which producers offer their goods and services. That means among other things that all the suppliers have equal access to the market and that there are no obstacles to entry. And also that they compete with one another for the favour of the consumer for the price and quality of the supply.

The sports market in general and the market for broadcasting rights in particular is peculiar from an economic point of view. In the first place the enterprises (clubs) that offer their products (the broadcasting right) on this market, are dependent on one another. They do not have full control over price and quality of the product they are offering and they need one another to make the offer. Secondly the market for broadcasting rights has the characteristics of a winner-take-all market. These markets show a natural tendency to concentrate around the suppliers who offer the relatively best (or most popular) product. These are the clubs who are just a bit better or more popular than the other clubs

In a completely free market in which clubs offer their rights individually, the more popular clubs always become richer at the expense of the less popular clubs. In the long term that reduces the quality of the product they offer, an exciting competition match. Because a poorer club that has less resources will in the long term have to pay for this with a loss of sports qualities and so become less attractive for the opponents in the competition.

An economically level playing-field for a market on which clubs offer their rights individually, thus in the long term leads to a distortion of sports equilibrium. A sporting level playing-field then as it were gets out of balance. And the more balanced sporting conditions, or the excitement in a competition, now form one of the characteristics of the broadcasting rights that makes it attractive to exploit these commercially.

3.3. Cross-ownership: BSkyB and Manchester United

The phenomenon of cross-ownership is increasingly attracting attention in the Western European sports world. This involves in particular interpenetration between sports organisations and media companies. Obviously this type of interpenetration can adversely affect a number of aspects essential to sport: an objective news service and fair tendering procedures for radio and television rights to be marketed[29]. To give a picture of the nature of the problems we first discuss some of the background to the concept of cross-ownership. We then present a few examples of cross-ownership in the countries around us. We go further into the best known case in this respect: the attempt of Rupert Murdoch's BSKyB to take over Manchester United.

The background
Different forms of cross-ownership are possible where the sports and media world is concerned. These all meet the definition of the concept 'concentration' in Article 27 of the Competition Act:
- a merger of a media company with a sports organisation;
- the direct or indirect acquisition of control by a media company over a sports organisation (downward vertical integration);
- the acquisition of control by a sports organisation over a media company (upward vertical integration);
- the creation of a structural concentrative joint venture (a structural joint venture without this resulting in the parent companies co-ordinating their competition behaviour).

For media companies there are appealing advantages of acquiring control of sports organisations, where TV-genic sports are concerned. By acquiring control the company can ensure structural access to the (TV rights for) certain sports events, the company can influence the organisation of sport in order to sell its own product (TV programmes) more attractively, it acquires the possibility of permanent sponsorship facilities, gains better control over programming costs etc.

In the Netherlands we have no legal restrictions on cross-ownership in the media world. A restriction from the Competition Act may however be imposed on cross-ownership. According to this act (section 5, Article 26 and following) the intention to merge must be notified to the Dutch Competition Authority, the NMa, in the case of:
- merger of two or more previously independent enterprises;
- the acquisition of further specified forms of control;
- the creation of a joint venture.

If the NMa has reason to assume that as a result of this merger an economic dominant position may arise or be reinforced, resulting in competition on the Dutch market or part of it being significantly impeded, it may prohibit the merger, or impose a license on it.

The practice
In the big European football countries the number of cases of cross-ownership is rapidly increasing. The main examples are:

---

[29] In the near future the Internet rights will also be added to this.

England

BSkyB   Manchester United, Manchester City, Chelsea and Leeds
                                  United
NTL   Newcastle
Granada   Liverpool

Italy

Fininvest/Mediaset   AC Milan
Stream   rights of the other 4 clubs from Series A, including
                                  Fiorentina, Lazio Roma and Parma. All four of these clubs
                                  have in exchange acquired a 6 percent interest in Stream.

Germany

UFA (Bertelsmann)   Borussia Dortmund, Hamburger SV, Herta BSC and FC
                                  Nürnberg

Spain

Canal+   Real Madrid (own channel)
Zeta   Mallorca and Antenna 3

France

Canal+   Paris Saint Germain
Pathé   Olympique Lyon
MG/UFA Sports   Girondins de Bordeaux
Kiosque (Canal+)   Olympique Marseille (own channel)

In Italy Juventus, AS Roma, Inter and AC Milan[30] have their own television network. In the Netherlands Heerenveen has recently started its own TV production company.

BSkyB and Manchester United

British Sky Broadcasting Group PLC (BSkyB) is a media concern in England that owns 6 basic channels, 6 cable TV channels and 1 pay-per-view channel. The company offers three sports channels and forms part of Rupert Murdoch's media conglomerate to which Fox TV also belongs. In the spring of 1999 BSkyB wanted to acquire full control of Manchester United football club. The take-over was presented to the Office of Fair Trading (OFT) that then prohibited the merger because it was against the general interest. In this the OFT looked mainly at the consequences of the merger for the market for broadcasting rights. This market would in the view of the OFT be dominated after the merger by BSkyB, certainly if the Restrictive Practices Court (RPC) was to decide that it would allow the collective sales of TV rights (which later proved to be the case) and no media companies other than BSkyB acquired control of football clubs. The Monopolies and Mergers Commission of the OFT examined four possible scenarios for the broadcasting rights market and on the basis of these came to its negative opinion. The scenarios were:

---

[30] Since 16 December 1999.

1. Maintain present situation: collective sales and one take-over
The broadcasting rights of the English competition are sold collectively by the Premier League (English football association). If BSkyB were to take over Manchester United, the company would as a member of the supplier Premier League obtain information on the sale of the broadcasting rights. As a result BSkyB would gain an advantage in its bid for the broadcasting rights with respect to other bidders. Since BSkyB already has a strong position on the market for broadcasting rights, the competition would ultimately be discouraged from bidding. The result of maintaining the present situation is then that the competition for the broadcasting rights is decreasing. This would ultimately result in less choice for the Premier League to sell and fewer opportunities for innovation in broadcasting Premier League football.

2. Individual sales of broadcasting rights and one take-over
A second scenario is that BSkyB/Manchester United would be the only take-over and that the broadcasting rights would be sold individually by the clubs. BSkyB would because of the merger gain a competitive advantage over the other bidders as it already owns the home rights of Manchester. Partly because of its strong present position the competition for broadcasting rights would decrease.

3. Collective sales and several take-overs
The consequence of the take-over could also be that several media companies would buy football clubs. The collective sales of broadcasting rights would then only continue if the media companies agreed to share the rights. This would mean that the rights would be owned by a limited group of media companies, which would also have the effect of distorting competition.

4. Individual sales and several take-overs
Finally there is also the possibility that several take-overs would occur and that clubs would sell their broadcasting rights individually. The result of this would be that there would hardly be any competition since the merged clubs would no longer offer their broadcasting rights to the market.

All the scenarios examined would in the view of the OFT lead to a considerable restriction of the competition between media organisations. In addition the take-over would also adversely affect the organisation of paid football. In first instance it would considerably disrupt the competitive balance in the English competition. Also via Manchester United BSkyB would gain an influence in the organisation of the Premier League, which could lead to an adverse effect on the long term interests of football. One could also imagine that the playing schedule would be organised in such a way that Manchester United would enjoy precedence over other clubs for attractive TV times.

In general cross-ownership does not in itself have to cause a problem. Just as other enterprises or private investors can take an investment in a club, so can a media company. Tensions arise when sales of broadcasting rights are under discussion. At that point the problem of wearing two hats may arise as described in the BSkyB – Manchester United case. When a media company is active on the market as both supplier and demander – of the same broadcasting rights package – there can be no question of a fair bidding procedure. In America and various European countries it does seem possible for a media company to exploit some of the rights itself (for example regional television or club channel) and leave some to others (for example the national rights).

In addition to these consequences cross-ownership may form a threat to an objective news service. There is a chance that biased reporting (quality) may occur in favour of their 'own' club. There is also a chance of the dominance (quantity) of news about their own club at the expense of news about other clubs or subjects.

In order to properly assess the permissibility of mergers between media companies and sports organisations, it is necessary to further examine what the effect of such mergers will be on the market. It is not possible to take a general measure. An assessment will have to be made for each case as to what the consequences will be for the relevant market(s) of an intended merger in this context. In this assessment the considerations of the OFT in the matter of Manchester United – BSkyB are extremely relevant.

Lessons and conclusions

Cross-ownership is not by definition reprehensible. Only in the case of market distortion is further attention required. So when assessing the 'dangers' of cross-ownership the situation regarding broadcasting rights must always be considered. In case of individual sales the question is whether cross-ownership in itself is a problem. It does become so if one media company owns the rights of so many clubs that this involves undesirable domination. In the case of collective sales of TV rights this involves media companies via their club interest having undesirable insider knowledge and abusing this.

Whether unlawful situations are involved as regard competition law will have to be assessed for each individual case. The definition of the relevant market and the economic consequences play an important part in this. With the growth in the phenomenon of cross-ownership it is perhaps advisable to draw up a few guidelines for a fair bidding procedure. A limit can then be set on the interest that media companies may have in a club, if they still want take part in the bidding procedure.

3.4. The position of an association with respect to individual sportsmen and women: the KNSB case

In Dutch skating commercialisation has really got going. With the arrival of commercial teams alongside the squad of the Royal Dutch Skating Association (Koninklijke Nederlandse Schaatsenrijdersbond – KNSB) an argument has flared up about the position of the KNSB in the new field of influence. In the media in recent years a great deal of attention has been paid to the relationship between the squad and 'the commercial skaters', which often focussed on the non-sporting aspects. Selection criteria, the availability of own coaches and the space for advertising statements on their clothing took a prime place.

In this paragraph we describe the effects that commercialisation has on skating in our country. We briefly cover the structure of Dutch skating. Then we discuss the case that the Association of Professional Skating Teams (Vereniging van Professionele Schaatsteams – VPST) recently brought against the KNSB because of an alleged abuse of power by laying down conditions for participation by skaters in international competitions. Finally we cover the possible (economic) consequences of the developments described for skating.

Structure of Dutch skating
KNSB
The KNSB is an association whose members (licensees) include skating clubs, districts and independent skaters. The skating clubs and districts have as members individual skaters who are members of the association via the clubs. All licensees must adhere to the statutes, regulations and resolutions of the KNSB. The KNSB has in Aegon a main sponsor who supports the association financially when carrying out its social functions. The sponsorship money of the KNSB mainly benefits mass sport. The KNSB also has a few 'squads' in which top-class skaters can carry out their profession. The KNSB just like each association is also responsible for sending national teams to European Championships, World Championships, the Olympic Games and World Cup competitions.

The squads
At the beginning of the year the KNSB invites top-class sportsmen and women to take part in one of the squads. If a skater accepts the invitation he/she (now) begins a three year membership. Squad members skate in national competitions in the association's kit.

VPST
Top-class skaters may choose to skate in a commercial team. The best known commercial teams are Sanex and Spaarselect. These teams have joined together in the VPST that does not come under the KNSB. Commercial teams do not simply transfer sponsor money for mass sport. The commercial skaters remain licence-holders of the KNSB.

National competitions
National skating competitions are organised by the KNSB. The competitors include skaters from squads, from commercial teams and individual skaters (independent skaters who do not form part of a team). Skaters may appear in the clothing of their own sponsor.

International competitions
The International Skating Union (ISU) organises the international competitions. The KNSB provides logistics here if the competitions are held in the Netherlands. Under the ISU events skaters from the same national team must wear identical competition clothing, that clearly shows the nationality of the skater in question. The regulations of the KNSB state that skaters who are selected for the national team must wear the association clothing, which in addition to the names of their own sponsors, bears the names of the association sponsor. For the national team selection is carried out from all the licence-holders: from the squads, the commercial teams and independent skaters.

VPST vs. KNSB: the 'fifth logo'
On 10 August 1998 the VPST submitted a complaint to the Dutch Competition Authority (Nederlands Mededingingsautoriteit – NMa) against the KNSB. This complaint accused the KNSB of abuse of a dominant position: the KNSB lays down certain conditions for participation by skaters in international competitions which the commercial teams see as restrictive. The NMa will give a ruling on this in the near future.

In addition to this case the VPST has applied for an injunction against the KNSB. The complaint of the VPST is directed against the conditions that the KNSB lays down for skaters to wear the sponsor names of the KNSB sponsors during international competitions. The VPST wants their members to be able to wear their own sponsor names during these competitions. True the association had offered to give up the so-called fifth logo – the 200 square centimetre emblem on the right leg – for the commercial skaters, but the compensation payment demanded was not negotiable for the VPST. To break the power of the KNSB the commercial teams were even prepared to appear this winter in neutral clothing (without sponsorship logos).

The KNSB is bringing an independent defence against this charge. Among other things it points out that the national teams are only put together on the basis of sports performance. An independent selection committee selects the best skaters from the licence-holders (squads and commercial teams and independent skaters). Commercial interests play no part in this. Secondly the KNSB states that the clothing of the national teams is the exclusive affair of the association. Just as in the KNVB all the players in the Dutch eleven wear the same KNVB kit, the same also applies for the skating association. The national teams then wear the association clothing during tournaments. The association also alleges that the advertising statements on the clothing form part of the sponsorship contract with Aegon and Deloitte & Touche. In exchange for advertising on the national clothing the KNSB receives resources for encouraging skating over the full range of the sport. The sponsorship statements on the clothing of the national teams are the main means for the association of generating this sponsorship income.

Before the case came to court, the two parties reached a compromise. During World Cup competitions commercial skaters can fill the space for the fifth logo with the name of their team's sponsor. During the European Championship and the three World Championships (WC allround, WC sprint, WC distances) the available space is for the association sponsors. The compromise with the commercial teams may mean that the KNSB receives less income as its sponsors will enjoy less exposure. This could be at the expense of mass sport.

Possible consequences for the sport (of skating)

In spite of the compromise that the KNSB and the VPST have agreed, it is not yet clear whether the KNSB is abusing its dominant position by specifying the skating costume to be worn. This will have to be shown by the NMa analysis. If the opinion of the NMa is in favour of the association and it is cleared of abuse of power, nothing will change. The association will retain its income from the sponsorships contracts as they now exist. The result may be that skaters no longer want to skate for the national team as they do not want to have rules imposed on them by the association. In the most extreme case the commercial skaters may set up their own association and in addition to the existing international competitions organise their own competitions. If the KNSB is charged with abuse of power, it may be that the skaters themselves will be able to decide their sponsorship statements during international competitions. This could mean a loss of income for the association and be at the expense of mass sport.

The same argument has arisen in cycling. Rabobank is the sponsor of the KNWU. It provides the KNWU with resources for its broad social objectives. As an important service in return Rabobank is the shirt sponsor for the national selections (pros, amateurs and juniors). In addition to the national teams Rabobank also sponsors the biggest national professional cycling team. There is also talk of a compromise in the cycling world. In the national selections riders may wear their own cycling shorts under the national shirt (Rabobank) bearing the names of their regular team sponsor (Rabobank, TVM or another professional team).

And in fact a similar arrangement is also noticeable in football. After Johan Cruijff made an issue of it in the 70s, the players in the Dutch team are allowed to wear their own boots under the national kit.

Lessons and conclusions

The central theme in this case is that in order to achieve their social objectives the associations are required to behave in some points like an entrepreneur. In addition to flows of public money some associations have the opportunity to earn extra resources via sponsoring.

By signing sponsorship contracts for national tournaments or selections the associations as 'public' bodies are coming into contact with 'private' markets and their forces. Sports rules (everyone wears the same kit) sometimes seem to conflict with the rules of free competition (no abuse of power). That may lead to tensions not only in the skating association. To date things have been solved by mutual agreement, but with the increasing number of conflicts it will be interesting to see where the EU, the NMa or the court will draw the line between the importance of sport and the importance of the market. Perhaps by a casuistic approach, perhaps by making a (partial) exception for sport.

3.5. Lessons from the United States

In the United States there are decades of experience in the commercialisation of sport. Sport in America is 'big business'. Although there are important differences between the American and Western European sports culture, within this study it is instructive to further explain a few aspects of the American sports world. This involves above all the way in which the competitive balance is handled in the four big American sports (basketball, baseball, American football and ice hockey). In the associations, the National Basketball Association (NBA), Major League Baseball (MLB), the National Football League (NFL) and the National Hockey League (NHL) there is a widely held understanding that the maintenance of a balanced – and thus exciting – competition is essential for the success of sport as a commercial product. In the continuation of this paragraph we briefly describe a number of methods that contribute to the monitoring of the competitive balance in the different American sports competitions. In addition to the pro sports world we briefly describe the state of affairs in the American college sports world. Finally we describe a number of developments and trends from the American sports world that may perhaps also take place in Western Europe.

Monitoring the competitive balance

In addition to the absolute quality of the game shown, the competitive balance is the most important determinant factor in the commercial value of a competition. In order to maximise the financial income in the long term the American sports associations use a number of tools to maintain competitive balance. The most important tools are:
- collective sales of television rights;
- regulated salary system;
- annual college draft;

Collective sales of television rights

Television rights are not the only source of income for sports teams and leagues. But according to the estimates of Financial World media income (in particular TV) in 1996 accounted for 38 percent of MLB income, 55 percent of NHL income, 37 percent of NBA income and 15 percent of NHL income. Television rights therefore form a considerable interest for professional sports organisations. In America a clear distinction must be made here between revenues from national and local broadcasting rights. In all the leagues the income from national TV rights are divided proportionately between all the clubs[31]. The agreement for these collective sales is laid down in the 1961 Sports Broadcasting Act. The Act rejected a judicial decision that the 'pooling' of TV rights by the NFL and CBS was illegal. The act includes rules (the so-called 'blackout rules') that protect teams from television broadcasts in their home region when they are playing a home match. The income from *national* TV rights is therefore used to support the so-called 'small market teams'. For the *local* TV rights the revenues only go to the selling sports organisation. This means that clubs in attractive sports markets (New York, Chicago) receive considerably more income from their local TV and radio rights than small market teams.

In addition to the income from TV rights the income from licensing (merchandise) is divided equally between the clubs. In 1998 each MLB team received 16.5 million dollars. In addition the thirteen richest MLB teams together had to pay 100 million dollars to the fifteen poorest teams. The New York Yankees put in 13 million dollars. Consideration is being given to an even greater redistribution which would promote the equality and hence the competition between the teams and increase the public interest in baseball even more.

Regulated salary system

In addition to the income side there is also an attempt 'to manage' the cost side of sports organisations to some extent. In the NBA and the NFL there is talk of a so-called 'salary cap', a limit on the total salary sum that a team can pay to its players. The aim of this is to try and keep the purchasing power of the richest clubs within some sort of limits. There is talk of a 'soft cap' that may be exceeded under certain conditions. In addition some competitions have fixed salary scales (minimum and maximum), based on the number of years a player has already been active. Where there are no salary scales (NFL, MLB) there is a system of salary arbitration. If player[32] and club do not agree on the financial remuneration this is fixed via arbitration. The statistics of the player in question – and what players of an equivalent quality earn in other clubs – play a central part in this.

Draft

All American pro competitions have the so-called 'draft' system, a sort of election in which clubs may each year select from the new talent coming available from the college sports world. The NFL has already had this system since 1935. College players who want to be considered for a pro contract can register for the draft. Then the clubs can make their choice in a number of rounds and in accordance with a pre-determined order. In this clubs who ended up low in the draft in the previous year have the first choice. By drafting the most talented players they can increase their competitiveness and the competitive balance

---

[31] There are a few exceptions for so-called expansion teams (new-entry organisations)

[32] Salary arbitration is only available for so-called free agents, experienced players who are (have been) associated with a club for a fixed number of years.

increases. The clubs are also permitted to trade their selection rights with one another before the draft. The condition for using a draft system is a strict separation between the professional sports world and (amateur) college sport.

Organisation of sport

The American professional sports have a different organisation to what we are familiar
with. Under the pressure of commercialisation, professionalization has some decades ago
already entered the field of influence in which sport takes place. We discuss briefly:
– the role of the associations;
– the clubs as franchises;
– the Collective Bargaining Agreement;
– owners of sports organisations.

The associations

The American associations have an important sports function: to organise the competition.
They prepare the playing schedules, provide the umpires, deal with protests, etcetera.
They are also very actively involved in the economic side of sport. They draw up rules of
behaviour for their members (clubs), aimed at maximising the joint revenues. In particular
this involves preventing economic competition between clubs and protecting the market
for new entrants. The American sports associations are headed by the so-called 'commissioners', chairmen with considerable (sanction) power.

The clubs as franchises

In the American professional sports world the attitude prevails that it is not so much the
clubs that form the offer on the entertainment market, but rather 'sport' as a whole. Much
more than in Europe sport is seen as a product to be sold jointly. Clubs are only part of a
bigger whole. It is not for nothing that clubs are called 'franchises'. When 'marketing'
basketball the image of 'the NBA' as a product plays an important part. Under the marketing umbrella of the NBA the clubs sell their merchandise articles jointly. The NBA logo is
on all the articles of all the clubs. The same applies for the NHL, the NFL and Major
League Baseball. The view that it is not the clubs but the league that in fact occupies the
central place plays an important part in American attitudes to sport and competition.
Many of the questions under discussion in Europe at present about possible cartel formation when clubs carry out economic activities jointly, have already been discussed at
length in America too. We have already discussed the 1961 Sports Broadcasting Act! But
there is already detailed legislation and jurisprudence on other questions at the interface of
sport and economics. An example of the interesting insights this can produce is the discussion on the question of whether (collective) league decisions hinder economic competition between clubs. Professor Gary Roberts of the University of Tulane had the following to say about this before the competition commission of the Senate for example[33]:
'*The Copperweld Corp. vs. Independent Tube Corp, 467 US 752 (1984) states whether
two or more separate legal persons who act jointly constitute a single firm or a voluntary
combination of competitors. (...) The deciding factor should be whether the single nature*

---

[33] Speech before the Subcommittee on Antitrust, Business Rights, and Competition, with reference to the question 'Should Congress stop the bidding war for sports franchises?', 29 November
1995.

of the joint enterprise is such that its existence flows from a single source of economic power, or instead from inherently independent sources of economic power that have simply chosen to operate jointly. (...) A sports league derives from a single source of economic power, namely the inherent reality that the league's product can only be produced through the total cooperation and integration of the member clubs, not independently by one team. Without doubt, the member clubs in a sports league are not 'independent sources of economic power previously pursuing separate interests,' for each has no capacity independently to produce anything of significant value, and thus cannot be an independent source of economic power. (...) To require the partners in an inherently joint partnership to compete against one another in some economic aspects is illogical and ultimately works to the detriment of consumers. General partnership/joint venture law reflects this by providing that partners not only are not required to compete against one another, they have a fiduciary duty not to compete against the venture or one another with respect to the venture's business, and not to expropriate for individual gain an asset or prospective business opportunity of the joint venture. (...) As such, the league's partners should not be required by antitrust law to do what partnership/joint venture law prohibits – to compete for individual gain against one another and the joint venture itself in ways related to the venture's business.'

The Collective Bargaining Agreement

The Collective Bargaining Agreement (CBA) is the contract between the leagues and the players' unions in which they lay down agreements about the organisation of sport. In the CBA the salary cap is fixed, as are the rules in accordance with which the minimum and maximum salaries are fixed. The CBA also includes rules relating to transfers (trades), the draft and many other matters. It is the CBA that protects American sports from breaking the competition legislation. After all a lot of the tools used (salary cap, draft) would conflict with the Sherman Act, if they had not come into being as a result of collective bargaining.

The owners

In America the professional sports organisations are virtually all in the hands of private parties[34]. Known examples are Ted Turner (CNN) who owns the Atlanta Braves (baseball) and the Atlanta Hawks (basketball), Rupert Murdoch (News Corporation/ Fox TV) with his Los Angeles Dodgers, the Disney Company (ESPN, ABC) with its Anaheim Angels (baseball) and Mighty Ducks (ice hockey) and Wayne Huizenga (Blockbuster Video), the owner of the three professional sports organisations that Miami was rich in, the Miami Dolphins (football), the Florida Panthers (ice hockey) and the Florida Marlins (baseball)[35]. The owners have joint consultation in which decisions are made on matters that relate to the economic value of their joint sports product. So a team owner who wants to sell or move his team must have the unanimous agreement of all the other owners.

In American professional sports all the parties involved (owners, associations, players) acknowledge that they need one another to achieve optimum results. More than we are accustomed to in Europe these parties form a single front with respect to the market (read:

---

[34] An exception is the American Football team of the Green Bay Packers, whose shares are largely in the hands of the local population.

media, consumers). Only after the size of the (financial) cake has been maximised in this way, do discussions as to its distribution start between them.

College sports

In addition to the professional competitions there are particularly interesting college competitions in America. Although colleges are technically not-for-profit institutions, certainly at the top colleges enormous amounts are spent on keeping sports teams on their feet[36]. In particular American football and basketball are popular. The National Collegiate Athletic Association (NCAA), the umbrella body for college sports, has for decades been selling the broadcasting rights for the football matches of its members as one package. The NCAA ensured a redistribution of the income of the strong football schools like Oklahoma, Miami and Notre Dame to the weaker schools. The NCAA also limited the transmission time of the big schools in favour of the weaker schools. In the early Eighties a few big football schools attacked these collective sales of TV rights. They claimed the ruling hindered free trade and contravened competition law. The court agreed with this: the NCAA was not eligible for an exemption from the Competition Act. In 1984 60 big football schools formed the College Football Association (CFA) that signed a national TV contract on behalf of the schools. The CFA also signed individual local TV contracts on behalf of its members.

The contract between the CFA and television company ABC was challenged in 1990 by the Federal Trade Commission (FTC). The contract was alleged to restrict competition between television companies. In 1991 the court did however rule that the FTC had no control over the CFA as 'it is not organized and does not carry on business either for its own profit or for the profit of its members'. The FTC Act requires this, but in the eyes of the court the money was used to improve the school system. A clear not-for-profit activity. The FTC attacked the judgement of the Commission with the argument that the court had wrongly ruled on the 'not-for-profit' status of the CFA. The source and application of the cash flow also played a part in this. The source of the money (sales of TV rights) was said to be a purely economic activity and hence fell under the scope of the FTC. The Commission found that this reasoning was not strong enough. In its judgement it followed the line of the Internal Revenue Service (IRS) that couples the sales of college TV rights with the promotion of education and amateur sport. The CFA in essence is nothing more than a body distributing the available funds.

The members of the CFA are still members of the NCAA, partly because they can as a result profit from the income from the NCAA basketball contract. There is a fear however that the big football schools and some big basketball schools will in the long term leave the NCAA and form their own conference. This Superconference is expected to draw the big sponsors away from the NCAA and hence strike a very sensitive blow to the 880 schools of the NCAA. However, because a Superconference – with controlled access to the profitable competitions – contravenes competition law, the big schools are for the time being choosing a strategy that is aimed at making the NCAA dance to their tune. By making a minimum transfer of resources to the weaker schools it can influence the NCAA and claim most of the income for itself.

---

[35] In 1988 Huizenga sold the Florida Marlins.

[36] Payments to players are not permitted, but the organisation around the teams is no different from that in the professional sports organisations (staff, facilities, travel).

What is perhaps waiting for us
The commercialisation of sport in America seems to be a few decades ahead of that in Europe. It is therefore sensible to look at what developments may possibly find their way to our sports markets. We will briefly discuss a few trends that do not seem very far off:
- rise of the farm system;
- the moving of clubs;
- top-class players with supporting cast.

Farm system
In America there is a lack of well organised amateur competitions. So there is no growth model in which young talent can mature and slowly climb upwards until it is ready for the real work. The professional sports organisations make up for this lack by maintaining their own rearing ponds of talent. In baseball in particular there is an extensive farm system, in which talent is tested and trained in return for payment. Below the absolute top-class level (the Major League) there are four competition levels: AAA (triple A), AA (double A), A (single A) and Rookie League. Young pro players are assessed each year at the start of the season and classified at the level for which they are suitable. All the baseball organisations have various teams, divided over different levels. In most cases they have one AAA team, one or two AA, A and Rookie League teams. Players who develop well are transferred during the season to higher teams.

In the Netherlands too we can see the outline of this development rising up. The big football clubs in particular seem to be moving towards such a scheme with one top-class selection in a top-class competition and a few satellite teams (or clubs) in lower-level competitions. For example Ajax is considering taking part in a European Superleague and is then thinking about playing a second team in the national competition. Various Dutch clubs are also busy setting up satellite clubs in various countries where talent can mature[37].

The moving of clubs
In America clubs are with some regularity moving to another city. Because there is a shortage in the number of clubs and the social and economic spin-off of a professional sports organisation is enormous, the clubs are succeeding in getting cities to bid against one another to accept a sports organisation with open arms. Local authorities try in particular to attract owners with new stadia. And owners use the threat of a possible move to force their present home local authority to make an extreme effort. Although a lot of water has to flow under the bridge before it actually comes to a move, is it not improbable that we in the Netherlands will also be faced with this phenomenon[38]. Here too the first cautious steps are already visible. Nesselande volleyball club is moving to Rotterdam because it has a new sports hall available there. What was once the Haarlem Basketball week, now takes place in Rotterdam because the Haarlem local authority did not want to meet the requirements of the organisers. Abroad too the first steps along the path to alienation are

---

[37] For example Ajax already has joint ventures with Beerschot (Belgium) and a club in South Africa, Heerenveen has a link with a Finnish club. Vice versa De Graafschap as a satellite club has a link with the Italian Udinese.

[38] The first impulsive response of 'this club belongs to this city' is expected to disappear as a result of commerce.

being taken. Two Scottish clubs have announced they would like to go into the English competition. The Portuguese cup final was recently played in Paris.

Top-class players with supporting cast
The enormous players' salaries – in combination with the salary cap – have in the NBA and the NFL led to remarkable compositions of various sports teams. Teams quite often only have one or a few superstars who earn an enormous amount of money and a large supporting cast like you see in the film industry. Every sports organisation is trying to lay hold of a superstar for sporting and financial reasons. Each of the four sports has around ten of these big earners. Because they account for a large part of the financial scope, there is 'little' over for the rest of the team.

Lessons and conclusions
The most important lesson from America is the need to 'manage' the competitive balance of a competition and the practical implementation of this.

Although their possible introduction will not take place over night, it is sensible to look further at the feasibility of the tools used in America. The introduction of a salary cap or the use of a draft system (at European level) certainly deserve attention with a view to the anticipated problems and questions.

We can also learn something from the organisation of professional sport in America with a view to the future. The role of a central organisation is central in this. The attitude that clubs are only franchise-enterprises of a national organisation could perhaps be used in some form in the Netherlands too. If all the football clubs in the KPN Telecompetition could operate on the basis of such a franchise-formula in the NV Eredivisie, that might put the competition discussion about broadcasting rights in a different light. Another lesson from America is also the input of all the parties involved in sport (leagues, owners and unions) to maximise their income via cooperation. Focussing on 'sport' instead of individual clubs is part of this. Only then can we talk about sharing out the cake.

With the arrival of the NVs and the floatation on the stock exchange of sports clubs in Europe, it is sensible to check how in America the phenomenon of 'club owner' is dealt with. The role of the unions is also interesting and the cross-ownership question regarding media companies is also under discussion.

The state of affairs in the NCAA shows a remarkable similarity with the threats of a split in the European football competitions (Superleague).

In Europe too (international) club links are rapidly being established that are similar to the American farm system. Director Kales of Ajax already anticipates an Ajax with a European team and a national team. It is sensible to look further at the way in which this system functions in America. Another phenomenon that (perhaps) will appear in the long term – certainly if return-hungry owners have the final say in the clubs – is playing off local authorities or regions against one another and (threatening them with) the clubs moving. With the rapidly increasing players' salaries in Western Europe it

---

may be that in the long term two types of players will be left: the superstars and their supporting cast.

The main conclusion is that in view of the speed at which commercialisation is increasing in European sport, it is advisable to learn as much as possible from experiences in America. After all they have many decades of experience in the questions that are increasingly facing us.

4. Conclusions, recommendations and solutions

4.1. Introduction

Section 2 gives a further analysis of the relationship between Community law and sport, particularly as regards competition law. We have stressed that the specific nature of sport does not always make it possible or desirable to treat sport as a normal economic activity. We also confirm that the European Commission and European jurisprudence recognise that sport has a great social significance. In this last section we discuss these specific characteristics of sport in relationship to Community and in particular to competition law. This involves looking at the options that may contribute to maintaining and where possible/ necessary restoring the equilibrium between the specific nature of sport and the application of Community law.

4.2. Social significance and competitive balance

European competition law in principle applies fully to the economic aspects of sport. This is most relevant in the case of paid or professional sport (pro sport), in particular football. With this observation the discussion could quickly be ended. However: the special aspects of sport are not only emphasised by the official sports associations, but also in a European context, which should be taken into account. In the Amsterdam Declaration on Sport and the Declaration at the Vienna Summit, reference was made to the social significance of sport and the need to respect existing sports structures. What does this mean in specific terms and what is the objective here? In particular at the European Conference on Sport in Olympia these basic principles were further developed.

In our view there are two essential aspects.

1. The social significance of sport
The social significance of sport is partly contained in its social function. Sport is socially significant because of amateur sport/mass sport in general and junior sport in particular (active recreation). Sport is also socially significant because of passive recreation (spectators in the stadia, TV viewers/media aspect). So sport is more than top-class sport that can be marketed within the context of the free competition. Top-class sport actually needs amateur sport: without a flow of talented youth there would be no top-class sport. In the existing sports structures the relationship between the top and grassroots has long been there.

The aspect of the social role means that amateur and junior sport should not only be a concern of individual clubs, but also of the association as a whole. The centre must therefore have some mechanism for drawing on funds to stimulate the base. Earlier on we called this vertical solidarity. This necessary support of the grassroots as such however has nothing to do with free competition; from that perspective it is an internal affair of sport. However, this vertical solidarity means that associations carry out economic activities that are partly aimed at supporting the grassroots (amateur, junior and disabled sport). Under certain circumstances such activities require protection in order to withstand the threats mentioned in section 2.

With this observation we touch on the wider discussion at which this report is directed: the social significance and the specific characteristics of sport require a slightly different application of Community law from one case to another than other sectors of the economy. We explain below whether and how far these needs of sport are met.

Sports associations play a prominent part in the European model of sport as far as working out the specific characteristics and social significance of sport is concerned. In certain circumstances this would justify special treatment of the associations' economic activities under Community law. Certainly if these activities – and the income generated by them – are to benefit the grassroots of sport and this cannot be achieved in any other way. It is also important to check to what extent the activities contribute to maintaining the competitive balance of the sports competition in question. Associations must be credible in the above-mentioned policy, which is expressed in plans for juniors and subsidies aimed at the grassroots.

In the media field (that is aimed at the public in the widest sense) the EU has already shaped the social significance by enacting the *Television without frontiers* Directive[39]. On the basis of this Directive Member States are authorised to designate events that must remain accessible to the public on the public network (at no extra cost). These expressly also include the bigger sports events. The Member States may submit a list of events to the European Commission for adoption.

2. In sport opponents are necessary: sports competitors and the importance of competitive balance

There must be every scope for sports competition, but this type of competition may not lead to opponents suffering economically and disappearing. In the long term this would also mean the end of competition. It is clear that there must be impartial structures to organise a competition (associations as 'third parties'). These do not have to be the existing associations in themselves however. They may also be newly set up associations competing with the existing associations. This in principle promotes free competition, which has long been the great benefit of European integration. In this respect there is little to protect even from a European perspective with regard to the existing sports structures.

The aspect of sports competition means that in an organisational sense there must be associations, whether these are the existing or 'commercial' leagues. They will in addition want to redistribute the income to some extent via whatever model to prevent too many competitions being walkovers (in this respect we refer to the term 'Mickey-Mouse League' as the name for the Dutch football competition in which relations of strength between the clubs are 'more lopsided' than in a number of other European countries). The

---

[39] Directive 97/36/EU to amend Directive 89/552/EEC.

competition must be exciting for the spectators and viewers, for only then can it be marketed to the optimum to advertisers, sponsors and media. One way of achieving this is to distribute the income of clubs and associations for example from sales of TV rights. Such a distribution may come about by collective sales of rights, or by means of a pro-rata contribution per club to a solidarity fund, if there is any redistribution of funds aimed at solidarity at all. In principle this restricts competition compared with normal competition and so may contravene European law.

4.3. Equilibrium

How can specific meaning be given to the aim for equilibrium between application of Community and competition law on the one hand and the social significance and the specific characteristics of sport on the other? The decision-making practice of the European Commission and the jurisprudence of the Court of Justice give rise to a casuistic search for that equilibrium. For example in the field of the collective sales of broadcasting rights where solidarity plays an essential part. The importance of solidarity is also obvious from a passage from the Bosman judgment:

'In view of the great social significance of sport and especially of football in the Community, it must be acknowledged that the maintenance of equilibrium between the clubs by ensuring a certain equality of chances and the uncertainty of the results and the encouragement of the recruitment and training of young players, are rightful objectives.

The above-mentioned collective action of associations in the interest of solidarity relates in particular to TV rights and sponsoring, whereby in particular the first subject mentioned has led to considerable argument and even jurisprudence. Additional conditions relating to the possible admissibility of collective sales, are a limited duration of the contracts and following fair bidding procedures.

A related element of solidarity is the position of supporters. Associations and clubs must ensure that big events and competitions remain accessible to the general public. Ticket sales for example may not be discriminating. There is a visible tendency to pass on the increasing costs in sport to the supporter through entrance prices and pay-per-view TV. Here too the aim is for an equilibrium prescribed on a European level.

Cross-ownership and multi-ownership[40] also deserve special concern from Community law. The European Commission assumes in case of multi-ownership that a ban – although restricting competition – may be justified where this is aimed at maintaining the unpredictability of results and hence a fair competition. It is conceivable that such ban regulations are admissible if they prohibit ownership of several clubs within a branch of sport, but not if this ban extends to clubs in other branches of sport. The desirability of allowing cross-ownership in sport is partly influenced by the answer to the question regarding the consequences on the objectivity of the news service and the consequences for the offer of TV rights (see Section 2.2. of this report).

Although in the BSkyB/ManUnited case cross-ownership was refused, at the same time it was also said that the ban did not mean a ban *per se*. Each case stands on its own and will be tested against the competition rules. In the majority of cases cross-ownership will be assessed according to the law of the Member States, so Community law or Euro-

---

[40] Several clubs in the hands of the same owner (see also paragraph 3.3).

pean competition law does not enter into it. In France (Canal+/Paris Saint Germain) and Italy (Mediaset/AC Milan) cross-ownership is permitted.

In the aim for equilibrium the question is justified of whether the actors in the different sports markets can give more clarity beforehand on the admissibility of their action on these markets. We shall discuss below the opportunities for this. In general it can be stated that the EU is prepared to take into account in the application of Community law the aim for the right equilibrium because of the social position and the specific characteristics of sport. For the application of competition law this may mean that the EU is prepared to grant exemptions. A link may be looked for here with European jurisprudence in the field of agricultural corporations[41]. An example of such an aim for equilibrium between Community law and the social significance of sport, is the *Television without frontiers* Directive. This ensures the accessibility of important events for the general public, even if application of the Directive in a formal sense conflicts with Community law (free movement of services) and competition law.

4.4. Equilibrium and free movement of persons, services and goods

Except for the horizontal relationship between associations ('old' and 'new') with one another and that of associations with TV stations and sponsors, the relationship between associations and sportsmen and women is also relevant (selection, sponsoring), as well as between associations and players' agents, and between sportsmen and women and clubs (in particular transfers). This may involve European competition law (including the abuse of a dominant position by the association) or the free movement of persons and services. In the Bosman case the Court first looked at the (then) Article 48 of the EC Treaty (free movement), which was sufficient (paragraph 138). This is the logical order, as without inadmissible restriction of free movement there can by definition be no question of an inadmissible restriction of competition.

It must be stated in advance that discrimination by nationality is never permitted in the selection of sportsmen and women and the composition of sports teams except where national teams and delegations are concerned. The social role of sport is however not an issue here where this relates to grassroots problems nor is the redistribution of income between clubs via the association. The practical case histories can simply be tested against the basic rules of European law (Articles 39 and 81 and 82 of the (new) EC Treaty) and lead to case law (cf. the opinions of the Solicitor-General in the matter of Deliege and Lehtonen). In addition the basic principle is that the sports rules to be justified must be spared as they do not fall under Community law (see already Walrave/Koch). An exceptional provision here may be useful, but is not necessary, though this is desirable in some circumstances for the collective action by associations.

The Bosman judgement clearly establishes that restriction of the number of foreigners to the EU in sports teams (unlike national teams) is inadmissible. UEFA and FIFA are now pleading for nationality clauses to be made possible again, as a large number of foreigners ruins the identity of national competitions and prevents the flow of our own youth to the top. In an integrated Europe the reintroduction of discrimination by nationality in

---

[41] Van Miert, 'Orientations preliminaires sur l'application des regles de concurrence au secteur du sport' (Preliminary guidance on the application of the competition rules to the sports sector), 15 February 1999.

sport may however be impossible to reintroduce. We shall have to learn to live with it and this relates to club policy and not association policy. The clubs would be able to adapt their policy at their own initiative and offer juniors more opportunities if that is what they want. It is interesting in this respect in the field of football that some top clubs at present are buying up clubs and setting up schools in non-EU or EA countries so that in due course talent can be transferred to the First World. That is in fact a form of development aid for one's own benefit. The question then arises of whether association policy (national, international) that generally benefits these countries can be regarded as grassroots policy within the framework of the application of Community law to the specific characteristics of sport. It must be remarked that such aid (see also FIFA) can be regarded as real football development aid, but this can only form a limited percentage of subsidy to the grassroots, as most money will still have to flow to national or European sport.

The free movement of services also plays an important part within sport. Reference has already been made to the restriction on the free movement of TV broadcasts in case of the application of the Television Directive as mentioned above. Other restrictions do not seem to be really feasible under the existing regulations. In the Deliege case an appeal is made for the free movement of services as a weapon against the application of selection criteria by the Belgian Judo Association. In this case the Solicitor-General of the European Court of Justice did however rule that such selection criteria should only be based on sports performance and not economic activities. Community law is not then applicable. Also for the free movement of sports goods there is no reason to depart from the usual application of Community law. The specific characteristics of sport only play a secondary part here.

4.5. Tools

In this paragraph we discuss specific possibilities for granting the specific characteristics and social significance of sport a better defined place in Community law. Different tools are conceivable here, some more obvious than the other. The different tools can be used separately or in a certain relation. We shall only comment on the feasibility and desirability of the options mentioned in a general sense.

I *Extension of the Declaration on Sport*

In the first place it is conceivable that a new Declaration will be written. By analogy with the Vienna Declaration the European government leaders can draw up a Declaration which acknowledges that because of the aim for equilibrium under certain circumstances there may be justification for granting exemptions from Community law and in particular competition law. Such circumstances must then be found in the previously mentioned aspects of horizontal and vertical solidarity, duration of the agreement, transparency of the way in which agreements come about and so on. At the Intergovernmental Conference in 2000 a successor to the Amsterdam Declaration with the same effect can then be adopted.

Another possibility is that one limits oneself to expressing the desirability that a sports exception will be drawn up which will leave unresolved the tool via which implementation will take place at IGC 2000. The question is whether this is desirable. There are many matters pending in the field of competition and it is important that the Commission deals with these matters using a clear guideline. It seems desirable to us that this is not left solely to case histories.

A possible text for a declaration relating to sport is the following:

'The EU stresses the social significance of sport as laid down in the Treaty of Amsterdam. The EU recognises that because of the specific nature of sport there may under certain circumstances (solidarity, transparency) be justification for granting exemptions for economic activities within the sports sector from Community law, where the economic activities in question in accordance with objective criteria fully or largely aim at or benefit (the organisation of) sport and/or are aimed at maintaining or reinforcing the competitive balance within sport.'

II *Revision of the EC Treaty*

On the basis of Article 48 of the Treaty relating to the EU (old Article N) Member States or the European Commission may submit drafts to the Council for the revision of the Treaties on which the EU is based. Ultimately the Member States have to reach agreement on such a revision during an IGC. If the Netherlands wants to include a sports exception in the Treaty, then it must submit a proposal to this end to the Council. Two options seem possible here:

(a) With regard to free movement:
It could be decided to add sport to the possible exceptions mentioned in Article 39 of the EC Treaty (public order, safety and health.) This approach is pushing it, as 'public order, safety and health' are of an entirely different order to a sports exception. Whether organised sport can be fully or partly classed as 'public health' (extrapolation) is the question.

(b) With regard to competition law:
A new provision could be added to the EC Treaty, on the basis of which activities in sport can be fully or partly exempted from the application of the competition regulations in the Treaty (Article 81 and 82 EC Treaty):

(i) Full exemption:
A full exemption for sport from the competition provisions of the Treaty, will have to lead to the incorporation of a new Article, that could be worded as follows:
'The competition provisions of Article 81 and Article 82 of the EC Treaty are declared not to apply for agreements and actual behaviour agreed with one another, to which two or more enterprises working in the sports sector are party – irrespective of which stage in the production or distribution chain they are in – and which fully or largely aim at or benefit (the organisation of) sport, contribute to the implementation of the social significance of sport or improve this, or are aimed at maintaining or reinforcing the competitive balance within sport'.

It is rather unrealistic to expect that a full exemption can be obtained for sport and the question is very much whether such an exemption is desirable. That does not in any case do justice to the way in which other sectors (for example culture) are dealt with under Community law.

(ii) Partial exemption:

In the EC Treaty on the other hand sport could be added as a criterion to Article 81 paragraph 3 of the EC Treaty. Since the conditions for exemption from Article 81 paragraph 3 of the EC Treaty must be met cumulatively, it is not likely and is perhaps excluded that sport will be added to this Article. It is more obvious to create clarity about the application of the existing conditions of the relevant Article (see below).

III *Rule of Reason approach*

There is a lot to be said for developing guidelines to make it easier for enterprises in the sports sector to themselves weigh up whether agreements and actual behaviour agreed between one another in sport are permitted under the competition regulations of the EC.

The above guidelines will always be applied to the specific circumstances of each case. Exemptions may be obtained under certain circumstances. For the sports sector this means that although certain types of agreements and behaviour fall under the scope of Article 81, paragraph 1 of the EC Treaty (collective sales, economic conditions for selection, conditional sales, ticketing, sponsorship agreements) such agreements and behaviour could be exempted. This is because they promote economic efficiency within the sports sector by ensuring better co-ordination between the participating enterprises ('Rule of Reason').

To sum up: the 'Rule of Reason' is based on the assumption that the efficiency-promoting effects of certain agreements (amateur, junior sport, solidarity, competitive balance) are more important than the possible competition-distorting effects of the restrictions that arise from the agreement or behaviour. Implementation of the 'Rule of Reason' approach in the application of competition law in sport may be achieved in the following ways:

(i) by establishing guidelines in a group exemption for certain agreements in sport.
The European Commission has in accordance with Regulation 19/65 the option of establishing group exemptions for agreements in the distribution sector and for agreements relating to patents and know-how. Similar authorisation regulations have been established relating to research and development, standards, specialisation and insurance (Regulation 2821/71 and Regulation 1543/91). The text of Regulation 19/65 was recently adapted to open up the way for establishing the new group exemption for vertical restrictions.

In view of the limited definition of the regulations, depending on the matters that would be included in a group exemption for sport, further amendment of the existing regulations will be necessary or even a completely new authorisation regulation. As a rule the Commission only uses its power to establish a group exemption if it has acquired sufficient experience with certain agreements and if it can thereby prevent a large number of applications with requests for individual exemptions. The Commission must before establishing a group exemption hear the interested parties and consult the Advisory committee for competition regulations and economic dominant positions.

Although it does not look as though a group exemption for sport will be achieved in the short term for the above reasons, this may contribute to the creation of clarity regarding the way in which equilibrium in sport can be brought about in an acceptable way. In any case a group exemption laid down in a Regulation is in our opinion a more suitable means of approaching the specific characteristics of sport than the other options mentioned above, especially where the decision-making practice of the European

Commission, the jurisprudence of the European Court of Justice, and in particular also the results of the first European Conference on Sport of May 1999 in Olympia show a certain consistent application of Community law to sport. In other words, the above-mentioned conditions to arrive at a group exemption for Sport – experience and prevention of many individual requests for exemption seem to be met.

(ii) by a casuistic approach based on the existing regulations.
Section 2.4. of this report indicates the way in which to date Community and competition law has been applied to economic activities in sport. The European Commission and the European Court of Justice have hence developed a line that can be continued and further developed without amendment or revision of the EC Treaty or by developing a group exemption. This does not however provide the required clarity and could in fact result in the European Commission being burdened with a large number of requests for exemption in the near future. It is possible to create clarity in advance by issuing a Notice as to how to deal with agreements in sport. Although these Notices have no formal legal force, they do contribute well to the required clarity beforehand.

IV *Exemption/discharge because of task of general economic importance*

An exception could exist if it can be assumed that the government has entrusted the sports organisations with a task of general economic importance (Article 86, paragraph 2, EC Treaty). Sports associations would then be entrusted with fulfilling a financially supporting role with respect to junior and amateur sport. The question is whether this basic principle is correct under the present regulations and if not whether it is desirable to give sports organisations such a task of general economic importance. In addition the question is also whether this is not much too difficult a means, especially too because it involves the obligations of authorities towards non-governmental sports organisations.

4.6. Conclusion

In the light of the considerations mentioned in this report, the most valid thing seems to us at present to aim for the agreement of a Declaration on Sport in a European context. This Declaration would have to include general principles regarding the relationship between sport and Community law. Such a Declaration would have to give the European Commission means of applying competition law to sport, taking into account the specific characteristics and the social significance of sport. The Helsinki Report on Sport that the European Commission has issued to the European Council, says among other things that sports associations must also promote amateur sport and help young people in society to integrate by playing sport. In that respect it states: *'These responsibilities should be translated effectively into practice by financial mechanisms or internal solidarity and the structural and solidarity-based relationship between competitive sport and amateur sport.'* To create clarity a first step would have to be taken to arrive at a group exemption in sport.

4.7. From politics to practice: the solutions

An important first step for putting the threats of sport higher on the political agenda is for the European Commission to draw up a Declaration on Sport. But this is a long process and in the meantime developments are in practice taking place at high speed because of economic forces and the Netherlands, with its open economy, is one of the first countries to be faced with the possible adverse consequences of these developments. It is also recommended that, at the same time as the political agenda is prepared, a look be taken outwards and the questions that require attention in the short term be established. This involves in particular the pressure on the existing horizontal and vertical solidarity that is among other things expressed in:

– the threat of a few European football clubs to leave the national competitions and set up a commercial Superleague;
– the threat that Dutch football will lose its link with the European top class and the resultant call by the Dutch top-class clubs for a 'more lopsided' redistribution of the income from TV rights;
– the remarkable distribution of income in the Champions League that just makes the gap between the 'haves' and 'have nots' all the greater;
– the discussion about the events list;
– the qualification problems of the Dutch volleyball team as a result of commercial selection criteria for a tournament in Japan;
– the threatened reduction in income for the KNSB to support mass sport because of the argument about sponsorship logos;
– the rapidly increasing interpenetration between sport and media;
– the growing stack of sports dossiers with the Dutch Competition Authority, NMa.

In other words: we are not talking about the future, but about problems that are very much of the moment. To keep these developments within socially desirable bounds, it is necessary in the short term to think about possible solutions. Of course it is not possible to formulate cut-and-dried answers. There is still too much turbulence for this. But during our study we have indeed heard a number of interesting and concrete options. This involves – in addition to the possible Declaration on Sport – the following solutions:

1) Promoting redistribution through positive incentives
For the time being the court has decided that clubs may sell their TV rights individually. Although the Dutch clubs have recently decided for the time being to still pull together, it is possible and even economically understandable that the big clubs will in the long term withdraw from the collective agreements. Even with individual sales, a lot depends on maintaining a certain amount of redistribution of funds. The government would be able to promote this solidarity by rewarding associations if they are able to effect a redistribution. One suggestion is to allow mass sport (as if it were a club) to join in the distribution of the money.

2) Changing the payment rules of the Champions League
The payment rules of the Champions League to winning clubs are partly based on the amount of TV income from the club's country of origin. This means that if Ajax beats Barcelona, it receives a smaller payment than Barcelona if it beats Ajax. These payment rules – drawn up by UEFA under pressure from a few European top-class clubs to start its own Superleague – are undesirable for several reasons. In the first place they increase the gap between the rich and poor clubs, which has a negative effect on the competitive balance of European competition. In the second place the discrimination by country of origin goes against the concept of European union.

3) The deduction of a 'solidarity levy' by participants in lucrative European competitions
Clubs that are able to qualify for lucrative tournaments like the Champions League know they will be assured a substantial financial injection. There is a lot to be said for passing on the enormous flows of money involved in European success in part to mass sport. This can be done by having the clubs transfer part of their income to a fund that is aimed at promoting mass sport in the club's home country (vertical solidarity). Such a scheme is also good for the competitive balance (horizontal solidarity) of both the European and national competitions.

4) Drawing up rules for cross-ownership
If it is possible to sell TV rights collectively via an exemption, it is important to prevent media companies being able to obtain an advantage in the bidding process by acquiring a club. In order to ensure level playing fields in such processes, consideration may be given to establishing limits for the interests that media companies may have in clubs. If it holds a certain interest in one or more of the clubs, the media company in question is excluded from bidding for the collective broadcasting rights.

5) Application of American measures to promote the competitive balance
In America the importance of 'managing' the competitive balance of professional sports competitions is recognised. Various tools are used for this that could perhaps also prove useful in Europe. Attention here goes in the first instance to a possible (European) salary cap. The draft system may also play a part. Further investigation will have to show which lessons from America may be relevant in the European situation.

ANNEX 1. COMPOSITION OF STEERING COMMITTEE

Table 1   Members of the steering committee

Mr R. Kramer, MA	Ministry of Health, Welfare and Sport
Mr L. Jorritsma, MA	Ministry of Health, Welfare and Sport
Mrs D. Höppener, LL.M.	Ministry of Health, Welfare and Sport
Mrs H. Zeinstra, MA	Ministry of Education, Culture and Science
Mr J. Stevens, LL.M.	Ministry of Education, Culture and Science
Mr W. Jansen, MA	Ministry of Economic Affairs

ANNEX 2. INTERLOCUTORS

To carry out this study we have, in addition to our own expertise, consulted a large number of existing sources. On the one hand that has been various memoranda that have been published on the subject and the literature on the subject, particularly that from the United States. These sources are indicated in Annex 3. On the other hand we have, in order to get a good idea of the situation that Dutch sport finds itself in, talked with a number of experts from sport and related sectors. This Annex contains a list of the interlocutors.

Table 2   Interlocutors

Mr F. van den Engel	Legal Adviser Canal+
Mr R. van der Hart	Director International Sport Consultancy
Mr F. Kales	General Manager AFC Ajax
Mr W. Moerer	Deputy General Manager Canal+
Mr J. van der Reijden	(in a personal capacity)
Mr B. Spaak	Director Pro Sport
Mr P. Vis	Deputy Managing Director Fox 8

ANNEX 3. LITERATURE CONSULTED

Arrondissementsrechtbank Rotterdam [Rotterdam District Court] (1999), *Vonnis van de meervoudige kamer voor de behandeling van burgerlijke zaken in de zaak van KNVB tegen Stichting Feyenoord, [Judgement of the full court dealing with civil cases in the case of KNVB v. Stichting Feyenoord]*
Case number/role number 98129/ HA ZA 98-1428, 9 September 1999

Borghans, L. and L.F.M. Groot (1998), *Superstardom and Monopolistic Power: Why Media Stars Earn More Than Their Marginal Contribution To Welfare*, Journal of Institutional and Theoretical Economics JITE, vol. 154

Dempsey, P. and K. Reilly (1998), *Big money beautiful game*, saving football from itself, Nicholas Brealy Publishing Limited

European Commission, 1999, *The Helsinki Report on Sport*, Report from the European Commission to the European Council with a view to safeguarding current sports structures, COM 1999 644 and /2

Fizel, J., E. Gustafson and J. Hadley (eds) (1999), *Sports Economics: Current Research*, London, Praeger

Frank, R.H. and P.J. Cook (1995), *The Winner Take-All Society*, The Free Press

Goeree, J.K. and M. Minkman (1999), *Balance in European Soccer?*, Working paper University of Virginia

Gorman, J. and Calhoun, K. (1994), *The Name of the Game, The Business of Sports, A unique look at today's pressures on team sports and how fans control success*, John Wiley & Sons, Inc.

Heartland Policy Study (1995), *Should Congress Stop the Bidding War for Sports Franchises, Hearing before the Subcommittee on Antitrust, Business Rights, and Competition Senate Committee on the Judiciary*, Heartland Policy Study, http://www.heartland.org

Kerckhoffs, R.F.M.J. (1997), *Economische gevolgen van het Bosman-arrest [Economic consequences of the Bosman judgement]*, Rechtseconomische Verkenningen Deel 7

KPMG Bureau voor Economische Argumentatie (1999), *Individuele exploitatie van uitzendrechten door eredivisieclubs [Individual exploitation of broadcasting rights by Premier League clubs]*, commissioned by Eredivisie NV

Koning, R.H. (1999), *Competitive Balance in Dutch Soccer*, Research Report 99B04, University of Groningen

Maassen, M.(1999), *Betaalde liefde – voetbal, van volkssport tot entertainment-industrie – [Paid amateur football, from national sport to entertainment industry]*, SUN

Neuman, G.R. and R.F. Tamura (1996), *Managing Competition: The Case of the National Football League*, Manuscript University of Iowa

Nitsche, Ingrid (TMC Asser Instituut) (2000), *Collective Marketing of Broadcasting Rights by Sports Associations in Europe*, European Competition Law Review, 2000, issue 4

OECD, *Communications Outlook 1999*

Pons, J.F. (1999), *Sport and European Competition Policy*, address in a personal capacity of the Deputy Director General of DGIV to the Twenty-sixth Annual Conference on International Antitrust Law & Policy in New York, 14-15 October 1999

Rumphorst, W. (1999), *Sports Broadcasting Rights and EC Competition Law*, Panel discussion on collective selling of sports television broadcasting rights, London, 12 October 1999

Quirk, J. and R.D. Fort (1999), *Hard Ball: The Abuse of Power in Pro Team Sports*, Princeton: Princeton University Press

Quirk, J. and R.D. Fort (1992), *Pay Dirt: The Business of Professional Team Sports*, Princeton: Princeton University Press

Restrictive Practices Court in England and Wales (1999), *Judgement of the Court, in the matter of the restrictive trade practices act 1976, and in the matter of an agreement between the football association Premier League Limited and the Football League Limited and their respective member clubs, and in the matter of an agreement relating to the supply of service facilitating the broadcasting on television of Premier League football matches and the supply of services consisting in the broadcasting on television of such matches*

Roberts, G.R. (1995), *Should Congress stop the biding war for sports franchises?*, Hearing before the Subcommittee on Antitrust, Business Rights and Competition, Senate Committee on the judiciary, November 29th 1995

Rosen, S. (1981), *The Economics of Superstars*, American Economic Review Vol. 71 No. 5

Rumphorst, W. (1999). *Collective Selling Of Sports Television Broadcasting Rights*, Panel Discussion, Sports Broadcasting Rights and EC Competition Law, International Conference, London, 12 October 1999

Siekmann, R. (TMC Asser Instituut)(1994), *Conferentie in Londen over TV-rechten en het Europese Mededingingsrecht [Conference in London on TV rights and European Competition Law]*, SPORTZAKEN 1994, No. 4,

Yamey, B.S. (1999), *Report by Professor Yamey in the U.K. Restrictive Practices Court Decision on Domestic T.V. Broadcasting arrangements*, FA Premier League Limited

CONTRIBUTORS

SIMON BOYES is a funded Research Student and member of the Sports Law Centre at Anglia Polytechnic University. Currently he is undertaking research towards a Ph.D. considering the implications of globalisation for regulatory practices in sport. Recent publications include, 'The Regulation of Sport and the Impact of the Human Rights Act 1998' (2000) *European Public Law* and 'The IOC, Transnational Doping Policy and the Problem of Globalization' in O'Leary, J. (ed) *Drugs and Doping in Sport: Socio-Legal Perspectives* (Cavendish, 2000). He is also a regular contributor to *Sports Law Bulletin*.

ANDREW CAIGER is Senior Lecturer in law and member of the Sports Law Centre at Anglia Polytechnic University. His current research interests include contract and competition law as it relates to sport. He has read conference papers in the UK, USA and South Africa. He has published previously in the area of European law including co-editing, *1996 Onwards: Lowering the Barriers Further* (John Wiley, 1996) (with D. Floudas) and 'Shift in the Power of English Professional Football' (2000) *New Zealand Journal of Industrial Relations* (with John O'Leary).

LAURA EDGAR is the National Computer Centre Research Fellow in Electronic Commerce Law at Queen Mary and Westfield College, University of London. She is currently carrying out research towards a Ph.D. on the challenges which electronic commerce poses to the international tax regime. She is involved in several EU-funded research projects and has written articles on various aspects of electronic commerce law. She is the Case Reviews Editor for *Electronic Business Law* and writes a legal column on electronic commerce issues for *Net Profit*.

KEN FOSTER is a Law Lecturer in the Law School at the University of Warwick. He has written on several aspects of sports law and is currently researching issues of governance in international sports federations and the impact of legal intervention on these organisations. Recent publications include 'European Football: Who's in Charge?' (2000) *Soccer and Society* and 'How can sport be regulated?' in Greenfield,S. and Osborn,G. (eds.) *Law and Sport in Contemporary Society* (Frank Cass, 2000).

SIMON GARDINER is Director of the Sports Law Centre at Anglia Polytechnic University. His particular research interests include sports governance, the regulation of sports violence, racism in sport and the construction of national identity in sport. He has published in a number of areas of sports law. His recent publications include co-author of *Sports Law* (Cavendish, 1998) and 'The Law and Hate Speech: 'Ooh Aah Cantona' and the Demonisation of 'the other' in *Fanatics: Power Identity & Fandom in Football* Brown, A. (ed.) (Routledge, 1998). He is also editor of the bi-monthly journal, *Sports Law Bulletin*.

JAMES T. GRAY is a founding partner of the Milwaukee law firm Pierski & Gray, LLP where he concentrates in the areas of sports law, real estate and estate planning. He is a Visiting Fellow at the Sports Law Centre at Anglia Polytechnic University and was the former assistant director of Marquette Universities' National Sports Law Institute. His expertise is particularly in the area of risk management from a legal, medical, ethical, insurance and sports body rule making perspective. He is the co-author of the two volume set, *Sports Law Practice* (Lexis, 1998) and co-author of *The Stadium Game* (NSLI, 1996), a treatise on the negotiation and drafting of sports facility contracts.

GREGORY IOANNIDIS is a post-graduate student in the Sports Law Centre at Anglia Polytechnic University. His research thesis concerns the criminalisation of the use of performance enhancing drugs in sport. He has published in a number of Greek journals and is co-author of 'Drugs, Health and Sporting Values' in O'Leary, J. (ed.) *Drugs and Doping in Sport: Socio-Legal Perspectives* (Cavendish, 2000) (with Edward Grayson).

DAVID MCARDLE is Research Fellow at De Montfort University, Bedford. His Ph.D. concerns sex discrimination in British and North American sports organisations. His current research interests are concerned with the regulation of professional football, the regulation of the entertainment industries by the European Union and the impact of anti-discrimination laws on British and North American sports organisations. He has published widely in journals in the United Kingdom, Australia and the United States. He is the author of *From Boot Money to Bosman* (Cavendish, 2000) and is the co-editor of the journal, *Entertainment Law*.

J PAUL MCCUTCHEON is Associate Professor of Law at the University of Limerick and Visiting Fellow at the Sports Law Centre, Anglia Polytechnic University. His research interests focus on contractual relations and procedural fairness in sport. He has published extensively in the areas of criminal law, criminal procedure and legal systems. His publications in the area of sports law include 'Negative Enforcement of Employment Contracts in the Sports Industries' (1997) *Legal Studies* and 'Sports Discipline, Natural Justice and Strict Liability' (1999) *Anglo-American Law Review*.

PHILIP MORRIS is Senior Lecturer in Business Law at the University of Stirling. He has researched and published extensively on the role of the Ombudsman in the public and private sectors, investor protection in British Offshore Finance Centres and legal regulation of sport. Recent publications in the area of sports law include 'Challenging Sports Bodies' Determinations' (1998) *Civil Justice Quarterly* (with Gavin Little), and 'The Court of Arbitration for Sport: A Study of the Extra-judicial Resolution of Sporting Disputes', in Stewart, W. (ed), *Sport and the Law: The Scots Perspective* (T&T Clark Ltd, 2000) (with Paul Spink).

TOM MORTIMER is a commercial and corporate lawyer within the Anglia Law School. His particular research interests are in the impact of European law on the corporate form; the use of the corporate form as a regulatory tool and in legal education issues. Recent publications include *Today's Law Teachers: Lawyers or Academics* (Cavendish, 1995) (with Patricia Leighton) and 'Corporate Mobility: an Analysis of the Cases Pertinent to Articles 52 and 58' Caiger, A. & Floudas, D. (eds.) *1996 Onwards: Lowering the Barriers Further*' (John Wiley, 1996).

JOHN O'LEARY is Lecturer in Law and member of the Sports Law Centre at Anglia Polytechnic University. His main research interests are contractual issues in professional sport and the regulation of drugs. He is co-author of *Sports Law* (Cavendish, 1998) and is editor of *Drugs and Doping in Sport: Socio-Legal Perspectives* (Cavendish, 2000). Other recent publications include 'The Re-regulation of Football and its Impact on Employment Contracts', in Collins, H. (ed.) *The Legal Regulation of the Employment Relation* (Kluwer Law International, 2000) (with Andrew Caiger).

DIMITRIOS P. PANAGIOTOPOULOS is Assistant Professor in Sport Law, Department of Physical Education, University of Athens. He is also Secretary General of the International Association of Sports Law and President of the Hellenic Centre of Research on Sports Law. He is editor in chief of *Pandektis: International Sport Law Review* and has published widely in sports law including, 'The Institutional Problem of The Greek Sport Federation: Structure, Organisation, Legal Nature and Function', (1995) *Marquette Sports Law Journal*.

RICHARD PARRISH is Lecturer at Edge Hill University College, Ormeskirk and Research Associate, Sports Law Centre at Anglia Polytechnic University. He is a political scientist with a specialism is European integration and EU public policy. He has a particular research interest in the relationship between sport and the EU. He is completing a Ph.D. entitled 'The Path to a European Union Sports Policy'. Recent publications include '"Sport and Policy" or "Sports Policy"? The Broadcasting of Sporting Events in the European Union' (1998) *Sport and the Law Journal*.

IAN PEARL is a post-graduate student at the Anglia Law School and research assistant at the Sports Law Centre. He is involved in research concerning the proposed tobacco-advertising directive. Preceding his law studies, he worked for a number of years as an assistant underwriter at Lloyds of London.

ANDRZEJ SZWARC is Professor of Law at Adama Mickiewicza University in Posnan, Poland. He is one of the eminent experts in sports law in Eastern Europe and has researched and written extensively in the area. He is President of the Polish Sports Law Association and edits the Polish sports law review, *Sport I Prawo*, which regularly produces special themed editions.

LUC SILANCE is a Barrister at the Brussels Bar and Honorary Professor at the University of Brussels (V.U.B.) in sports law. As an athletics coach, he was Secretary General of the Belgian Olympic Committee (1964-1968), member of the Juridical Department of the Belgian Olympic Committee (1968-1972) and Counsellor to the International Olympic Committee under presidency of Lord Killanin. He is also a former President of the Belgium track and field federation. He has published widely in the area of sports law and is author of *Les sports et le droit* (De Boeck Université, 1998).

PAUL SPINK is Lecturer in Law at the University of Stirling. He has published work in a variety of fields, in particular in the field of European Union Law and on the emerging nexus between sport and the law. Recent publications include, 'Blowing the Whistle on Football's Domestic Transfer Fee', (1999) *Juridical Review* and 'The Court of Arbitration for Sport: A Study of the Extra-judicial Resolution of Sporting Disputes', in Stewart, W.

(ed), *Sport and the Law: The Scots Perspective* (T&T Clark Ltd, 2000) (with Philip Morris).

KLAUS VIEWEG is Professor and Dean of the Law Faculty of the University of Erlangen-Nürnberg. His Ph.D. was completed in 1981 at University of Münster. Since 1992 he has been a member of the executive board of the International Association of Sports Law. His research interests include doping in sport and the regulation of sponsorship agreements. He is author of numerous articles concerning sports law including *Doping – Realität und Recht* (1998), *Vermarktungsrechte im Sport* (2000) and *Das Sportereignis – Ökonomische und rechtliche Fragen der Sportübertragungsrechte* (2000). He is also editor of the sports law review: *SpuRt, Zeitschrift für Sport und Recht.*

ROGER WELCH is Senior Lecturer in law at the University of Portsmouth. He is a co-author of *Sports Law* (Cavendish, 1998) and has written on the relationship between employment law and the world of sport. He has written extensively on the issue of trade union rights in both a national and an international context. Recent publications include 'The Winds of Change in Professional Football: The Impact of the *Bosman* Ruling' (1998) *Contemporary Issues in Law* (with Simon Gardiner) and 'A Snort and a Puff: Recreational Drugs and Discipline in Professional Sport' in O'Leary, J. (ed.) *Drugs in Sport: Socio-Legal Perspectives* (Cavendish, 2000).

TABLE OF CASES

INDEX